Nineteenth-Century Southern Fiction

A CHARLES E. MERRILL LITERARY TEXT

CHARLES E. MERRILL LITERARY TEXTS

Under the General Editorship of
Matthew J. Bruccoli and Joseph Katz

Anthologies by genre, period, theme, or other significant
principle for the study of American literature. Each volume
provides reliable texts introduced by a noted authority.

Nineteenth-Century Southern Fiction

Edited by

John Caldwell Guilds
University of South Carolina

Charles E. Merrill Publishing Company
A Bell & Howell Company
Columbus, Ohio

G 955n

ISBN: 0-675-09308-2

Library of Congress Catalog Number: 76-124354

1 2 3 4 5 6 7 8 9 10 — 79 78 77 76 75 74 73 72 71 70

Printed in the United States of America

Contents

v

Introduction

The eleven stories and tales included in this collection represent the excellence and versatility of fiction writers of the nineteenth-century South, but the criterion for selection has been more utilitarian than aesthetic. Short novels usually considered too long for anthologies—and perhaps too insignificant for separate textbook publication—have deliberately been chosen, along with some shorter pieces not readily available. These shorter pieces are balanced against a few frequently anthologized stories which have been included as a convenience to the reader who, already familiar with their virtues, desires some semblance of full representation. *Nineteenth-Century Southern Fiction* is designed primarily, then, as a supplementary text—for general courses in Southern literature or history, for specialized courses in the short story or the novel, or for period courses in American literature—rather than as a full-course anthology. But whatever its use, this volume brings together, in perhaps unique combination, the long and the short, the well known and the little known, the accessible and the relatively inaccessible, all complete in themselves.

The selections vary considerably in content, style, purpose, and scope. Nevertheless, they can be divided with some logic into three broad classifications:

I. *Traditional romantic tales:* John Pendleton Kennedy's "A Legend of Maryland," James Lane Allen's *A Kentucky Cardinal,* William Alexander Caruthers's "Love and Consumption," and Edgar Allan Poe's "The Gold-Bug."

II. *Tall tales and hunting stories:* Augustus Baldwin Longstreet's "The Horse Swap," William Elliott's "The Fire Hunter," Thomas Bangs Thorpe's "The Big Bear of Arkansas," and William Gilmore Simms's "How Sharp Snaffles Got His Capital and Wife."

1

III. *Stories of manners (social satire)*: George Washington Cable's
Madame Delphine, Charles Waddell Chesnutt's "A Matter of Principle,"
and Katherine O'Flaherty Chopin's "Athénaise: A Story of A Temperament."

There is overlapping, of course, and there are major differences among
stories in each group; but these rough divisions prove useful not only for
discussion purposes, but for demonstrating the characteristic patterns in
fiction writing of the nineteenth-century South.

Two of the stories included in the first category are perhaps long
enough to be considered short novels: "A Legend of Maryland" (1860) and
A Kentucky Cardinal (1894). Kennedy's "legend," written in the rambling
yet picturesque style of *Swallow Barn,* has literary merit as an example of
how history, in the hands of the artist, "becomes a world of living figures,—
a theatre that presents to us a majestic drama . . ." (below, p. 11). "A
Legend of Maryland" is based upon Kennedy's research in the state archives concerning the life of Colonel George Talbot, a minor figure in *Rob
of the Bowl,* whose seventeenth-century political murder of a customs collector of the king set into motion a series of actions not only illustrative of
the flight-pursuit, freedom-prisoner theme, but also of the animosities between colonial Maryland and Virginia. In some ways the story is reminis-
cent of Hawthorne, if only because the device of the old legend's discovery
is similar to "The Custom-House" introduction to *The Scarlet Letter.*

Allen's *A Kentucky Cardinal* is even better, with some of the qualities
of stories of manners as well as of traditional romantic stories. It is a remarkable work for its period, seeming surprisingly modern in tone and style—
called by Allen's biographer "the story which of all his works is most likely to
endure as a minor classic of our literature."[1] A strain of light humor and
gentle irony pervades the first part, becoming sharper, perhaps bitter,
toward the end. It is significant that Allen made careful and important
alterations in the story when he revised it for book publication, the most
crucial of which is the addition of the final line, "Ah, but the long, long
silence of the trees!," a dissonant note giving ambivalence to the harmonic
chord of the conclusion. Though *A Kentucky Cardinal* is romantic throughout—at least in its almost Wordsworthian sensitivity to nature—it is relatively realistic in tone, definitely not sentimentalized.

Structurally, *A Kentucky Cardinal* seems to be built around a two-part
movement, which harmonizes with its two themes—Nature and Love. In
the first half, Nature is the dominant theme: thus we move chapter by
chapter, month by month from January to September, through a kind of

---

[1]Grant C. Knight, *James Lane Allen and the Genteel Tradition* (Chapel Hill, 1935),
p. 97.

prose poem of the seasons, rich in imagery. In the second half, Love becomes the dominant theme, and Nature diminishes in importance as Love ascends. Allen achieves this structurally by the break in chronology caused by the narrator's fever. The tone and technique of the whole is that of the journal or diary, with a chapter given to each month. Thus, logically, the journal must break off during his fever and pick up when he is well enough to begin writing again.

Adding to the effectiveness of the book's structure is the ambiguous symbolism of the cardinal itself. If Adam is identified with the cardinal (and he seems to identify himself with it), the ambivalence of the ending is greatly increased. Another interpretation is suggested, however, by the striking, if terrible, sight of the young pigs tearing apart the dead cardinal. Could Allen be dealing indirectly with the slavery issue? Adam avoids meeting Negroes in the fields because he is bothered by thoughts of man being in bondage; yet he himself keeps slaves (presumably his servants are slaves). It is tempting to see the cardinal as symbolic of the South.

On the allegorical level, we have Adam tending his garden and happy there, yet lonely for Eve. She appears, to be sure, and tempts him with the one forbidden act. He commits the forbidden act, violating his own nature and sinning against Nature. Both Adam and Georgiana are made sadder and wiser by the act, and though they are reconciled at last, we wonder at the price they have paid—and at the duration of their happiness.

Unlike Allen, Caruthers is not successful in avoiding sentimentality in his only published short story, "Love and Consumption" (1842). The story, written in Savannah, Georgia, as was *The Knights of the Horse-Shoe* for the most part, also has the same Virginia setting as the novel. It is perhaps significant that Caruthers interrupted work on a projected but never completed novel "founded upon real and recent events in the social world of Georgia," his adopted state, to write this tale of the Great Valley of Virginia, his native state. But "Love and Consumption" is noteworthy primarily as an early example of the domestic tale, and to a lesser degree for the insight it offers into Caruthers' strong religious orthodoxy. Its possible autobiographical import, as a story of the wages of consumption written by a physician who himself was to die of tuberculosis four years later, adds some interest. Though it is a representative work of a neglected Southern writer of substantial ability, "Love and Consumption" suffers from the faults of its genre—it is didactic, moralistic, and bathetic. Perhaps the situation posed in "Love and Consumption" is better suited to comedy of manners than to pseudo-tragedy. Caruthers succeeds in maintaining interest, however, by suspending resolution to the very end.

Probably the best of the traditional stories is Poe's famous "The Gold-Bug," winner of the hundred-dollar first prize in the short story contest sponsored in 1843 by the *Dollar Newspaper* of Philadelphia. One of Poe's own favorites, "The Gold-Bug" has achieved its enviable reputation as a near perfect work of art as much for its skill in capturing the strangely beautiful setting and atmosphere of Sullivan's Island as for its more dramatic narrative power in sustaining mystery and suspense until the exactly appropriate moment. Though the story is sometimes quite rightly included among Poe's tales of ratiocination, and has been much praised for its ingenuity and imagination in analysis, part of its charm lies in its successful portrayal of the interesting human interplay between Legrand and Jupiter, a benevolent Southern master and his overly solicitous slave, in a purely non-political context. In this sense—as well as in its artistic use of the languid Charleston setting—"The Gold-Bug" is the most truly "Southern" story written by the greatest fiction writer of the nineteenth-century South, an adopted Southerner who advocated international rather than regional literature.

The four tall tales and hunting stories possess a verve, a gutty flavor, and frequently the gusty humor and almost myth-like quality characteristic of the best stories in the tradition of the Southwestern frontier. One of the very earliest of these stories is Longstreet's "The Horse Swap" (1833), first published two years before its inclusion in *Georgia Scenes* (1835), the book frequently used as a landmark for the beginning of Southwestern humor. Poe himself, in an early review of *Georgia Scenes,* was among the first critics to recognize the peculiar merits of "The Horse Swap," calling it

> a vivid narration of an encounter between the wits of two Georgian horse-jockies. This is most excellent in every respect—but especially so in its delineations of Southern bravado, and the keen sense of the ludicrous evinced in the portraiture of the steeds. We think the following free and easy sketch of a *hoss* superior, in joint humor and verisimilitude, to any thing of the kind we have ever seen.[2]

Not only did "The Horse Swap" help to usher in a new, distinctively Southern kind of humor, it also established what has become a specialized genre within a genre—the literature of the horse-trade, made most notable, of course, by Faulkner's "Spotted Horses." One of Longstreet's finest insights is his recognition of the peculiar etiquette of horse-swapping: absolute silence by onlookers enhancing the dignity of the dickering of the traders, whose reputations for shrewdness are highly prized.

Elliott's "The Fire Hunter" (1846) does not possess the usual ingredients of a tall tale, but its subject—the hunt—and its use of salty, realistic dialect place it within the frontier tradition. Though it contains an easy, masculine humor, it possesses none of the comic; it approaches the tragic in its portrayal of the consequences of the illegal fire hunt. It is in the best

---

[2]*Southern Literary Messenger,* II (March, 1836), 288.

sense a hunting story for hunters told by a lover of hunting. Written in the cool, clean understated prose of a writer thoroughly conversant with the ways of nature, it indirectly protests against the stupidity of man, whose attempt to destroy an almost mythical creature of nature ironically leads to self-destruction. Like the bears of Faulkner and Thorpe, the deer of Elliott's "The Fire Hunter" is larger than reality, larger than the small hunters who cheat, who fail to follow the time-honored ritual of the hunt. Elliott's modest claim in the preface to *Carolina Sports* that the popularity of his "Sketches" was "determined less by the skill of the artist, than by the novelty of the subject" belies his accomplishment in this quiet, straightforward story with its simple air of dignity.

In the words of Thorpe's biographer, "In all the body of frontier literature, 'The Big Bear of Arkansas' is the masterpiece of its kind, created from Thorpe's habits of close observation, his interest in the literary conventions of the American frontiersman, and his opportunity to observe at first hand the actual farmer and hunter of the Old Southwest."[3] "The Big Bear of Arkansas" (1846) fully captures the language and the spirit of the frontier and creates in its central figure, Jim Doggett, a Davy Crockett-type character far more believable than the real Crockett. The humor of "The Big Bear" is the humor of character—not, primarily, of situation—and therein lies its superiority in a genre too often dependent upon discomfort of body or awkwardness of situation for its comedy. The tale of the hunt of a gigantic bear by the greatest bear hunter in Arkansas artistically infuses both the bear and the hunter with epic qualities—the bear is definitely associated with the supernatural—and in the process the tall tale itself becomes a kind of miniature epic.

One of the few tales to rival the excellence of "The Big Bear of Arkansas" in the tradition of Southwestern humor is Simms's "How Sharp Snaffles Got His Capital and Wife" (1870). Indeed, one of the serious shortcomings of American literary scholarship has been its failure to recognize the merits of Simms as a writer of short fiction in general; "Sharp Snaffles" and its sequel " 'Bald-Head Bill Bauldy,' and How He Went Through the Flurriday Campaign!" almost certainly place him first in the genre of the tall tale. Unfortunately for Simms and his readers, he was late in fully recognizing his true forte (although evidence of it came early in his long career): "Sharp Snaffles" was not published until after his death and "Bald-Head Bill Bauldy" was left in manuscript until its publication in the Centennial Simms.[4] "How Sharp Snaffles Got His Capital and Wife" is an authentic American folk tale based upon Simms's own experiences at a hunter's camp

---

[3]Milton Rickels, *Thomas Bangs Thorpe, Humorist of the Old Southwest* (Baton Rouge, 1962), p. 60.

[4]John C. Guilds, General Editor, *The Centennial Edition of the Writings of William Gilmore Simms,* II (Columbia, South Carolina, 1971), 466–521.

in the mountains of North Carolina, but the author also draws upon literary sources (Baron Munchausen and William Crafts, among others, have been suggested) to weld together a little masterpiece capturing the essence of the language, the physical vitality, and the bouyant spirit of the backwoods. As with "The Big Bear of Arkansas," it is the character of the story-teller even more than the episodes he relates that creates the humor and irrepressible charm of the story. The art of story-telling in the best tongue-in-cheek Chaucerian manner comes to life again in "How Sharp Snaffles Got His Capital and Wife."

The remaining type of story represented in this anthology—the story of manners dealing with social or psychological problems—includes three of the most interesting stories written by Southern authors in the late nineteenth century. Two of the stories—Cable's *Madame Delphine* and Chesnutt's "A Matter of Principle"—deal with problems of racial discrimination, while the third—Kate Chopin's "Athénaïse: A Story of A Temperament"—probes the inner consciousness of a liberated young woman, anticipatory of twentieth-century existentialism. It is significant that a tone of irony—the characteristic mode of twentieth-century literature—pervades all three of the tales.

Madame Delphine (1881), published in book form after its serial publication in *Scribner's Monthly* earlier that same year, was the natural outgrowth of Cable's growing awareness of the tragic plight of quadroons in his native New Orleans—a subject he had already more than touched upon in " 'Tite Poulette" (1874) and *The Grandissimes* (1880). But *Madame Delphine* faced the issue much more squarely than did " 'Tite Poulette," a romanticized, sentimentalized treatment of the same racial dilemma—the light-skinned mulatto denied acceptance both by the white race he aspires to and by the black race he condescendingly is assigned to by the whites. In an 1896 preface Cable said that he wrote *Madame Delphine* because a quadroon who had read " 'Tite Poulette" wrote him an unforgettable letter, saying in effect, "If you have a whole heart for the cruel case of us poor quadroons, change the story even yet, and tell the inmost truth of it. Madame John lied! The girl was her own daughter; but like many and many a real quadroon mother, as you surely know, Madame John perjured her own soul to win for her child a legal and honorable alliance with the love-mate and life-mate of her choice."[5] Cable's response to this challenge produced a short novel which Arlin Turner (in the definitive biography) calls "as delicate as anything Cable ever wrote. Revelation comes through glimpses here and there, but with more naturalness than

---

[5]Quoted in Arlin Turner, *George Washington Cable: A Biography* (Durham, 1956), p. 105.

in the earlier stories. With a touch of suggestion, a figure of speech, an ironic turn of thought, a hint of feelings only half expressed, the reader is gently led through events that have an effect as delicate as the odor of orange blossoms but also as haunting and unforgettable."[6]

Chesnutt, the only prominent Negro fiction writer of the nineteenth-century South, deals with the color question with rarer insight, perhaps, and deeper irony in "A Matter of Principle" (1899), included in the collection entitled *The Wife of His Youth and Other Stories of the Color Line*. In "A Matter of Principle" Chesnutt possesses the gift of all satirists, the ability to cut both ways with blades so keenly honed that the wounds are practically painless. Chesnutt himself suggested to his editor, Walter Hines Page, in 1897 that "A Matter of Principle" be classified "under the general heading 'The Blue Veins',"[7] a term he best explains in the opening paragraphs of *The Wife of His Youth*:

> The original Blue Veins were a little society of colored persons organized in a certain Northern city shortly after the war. Its purpose was to establish and maintain correct social standards among a people whose social condition presented almost unlimited room for improvement. By accident, combined perhaps with some natural affinity, the society consisted of individuals who were, generally speaking, more white than black. Some envious outsider made the suggestion that no one was eligible for membership who was not white enough to show blue veins. The suggestion was readily adopted by those who were not of the favored few, and since that time the society, though possessing a longer and more pretentious name, has been known far and wide as the "Blue Vein Society," and its members as the "Blue Veins."[8]

An even more subtle touch is displayed by Kate Chopin in "Athénaise: A Story of A Temperament" (1896), a story as remarkable for its crisp, economical style as for its sexual candor. "Athénaise" contains none of the prolixity and embellished affectation characteristic of female authors of the nineteenth century; it is clear and straightforward, yet at once suggestive and imaginative—and at times symbolic, as in the episode at the oak tree. Cazeau recalls a childhood incident that occurred at the oak: his father is returning a runaway slave, who stops at the oak to rest; now Cazeau is returning a runaway wife and the thought of her being a slave to him sickens him. This freedom-restraint, flight-pursuit motif seems a recurring theme in nineteenth-century Southern fiction; but if it at all

---

[6]Turner, *Cable*, p. 107.

[7]Helen M. Chesnutt, *Charles W. Chesnutt: Pioneer of the Color Line* (Chapel Hill, 1952), p. 78.

[8]*The Wife of His Youth and Other Stories of the Color Line* (Boston and New York, 1899), pp. 1–2.

reflects a submerged feeling of guilt on the author's part, in the artistry of Kate Chopin it is skillfully subordinated to the main theme: the psychological liberation of a sensuous young woman through discovery of self. In Athénaise's case, ironically, it is knowledge of her biological entrapment—pregnancy—that releases her pent-up psyche, freeing her to respond passionately to Cazeau for the first time since her marriage. In "Athénaise: A Story of A Temperament" Kate Chopin approaches the excellence of her masterpiece, *The Awakening* (1899), though as yet her growing reputation is based primarily upon the novel.

John Pendleton Kennedy
(1795-1870)

John Pendleton Kennedy grew up in Baltimore where his Scotch-Irish father, John Kennedy, was a merchant. His mother, Nancy Pendleton, came from an aristocratic Virginia family. Kennedy frequently visited his relations in Virginia and later drew on these experiences for *Swallow Barn.* He was educated at a Baltimore academy, which later merged with another academy to form Baltimore College, from which he graduated in 1812. His education was typical of that day, his literary interests centering primarily in the classics and English literature, and by his own account he was a diligent and avid student.

After his graduation from Baltimore College, Kennedy began reading law, and in 1816 began practice. Though he evidently found literary endeavors more to his taste, he never wholly abandoned law in their favor; the practice of law along with other business and political pursuits provided the economic stability which a writing career could not supply. He served in the Maryland legislature, was a Whig Congressman in Washington for three terms, and acted as Secretary of the Navy under President Fillmore.

Soon after he began his legal practice in Baltimore he also began his literary pursuits. For a year he and Peter Hoffman Cruse published a fortnightly periodical called the *Red Book* (1818–1819). For this pamphlet he supplied lightly satirical sketches and essays in the tradition of the *Spectator.* Throughout his career, Kennedy displayed an eighteenth-century manner and taste, a preference for the polished and genteel over the melodramatic or fantastic.

His first and best known work, *Swallow Barn,* published in 1832, displays this tendency. It is neither a novel nor a romance, though it does contain a slight narrative element. It is best described as a series of sketches of plantation life in the Old Dominion, which faithfully reproduces the manners and tone of early nineteenth-century Virginia. Two subsequent works, *Horse Shoe Robinson* (1835) and *Rob of the Bowl* (1838), are historical

9

romances in the tradition of Cooper and Scott. Though the hero of *Horse Shoe Robinson* is Kennedy's best achievement in characterization, both of these novels are of lesser importance than *Swallow Barn* because they deal with material remote to Kennedy's own experience. The strength of *Swallow Barn*, on the other hand, is precisely that it is drawn from first hand observation of familiar surroundings. Kennedy's later publications include *Quodlibet* (1840), a satire of Jacksonian democracy; a biography, *Memoirs of the Life of William Wirt* (1849); a number of addresses; a few essays and sketches; and the historical short story, "A Legend of Maryland," probably the most significant work of the author's last twenty years. The opening paragraphs of "A Legend of Maryland" contain an important statement of Kennedy's concept of history and historical romance, a concept which doubtless owes something to Scott, and perhaps to Macaulay.

Textual note

In an earlier form this story was published under the title "A Legend of the Chesapeake" in the *Southern Literary Messenger*, XXIV (March, 1857), 223–235, with the following note from the editor:

> The following narrative is the substance of a Lecture, delivered, a year ago, before the Maryland Institute by the Hon. John P. Kennedy, which has had hitherto only a local circulation as published in the Baltimore *Patriot*. It is the intention of the distinguished author to amplify his materials hereafter and give to this episode in the colonial annals of Maryland something more of historic dignity, but in the mean time we are sure the readers of the Messenger will receive with pleasure a paper so imbued with the spirit of the zealous antiquarian and so marked by the graces of the accomplished writer.

In its final form "A Legend of Maryland: 'An Owre True Tale' " was published in the *Atlantic Monthly*, VI (July, 1860), 29–44; (August, 1860), 141–152. After Kennedy's death it was reprinted by Henry T. Tuckerman in *At Home and Abroad* (New York, 1872), pp. 37–87. The *Atlantic Monthly* publication serves as copy-text.

A Legend of Maryland

An Owre True Tale

The framework of modern history is, for the most part, constructed out of the material supplied by national transactions described in official documents and contemporaneous records. Forms of government and their organic changes, the succession of those who have administered them, their legislation, wars, treaties, and the statistics demonstrating their growth or decline, —these are the elements that furnish the outlines of history. They are the dry timbers of a vast old edifice; they impose a dry study upon the antiquary, and are still more dry to his reader.

But that which makes history the richest of philosophies and the most genial pursuit of humanity is the spirit that is breathed into it by the thoughts and feelings of former generations, interpreted in actions and incidents that disclose the passions, motives, and ambition of men, and open to us a view of the actual life of our forefathers. When we can contemplate the people of a past age employed in their own occupations, observe their habits and manners, comprehend their policy and their methods of pursuing it, our imagination is quick to clothe them with the flesh and blood of human brotherhood and to bring them into full sympathy with our individual nature. History then becomes a world of living figures,—a theatre that presents to us a majestic drama, varied by alternate scenes of the grandest achievements and the most touching episodes of human existence.

In the composing of this drama the author has need to seek his material in many a tangled thicket as well as in many an open field. Facts accidentally encountered, which singly have but little perceptible significance, are sometimes strangely discovered to illustrate incidents long obscured and incapable of explanation. They are like the lost links of a chain, which, being found, supply the means of giving cohesion and completeness to the heretofore useless fragments. The scholar's experience is full of these reunions of illustrative incidents gathered from regions far apart in space, and often in time. The historian's skill is challenged to its highest task in the effort to draw together those tissues of personal and local adventure which, at first without seeming or suspected dependence, prove, when brought into their proper relationship with each other, to be unerring exponents of events of highest concern.

It is pleasant to fall upon the course of one of these currents of adventure,—to follow a solitary rivulet of tradition, such as by chance we now and then find modestly flowing along through the obscure coverts of time, and to be able to trace its progress to the confluence of other streams,—and finally to see it grow, by the aid of these tributaries, to the proportions of an ample river, which waters the domain of authentic history and bears upon its bosom a clear testimony to the life and character of a people.

The following legend furnishes a striking and attractive exemplification of such a growth, in the unfolding of a romantic passage of Maryland history, of which no annalist has ever given more than an ambiguous and meagre hint. It refers to a deed of bloodshed, of which the only trace that was not obliterated from living rumor so long as a century ago was to be found in a vague and misty relic of an old memory of the provincial period of the State. The facts by which I have been enabled to bring it to the full light of an historical incident, it will be seen in the perusal of this narrative, have successively, and by most curious process of development, risen into view through a series of accidental discoveries, which have all combined, with singular coincidence and adaptation, to furnish an unquestionable chapter of Maryland history, altogether worthy of recital for its intrinsic interest, and still more worthy of preservation for the elements it supplies towards a correct estimate of the troubles which beset the career and formed the character and manners of the forefathers of the State.

Chapter I

Talbot's Cave

It is now many years ago,—long before I had reached manhood,—that, through my intimacy with a friend, then venerable for his years and most attractive to me by his store of historical knowledge, I became acquainted with a tradition touching a strange incident that had reference to a mysterious person connected with a locality on the Susquehanna River near Havre de Grace. In that day the tradition was repeated by a few of the oldest inhabitants who dwelt in the region. I dare say it has now entirely run out of all remembrance amongst their descendants, and that I am, perhaps, the only individual in the State who has preserved any traces of the facts to which I allude.

There was, until not long ago, a notable cavern at the foot of a rocky cliff about a mile below the town of Port Deposit. It was of small compass, yet sufficiently spacious to furnish some rude shelter against the weather to one who might seek refuge within its solitary chamber. It opened upon the river just where a small brook comes brattling down the bank, along the base of a hill of some magnitude that yet retains the stately name of Mount Ararat. The visitor of this cavern might approach it by a boat from the river, or by a rugged path along the margin of the brook and across the ledges of the rock. This rough shelter went by the name of Talbot's Cave down to a very recent period, and would still go by that name, if it were yet in existence. But it happened, not many years since, that Port Deposit was awakened to a sudden notion of the value of the granite of the cliff, and, as commerce is a most ruthless contemner of all romance, and never hesitates between a speculation of profit and a speculation of history, Talbot's Cave soon began to figure conspicuously in the Price Current, and in a very little while disappeared, like a witch from the stage, in blasts of sulphur fire and rumbling thunder, under the management of those effective scene-shifters, the quarrymen. A government contract, more potent than the necromancy of the famed wizard Michael Scott, lifted this massive rock from its base, and, flying with it full two hundred miles, buried it fathoms below the surface of the Atlantic, at the Rip Raps, near Hampton Roads; and thus it happens that I cannot vouch the ocular proof of the Cave to certify the legend I am about to relate.

The tradition attached to this spot had nothing but a misty and spectral outline. It was indefinite in the date, uncertain as to persons, mysterious as to the event, — just such a tradition as to whet the edge of one's curiosity and to leave it hopeless of gratification. I may relate it in a few words.

Once upon a time, somewhere between one and two hundred years ago, there was a man by the name of Talbot, a kinsman of Lord Baltimore, who had committed some crime, for which he fled and became an outlaw and was pursued by the authorities of the Province. To escape these, he took refuge in the wilderness on the Susquehanna, where he found this cave, and used it for concealment and defence for some time—how long, the tradition does not say. This region was then inhabited by a fierce tribe of Indians, who are described on Captain John Smith's map as the "Sasquesahannocks," and who were friendly to the outlaw' and supplied him with provisions. To these details was added another, which threw an additional interest over the story,—that Talbot had a pair of beautiful English hawks, such as were most prized in the sport of falconry, and that these were the companions of his exile, and were trained by him to pursue and strike the wild duck that abounded, then as now, on this part of the river; and he thus found amusement to beguile his solitude, as well as sustenance in a luxurious article of food, which is yet the pride of gastronomic science, and the envy of *bons vivants* throughout this continent.

These hawks my aged friend had often himself seen, in his own boyish days, sweeping round the cliffs and over the broad expanse of the Susquehanna. They were easily distinguished, he said, by the residents of that district, by their peculiar size and plumage, being of a breed not known to our native ornithology, and both being males. For many years, it was affirmed,—long after the outlaw had vanished from the scene,—these gallant old rovers of the river still pursued their accustomed game, a solitary pair, without kindred or acquaintance in our woods. They had survived their master,—no one could tell how long,—but had not abandoned the haunts of his exile. They still for many a year saw the wilderness beneath their daily flight giving place to arable fields, and learned to exchange their wary guard against the Indian's arrow for a sharper watch of the Anglo-Saxon rifle. Up to the last of their appearance the country-people spoke of them as Talbot's hawks.

This is a summary of the story, as it was told to me. No inquiry brought me any addition to these morsels of narrative. Who this Talbot was,—what was his crime,—how long he lived in this cave, and at what era,—were questions upon which the oracle of my tradition was dumb.

Such a story would naturally take hold of the fancy of a lover of romance, and kindle his zeal for an enterprise to learn something more about it; and I may reasonably suppose that this short sketch has already stirred the bosoms of the novel-reading portion, at least, of my readers with a desire that I should tell them what, in my later researches, I have found to explain this legend of the Cave. Even the outline I have given is suggestive of inferences to furnish quite a plausible chapter of history.

First, it is clear, from the narrative, that Talbot was a gentleman of rank in the old Province,—for he was kinsman to the Lord Proprietary; and there is one of the oldest counties of Maryland that bears the name of his family,—perhaps called so in honor of himself. Then he kept his hawks, which showed him to be a man of condition, and fond of the noble sport which figures so gracefully in the annals of Chivalry.

Secondly, this hawking carries the period of the story back to the time of one of the early Lords Baltimore; for falconry was not common in the eighteenth century: and yet the date could not have been much earlier than that century, because the hawks had been seen by old persons of the last generation somewhere about the period of our Revolution; and this bird does not live much over a hundred years. So we fix a date not far from sixteen hundred and eighty for Talbot's sojourn on the river.

Thirdly, the crime for which he was outlawed could scarcely have been a mean felony, perpetrated for gain, but more likely some act of passion,—a homicide, probably, provoked by a quarrel, and enacted in hot blood. This Talbot was too well conditioned for a sordid crime; and his flight to the wilderness and his abode there would seem to infer a man of strong purpose and self-reliance.

And, lastly, as he must have had friends and confederates on the frontier, to aid him in his concealment, and to screen him from the pursuit of the government officers, and, moreover, had made himself acceptable to the Indians, to whose power he had committed himself, we may conclude that he possessed some winning points of character; and I therefore assume him to have been of a brave, frank, and generous nature, capable of attracting partisans and enlisting the sympathies and service of bold men for his personal defence.

So, with the help of a little obvious speculation, founded upon the circumstantial evidence, we weave the network of quite a natural story of Talbot; and our meagre tradition takes on the form, and something of the substance, of an intelligible incident.

Chapter II

Strange Revelations

At this point I leave the hero of my narrative for a while, in order that I may open another chapter.

Many years elapsed, during which the tradition remained in this unsatisfactory state, and I had given up all hope of further elucidation of it, when an accidental discovery brought me once more upon the tracks of inquiry.

There was published in the city of Baltimore, in the year 1808, a book whose title was certainly as little adapted to awaken the attention of one in quest of a picturesque legend as a treatise on Algebra. It was called "The Landholder's Assistant," and was intended, as its name imported, to assist that lucky portion of mankind who possessed the soil of Maryland in their pursuit of knowledge touching the mysteries of patents, warrants, surveys, and such like learning, necessary to getting land or keeping what they had. The character and style of this book, in its exterior aspect, were as unpromising as its title. It was printed by Messrs. Dobbin & Murphy, on rather dark paper, in a muddy type,—such as no Mr. Dobbin nor Mr. Murphy of this day would allow to bear his imprimatur,—though in 1808, I doubt not, it was considered a very creditable piece of Baltimore typography. This unpretending volume was compiled by Chancellor Kilty. It is a very instructive book, containing much curious matter, is worthy of better adornment in the form of its presentation to the world, and ought to have a title more suggestive of its antiquarian lore. I should call it "Fossil Remains of Old Maryland Law, with Notes by an Antiquary."

It fell into my hands by a purchase at auction, some twenty years after I had abandoned the Legend of the Cave and the Hawks as a hopeless quest. In running over its contents, I found that a Colonel George Talbot was once the Surveyor-General of Maryland; and in two short marginal notes (the substance of which I afterwards found in Chalmers's "Annals") it was said that "he was noted in the Province for the murder committed by him on Christopher Rousby, Collector of the Customs,"—the second note adding that this was done on board a vessel in Patuxent River, and that Talbot "was conveyed for trial to Virginia, from whence he made his escape; and after being retaken, and" (as the author expresses his belief) "tried and convicted, was finally pardoned by King James the Second."

These marginal notes, though bringing no clear support to the story of the Cave, were embers, however, of some old fire not entirely extinct, which emitted a feeble gleam upon the path of inquiry. The name of the chief actor coincided with that of the tradition; the time, that of James the Second, conformed pretty nearly to my conjecture derived from the age of the hawks; and the nature of the crime was what I had imagined. There was just enough in this brief revelation to revive the desire for further investigation. But where was the search to be made? No history that I was aware of, no sketch of our early time that I had ever seen, nothing in print was known to be in existence that could furnish a clue to the story of the Outlaw's Cave.

And here the matter rested again for some years. But after this lapse, chance brought me upon the highway of further development, which led me in due time to a strange realization of the old proverb that "Murder will out,"—though, in this case, its discovery could bring no other retribution than the settlement of an historical doubt, and give some posthumous fame to the subject of the disclosure.

In the month of May, 1836, I had a motive and an opportunity to make a visit to the County of St. Mary's. I had been looking into the histories of our early Maryland settlement, as they are recounted in the pages of Bozman, Chalmers, and Grahame, and found there some inducements to persuade me to make an exploration of the whereabouts of the old city which was planted near the Potomac by our first pilgrims. Through the kindness of a much valued friend, whose acquirements and taste—both highly cultivated—rendered him a most effective auxiliary in my enterprise, I was supplied with an opportunity to spend a week under the hospitable roof of Mr. Carberry, the worthy Superior of the Jesuit House of St. Inigoes on the St. Mary's River, within a short distance of the plain of the ancient city.

Mr. Campbell and myself were invited by our host to meet him, on an appointed day, at the Church of St. Nicholas on the Patuxent, near the landing at Town Creek, and we were to travel from there across to St. Inigoes in his carriage,—a distance of about fifteen miles.

Upon our arrival at St. Nicholas, we found a full day at our disposal to look around the neighborhood, which, being the scene of much historical interest in our older annals, presented a pleasant temptation to our excursion. Our friendly guide, Mr. Carberry, took us to Drum Point, the southern headland of the Patuxent at its entrance into Chesapeake Bay. Here was, at that time, and perhaps still is, the residence of the Carroll family, whose ancestors occupied the estate for many generations. The dwelling-house was a comfortable wooden building of the style and character of the present day, with all the appurtenances proper to a convenient and pleasant country homestead. Immediately in its neighborhood—so near that it might be said to be almost within the curtilage of the dwelling—stood an old brick ruin of what had apparently been a substantial mansion-house. Such a monument of the past as this, of course, could not escape our special attention, and, upon inquiry, we were told that it was once, a long time ago, the family home of the Rousbys, the ancestors of the present occupants of the estate; that several generations of this family, dating back to the early days of the Province, had resided in it; and that when it had fallen into decay, the modern building was erected, and the old one suffered to crumble into the condition in which we saw it. I could easily understand and appreciate the sentiment that preserved it untouched as part and parcel in the family associations of the place, and as a relic of the olden time which no one was willing to disturb.

The mention of the name of the Rousbys, here on the Patuxent River, was a sudden and vivid remembrancer to me of the old story of Talbot, and gave new encouragement to an almost abandoned hope of solving this mystery.

Chapter III

A Graveyard and an Epitaph

Within a short distance of this spot, perhaps not a mile from Drum Point, there is a small creek which opens into the river and bears the name of Mattapony. In early times there was a notable fort here, and connected with it a stately mansion, built by Charles Calvert, Lord Baltimore, for his own occasional residence. The fort and mansion are often mentioned in the Provincial records as the place where the Council sometimes met to transact business; and accordingly many public acts are dated from Mattapony.

Calvert was doubtless attracted to this spot by the pleasant scenery of the headland which here looks out upon the noble water-view of the Chesapeake, and by its breezy position as an agreeable refuge from the heats of summer.

Our party, therefore, determined to set out upon a search for some relics of the mansion and fort; and as a guide in this enterprise, we engaged an old negro who seemed to have a fair claim in his own conceit to be regarded both as the Solomon and the Methuselah of the plantation. He was a wrinkled, wise-looking old fellow, with a watery eye and a grizzled head, and might, perhaps, have been about eighty; but, from his own account, he left us to infer that he was not much behind that great patriarch of Scripture whose years are described as one hundred and threescore and fifteen.

Finding that he was native to the estate, and had lived here all his life, we interrogated him with some confidence in his ability to contribute something useful to the issue of our pursuit. Amongst all the Solomons of this world, there is not one so consciously impressed with the unquestionable verity of his wisdom and the intensity of his knowledge as one of these veterans of an old family-estate upon which he has spent his life. He is always an aristocrat of the most uncompromising stamp, and has a contemptuous disdain and intolerance for every form of democracy. Poor white people have not the slightest chance of his good opinion. The pedigree and history of his master's family possess an epic dignity in his imagination; and the liberty he takes with facts concerning them amounts to a grand poetical hyperbole. He represents their wealth in past times to have amounted to something of a fabulous superfluity, and their magnificence so unbounded, that he stares at you in describing it, as if its excess astonished himself.

When we now questioned our venerable conductor, to learn what he could tell us of the old Proprietary Mansion, he said, in his way, he "membered it, as if it was built only yesterday: he was fotch up so near it, that he could see it now as if it was standing before him: if *he* couldn't pint out where it stood, it was time for him to give up: it was a mighty grand brick house,"—laying an emphasis on *brick*, as a special point in his notion of its grandeur; and then he added, with all the gravity of which his very solemn visage was a copious index, that "Old Master Baltimore, who built it, was a real fine gentleman. He knowed him so well! He never gave anything but gold to the servants for tending on him. Bless you! he wouldn't even think of silver! Many a time has he given me a guinea for waiting on him."

This account of Old Master Baltimore, and his magnificent contempt of silver, and the intimacy of our patriarch with him, rather startled us, and

I began to fear that the story of the house might turn out to be as big a lie as the acquaintance with the Lord Proprietary,—for Master Baltimore had then been dead just one hundred and twenty-one years. But we went on with him, and were pleasantly disappointed when he brought us upon a hill that sloped down to the Mattapony, and there traced out for us, by the depression of the earth, the visible lines of an old foundation of a large building, the former existence of which was further demonstrated by some scattered remains of the old imported brick of the edifice which were imbedded in the soil.

This spot had a fine outlook upon the Bay, and every advantage of locality to recommend its choice for a domestic establishment. We could find nothing to indicate the old fort except the commanding character of the hill with reference to the river, which might warrant a conjecture as to its position. I believe that the house was included within the ramparts of the fortification, as I perceive in some of the old records that the fortification itself was called the Mattapony House, which was once beleaguered and taken by Captain John Coode and Colonel Jowles.

After we had examined all that was to be seen here, our next point of interest was a graveyard, which, we had been informed by some of the household at Mrs. Carroll's, had been preserved upon the estate from a very early period. Our old gossip professed to know all about this, from its very first establishment. It was in another direction from the mansion-house, about a mile distant, on the margin of an inlet from the Bay, called Harper's Creek; and thither we accordingly went. Before we reached the spot, the old negro stopped at a cabin that lay in our route and provided himself with a hoe, which, borne upon his shoulder, gave a somewhat mysterious significance to the office he had assumed. He did not explain the purpose of this equipment to us, and we forbore to question him. After descending to the level of the tide and passing through some thickets of wild shrubbery, we arrived upon a grassy plain immediately upon the border of the creek; and there, in a quiet, sequestered nook of rural landscape, the smooth and sluggish little inlet begirt with water-lilies and reflecting wood and sky and the green hill-side upon its surface, was the chosen resting-place of the departed generations of the family. A few simple tombstones—some of them darkened by the touch of Time—lay clustered within an old inclosure. The brief memorials engraved upon them told us how inveterately Death had pursued his ancient vocation and gathered in his relentless tribute from young and old in times past as he does to-day.

Here was a theme for a sermon from the patriarch, who now leaned upon his hoe and shook his head with a slow ruminative motion, as if he hoped by this action to disengage from it some profound moral reflections, and then began to enumerate how many of these good people he had helped to bury; but before he had well begun this discourse we had turned away and were about leaving the place, when he recalled us by saying, "I have got one tombstone yet to show you, as soon as I can clear it off with the hoe: it belongs to old Master Rousby, who was stobbed aboard ship, and is, besides that, the grandest tombstone here."

Here was another of those flashes of light by which my story seemed to be preordained to a prosperous end. We eagerly encouraged the old man to this task, and he went to work in removing the green sod from a large slab which had been entirely hidden under the soil, and in a brief space revealed to us a tombstone fully six feet long, upon which we were able to read, in plainly chiselled letters, an inscription surmounted by a carved heraldic shield with its proper quarterings and devices.

Our group at this moment would have made a fine artistic study. There was this quiet landscape around us garnished with the beauty of May; there were the rustic tombs,—the old negro, with a countenance surcharged with the expression of solemn satisfaction at his employment, bending his aged figure over the broad, carved stone, and scraping from it the grass which had not been disturbed perhaps for a quarter of a century; and there was our own party looking on with eager interest, as the inscription every moment became more legible. That interest may be imagined, on reading the inscription, which, when brought to the full light of day, revealed these words:—

"Here lyeth the body of Xph^r Rousbie Esquire, who was taken out of this world by a violent death received on board his Majesty's ship The Quaker Ketch, Capt. Thos. Allen Commander, the last day of October 1684. And also of M^r. John Rousbie, his brother, who departed this naturall life on board the Ship Baltimore, being arrived in Patuxen the first day of February 1685."

This was a picturesque incident in its scenic character, but a still more engaging one as an occurrence in the path of discovery. Here was most unexpectedly brought to view a new link in the chain of our story. It was a pleasant surprise to have such a fact as this breaking upon us from an ambuscade, to help out a half-formed narrative which I had feared was hopeless of completion. The inscription is a necessary supplement to the marginal notes. As an insulated monument, it is meagre in its detail, and stands in need of explanation. It does not describe Christopher Rousby as the Collector of the Customs; it does not affirm that he was murdered; it makes no allusion to Talbot: but it gives the name of the ship and its commander, along with the date of the death. "The Landholder's Assistant" supplies all the facts that are wanting in this brief statement. These two memorials help each other and enlarge the common current of testimony, like two confluent streams coming from opposite sources. From the two together we learn that Colonel Talbot, the Surveyor-General in 1684, killed Mr. Christopher Rousby on board of a ship of war; and we are apprised that Rousby was a gentleman of rank and authority in the Province, holding an important commission from the King. The place at which the tomb is found shows also that he was the owner of a considerable landed estate and a near neighbor of the Lord Proprietary.

The story, however, requires much more circumstance to give it the interest which we hope yet to find in it.

Chapter IV

Dryasdust

I have now to change my scene, and to pursue in another quarter more important investigations. I break off with some regret from my visit to St. Mary's, because it had many attractions of its own, which would form a pleasant theme for description. Some of the results of that visit I embodied, several years ago, in a fiction which I fear the world will hardly credit me in saying has as much history in it as invention.* But my journey had no further connection with the particular subject before us, after the discovery of the tomb. I therefore take my leave, at this juncture, of good Father Carberry and St. Inigoes, and also of my companion in this adventure,—pausing but a moment to say, that the Superior of St. Inigoes has, some time since, gone to his account, and that I am not willing to part with him in my narrative without a grateful recognition of the esteem I have for his memory, in which I share with all who were acquainted with him,—an esteem won by the simple, unostentatious merit of his character, his liberal religious sentiment, and his frank and cordial hospitality, which had the best flavor of the good old housekeeping of St. Mary's,—a commendation which every one conversant with that section of Maryland will understand to imply what the Irish schoolmaster, in one of Carleton's tales, calls "the hoighth of good living."

After my return from this excursion, I resolved to make a search amongst the records at Annapolis, to ascertain whether any memorials existed which might furnish further information in regard to the events to which I had now got a clue. And here comes in a morsel of official history which will excuse a short digression.

The Legislature had, about this time, directed the Executive to cause a search through the government buildings, with a view to the discovery of old state papers and manuscripts, which, having been consigned, time out

---

Rob of the Bowl [Kennedy's note].

of mind, to neglect and oblivion, were known only as heaps of promiscuous lumber, strewed over the floors of damp cellars and unfrequented garrets. The careless and unappreciative spirit of the proper guardians of our archives in past years had suffered many precious folios and separate papers to be disposed of as mere rubbish; and the not less culpable and incurious indolence of their successors, in our own times, had treated them with equal indifference. The attention of the Legislature was awakened to the importance of this investigation by Mr. David Ridgely, the State Librarian, and he was appointed by the Executive to undertake the labor. Never did beagle pursue the chase with more steady foot than did this eager and laudable champion of the ancient fame of the State his chosen duty. He rummaged old cuddies, closets, vaults, and cocklofts, and pried into every recess of the Chancery, the Land Office, the Committee-Rooms, and the Council-Chamber, searching up-stairs and down-stairs, wherever a truant paper was supposed to lurk. Groping with lantern in hand and body bent, he made his way through narrow passages, startling the rats from their fastnesses, where they had been intrenched for half a century, and breaking down the thick drapery—the Gobelin tapestry I might call it—woven by successive families of spiders from the days of the last Lord Proprietary. The very dust which was kicked up in Annapolis, as the old newspapers tell us, at the passage of the Stamp Act, was once more set in motion by the foot of this resolute and unwearied invader, and everywhere something was found to reward the toil of the search. But the most valuable discoveries were made in the old Treasury,—made, alas! too late for the full fruition of the Librarian's labor. The Treasury, one of the most venerable structures in the State, is that lowly and quaint little edifice of brick which the visitor never fails to notice within the inclosure of the State-House grounds. It was originally designed for the accommodation of the Governor and his Council, and for the sessions of the Upper House of the Provincial Legislature; the Burgesses, at that time, holding their meetings in the old State House, which occupied the site of the present more imposing and capacious building: this latter having been erected about the year 1772.

In some dark recess of the Treasury Office Mr. Ridgely struck upon a mine of wealth, in a mouldy wooden box, which was found to contain many missing Journals of the Provincial Council, some of which bore date as far back as 1666. It was a sad disappointment to him, when his eye was greeted with the sight of these folios, to see them crumble, like the famed Dead-Sea Apples, into powder, upon every attempt to handle them. The form of the books was preserved and the character of the writing distinctly legible, but, from the effect of moisture, the paper had lost its cohesion, and fell to pieces at every effort to turn a leaf. I was myself a witness to this tantalizing deception, and, with the Librarian, read enough to show the date and character of the perishing record.

Through this accident, the Council Journals of a most interesting period, embracing several years between 1666 and 1692, were irretrievably lost. Others sustained less damage, and were partially preserved. Some few survived in good condition.

Our Maryland historians have had frequent occasion to complain of the deficiency of material for the illustration of several epochs in the Provincial existence, owing to the loss of official records. No research has supplied the means of describing the public events of these intervals, beyond some few inferences, which are only sufficient to show that these silent periods were marked by incidents of important interest. The most striking of these privations occurs towards the end of the seventeenth century,— precisely that period to which the crumbling folios had reference.

This loss of the records has been ascribed to their frequent removals during periods of trouble, and to the havoc made in the rage of parties. The Province, like the great world from which it was so far remote, was distracted with what are sometimes called religious quarrels, but what I prefer to describe as exceedingly irreligious quarrels, carried on by men professing to be Christians, and generated in the heat of disputes concerning the word of the great Teacher of "peace on earth." Out of these grew any quantity of rebellion and war, tinctured with their usual flavor of persecution. For at this era the wars of Christendom were chiefly waged in support of dogmas and creeds, and took a savage hue from the fury of religious bigotry. The wars of Europe since that period have arisen upon commercial and political questions, and religion has been freed from the dishonor of promoting these bloody strifes so incompatible with its high office. In these quarrels of the fathers of Maryland, the archives of government were seized more than once, and, perhaps, destroyed. On one occasion they were burnt. And so, amongst all these disorders, it has fallen out that the full development of the State history has been rendered impossible.

Mr. Ridgely's foray, however, into this domain of dust and darkness has happily rescued much useful matter to aid the future chronicler in supplying the deficiency of past attempts to trace the path of our modest annals through these silent intervals. Incidentally the Librarian's work has assisted my story; for, although the recovered folios did not touch the exact year of my search, the pursuit of them led me to what I may claim as a discovery of my own. I found what I could not say was wholly lost, but what, until Mr. Ridgely's exploration drew attention to the records, might have been said to have shrunk from all notice of the present generation, and to be fast falling a prey to the tooth of time and the visit of the worm. A few years more

of neglect and the ill usage of careless custodians, and it would have passed
to that depository of things lost upon the earth, which fable has placed in
the moon. It was my good fortune, in this upturning of relics of the past, to
lay my hand upon a sadly tattered and decayed MS. volume,—unbound,
without beginning and without end, coated with the dust which had been
gathering upon it ever since Chalmers and Bozman had done their work of
deciphering its quaint old text. It lay in the state of rubbish, in an old
case, where many documents of the same kind had been consigned to the
same oblivion, and with it had been sleeping for as many years, perhaps, as
the Beauty in the fairy tale,—happily destined, at last, to be awakened, as
she was, by one who by his perseverance had won a title to herself.

This manuscript was now, in this day of revival, brought out from its
hiding-place, and, upon inspection, proved to be a Journal of the Council
for some few years including the very date of the death of the Collector on
the Patuxent.

The record was complete, neatly written in the peculiar manuscript
character of that age, so difficult for a modern reader to decipher. Its queer
old-fashioned spelling suggested the idea that our ancestors considered both
consonants and vowels too weak to stand alone, and that therefore they
doubled them as often as they could; and there was such an actual identification of its antiquity in its exterior aspect as well as in its forms of speech,
that, when I have sat poring over it alone at midnight in my study, as I
have often done, I have turned my eye over my shoulder, expecting to see
the apparition of Master John Llewellin—who subscribes his name with a
very energetic flourish as Clerk of the Council—standing behind me in
grave-colored doublet and trunk-hose, with a starched ruff, a wide-awake
hat drawn over his brow, and a short black feather falling amongst the locks
of his dark hair towards his back.

This Journal lets in a blaze of light upon the old tradition of Talbot's
Cave. The narrative of what it discloses it is now my purpose to make as
brief as is compatible with common justice to my subject.

Chapter V

A Fragment of History

Charles Calvert, Lord Baltimore, the son of Cecilius, was, according to
the testimony of all our annalists, a worthy gentleman and an upright ruler.
He was governor of Maryland, by the appointment of his father, from 1662
to 1675, and after that became the Lord Proprietary by inheritance, and
administered the public affairs in person. His prudence and judgment won
him the esteem of the best portion of his people, and the Province prospered
in his hands.

All our histories tell of the troubles that beset the closing years of his residence in Maryland. They arose partly out of his religion, and in part out of the jealousy of the crown concerning the privileges of his charter.

He was a Roman Catholic; but, like his father, liberal and tolerant in opinion, and free from sectarian bias in the administration of his government. Apart from the influence of his father's example, the training of his education, his real attachment to the interests of the Province, and his own natural inclination,—all of which pointed out to him the duty as well as the advantage of affording the utmost security to the freedom of religious opinion,—the conditions under which he held his proprietary rights rendered a departure from this policy the most improbable accusation that could be made against him. The public mind of England at that period was fevered to a state of madness by the domestic quarrel that raged within the kingdom against the Catholics. The people were distracted with constant alarms of Popish plots for the overthrow of the government. The King, a heartless profligate, absorbed in frivolous pleasures, scarcely entertained any grave question of state affairs that had not some connection with his hatreds and his fears of Catholics and Dissenters. Then, also, the Province itself was composed, in far the greater part, of a Protestant population,— computed by some contemporary writers at the proportion of thirty to one, —a population who were guaranteed freedom of conscience by the Charter, and who possessed all necessary power both legal and physical to enforce it.

Under such circumstances as these, how is it possible to impute designs against the old established toleration, which had marked the history of Maryland from its first settlement to that day, to so prudent and careful a ruler as Charles Calvert, without imputing to him, at the same time, a folly so absurd as to belie every opinion that has ever been uttered to his advantage?

Yet, notwithstanding these improbabilities, the accusation was made and affected to be believed by the King and his Council; the result of which was that a royal order was sent to the Proprietary, commanding him to dismiss every Catholic from employment in the Province, and to supply their places by the appointment of Protestants.

The most plausible theory upon which I can account for this harsh proceeding is suggested by the fact that parties in the Province took the same complexion with those in the mother country and ran parallel with them,—that the same excitements which agitated the minds of the people in England were industriously fomented here, where no similar reason for them existed, as the volunteer work of demagogues who saw in them the means of promoting their own interest,—that, in fact, this opposition to the Proprietary grew out of a failing in our ancestors which has not yet been cured in their descendants, a weakness in favor of the loaves and fishes. The party in the majority carried the elections, and felt, of course, as all parties do who perform such an exploit, that they had made a very gigantic sacrifice for the good of the country and deserved to be remunerated for such an act of heroism, and thereupon set up and asserted that venerable doctrine which has been erroneously and somewhat vaingloriously claimed as the conception of a modern statesman, namely,—"that to the victors belong the spoils." I rejoice in the discovery that a dogma so profound and so convenient has the sanction of antiquity to commend it to the platform of the patriots of our own time.

I must in a few words notice another charge against Lord Baltimore, which was even more serious than the first, and to which the cupidity of the King lent a willing ear. Parliament had passed an act for levying certain duties on the trade of the Southern Colonies, which were very oppressive to the commerce of Maryland. These duties were gathered by Collectors specially appointed for the occasion, who held their commissions from the Crown, and who were stationed at the several ports of entry of the Province. The frequent evasion of these duties gave rise to much ill-will between the Collectors and the people. Lord Baltimore was charged with having connived at these evasions, and with obstructing the collection of the royal revenue. His chief accusers were the Collectors, who, being Crown officers, seemed naturally to array themselves against him. Although there was really no foundation for this complaint, yet the King, who never threw away a chance to replenish his purse, compelled the Proprietary to pay by way of retribution a large sum into the Exchequer.

I have no need to dwell upon this subject, and have referred to it only because it explains the relation between Lord Baltimore and Christopher Rousby, and has therefore some connection with my story. Rousby was an enemy to the Proprietary; and from a letter preserved by Chalmers it appears there was no love lost between them. Lord Baltimore writes to the Earl of Anglesey, the President of the King's Council, in 1681,—"I have already written twice to your Lordship about Christopher Rousby, who I desired might be removed from his place of Collector of his Majesty's Customs,—he having been a great knave, and a disturber of the trade and peace of the Province"; which letter, it seems, had no effect,—as Christopher Rousby was continued in his post. He was doubtless emboldened by the failure of this remonstrance against him to exhibit his ill-will towards the Proprietary in more open and more vexatious modes of annoyance.

All these embarrassments threw a heavy shadow over the latter years of Lord Baltimore's life, and now drove him to the necessity of making a visit to England for the purpose of personal explanation and defence before the King. He accordingly took his departure in the month of June, 1684, intending to return in a few months; but a tide of misfortune that now set in upon him prevented that wish, and he never saw Maryland again.

In about half a year after Calvert's arrival in England, King Charles the Second was gathered to his fathers, and his brother, the Duke of York, a worse man, a greater hypocrite, and a more crafty despot, reigned in his stead.

James the Second was a Roman Catholic, and Calvert, on that score alone, might have expected some sympathy and favor: he might, at least, have expected justice. But James was heartless and selfish. The Proprietary found nothing but cold neglect, and a contemptible jealousy of the prerogatives and power conferred by his charter. James himself claimed to be a proprietary on this continent by virtue of extensive royal grants, and was directly interested with William Penn in defeating the claims of the Baltimore family to the country upon the Delaware; he was, therefore, in fact, the secret and prepossessed enemy of Calvert. Instead of protection from the Crown, Calvert found proceedings instituted in the King's Bench to annul his charter, which, but for the abrupt termination of this short, disgraceful reign in abdication and flight, would have been consummated under James's own direction. The Revolution of 1688 brought up other influences more hostile still to the Proprietary; and the Province, which was always sedulous to follow the fashions of London, was not behindhand on this occasion, but made, also, its revolution, in imitation of the great one. The end of all was the utter subversion of the Charter, and a new government of Maryland under a royal commission. How this was accomplished our historians are not able to tell. From 1688 to 1692 is one of our dark intervals of which I have spoken. It begins with a domestic revolution and ends with the appointment of a Royal Governor, and that is pretty nearly all we know about it. After this, there was no Proprietary dominion in Maryland, until it was restored upon the accession of George the First in 1715; when it reappears in the second Charles Calvert, a minor, the grandson of the late Proprietary. This gentleman was the son of Benedict Leonard Calvert, and was educated in the Protestant faith, which his father had adopted as more consonant with the prosperity of the family and the hopes of the Province.

Before Lord Baltimore took his departure, he made all necessary arrangements for the administration of the government during his absence. The chief authority he invested in his son Benedict Leonard, to whom I referred just now,—at that time a youth of twelve or fourteen years of age. My old record contains the commission issued on this occasion, which is of the most stately and royal breadth of phrase, and occupies paper enough to make a deed for the route of the Pacific Railroad. In this document "our dearly beloved son Benedict Leonard Calvert" is ordained and appointed to be "Lieutenant General, Chief Captain, Chief Governor and Commander, Chief Admiral both by sea and land, of our Province of Maryland, and of all our Islands, Territories, and Dominions whatsoever, and of all and singular our Castles, Forts, Fortresses, Fortifications, Munitions, Ships, and Navies in our said Province, Islands, Territories, and Dominions aforesaid."

I hope to be excused for the particularity of my quotation of this young gentleman's titles, which I have given at full length only by way of demonstration of the magnificence of our old Palatine Province of Maryland, and to excite in the present generation a becoming pride at having fallen heirs to such a principality; albeit Benedict Leonard's more recent successors to these princely prerogatives may have reason to complain of that relentless spirit of democracy which has shorn them of so many worshipful honors. But we republicans are philosophical, and can make sacrifices with a good grace.

As it was quite impossible for this young Lieutenant General to go alone under such a staggering weight of dignities, the same commission puts him in leading-strings by the appointment of nine Deputy or Lieutenant Governors who are charged with the execution of all his duties. The first-named of these deputies is "our dearly beloved Cousin," Colonel George Talbot, who is associated with "our well-beloved Counsellor," Thomas Tailler, Colonel Vincent Low, Colonel Henry Darnall, Colonel William Digges, Colonel William Stevens, Colonel William Burgess, Major Nicholas Sewall, and John Darnall, Esquire. These same gentlemen, with Edward Pye and Thomas Truman, are also commissioned to be of the Privy Council, "for and in relation to all matters of State."

These appointments being made and other matters disposed of, Charles Calvert took leave of his beautiful and favorite Maryland, never to see this fair land again.

Chapter VI

A Border Chieftain

I have now to pursue the narrative of my story as I find the necessary material in the old Council Journal. I shall not incumber this narrative with literal extracts from these proceedings, but give the substance of what I find there, with such illustration as I have been able to glean from other sources.

Colonel George Talbot, whom we recognize as the first-named in the commission of the nine Deputy Governors and of the Privy Council, seems to have been a special favorite of the Proprietary. He was the grandson of the first Baron of Baltimore, the Secretary of State of James the First. His father was an Irish baronet, Sir George Talbot, of Cartown in Kildare, who had married Grace, one of the younger sisters of Cecilius, the second Proprietary and father of Charles Calvert. He was, therefore, as the commission describes him, the cousin of Lord Baltimore, who had now invested him with a leading authority in the administration of the government.

He was born in Ireland, and from some facts connected with his history I infer that he did not emigrate to Maryland until after his marriage, his wife being an Irish lady.

That he was a man of consideration in the Province, with large experience in its affairs, is shown by the character of the employments that were intrusted to him. He had been, for some years before the departure of Lord Baltimore on his visit to England, a conspicuous member of his Council. He had, for an equal length of time, held the post of Surveyor-General, an office of high responsibility and trust. But his chief employment was of a military nature, in which his discretion, courage, and conduct were in constant requisition. He had the chief command, with the title and commission of Deputy Governor, over the northern border of the Province, a region continually exposed to the inroads of the fierce and war-like tribe of the "Sasquesahannocks."

The country lying between the Susquehanna and the Delaware, that which now coincides with parts of Harford and Cecil Counties in Maryland and the upper portion of the State of Delaware, was known in those days as New Ireland, and was chiefly settled by emigrants from the old kingdom whose name it bore. This region was included within the range of Talbot's command, and was gradually increasing in population and in farms and houses scattered over a line of some seventy or eighty miles from east to west, and slowly encroaching upon the thick wilderness to the north, where surly savages lurked and watched the advance of the white man with jealous anger.

The tenants of this tract held their lands under the Proprietary grants, coupled with a condition, imposed as much by their own necessities as by the law, to render active service in the defence of the frontier as a local militia. They were accordingly organized on a military establishment, and kept in a state of continual preparation to repel the unwelcome visits of their hostile neighbors.

A dispute between Lord Baltimore and William Penn, founded upon the claim of the former to a portion of the territory bounding on the Delaware, had given occasion to border feuds, which had imposed upon our Proprietary the necessity of building and maintaining a fort on Christiana Creek, near the present city of Wilmington; and there were also some few block-houses or smaller fortified strongholds along the line of settlement towards the Susquehanna. These forts were garrisoned by a small force of musketeers maintained by the government. The Province was also at the charge of a regiment of cavalry, of which Talbot was the Colonel, and parts of which were assigned to the defence of this frontier.

If we add to these a corps of rangers, who were specially employed in watching and arresting all trespassers upon the territory of the Province, it will complete our sketch of the military organization of the frontier over which Talbot had the chief command. The whole or any portion of this force could be assembled in a few hours to meet the emergencies of the time. Signals were established for the muster of the border. Beacon fires on the hills, the blowing of horns, and the despatch of runners were familiar to the tenants, and often called the ploughman away from the furrow to the appointed gathering-place. Three musket-shots fired in succession from a lonely cabin, at dead of night, awakened the sleeper in the next homestead; the three shots, repeated from house to house, across this silent waste of forest and field, carried the alarm onward; and before break of day a hundred stout yeomen, armed with cutlass and carbine, were on foot to check and punish the stealthy foray of the Sasquesahannock against the barred and bolted dwellings where mothers rocked their children to sleep, confident in the protection of this organized and effective system of defence.

In this region Talbot himself held a manor which was called New Connaught, and here he had his family mansion, and kept hospitality in rude woodland state, as a man of rank and command, with his retainers and friends gathered around him. This establishment was seated on Elk River, and was, doubtless, a fortified position. I picture to my mind a capacious dwelling-house built of logs from the surrounding forest; its ample hall furnished with implements of war, pikes, carbines, and basket-hilted swords, mingled with antlers of the buck, skins of wild animals, plumage of birds, and other trophies of the hunter's craft; the large fireplace surrounded with hardy woodsmen, and the tables furnished with venison, wild fowl, and fish, the common luxuries of the region, in that prodigal profusion to which our forefathers were accustomed, and which their descendants still regard as the essential condition of hearty and honest housekeeping. This mansion I fancy surrounded by a spacious picketed rampart, presenting its bristling points to the four quarters of the compass, and accessible only through a gateway of ponderous timber studded thick with nails: the whole offering defiance to the grim savage who might chance to prowl within the frown of its midnight shadow.

Here Talbot spent the greater portion of the year with his wife and children. Here he had his yacht or shallop on the river, and often skimmed this beautiful expanse of water in pursuit of its abundant game,—those hawks of which tradition preserves the memory his companions and auxiliaries in this pastime. Here, too, he had his hounds and other hunting-dogs to beat up the game for which the banks of Elk River are yet famous.

This sylvan lodge was cheered and refined by the presence of his wife and children, whose daily household occupations were assisted by numerous servants chosen from the warm-hearted people who had left their own Green Isle to find a home in this wilderness.

Amidst such scenes and the duties of her station we may suppose that Mrs. Talbot, a lady who could not but have relinquished many comforts in her native land for this rude life of the forest, found sufficient resource to quell the regrets of many fond memories of the home and friends she had left behind, and to reconcile her to the fortunes of her husband, to whom, as we shall see, she was devoted with an ardor that no hardship or danger could abate.

Being the dispenser of her husband's hospitality,—the bread-giver, in the old Saxon phrase,—the frequent companion of his pastime, and the bountiful friend, not only of the families whose cottages threw up their smoke within view of her dwelling, but of all who came and went on the occasions of business or pleasure in the common intercourse of the frontier, we may conceive the sentiment of respect and attachment she inspired in this insulated district, and the service she was thus enabled to command.

This is but a fancy picture, it is true, of the home of Talbot, which, for want of authentic elements of description, I am forced to draw. It is suggested by the few scattered glimpses we get in the records of his position and circumstances, and may, I think, be received at least as near the truth in its general aspect and characteristic features.

He was undoubtedly a bold, enterprising man,—impetuous, passionate, and harsh, as the incidents of his story show. He was, most probably, a soldier trained to the profession, and may have served abroad, as nearly all gentlemen of that period were accustomed to do. That he was an ardent and uncompromising partisan of the Proprietary in the dissensions of the Province seems to be evident. I suppose him, also, to have been warm-hearted, proud in spirit, and hasty in temper,—a man to be loved or hated by friend or foe with equal intensity. It is material to add to this sketch of him, that he was a Roman Catholic,—as we have record proof that all the Deputy Governors named in the recent commission were, I believe, without exception,—and that he was doubtless imbued with the dislike and indignation which naturally fired the gentlemen of his faith against those who were then supposed to be plotting the overthrow of the Proprietary government, by exciting religious prejudice against the Baltimore family.

Chapter VII

The Old City

Let me now once more shift the scene. In the summer of 1684, the peaceful little port of St. Mary's was visited by a phenomenon of rare occurrence in those days. A ship of war of the smaller class, with the Cross of St. George sparkling on her broad flag, came gliding to an anchorage abreast the town. The fort of St. Inigoes gave the customary salute, which I have reason to believe was not returned. Not long after this, a bluff, swaggering, vulgar captain came on shore. He made no visit of respect or business to any member of the Council. He gave no report of his character or the purpose of his visit, but strolled to the tavern,—I suppose to that kept by Mr. Cordea, who, in addition to his calling of keeper of the ordinary, was the most approved shoemaker of the city,—and here regaled himself with a potation of strong waters. It is likely that he then repaired to Mr. Blakiston's, the King's Collector,—a bitter and relentless enemy of the Lord Proprietary,—and there may have met Kenelm Chiseldine, John Coode, Colonel Jowles, and others noted for their hatred of the Calvert family, and in such company as this indulged himself in deriding Lord Baltimore and his government. During his stay in the port, his men came on shore, and, imitating their captain's unamiable temper, roamed in squads about the town and its neighborhood, conducting themselves in a noisy, hectoring manner towards the inhabitants, disturbing the repose of the quiet burghers, and shocking their ears with ribald abuse of the authorities. These roystering sailors—I mention it as a point of historical interest—had even the audacity to break into Alderman Garret Van Swearingen's garden, and to pluck up and carry away his cabbages and other vegetables, and—according to the testimony of Mr. Cordea, whose indignation was the more intense from his veneration for the Alderman, and from the fact that he made his Worship's shoes—they would have killed one of his Worship's sheep, if his (Cordea's) man had not prevented them; and after this, as if on purpose more keenly to lacerate his feelings, they brought these cabbages to Cordea's house, and there boiled them before his eyes,—he being sick and not able to drive them away.

After a few days spent in this manner, the swaggering captain—whose name, it was soon bruited about, was Thomas Allen, of his Majesty's Navy—went on board of his ketch,—or brig, as we should call it,—the Quaker, weighed anchor, and set sail towards the Potomac, and thence stood down the Bay upon the coast of Virginia. Every now and then, after his departure, there came reports to the Council of insults offered by Captain Allen to the skippers of sundry Bay craft and other peaceful traders on the Chesapeake; these insults consisting generally in wantonly compelling them to heave to and submit to his search, in vexatiously detaining them, overhauling their papers, and offending them with coarse vituperation of themselves, as well as of the Lord Proprietary and his Council.

About a month later the Quaker was observed to enter the Patuxent

River, and cast anchor just inside of the entrance, near the Calvert County shore, and opposite Christopher Rousby's house at Drum Point. This was —says my chronicle—on Thursday, the 30th of October, in this year 1684. As yet Captain Allen had not condescended to make any report of his arrival in the Province to any officer of the Proprietary.

On Sunday morning, the 2d of November, the city was thrown into a state of violent ebullition—like a little red-hot tea-kettle—by the circulation of a rumor that got wind about the hour the burghers were preparing to go to church. It was brought from Patuxent late in the previous night, and was now whispered from one neighbor to another, and soon came to boil with an extraordinary volume of steam. Stripping it of the exaggeration natural to such an excitement, the rumor was substantially this: That Colonel Talbot, hearing of the arrival of Captain Allen in the Patuxent on Thursday, and getting no message or report from him, set off on Friday morning, in an angry state of mind, and rode over to Patuxent, determined to give the unmannerly captain a lesson upon his duty. That as soon as he reached Mattapony House, he took his boat and went on board the ketch. That there he found Christopher Rousby, the King's Collector, cronying with Captain Allen, and upholding him in his disrespect to the government. That Colonel Talbot was very sharp upon Rousby, not liking him for old grudges, and more moved against him now; and that he spoke his mind both to Captain Allen and Christopher Rousby, and so got into a high quarrel with them. That when he had said all he desired to say to them, he made a move to leave the ketch in his boat, intending to return to Mattapony House; but they who were in the cabin prevented him, and would not let him go. That thereupon the quarrel broke out afresh, and became more bitter; and it being now in the night, and all in a great heat of passion, the parties having already come from words to blows, Talbot drew his skean, or dagger, and stabbed Rousby to the heart. That nothing was known on shore of the affray till Saturday evening, when the body was brought to Rousby's house; after which it became known to the neighborhood; and one of the men of Major Sewall's plantation, which adjoined Rousby's, having thus heard of it, set out and rode that night over to St. Mary's with the news, which he gave to the Major before midnight. It was added, that Colonel Talbot was now detained on board of the ketch, as a prisoner, by Captain Allen.

This was the amount of the dreadful story over which the gossips of St. Mary's were shaking their wise heads and discoursing on "crowner's quest law" that Sunday morning.

As soon as Major Sewall received these unhappy midnight tidings, he went instantly to his colleague, Colonel Darnall, and communicated them to him; and they, being warm friends of Talbot's, were very anxious to get him out of the custody of this Captain Allen. They therefore, on Sunday morning, issued a writ directed to Roger Brooke, the sheriff of Calvert County, commanding him to arrest the prisoner and bring him before the Council. Their next move was to ride over—the same morning—to Patuxent, taking with them Mr. Robert Carvil, and John Llewellin, their secretary. Upon reaching the river, all four went on board the ketch to learn the particulars of the quarrel. These particulars are not preserved in the record; and we have nothing better than our conjectures as to what they disclosed. We know nothing specific of the cause or character of the quarrel. The visitors found Talbot loaded with irons, and Captain Allen in a brutal state of exasperation, swearing that he would not surrender his prisoner to the authorities of the Province, but would carry him to Virginia and deliver him to the government there, to be dealt with as Lord Effingham should direct. He was grossly insulting to the two members of the Council who had come on this inquiry; and after they had left his vessel, in the pinnace, to return to the shore, he affected to believe that they had some concealed force lying in wait to seize the pinnace and its crew, and so ordered them back on board, but after a short detention thought better of it, and suffered them again to depart.

The contumacy of the captain, and the declaration of his purpose to carry away Talbot out of the jurisdiction of the Province within which the crime was committed, and to deliver him to the Governor of Virginia, was a grave assault upon the dignity of the government and a gross contempt of the public authorities, which required the notice of the Council. A meeting of this body was therefore held on the Patuxent, at Rich Neck, on the morning of the 4th of November. I find that five members were present on that occasion. Besides Colonel Darnall and Major Sewall, there were Counsellor Tailler and Colonels Digges and Burgess. Here the matter was debated and ended in a feeble resolve,—that, if this Captain Allen should persist in his contumacy and take Talbot to Virginia, the Council should immediately demand of Lord Effingham his redelivery into this Province. Alas, they could only scold! This resolution was all they could oppose to the bullying captain and the guns of the troublesome little Quaker.

Allen, after hectoring awhile in this fashion, and raising the wrath of the Colonels of the Council until they were red in the cheeks, defiantly took his departure, carrying with him his prisoner, in spite of the vehement indignation of the liegemen of the Province.

We may imagine the valorous anger of our little metropolis at this act or crime of lese-majesty. I can see the group of angry burghers, collected on the porch of Cordea's tavern, in a fume as they listen to Master John

Llewellin's account of what had taken place,—Llewellin himself as peppery as his namesake when he made Ancient Pistol eat his leek; and I fancy I can hear Alderman Van Swearingen's choleric explosion against Lord Effingham, supposing his Lordship should presume to slight the order of the Council in respect to Talbot's return.

But these fervors were too violent to last. Christopher Rousby was duly deposited under the greensward upon the margin of Harper's Creek, where I found him safe, if not sound, more than a hundred and fifty years afterwards. The metropolis gradually ceased to boil, and slowly fell to its usual temperature of repose, and no more disturbed itself with thoughts of the terrible captain. Talbot, upon being transferred to the dominion of Virginia, was confined in the jail of Gloucester County, in the old town of Gloucester, on the northern bank of York River.

The Council now opened their correspondence with Lord Effingham, demanding the surrender of their late colleague. On their part, it was marked by a deferential respect, which, it is evident, they did not feel, and which seems to denote a timid conviction of the favor of Virginia and the disgrace of Maryland in the personal feelings of the King. It is manifest they were afraid of giving offence to the lordly governor of the neighboring Province. On the part of Lord Effingham, the correspondence is cavalier, arrogant, and peremptory.

The Council write deploringly to his Lordship. They "pray"—as they phrase it—"in humble, civil, and obliging terms, to have the prisoner safely returned to this government." They add,—"Your Excellency's great wisdom, prudence, and integrity, as well as neighborly affection and kindness for this Province, manifested and expressed, will, we doubt not, spare us the labor of straining for arguments to move your Excellency's consideration to this our so just and reasonable demand." Poor Colonel Darnall, Poor Colonel Digges, and the rest of your Colonels and Majors,—to write such whining hypocrisy as this! George Talbot would not have written to Lord Effingham in such phrase, if one of you had been unlawfully transported to his prison and Talbot were your pleader!

The nobleman to whom this servile language was addressed was a hateful despot, who stands marked in the history of Virginia for his oppressive administration, his arrogance, and his faithlessness.

To give this beseeching letter more significance and the flattery it contained more point, it was committed to the charge of two gentlemen who were commissioned to deliver it in person to his Lordship. These were Mr. Clement Hill and Mr. Anthony Underwood.

Effingham's answer was cool, short, and admonitory. The essence of it is in these words:—"We do not think it warrantable to comply with your desires, but shall detain Talbot prisoner until his Majesty's particular commands be known therein." A postscript is added of this import:—"I recommend to your consideration, that you take care, as far as in you lies, that, in the matter of the Customs, his Majesty receive no further detriment by this unfortunate accident."

One almost rejoices to read such an answer to the fulsome language which drew it out. This correspondence runs through several such epistles. The Council complain of the rudeness and coarse behavior of Captain Allen, and particularly of his traducing Lord Baltimore's government and attempting to excite the people against it. Lord Effingham professes to disbelieve such charges against "an officer who has so long served his King with fidelity, and who could not but know what was due to his superiors."

Occasionally this same faithful officer, Captain Allen himself, reappears upon the stage. We catch him at a gentleman's house in Virginia, boasting over his cups—for he seems to have paid habitual tribute to a bowl of punch—that he will break up the government of Maryland, and annex this poor little Province of ours to Virginia: a fact worth notice just now, as it makes it clear that annexation is not the new idea of the Nineteenth Century, but lived in very muddy brains a long time ago. I now quit this correspondence to look after a bit of romance in a secret adventure.

Chapter VIII

A Plot

We must return to the Manor of New Connaught upon the Elk River.

There we shall find a sorrowful household. The Lord of the Manor is in captivity; his people are dejected with a presentiment that they are to see him no more; his wife is lamenting with her children, and counting the weary days of his imprisonment.

> "His hounds they all run masterless,
> His hawks they flee from tree to tree."

Everything in the hospitable woodland home is changed. November, December, January had passed by since Talbot was lodged in the Gloucester prison, and still no hope dawned upon the afflicted lady. The forest around her howled with the rush of the winter wind, but neither the wilderness nor the winter was so desolate as her own heart. The fate of her husband was in the hands of his enemies. She trembled at the thought of his being forced to a trial for life in Virginia, where he would be deprived of that friendly sympathy so necessary even to the vindication of innocence, and where he ran the risk of being condemned without defence, upon the testimony of exasperated opponents.

But she was a strong-hearted and resolute woman, and would not despair. She had many friends around her,—friends devoted to her husband and herself. Amongst these was Phelim Murray, a cornet of cavalry under the command of Talbot,—a brave, reckless, true-hearted comrade, who had often shared the hospitality, the adventurous service, and the sports of his commander.

To Murray I attribute the planning of the enterprise I am now about to relate. He had determined to rescue his chief from his prison in Virginia. His scheme required the coöperation of Mrs. Talbot and one of her youngest children,—the pet boy, perhaps, of the family, some two or three years old,—I imagine, the special favorite of the father. The adventure was a bold one, involving many hardships and perils. Towards the end of January, the lady, accompanied by her boy with his nurse, and attended by two Irish men-servants, repaired to St. Mary's, where she was doubtless received as a guest in the mansion of the Proprietary, now the residence of young Benedict Leonard and those of the family who had not accompanied Lord Baltimore to England.

Whilst Mrs. Talbot tarried here, the Cornet was busy in his preparations. He had brought the Colonel's shallop from Elk River to the Patuxent, and was here concerting a plan to put the little vessel under the command of some ostensible owner who might appear in the character of its master to any over-curious or inopportune questioner. He had found a man exactly to his hand in a certain Roger Skreene, whose name might almost be thought to be adopted for the occasion and to express the part he had to act. He was what we may call the sloop's husband, but was bound to do whatever Murray commanded, to ask no questions, and to be profoundly ignorant of the real objects of the expedition. This pliant auxiliary had, like many thrifty— or more probably thriftless—persons of that time, a double occupation. He was amphibious in his habits, and lived equally on land and water. At home he was a tailor, and abroad a seaman, frequently plying his craft as a skipper on the Bay, and sufficiently known in the latter vocation to render his present employment a matter to excite no suspicious remark. It will be perceived in the course of his present adventure that he was quite innocent of any avowed complicity in the design which he was assisting.

Murray had a stout companion with him, a good friend to Talbot, probably one of the familiar frequenters of the Manor House of New Connaught,—a bold fellow, with a hand and a heart both ready for any perilous service. He may have been a comrade of the Cornet's in his troop. His name was Hugh Riley,—a name that has been traditionally connected with dare-devil exploits ever since the days of Dermot McMorrogh. There have been, I believe, but few hard fights in the world, to which Irishmen have had anything to say, without a Hugh Riley somewhere in the thickest part of them.

The preparations being now complete, Murray anchored his shallop near a convenient landing,—perhaps within the Mattapony Creek.

In the dead of winter, about the 30th of January, 1685, Mrs. Talbot, with her servants, her child, and nurse, set forth from the Proprietary residence in St. Mary's, to journey over to the Patuxent,—a cold, bleak ride of fifteen miles. The party were all on horseback: the young boy, perhaps, wrapped in thick coverings, nestling in the arms of one of the men: Mrs. Talbot braving the sharp wind in hood and cloak, and warmed by her own warm heart, which beat with a courageous pulse against the fierce blasts that swept and roared across her path. Such a cavalcade, of course, could not depart from St. Mary's without observation at any season; but at this time of the year so unusual a sight drew every inhabitant to the windows, and set in motion a current of gossip that bore away all other topics from every fireside. The gentlemen of the Council, too, doubtless had frequent conference with the unhappy wife of their colleague, during her sojourn in the Government House, and perhaps secretly counselled with her on her adventure. Whatever outward or seeming pretext may have been adopted for this movement, we can hardly suppose that many friends of the Proprietary were ignorant of its object. We have, indeed, evidence that the enemies of the Proprietary charged the Council with a direct connivance in the scheme of Talbot's escape, and made it a subject of complaint against Lord Baltimore that he afterwards approved of it.

Upon her arrival at the Patuxent, Mrs. Talbot went immediately on board of the sloop, with her attendants. There she found the friendly cornet and his comrade, Hugh Riley, on the alert to distinguish their loyalty in her cause. The amphibious Master Skreene was now at the head of a picked crew,—the whole party consisting of five stout men, with the lady, her child, and nurse. All the men but Skreene were sons of the Emerald Isle,—of a race whose historical boast is the faithfulness of their devotion to a friend in need and their chivalrous courtesy to woman, but still more their generous and gallant championship of woman in distress. On this occasion this national sentiment was enhanced when it was called into exercise in behalf of the sorrowful lady of the chief of their border settlements.

They set sail from the Patuxent on Saturday, the 31st of January. On Wednesday, the fifth day afterwards, they landed on the southern bank of the Rappahannock, at the house of Mr. Ralph Wormeley, near the mouth of the river. This long voyage of five days over so short a distance would seem to indicate that they departed from the common track of navigation to avoid notice.

The next morning Mr. Wormeley furnished them horses and a servant, and Mrs. Talbot, with the nurse and child, under the conduct of Cornet Murray, set out for Gloucester,—a distance of some twenty miles. The day following,—that is, on Friday,—the servant returned with the horses, having left the party behind. Saturday passed and part of Sunday, when, in the evening, Mrs. Talbot and the Cornet reappeared at Mr. Wormeley's. The child and nurse had been left behind; and this was accounted for by Mrs. Talbot's saying she had left the child with his father, to remain with him until she should return to Virginia. I infer that the child was introduced into this adventure to give some seeming to the visit which might lull suspicion and procure easier access to the prisoner; and the leaving of him in Gloucester proves that Mrs. Talbot had friends, and probably confederates there, to whose care he was committed.

As soon as the party had left the shallop, upon their first arrival at Mr. Wormeley's, the wily Master Skreene discovered that he had business at a landing farther up the river; and thither he straightway took his vessel,—Wormeley's being altogether too suspicious a place for him to frequent. And now, when Mrs. Talbot had returned to Wormeley's, Roger's business above, of course, was finished, and he dropped down again opposite the house on Monday evening; and the next morning took the Cornet and the lady on board. Having done this, he drew out into the river. This brings us to Tuesday, the 10th of February.

As soon as Mrs. Talbot was once more embarked in the shallop, Murray and Riley (I give Master Skreene's own account of the facts, as I find it in his testimony subsequently taken before the Council) made a pretext to go on shore, taking one of the men with them. They were going to look for a cousin of this man,—so they told Skreene,—and besides that, intended to go to a tavern to buy a bottle of rum: all of which Skreene gives the Council to understand he verily believed to be the real object of their visit.

The truth was, that, as soon as Murray and Riley and their companion had reached the shore, they mounted on horseback and galloped away in the direction of Gloucester prison. From the moment they disappeared on this gallop until their return, we have no account of what they did. Roger Skreene's testimony before the Council is virtuously silent on this point.

After this party was gone, Mrs. Talbot herself took command, and, with a view to more privacy, ordered Roger to anchor near the opposite shore of the river, taking advantage of the concealment afforded by a small inlet on the northern side. Skreene says he did this at her request, because she expressed a wish to taste some of the oysters from that side of the river, which he, with his usual facility, believed to be the only reason for getting into this unobserved harbor; and, merely to gratify this wish, he did as she desired.

The day went by slowly to the lady on the water. Cold February, a little sloop, and the bleak roadstead at the mouth of the Rappahannock brought but few comforts to the anxious wife, who sat muffled upon that unstable deck, watching the opposite shore, whilst the ceaseless plash of the waves breaking upon her ear numbered the minutes that marked the weary hours, and the hours that marked the still more weary day. She watched for the party who had galloped into the sombre pine-forest that sheltered the road leading to Gloucester, and for the arrival of that cousin of whom Murray spoke to Master Skreene.

But if the time dragged heavily with her, it flew with the Cornet and his companions. We cannot tell when the twenty miles to Gloucester were thrown behind them, but we know that the whole forty miles of going and coming were accomplished by sunrise the next morning. For the deposition tells us that Roger Skreene had become very impatient at the absence of his passengers,—at least, so he swears to the Council; and he began to think, just after the sun was up, that, as they had not returned, they must have got into a revel at the tavern, and forgotten themselves; which careless demeanor of theirs made him think of recrossing the river and of going ashore to beat them up; when, lo! all of a sudden, he spied a boat coming round the point within which he lay. And here arises a pleasant little dramatic scene, of some interest to our story.

Mrs. Talbot had been up at the dawn, and watched upon the deck, straining her sight, until she could see no more for tears; and at length, unable to endure her emotion longer, had withdrawn to the cabin. Presently Skreene came hurrying down to tell her that the boat was coming,—and, what surprised him, there were *four* persons in it. "Who is this fourth man?" he asked her, with his habitual simplicity, "and how are we to get him back to the shore again?"—a very natural question for Roger to ask, after all that had passed in his presence! Mrs. Talbot sprang to her feet,— her eyes sparkling, as she exclaimed, with a cheery voice, "Oh, his cousin has come!"—and immediately ran upon the deck to await the approaching party. There were pleasant smiling faces all around, as the four men came over the sloop's side; and although the testimony is silent as to the fact, there might have been some little kissing on the occasion. The new-comer was in a rough dress, and had the exterior of a servant; and our skipper says in his testimony, that "Mrs. Talbot spoke to him in the Irish language": very volubly, I have no doubt, and that much was said that was never translated. When they came to a pause in this conversation, she told Skreene, by way of interpretation, "he need not be uneasy about the stranger's going on shore, nor delay any longer, as this person had made up his mind to go with them to Maryland."

So the boat was made fast, the anchor was weighed, the sails were set, and the little sloop bent to the breeze and kissed the wave, as she rounded the headland and stood up the Bay, with Colonel George Talbot encircling with his arm his faithful wife, and with the gallant Cornet Murray sitting at his side.

They had now an additional reason for caution against search. So Murray ordered the skipper to shape his course over to the eastern shore, and to keep in between the islands and the main. This is a broad circuit outside of their course; but Roger is promised a reward by Mrs. Talbot, to compensate him for his loss of time; and the skipper is very willing. They had fetched a compass, as the Scripture phrase is, to the shore of Dorset County, and steered inside of Hooper's Island, into the mouth of Hungary River. Here it was part of the scheme to dismiss the faithful Roger from further service. With this view they landed on the island and went to Mr. Hooper's house, where they procured a supply of provisions, and immediately afterwards reëmbarked,—having clean forgotten Roger, until they were once more under full sail up the Bay, and too far advanced to turn back!

The deserted skipper bore his disappointment like a Christian; and being asked, on Hungary River, by a friend who met him there, and who gave his testimony before the Council, "What brought him there?" he replied, "He had been left on the island by Madam Talbot." And to another, "Where Madam Talbot was?" he answered, " She had gone up the Bay to her own house." Then, to a third question, "How he expected his pay?" he said, "He was to have it of Colonel Darnall and Major Sewall; and that Madam Talbot had promised him a hogshead of tobacco extra, for putting ashore at Hopper's Island." The last question was, "What news of Talbot?" and Roger's answer, "He had not been within twenty miles of him; neither did he know anything about the Colonel"!! But, on further discourse, he let fall, that "he knew the Colonel never would come to a trial,"—"that *he* knew this; but neither man, woman, nor child should know it, but those who knew it already."

So Colonel George Talbot is out of the hands of the proud Lord Effingham, and up the Bay with his wife and friends; and is buffeting the wintry head-winds in a long voyage to the Elk River, which, in due time, he reaches in safety.

Chapter IX

Troubles in Council

Let us now turn back to see what is doing at St. Mary's.

On the 17th of February comes to the Council a letter from Lord Effingham. It has the superscription, "These, with the greatest care and speed." It is dated on the 11th of February from Poropotanck, an Indian point on the York River above Gloucester, and memorable as being in the nighborhood of the spot where, some sixty years before these events, Pocahontas saved the life of that mirror of chivalry, Captain John Smith.

The letter brings information "that last night [the 10th of February] Colonel Talbot escaped out of prison,"—a subsequent letter says, "by the corruption of his guard,"—and it is full of admonition, which has very much the tone of command, urging all strenuous efforts to recapture him, and particularly recommending a proclamation of "hue and cry."

And now, for a month, there is a great parade in Maryland of proclamation, and hue and cry, and orders to sheriffs and county colonels to keep a sharp look-out everywhere for Talbot. But no person in the Province seems to be anxious to catch him, except Mr. Nehemiah Blakiston, the Collector, and a few others, who seem to have been ministering to Lord Effingham's spleen against the Council for not capturing him. His Lordship writes several letters of complaint at the delay and ill success of this pursuit, and some of them in no measured terms of courtesy. "I admire," he says in one of these, "at any slow proceedings in service wherein his Majesty is so concerned, and hope you will take off all occasions of future trouble, both unto me and you, of this nature, by manifesting yourselves zealous for his Majesty's service." They answer, that all imaginable care for the apprehending of Talbot has been taken by issuing proclamations, etc.,— but all have proved ineffectual, because Talbot upon all occasions flies and takes refuge "in the remotest parts of the woods and deserts of this Province."

At this point we get some traces of Talbot. There is a deposition of Robert Kemble of Cecil County, and some other papers, that give us a few particulars by which I am enabled to construct my narrative.

Colonel Talbot got to his own house about the middle of February,— nearly at the same time at which the news of his escape reached St. Mary's. He there lay warily watching the coming hue and cry for his apprehension. He collected his friends, armed them, and set them at watch and ward, at all his outposts. He had a disguise provided, in which he occasionally ventured abroad. Kemble met him, on the 19th of February, at George Oldfield's, on Elk River; and although the Colonel was disguised in a flaxen wig, and in other ways, Kemble says he knew him by hearing him cough in the night, in a room adjoining that in which Kemble slept. Whilst this witness was at Oldfield's, "Talbot's shallop," he says, "was busking and turning before Oldfield's landing for several hours." The roads leading towards Talbot's house were all guarded by his friends, and he had a report made to him of every vessel that arrived in the river. By way of more permanent concealment, until the storm should blow over, he had made preparations to build himself a cabin, somewhere in the woods out of the range of the thoroughfares of the district. When driven by a pressing emergency which required more than ordinary care to prevent his apprehension, he betook himself to the cave on the Susquehanna, where, most probably, with a friend or two,—Cornet Murray I hope was one of them,— he lay perdu for a few days at a time, and then ventured back to speak a word of comfort and encouragement to the faithful wife who kept guard at home.

In this disturbed and anxious alternation of concealment and flight Talbot passed the winter, until about the 25th of April, when, probably upon advice of friends, he voluntarily surrendered himself to the Council at St. Mary's, and was committed for trial in the provincial Court. The fact of the surrender was communicated to Lord Effingham by the Council, with a request that he would send the witnesses to Maryland to appear at his trial. Hereupon arose another correspondence with his Lordship, which is worthy of a moment's notice. Lord Effingham has lost nothing of his arrogance. He says, on the 12th of May, 1685, "I am so far from answering your desires, that I do hereby demand Colonel Talbot as my prisoner, in the King of England's name, and that you do forthwith convey him into Virginia. And to this my demand I expect your ready performance and compliance, upon your allegiance to his Majesty."

I am happy to read the answer to this insolent letter, in which it will be seen that the spirit of Maryland was waked up on the occasion to its proper voice.—It is necessary to say, by way of explanation to one point in this answer, that the Governor of Virginia had received the news of the accession and proclamation of James the Second, and had not communicated it to the Council in Maryland. The Council give an answer at their leisure, having waited till the 1st of June, when they write to his Lordship, protesting against Virginia's exercising any superintendence over Maryland, and peremptorily refusing to deliver Talbot. They tell him "that we are desirous and conclude to await his Majesty's resolution, [in regard to the prisoner,] which we question not will be agreeable to his Lordship's Charter, and, consequently, contrary to your expectations. In the mean time we cannot but resent in some measure, for we are willing to let you see that we observe, the small notice you seem to take of this Government, (contrary to that amicable correspondence so often promised, and expected by us,) in not holding us worthy to be advised of his Majesty's being proclaimed, without which, certainly, we have not been enabled to do our duty in that particular. Such advice would have been gratefully received by your Excellency's humble servants." Thanks, Colonels Darnall and Digges and you other Colonels and Majors, for this plain outspeaking of the old Maryland heart against the arrogance of the "Right Honorable Lord Howard, Baron of Effingham, Captain General and Chief Governor of his Majesty's Colony of Virginia," as he styles himself! I am glad to see this change of tone, since that first letter of obsequious submission.

Perhaps this change of tone may have had some connection with the recent change on the throne, in which the accession of a Catholic monarch may have given new courage to Maryland, and abated somewhat the confidence of Virginia. If so, it was but a transitory hope, born to a sad disappointment.

The documents afford but little more information.

Lord Baltimore, being in London, appears to have interceded with the King for some favor to Talbot, and writes to the Council on the third of July, "that it formerly was and still is the King's pleasure, that Talbot shall be brought over, in the Quaker Ketch, to England, to receive his trial there; and that, in order thereto, his Majesty had sent his commands to the Governor of Virginia to deliver him to Captain Allen, commander of said ketch, who is to bring him over." The Proprietary therefore directs his Council to send the prisoner to the Governor of Virginia, "to the end that his Majesty's pleasure may be fulfilled."

This letter was received on the 7th of October, 1685, and Talbot was accordingly sent, under the charge of Gilbert Clarke and a proper guard, to Lord Effingham, who gives Clarke a regular business receipt, as if he had brought him a hogshead of tobacco, and appends to it a short apologetic explanation of his previous rudeness, which we may receive as another proof of his distrust of the favor of the new monarch. "I had not been so urgent," he says, "had I not had advices from England, last April, of the measures that were taken there concerning him."

After this my chronicle is silent. We have no further tidings of Talbot. The only hint for a conjecture is the marginal note of "The Landholder's Assistant," got from Chalmers: "He was, I believe," says the note, "tried and convicted, and finally pardoned by James the Second."

This is probably enough. For I suppose him to have been of the same family with that Earl of Tyrconnel equally distinguished for his influence with James the Second as for his infamous life and character, who held at this period unbounded sway at the English Court. I hope, for the honor of our hero, that he preserved no family-likeness to that false-hearted, brutal, and violent favorite, who is made immortal in Macaulay's pages as Lying Dick Talbot. Through his intercession his kinsman may have been pardoned, or even never brought to trial.

Chapter X

Conclusion

This is the end of my story. But, like all stories, it requires that some satisfaction should be given to the reader in regard to the dramatic proprieties. We have our several heroes to dispose of. Phelim Murray and Hugh Riley, who had both been arrested by the Council to satisfy public opinion as to their complicity in the plot for the escape, were both honorably discharged,—I suppose being found entirely innocent! Roger Skreene swore himself black and blue, as the phrase is, that he had not the least suspicion of the business in which he was engaged; and so he was acquitted! I am also glad to be able to say that our gallant Cornet Murray, in the winding-up of this business, was promoted by the Council to a captaincy of cavalry, and put in command of Christiana Fort and its neighborhood, to keep that formidable Quaker, William Penn, at a respectful distance. It would gratify me still more, if I could find warrant to add, that the Cornet enjoyed himself, and married the lady of his choice, with whom he has, unknown to us, been violently in love during these adventures, and that they lived happily together for many years. I hope this was so,— although the chronicle does not allow one to affirm it,—it being but a proper conclusion to such a romance as I have plucked out of our history.

And so I have traced the tradition of the Cave to the end. What I have been able to certify furnishes the means of a shrewd estimate of the average amount of truth which popular traditions generally contain. There is always a fact at the bottom, lying under a superstructure of fiction,— truth enough to make the pursuit worth following. Talbot did not live in the Cave, but fled there occasionally for concealment. He had no hawks with him, but bred them in his own mews on the Elk River. The birds seen in after times were some of this stock, and not the solitary pair they were supposed to be. I dare say an expert naturalist would find many specimens of the same breed now in that region. But let us not be too critical on the tradition, which has led us into a quest through which I have been able to supply what I hope will be found to be a pleasant insight into that little world of action and passion,—with its people, its pursuits, and its gossips,—that, more than one hundred and seventy years ago, inhabited the beautiful banks of St. Mary's River and wove the web of our early Maryland history.

Postscript

I have another link in the chain of Talbot's history, furnished me by a friend in Virginia. It comes since I have completed my narrative, and very accurately confirms the conjecture of Chalmers, quoted in the note of "The Landholder's Assistant." "As for Colonel Talbot, he was conveyed for trial to Virginia, from whence he made his escape, and, after being retaken, and, *I believe*, tried and convicted, was finally pardoned by King James II." This is an extract from the note. It is now ascertained that Talbot was not taken to England for trial, as Lord Baltimore, in his letter of the 6th of July, 1685, affirmed it was the King's pleasure he should be; but that he was tried and convicted in Virginia on the 22d of April, 1686, and on the 26th of the same month, reprieved by order of the King; after which we may presume he received a full pardon, and perhaps was taken to England in obedience to the royal command, to await it there. The conviction and reprieve are recorded in a folio of the State Records of Virginia at Richmond, on a mutilated and scarcely legible sheet,—a copy of which I present to my reader with all its obliterations and broken syllables and sad gashes in the text, for his own deciphering. The MS. is in keeping with the whole story, and may be looked upon as its appropriate emblem.

The story has been brought to light by chance, and has been rendered intelligible by close study and interpretation of fragmentary and widely separated facts, capable of being read only by one conversant with the text of human affairs, and who has the patience to grope through the trackless intervals of time, and the skill to supply the lost words and syllables of history by careful collation with those which are spared. How faithfully this accidentally found MS. typifies such a labor, the reader may judge from the literal copy of it I now offer to his perusal.

OLD SEAL.   "By his Excellency

"Whereas his most Sacred Majesty has been Graciously pleased by his Royall Com'ands to Direct and Com'and Me ffrancis Lord Howard of Effingham his Maj^ties Lieut and Govr. Gen^ll. of Virginia that if George Talbott Esqr. upon his Tryall should be found Guilty of Killing Mr Christopher Rowsby, that Execution should be suspended untill his Majesties pleasure should be further signified unto Me; And forasmuch as the sd George Talbott was Indicted upon the Statute of Stabbing and hath Received a full and Legall Tryall in open Court on ye Twentieth and One and Twentieth dayes of this Instant Aprill, before his Majesties Justices of Oyer and Terminer, and found Guilty of ye aforesaid fact and condemned

for the Same, I, therefore, ffrancis Lord Howard, Baron of ffingham, his
Majesties Lieu^t and Govr. Gen^ll. of Virginia, by Virtue of ajties
Royall Com'ands to Me given there doe hereby Suspend tion
of the Sentence of death his Maj^ties Justices
Terminer on the till his Majesties
erein be nor any
fail as yo uttmost
and for y^r soe doing this sh
Given under my and Seale
the 26th day of Apri

EFFINGHAM

To his Majesties Justices
of Oyer and Terminer.

Recordatur E Chillon Genl Car

[Endorsed]
Talbott's Repreif
from Ld Howard
1686 for Killing Ch^r. Rousby
Examined Sept. 24th
26th Aprill 1686
Sentence of
ag^t Col Ta
Suspended
Aprill 26   1 86"

James Lane Allen
(1849-1925)

James Lane Allen was born December 21, 1849, near Lexington, Kentucky, the seventh and last child of Richard and Helen Jane Foster Allen. Allen's mother was the dominating influence in his childhood and throughout his life. It was she who early introduced him to Nature, especially to birds, as the introduction to the revised edition of *A Kentucky Cardinal* makes clear; and it was she to whom he dedicated that work, as well as five of his other books.

In the autumn of 1872, after his graduation from the University of Kentucky, Allen began teaching at a nearby school. The family's financial situation made it necessary for him to contribute to their income, and the death of his father in November, 1872, left the support of his mother to him. The next year, 1873, he went to Missouri, where he was an instructor in Greek and mathematics at Richmond College. After a year, he again moved to Lexington, Missouri, where in 1874-75 he was master of a boys' school. The following year, apparently convinced of the need for an advanced degree, he returned to the University of Kentucky and enrolled as a candidate for a Master of Arts degree, which he received in 1877, at the same time becoming principal of the Academy of the University, his old preparatory school. Two years later he moved to Bethany College in West Virginia, where he was given an honorary Master of Arts degree and a professorship of Latin Languages and Literature—the highest academic position he ever held. But stifled by the orthodox dogmatism of the institution and the other members of the faculty, he resigned his chair in 1883 and returned to Lexington. He taught in a private boys' school there for one more year and then abandoned the teaching profession forever.

Dissatisfied with teaching, Allen had begun in the 1880's to consider another vocation. He had no trouble finding magazines willing to print his essays, and for the next few years he published numerous essays and a few poems. By 1884 Allen felt his literary reputation well enough established to rely entirely upon his pen for a living. At this time Allen made his first trip to New York, saw several editors, and soon returned to Lexington. He spent the next five years there and in Cincinnati, writing several "local color" articles and travelogues for the New York *Evening Post* and *Harper's Magazine*.

Allen's first important short story was "The White Cowl," published in *The Century* in September, 1888. Though marred by some defects, this story of a fallen and restored priest marks the beginning of Allen's efforts to deal seriously with themes of lasting value. His first book, *Flute and Violin and Other Kentucky Tales*, was published in January, 1891. The next year his second volume appeared, a collection of travelogues and journalistic essays of the local color variety entitled *The Blue Grass Region of Kentucky*. In June of 1892 *Lippincott's Magazine* brought out a new story by Allen, "John Gray: A Kentucky Tale of the Olden Time"; the following year the story was issued in book form by Lippincott, although it was not a great success.

The first stage of Allen's development as an artist some critics have called his Romantic period; Allen himself applied the phrase "the Feminine Principle" to the motivating force in his early work, the best of which is "A Kentucky Cardinal." The story was first published in two installments in *Harper's Magazine* in May and June of 1894, and later the same year brought out in book form by Harper and Brothers. Perhaps because of the popularity of *A Kentucky Cardinal*, Allen followed it the next year with a sequel, *Aftermath*, which deals with the life of Adam Moss and Georgiana after their marriage. It fails to live up to the excellence of its predecessor.

In 1896 Allen had published a novel which marked the beginning of a new trend in his work. This book, *Summer in Arcady: A Tale of Nature*, exhibited the techniques and subject matter of realism, or as Allen termed it, "the Masculine Principle." The subject of the work is the sexual awakening of a young girl and boy, and though it is difficult now to find anything even slightly shocking in it, it was attacked by critics and public for its frankness. Following the furor created by *Summer in Arcady*, and perhaps because of it, Allen returned to his former style in his next book. *The Choir Invisible*, published in 1897, dealt with the same material as *John Gray*, but it became an immediate success and remains Allen's most popular novel.

After 1900 Allen returned to the realistic and experimental novel, baffling and antagonising his readers and thereby losing his popularity. *The Reign of Law* dealt with evolution—a subject which had interested Allen since his college days—and produced a quarrel with religious fundamentalists and critics. Following a six-year interval of silence, Allen brought out *The Bride of the Mistletoe*, the first volume of a projected trilogy.

Probably ahead of its time, this work dealt with myth and marital relationships and succeeded only in confusing and angering most readers, as did its sequel *The Doctor's Christmas Eve*. From this time on, Allen's popularity waned, his health and finances deteriorated, and he eked out a meagre living with magazine stories and a few novels. More than ever a solitary being in his old age, he continued to write diligently and endure his hardships with equanimity. He died in New York City, February 18, 1925, and was buried three days later in Lexington, Kentucky.

Textual note

The text used here is the 1900 "New Edition Revised with A New Preface," published by the MacMillan Company. "A Kentucky Cardinal" was first published in *Harper's New Monthly Magazine* in two installments, May and June, 1894. Allen made extensive revisions for the book publication by Harper and Brothers later the same year. The book went through various reprintings and editions, but the 1900 Revised Edition is the last in which Allen had a hand.

A Kentucky Cardinal

I

All this New-year's Day of 1850 the sun shone cloudless but wrought
no thaw. Even the landscapes of frost on the window-panes did not melt a
flower, and the little trees still keep their silvery boughs arched high above
the jewelled avenues. During the afternoon a lean hare limped twice across
the lawn, and there was not a creature stirring to chase it. Now the night
is bitter cold, with no sounds outside but the cracking of the porches as
they freeze tighter. Even the north wind seems grown too numb to move.
I had determined to convert its coarse, big noise into something sweet—as
may often be done by a little art with the things of this life—and so
stretched a horse-hair above the opening between the window sashes; but
the soul of my harp has departed. I hear but the comfortable roar and snap
of hickory logs, at long intervals a deeper breath from the dog stretched
on his side at my feet, and the crickets under the hearth-stones. They have
to thank me for that nook. One chill afternoon I came upon a whole
company of them on the western slope of a woodland mound, so lethargic
that I thumped them repeatedly before they could so much as get their
senses. There was a branch near by, and the smell of mint in the air, so
that had they been young Kentuckians one might have had a clew to the
situation. With an ear for winter minstrelsy, I brought two home in a
handkerchief, and assigned them an elegant suite of apartments under a
loose brick.

But the finest music in the room is that which streams out to the ear
of the spirit in many an exquisite strain from the hanging shelf of books
on the opposite wall. Every volume there is an instrument which some
melodist of the mind created and set vibrating with music, as a flower
shakes out its perfume or a star shakes out its light. Only listen, and they

soothe all care, as though the silken soft leaves of poppies had been made vocal and poured into the ear.

Towards dark, having seen to the comfort of a household of kind, faithful fellow-beings, whom man in his vanity calls the lower animals, I went last to walk under the cedars in the front yard, listening to that music which is at once so cheery and so sad—the low chirping of birds at dark winter twilights as they gather in from the frozen fields, from snow-buried shrubbery and hedge-rows, and settle down for the night in the depths of the evergreens, the only refuge from their enemies and shelter from the blast. But this evening they made no ado about their home-coming. To-day perhaps none had ventured forth. I am most uneasy when the red-bird is forced by hunger to leave the covert of his cedars, since he, on the naked or white landscapes of winter, offers the most far-shining and beautiful mark for Death. I stepped across to the tree in which a pair of these birds roost, and shook it, to make sure they were at home, and felt relieved when they fluttered into the next with the quick startled notes they utter when aroused.

The longer I live here, the better satisfied I am in having pitched my earthly camp-fire, gypsylike, on the edge of a town, keeping it on one side, and the green fields, lanes, and woods on the other. Each, in turn, is to me as a magnet to the needle. At times the needle of my nature points towards the country. On that side everything is poetry. I wander over field and forest, and through me runs a glad current of feeling that is like a clear brook across the meadows of May. At others the needle veers round, and I go to town—to the massed haunts of the highest animal and cannibal. That way nearly everything is prose. I can feel the prose rising in me as I step along, like hair on the back of a dog, long before any other dogs are in sight. And, indeed, the case is much that of a country dog come to town, so that growls are in order at every corner. The only being in the universe at which I have ever snarled, or with which I have rolled over in the mud and fought like a common cur, is Man.

Among my neighbours who furnish me much of the plain prose of life, the nearest hitherto has been a bachelor named Jacob Mariner. I called him my raincrow, because the sound of his voice awoke apprehensions of falling weather. A visit from him was an endless drizzle. For Jacob came over to expound his minute symptoms; and had everything that he gave out on the subject of human ailments been written down, it must have made a volume as large, as solemn, and as inconvenient as a family Bible. My other nearest neighbour lives across the road—a widow, Mrs. Walters. I call Mrs. Walters my mocking-bird, because she reproduces by what is truly a divine arrangement of the throat the voices of the town. When she flutters across to the yellow settee under the grape-vine and balances herself lightly with expectation, I have but to request that she favour me with a little singing, and as soon the air is vocal with every note of the village songsters. After this, Mrs. Walters usually begins to flutter in a motherly way around the subject of *my* symptoms.

Naturally, it has been my wish to bring about between this raincrow and mocking-bird the desire to pair with one another. For, if a man always wanted to tell his symptoms, and a woman always wished to hear about them, surely a marriage compact on the basis of such a passion ought to open up for them a union of everflowing and indestructible felicity. They should associate as perfectly as the compensating metals of a pendulum, of which the one contracts as the other expands. And then I should be a little happier myself. But the perversity of life! Jacob would never confide in Mrs. Walters. Mrs. Walters would never inquire for Jacob.

Now poor Jacob is dead, of no complaint apparently, and with so few symptoms that even the doctors did not know what was the matter, and the upshot of this talk is that his place has been sold, and I am to have new neighbours. What a disturbance to a man living on the edge of a quiet town!

Tidings of the calamity came to-day from Mrs. Walters, who flew over and sang—sang even on a January afternoon—in a manner to rival her most vociferous vernal execution. But the poor creature was so truly distressed that I followed her to the front gate, and we twittered kindly at each other over the fence, and ruffled our plumage with common disapproval. It is marvellous how a member of her sex will conceive dislike of people that she has never seen; but birds are sensible of heat or cold long before either arrives, and it may be that this mocking-bird feels something wrong at the quill end of her feathers.

II

Mrs. Walters this morning with more news touching our incoming neighbours. Whenever I have faced towards this aggregation of unwelcome individuals, I have beheld it moving towards me as a thick gray mist, shutting out nature beyond. Perhaps they are approaching this part of the earth like a comet that carries its tail before it, and I am already enveloped in a disturbing, befogging nebulosity.

There is still no getting the truth, but it appears that they are a family of consequence in their way—which, of course, may be a very poor way. Mrs. Margaret Cobb, mother, lately bereaved of her husband, Joseph Cobb, who fell among the Kentucky boys at the battle of Buena Vista. A son, Joseph Cobb, now cadet at West Point, with a desire to die like his father, but destined to die—who knows?—in a war that may break out in this country about the negroes. Then there is a daughter, Miss Georgiana Cobb,

who embroiders blue-and-pink-worsted dogs on black foot-cushions, makes
far-off crayon trees that look like sheep in the act of variously getting up
and lying down on a hill-side, and, when the dew is falling and the moon
is the shape of the human lips, touches her guitar with maidenly solicitude.
Lastly, a younger daughter, who is in the half-fledged state of becoming
educated.

While not reconciled, I am resigned. The young man when at home
may wish to practise the deadly vocation of an American soldier of the
period over the garden fence at my birds, in which case he and I could
readily fight a duel, and help maintain an honoured custom of the com-
monwealth. The older daughter will sooner or later turn loose on my heels
one of her pack of blue dogs. If this should befall me in the spring, and I
survive the dog, I could retort with a dish of strawberries and a copy of
"Lalla Rookh"; if in the fall, with a basket of grapes and Thomson's
"Seasons," after which there would be no further exchange of hostilities.
The younger daughter, being a school-girl, will occasionally have to be
subdued with green apples and salt. The mother could easily give trouble;
or she might be one of those few women to know whom is to know the best
that there is in all this faulty world.

The middle of February. The depths of winter reached. Thoughtful,
thoughtless words—the depths of winter. Everything gone inward and
downward from surface and summit, Nature at low tide. In its time will
come the height of summer, when the tides of life will rise to the tree-tops,
or be dashed as silvery insect spray all but to the clouds. So bleak a season
touches my concern for birds, which never seem quite at home in this
world; and the winter has been most lean and hungry for them. Many
snows have fallen—snows that are as raw cotton spread over their break-
fast-table, and cutting off connection between them and its bounties. Next
summer I must let the weeds grow up in my garden, so that they may have
a better chance for seeds above the stingy level of the universal white. Of
late I have opened a pawnbroker's shop for my hard-pressed brethren in
feathers, lending at a fearful rate of interest; for every borrowing Lazarus
will have to pay me back in due time by monthly instalments of singing.
I shall have mine own again with usury. But were a man never so usurious,
would he not lend a winter seed for a summer song? Would he refuse to
invest his stale crumbs in an orchestra of divine instruments and a choir of
heavenly voices? And to-day, also, I ordered from a nursery-man more
trees of holly, juniper, and fir, since the storm-beaten cedars will have to
come down. For in Kentucky, when the forest is naked, and every shrub
and hedge-row bare, what would become of our birds in the universal
rigour and exposure of the world if there were no evergreens—Nature's
hostelries for the homeless ones? Living in the depths of these, they can

keep snow, ice, and wind at bay; prying eyes cannot watch them, nor enemies so well draw near; cones or seed or berries are their store; and in those untrodden chambers each can have the sacred company of his mate. But wintering here has terrible risks which few run. Scarcely in autumn have the leaves begun to drop from their high perches silently downward when the birds begin to drop away from the bare boughs silently southward. Lo! some morning the leaves are on the ground, and the birds have vanished. The species that remain, or that come to us then, wear the hues of the season, and melt into the tone of Nature's background—blues, grays, browns, with touches of white on tail and breast and wing for coming flecks of snow.

Save only him—proud, solitary stranger in our unfriendly land—the fiery grosbeak. Nature in Kentucky has no wintry harmonies for him. He could find these only among the tufts of the October sumac, or in the gum-tree when it stands a pillar of red twilight fire in the dark November woods, or in the far depths of the crimson sunset skies, where, indeed, he seems to have been nested, and whence to have come as a messenger of beauty, bearing on his wings the light of his diviner home.

With almost everything earthly that he touches this high herald of the trees is in contrast. Among his kind he is without a peer. Even when the whole company of summer voyagers have sailed back to Kentucky, singing and laughing and kissing one another under the enormous green umbrella of Nature's leaves, he still is beyond them all in loveliness. But when they have been wafted away again to brighter skies and to soft islands over the sea, and he is left alone on the edge of that Northern world which he has dared invade and inhabit, it is then, amid black clouds and drifting snows, that the gorgeous cardinal stands forth in the ideal picture of his destiny. For it is then that his beauty is most conspicuous, and that Death, lover of the peerless, strikes at him from afar. So that he retires to the twilight solitude of his wild fortress. Let him even show his noble head and breast at a slit in its green window-shades, and a ray flashes from it to the eye of a cat; let him, as spring comes on, burst out in desperation and mount to the tree-tops which he loves, and his gleaming red coat betrays him to the poised hawk as to a distant sharpshooter; in the barn near by an owl is waiting to do his night marketing at various tender-meat stalls; and, above all, the eye and heart of man are his diurnal and nocturnal foe. What wonder if he is so shy, so rare, so secluded, this flame-coloured prisoner in dark-green chambers, who has only to be seen or heard and Death adjusts an arrow!

No vast Southern swamps or forest of pine here into which he may plunge. If he shuns man in Kentucky, he must haunt the long lonely river valleys where the wild cedars grow. If he comes into this immediate swarming pastoral region, where the people, with ancestral love of privacy, and not from any kindly thought of him, plant evergreens around their country homes, he must live under the very guns and amid the pitfalls of the enemy. Surely, could the first male of the species have foreseen how, through the generations of his race to come, both their beauty and their song, which were meant to announce them to Love, would also announce them to Death, he must have blanched snow-white with despair and turned as mute as stone. Is it this flight from the inescapable just behind that makes the singing of the red-bird thoughtful and plaintive, and, indeed, nearly all the wild sounds of Nature so like the outcry of the doomed? He will sit for a long time silent and motionless in the heart of a cedar, as if absorbed in the tragic memories of his race. Then, softly, wearily, he will call out to you and to the whole world: *Peace . . Peace . . Peace . . Peace . . Peace!*—the most melodious sigh that ever issued from the clefts of a dungeon.

For colour and form, brilliant singing, his very enemies, and the bold nature he has never lost, I have long been most interested in this bird. Every year several pairs make their appearance about my place. This winter especially I have been feeding a pair; and there should be finer music in the spring, and a lustier brood in summer.

III

March has gone like its winds. The other night as I lay awake with that yearning which often beats within, there fell from the upper air the notes of the wild gander as he wedged his way onward by faith, not by sight, towards his distant bourn. I rose and, throwing open the shutters, strained eyes towards the unseen and unseeing explorer, startled, as a half-asleep soldier might be startled by the faint bugle-call of his commander, blown to him from the clouds. What far-off lands, streaked with mortal dawn, does he believe in? In what soft sylvan waters will he bury his tired breast? Always when I hear his voice, often when not, I too desire to be up and gone out of these earthly marshes where hunts the dark Fowler,—gone to some vast, pure, open sea, where, one by one, my scattered kind, those whom I love and those who love me, will arrive in safety, there to be together.

March is a month when the needle of my nature dips towards the country. I am away, greeting everything as it wakes out of winter sleep, stretches arms upward and legs downward, and drinks goblet after goblet of young sunshine. I must find the dark green snowdrop, and sometimes help to remove from her head, as she lifts it slowly from her couch, the frosted nightcap, which the old Nurse would still insist that she should wear. The pale green tips of daffodils are a thing of beauty. There is the sun-struck brook of the field, underneath the thin ice of which drops form and fall, form and fall, like big round silvery eyes that grow bigger and brighter with astonishment that you should laugh at them as they vanish. But most I love to see Nature do her spring house-cleaning in Kentucky, with the rain-clouds for her water-buckets and the winds for her brooms. What an amount of drenching and sweeping she can do in a day! How she dashes pailful and pailful into every corner, till the whole earth is as clean as a new floor! Another day she attacks the piles of dead leaves, where they have lain since last October, and scatters them in a trice, so that every cranny may be sunned and aired. Or, grasping her long brooms by the handles, she will go into the woods and beat the icicles off the big trees as a housewife would brush down cobwebs; so that the released limbs straighten up like a man who has gotten out of debt, and almost say to you, joyfully, "Now, then, we are all right again!" This done, she begins to hang up soft new curtains at the forest windows, and to spread over her floor a new carpet of an emerald loveliness such as no mortal looms could ever have woven. And then, at last, she sends out invitations through the South, and even to some tropical lands, for the birds to come and spend the summer in Kentucky. The invitations are sent out in March, and accepted in April and May, and by June her house is full of visitors.

Not the eyes alone love Nature in March. Every other sense hies abroad. My tongue hunts for the last morsel of wet snow on the northern root of some aged oak. As one goes early to a concert-hall with a passion even for the preliminary tuning of the musicians, so my ear sits alone in the vast amphitheatre of Nature and waits for the earliest warble of the blue-bird, which seems to start up somewhere behind the heavenly curtains. And the scent of spring, is it not the first lyric of the nose—that despised poet of the senses?

But this year I have hardly glanced at the small choice edition of Nature's spring verses. This by reason of the on-coming Cobbs, at the mere mention of whom I feel as though I were plunged up to my eyes in a vat of the prosaic. Some days ago workmen went into the house and all but scoured the very memory of Jacob off the face of the earth. Then there has been need to quiet Mrs. Walters.

Mrs. Walters does not get into our best society; so that the town is to her like a pond to a crane: she wades round it, going in as far as she can, and snatches up such small fry as come shoreward from the middle. In this way lately I have gotten hints of what is stirring in the vasty deeps of village opinion.

Mrs. Cobb is charged, among other dreadful things, with having ordered of the town manufacturer a carriage that is to be as fine as President Taylor's and with marching into church preceded by a servant, who bears her prayer-book on a velvet cushion. What if she rode in Cinderella's coach, or had her prayer-book carried before her on the back of a Green River turtle? But to her sex she promises to be an invidious Christian. I am rather disturbed by the gossip regarding the elder daughter. But this is so conflicting that one impression is made only to be effaced by another.

A week ago their agent wanted to buy my place. I was so outraged that I got down my map of Kentucky to see where these peculiar beings originate. They come from a little town in the southwestern corner of the State, on the Ohio River, named Henderson—named from that Richard Henderson who in the year 1775 bought about half of Kentucky from the Cherokees, and afterwards, as president of his purchase, addressed the first legislative assembly ever held in the West, seated under a big elm tree outside the walls of Boonsborough fort. These people must be his heirs, or they would never have tried to purchase my few Sabine acres. It is no surprise to discover that they are from the Green River country. They must bathe often in that stream. I suppose they wanted my front yard to sow it in penny-royal, the characteristic growth of those districts. They surely distil it and use it as a perfume on their handkerchiefs. It was per- haps from the founder of this family that Thomas Jefferson got authority for his statement that the Ohio is the most beautiful river in the world— unless, indeed, the President formed that notion of the Ohio upon lifting his eyes to it from the contemplation of Green River. Henderson! Green River region! To this town and to the blue-grass country as Bœotia to Attica in the days of Pericles. Hereafter I shall call these people my Green River Bœotians.

A few days later their agent again, a little frigid, very urgent—this time to buy me out on my own terms, *any* terms. But what was back of all this, I inquired. I did not know these people, had never done them a favour. Why, then, such determination to have me removed? Why such bitterness, vindictiveness, ungovernable passion?

That was the point, he replied. This family had never wronged *me*. I had never even seen *them*. Yet they had heard of nothing but my intense dislike of them and opposition to their becoming my neighbours. They could not forego their plans, but they were quite willing to give me the chance of leaving their vicinity, on whatever I might regard the most advantageous terms.

Oh, my mocking-bird, my mocking-bird! When you have been sitting on other front porches, have you, by the divine law of your being, been reproducing your notes as though they were mine, and even pouring forth the little twitter that was meant for your private ear?

As March goes out, two things more and more I hear—the cardinal has begun to mount to the bare tops of the locust-trees and scatter his notes downward, and over the way the workmen whistle and sing. The bird is too shy to sit in any tree on that side of the yard. But his eye and ear are studying them curiously. Sometimes I even fancy that he sings to them with a plaintive sort of joy, as though he were saying, "Welcome—go away!"

IV

The Cobbs will be the death of me before they get here. The report spread that they and I had already had a tremendous quarrel, and that, rather than live beside them, I had sold them my place. This set flowing towards me for days a stream of people, like a line of ants passing to and from the scene of a terrific false alarm. I had nothing to do but sit perfectly still and let each ant, as it ran up, touch me with its antennæ, get the counter-sign, and turn back to the village ant-hill. Not all, however. Some remained to hear me abuse the Cobbs; or, counting on my support, fell to abusing the Cobbs themselves. When I made not a word of reply, except to assure them that I really had not quarrelled with the Cobbs, had nothing against the Cobbs, and was immensely delighted that the Cobbs were coming, they went away amazingly cool and indignant. But for days I continued to hear such things attributed to me that, had that young West-Pointer been in the neighbourhood, and known how to shoot, he must infallibly have blown my head off me, as any Kentucky gentleman would.

Others of my visitors, having heard that I was not to sell my place, were so glad of it that they walked around my garden and inquired about my health and the prospect for fruit. For the season has come when the highest animal begins to pay me some attention. During the winter, having little to contribute to the community, I drop from communal notice. But there are certain ladies who bow sweetly to me when my roses and honey-suckles burst into bloom; a fat old cavalier of the South begins to shake hands with me when my asparagus bed begins to send up its tender stalks; I am in high favour with two or three young ladies at the season of lilies and sweet-pea; there is one old soul who especially loves rhubarb pies, which she makes to look like little latticed porches in front of little green skies, and it is she who remembers me and my row of pie-plant; and still another, who knows better than cat-birds when currants are ripe. Above all, there is a preacher, who thinks my sins are as scarlet so long as my strawberries are, and plants himself in my bed at that time to reason with me of Judgment to come; and a doctor, who gets despondent about my constitution in pear-time—after which my health seems to return, but never my pears.

So that, on the whole, from May till October I am the bright side of the moon, and the telescopes of the town are busy observing my phenomena; after which it is as though I had rolled over on my dark side, there to lie forgotten till once more the sun entered the proper side of the zodiac. But let me except always the few steadily luminous spirits I know, with whom is no variableness, neither shadow of turning. If any one wishes to become famous in a community, let him buy a small farm on the edge of it and cultivate fruits, berries, and flowers, which he freely gives away or lets be freely taken.

All this has taken freely of my swift April days. Besides, I have made me a new side-porch, made it myself, for I like to hammer and drive things home, and because the rose on the old one had rotted it from post to shingle. And then, when I had tacked the rose in place again, the little old window opening above it made that side of my house look like a boy in his Saturday hat and Sunday breeches. So in went a large new window; and now these changes have mysteriously offended Mrs. Walters, who says the town is laughing at me for trying to outdo the Cobbs. The highest animal is the only one who is divinely gifted with such noble discernment. But I am not sorry to have my place look its best. When they see it, they will perhaps understand why I was not to be driven out by a golden cracker on their family whip. They could not have bought my little woodland pasture, where for a generation has been picnic and muster and Fourth-of-July ground, and where the brave fellows met to volunteer for the Mexican war. They could not have bought even the heap of brush behind my wood-pile, where the brown thrashers build.

V

In May I am of the earth, earthy. The soul loses its wild white pinions; the heart puts forth its short, powerful wings, heavy with heat and colour, that flutter, but do not lift it off the ground. The month comes and goes, and not once do I think of raising my eyes to the stars. The very sunbeams fall on the body as a warm golden net, and keep thought and feeling from escape. Nature uses beauty now not to uplift, but to entice. I find her intent upon the one general business of seeing that no type of her creatures gets left out of the generations. Studied in my yard full of birds, as with a condensing glass of the world, she can be seen enacting among them the dramas of history. Yesterday, in the secret recess of a walnut, I saw the beginning of the Trojan war. Last week I witnessed the battle of Actium fought out in mid-air. And down among my hedges—indeed, openly in my very barn-yard—there is a perfectly scandalous Salt Lake City.

And while I am watching the birds, they are watching me. Not a little fop among them, having proposed and been accepted, but perches on a limb, and has the air of putting his hands mannishly under his coat-tails and crying out at me, "Hello! Adam, what were you made for?" "You attend to your business, and I'll attend to mine," I answer. "You have one May; I have twenty-five!" He didn't wait to hear. He caught sight of a pair of clear brown eyes peeping at him out of a near tuft of leaves, and sprang thither with open arms and the sound of a kiss.

But if I have twenty-five Mays remaining, are not some Mays gone? Ah, well! Better a single May with the right mate, than the full number with the wrong. And where is she—the right one? If she ever comes near my yard and answers my whistle, I'll know it; and then I'll teach these popinjays in blue coats and white pantaloons what Adam was made for.

But the wrong one—there's the terror! Only think of so composite a phenomenon as Mrs. Walters, for instance, adorned with limp nightcap and stiff curl-papers, like garnishes around a leg of roast mutton, waking up beside me at four o'clock in the morning as some gray-headed love-bird of Madagascar, and beginning to chirp and trill in an ecstasy!

The new neighbours have come—mother, younger daughter, and servants. The son is at West Point; and the other daughter lingers a few days, unable, no doubt, to tear herself away from her beloved penny-royal and dearest Green River. They are quiet; have borrowed nothing from any one in the neighbourhood; have well-dressed, well-trained servants; and one begins to be a little impressed. The curtains they have put up at the windows suggest that the whole nest is being lined with soft, cool, spotless loveliness, which is very restful and beguiling.

No one has called yet, since they are not at home till June; but Mrs. Walters has done some tall wading lately, and declares that people do not know what to think. They will know when the elder daughter arrives; for it is the worst member of the family that settles what the world shall think of the others.

If only she were not the worst! If only as I sat here beside my large new window, around which the old rose-bush has been trained and now is blooming, I could look across to her window where the white curtains hang, and feel that behind them sat, shy and gentle, the wood-pigeon for whom through Mays gone by I have been vaguely waiting!

And yet I do not believe that I could live a single year with only the sound of cooing in the house. A wood-pigeon would be the death of me.

VI

This morning, the 3d of June, the Undine from Green River rose above the waves.

The strawberry bed is almost under their windows. I had gone out to pick the first dish of the season for breakfast; for while I do not care to eat except to live, I never miss an opportunity of living upon strawberries.

I was stooping down and bending the wet leaves over, so as not to miss any, when a voice at the wondow above said, timidly and playfully,

"Are you the gardener?"

I picked on, turning as red as the berries. Then the voice said again,

"Old man, are you the gardener?"

Of course a person looking down carelessly on the stooping figure of *any* man, and seeing nothing but a faded straw hat, and arms and feet and ankles bent together, might easily think him decrepit with age. Some things touch off my temper. But I answered, humbly,

"I am the gardener, madam."

"How much do you ask for your strawberries?"

"The gentleman who owns this place does not sell his strawberries. He gives them away, if he likes people. How much do you ask for *your* strawberries?"

"What a nice old gentleman! Is he having those picked to give away?"

"He is having these picked for his breakfast."

"Don't you think he'd like you to give me those, and pick him some more?"

"I fear not, madam."

"Nevertheless, you might. He'd never know."

"I think he'd find it out."

"You are not afraid of him, are you?"

"I am when he gets mad."

"Does he treat you badly?"

"If he does, I always forgive him."

"He doesn't seem to provide you with very many clothes."

I picked on.

"But you seem nicely fed."

I picked on.

"What is his name, old man? Don't you like to talk?"

"Adam Moss."

"Such a green, cool, soft name! It is like his house and yard and garden. What does he do?"

"Whatever he pleases."

"You must not be impertinent to me, or I'll tell him. What does he like?"

"Birds—red-birds. What do *you* like?"

"Red-birds! How does he catch them? Throw salt on their tails?"

"He is a lover of Nature, madam, and particularly of birds."

"What does *he* know about birds? Doesn't he care for people?"

"He doesn't think many worth caring for."

"Indeed! And *he* is perfect, then, is he?"

"He thinks he is nearly as bad as any; but that doesn't make the rest any better."

"Poor old gentleman! He must have the blues dreadfully. What does he do with his birds? Eat his robins, and stuff his cats, and sell his red-birds in cages?"

"He considers it part of his mission in life to keep them from being eaten or stuffed or caged."

"And you say he is nearly a hundred?"

"He is something over thirty years of age, madam."

"Thirty? Surely we heard he was very old. And does he live in that beautiful little old house all by himself?"

"*I* live with him!"

"*You!* Ha! ha! ha! And what is *your* name, you dear good old man?"

"Adam."

"*Two* Adams living in the same house! Are you the *old* Adam? I have heard so much of him."

At this I rose, pushed back my hat, and looked up at her.

"*I* am Adam Moss," I said, with distant politeness. "You can have these strawberries for your breakfast if you want them."

There was a low quick "Oh!" and she was gone, and the curtains closed over her face. It was rude; but neither ought she to have called me the old Adam. I have been thinking of one thing: why should she speak slightingly of my knowledge of birds? What does she know about them? I should like to inquire.

Late this afternoon, I dressed up in my high gray wool hat, my fine long-tailed blue cloth coat with brass buttons, my pink waist-coat, frilled shirt, white cravat, and yellow nankeen trousers, and walked slowly several times around my strawberry bed. Did not see any more ripe strawberries.

Within the last ten days I have called twice upon the Cobbs, urged no doubt by an extravagant readiness to find them all that I feared they were not. How exquisite in life is the art of not seeing many things, and of forgetting many that have been seen! They received me as though nothing unpleasant had happened. Nor did the elder daughter betray that we had met. She has not forgotten, for more than once I surprised a light in her eyes as though she were laughing. She has not, it is certain, told even her mother and sister. Somehow this fact invests her character with a charm as of subterranean roominess and secrecy. Women who tell everything are like finger-bowls of clear water.

But it is Sylvia that pleases me. She must be about seventeen; and so demure and confiding that I was ready to take her by the hand, lead her to the garden-gate, and say: Dear child, everything in here—butterflies, flowers, fruit, honey, everything—is yours; come and go and gather as you like.

Yesterday morning I sent them a large dish of strawberries, with a note asking whether they would walk during the day over to my woodland pasture, where the soldiers had a barbecue before setting out for the Mexican war. The mother and Sylvia accepted. Our walk was a little over-shadowed by their loss; and as I thoughtlessly described the gayety of that scene—the splendid young fellows dancing in their bright uniforms, and now and then pausing to wipe their foreheads, the speeches, the cheering, the dinner under the trees, and, a few days later, the tear-dimmed eyes, the hand-wringing and embracing, and at last the marching proudly away, each with a Bible in his pocket, and many never, never to return—I was sorry that I had not foreseen the sacred chord I was touching. But it made good friends of us more quickly, and they were well-bred, so that we re-turned to all appearance in gay spirits. The elder daughter came to meet us, and went at once silently to her mother's side, as though she had felt the separation. I wondered whether she had declined to go because of the memory of her father. As we passed my front gate, I asked them to look at my flowers. The mother praised also the cabbages, thus showing an ad-mirably balanced mind; the little Sylvia fell in love with a vine-covered arbour; the elder daughter appeared to be secretly watching the many birds about the grounds, but when I pointed out several less-known species, she lost interest.

What surprises most is that they are so refined and intelligent. It is greatly to be feared that we Kentuckians in this part of the State are profoundly ignorant as to the people in other parts. I told Mrs. Walters this, and she, seeing that I am beginning to like them, is beginning to like them herself. Dear Mrs. Walters! Her few ideas are like three or four marbles on a level floor: they have no power to move themselves, but roll equally well in any direction you push them.

This afternoon I turned a lot of little town boys into my strawberry bed, and now it looks like a field that had been harrowed and rolled. I think they would gladly have pulled up some of the plants to see whether there might not be berries growing on the roots.

It is unwise to do everything that you can for people at once; for when you can do nothing more, they will say you are no longer like yourself, and turn against you. So I have meant to go slowly with the Cobbs in my wish to be neighbourly, and do not think that they could reasonably be spoiled on one dish of strawberries in three weeks. But the other evening Mrs. Cobb sent over a plate of golden sally-lunn on a silver waiter, covered with a snow-white napkin; and acting on this provocation, I thought they could be trusted with a basket of cherries.

So next morning, in order to save the ripening fruit on a rather small tree of choice variety, I thought I should put up a scarecrow, and to this end rummaged a closet for some last winter's old clothes. These I crammed with straw, and I fastened the resulting figure in the crotch of the tree, tying the arms to the adjoining limbs, and giving it the dreadful appearance of shouting, "Keep out of here, you rascals, or you'll get hurt!" And, in truth, it did look so like me that I felt a little uncanny about it myself.

Returning home late, I went at once to the tree, where I found not a quart of cherries, and the servants told of an astonishing thing: that no sooner had the birds discovered who was standing in the tree, wearing the clothes in which he used to feed them during the winter, than the news spread like wildfire to the effect that he had climbed up there and was calling out: "Here is the best tree, fellows! Pitch in and help yourselves!" So that the like of the chattering and fetching away was never seen before. This was the story; but little negroes love cherries, and it is not incredible that the American birds were assisted in this instance by a large family of fat young African spoon bills.

Anxious to save another tree, and afraid to use more of my own clothes, I went over to Mrs. Walters, and got from her an old bonnet and veil, a dress and cape, and a pair of her cast-off yellow gaiters. These garments I strung together and prepared to look lifelike as nearly as a stuffing of hay would meet the inner requirements of the case. I then seated the dread apparition in the fork of a limb, and awaited results. The first thief was an old jay, who flew towards the tree with his head turned to one side to see whether any one was overtaking him. But scarcely had he alighted when he uttered a scream of horror that was sickening to hear, and dropped on the grass beneath, after which he took himself off with a silence and speed that would have done credit to a passenger-pigeon. That tree was rather avoided for some days, or it may have been let alone merely because others were ripening; so that Mrs. Cobb got her cherries, and I sent Mrs. Walters some also for the excellent loan of her veil and gaiters.

As the days pass I fall in love with Sylvia, who has been persuaded to turn my arbour into a reading-room, and is often to be found there of mornings with one of Sir Walter's novels. Sometimes I leave her alone, sometimes lie on the bench facing her, while she reads aloud, or, tiring, prattles. Little half-fledged spirit, to whom the yard is the earth and June eternity, but who peeps over the edge of the nest at the chivalry of the ages, and fancies that she knows the world. The other day, as we were talking, she tapped the edge of her *Ivanhoe* with a slate-pencil—for she is also studying the Greatest Common Divisor—and said, warningly, "You must not make epigrams; for if you succeeded you would be brilliant, and everything brilliant is tiresome."

"Who is your authority for *that* epigram, Miss Sylvia?" I said, laughing.

"Don't you suppose that I have any ideas but what I get from books?"

"You may have all wisdom, but those sayings proceed only from experience."

"I have my intuitions; they are better than experience."

"If you keep on, you will be making epigrams presently, and then I shall find you tiresome, and go away."

"You couldn't. I am your guest. How unconventional I am to come over and sit in your arbour? But is it Georgiana's fault."

"Did *she* tell you to come?"

"No; but she didn't keep me from coming. Whenever any one of us does anything improper we always say to each other, 'It's Georgiana's fault. She ought not to have taught us to be so simple and unconventional.' "

"And is she the family governess?"

"She governs the family. There doesn't seem to be any real government, but we all do as she says. You might think at first that Georgiana was the most light-headed member of the family, but she isn't. She's deep. I'm shallow in comparison with her. She calls me sophisticated, and introduces me as the elder Miss Cobb, and says that if I don't stop reading Scott's novels and learn more arithmetic she will put white caps on me, and make me walk to church in carpet slippers and with grandmother's stick."

"But you don't seem to have stopped, Miss Sylvia."

"No; but I'm stopping. Georgiana always gives us time, but we get right at last. It was two years before she could make my brother go to West Point. He was wild and rough, and wanted to raise tobacco, and float with it down to New Orleans, and have a good time. Then when she had gotten him to go she was afraid he'd come back, and so she persuaded my mother to live here, where there isn't any tobacco, and where I could be sent to school. That took her a year, and now she is breaking up my habit of reading nothing but novels. She gets us all down in the end. One day when she and Joe were little children they were out at the wood-pile, and Georgiana was sitting on a log eating a jam biscuit, with her feet on the log in front of her. Joe had a hand-axe, and was chopping at anything till he caught sight of her feet. Then he went to the end of the log, and whistled like a steamboat, and began to hack down in that direction, calling out to her: 'Take your toes out of the way, Georgiana. I am coming down the river. The current is up and I can't stop.' 'My toes were there first,' said Georgiana, and went on eating her biscuit. 'Take them out of the way, I tell you,' he shouted as he came nearer, 'or they'll get cut off.' 'They were there first,' repeated Georgiana, and took another delicious nibble. Joe cut straight along, and went *whack!* right into her five toes. Georgiana screamed with all her might, but she held her foot on the log, till Joe dropped the hatchet with horror, and caught her in his arms. 'Georgiana, I *told* you to take your toes away,' he cried; 'you are such a little fool,' and ran with her to the house. But she always had control over him after that."

To-day I saw Sylvia enter the arbour, and shortly afterwards I followed with a book.

"When you stop reading novels and begin to read history, Miss Sylvia, here is the most remarkable history of Kentucky that was ever written or ever will be. It is by my father's old teacher of natural history in Transylvania University, Professor Rafinesque, who also had a wonderful botanical garden on this side of the town; perhaps the first ever seen in this country."

"I know all about it," replied Sylvia, resenting this slight upon her erudition. "Georgiana has my father's copy, and his was presented to him by Mr. Audubon."

"Audubon!" I said, with a doubt.

"Never heard of Audubon?" cried Sylvia, delighted to show up my ignorance.

"Only of the great Audubon, Miss Sylvia; the *great,* the very *great* Audubon."

"Well, this was the *great,* the very *great* Audubon. He lived in Henderson, and kept a corn-mill. He and my father were friends, and he gave my father some of his early drawings of Kentucky birds. Georgiana has them now, and that is where she gets her love of birds—from my father, who got his from the *great,* the very *great* Audubon."

"Would Miss Cobb let me see these drawings?" I asked, eagerly.

"She might; but she prizes them as much as if they were stray leaves out of the only Bible in the world."

As Sylvia turned inside out this pocket of her mind, there had dropped out a key to her sister's conduct. Now I understood her slighting attitude towards my knowledge of birds. But I shall feel some interest in Miss Cobb from this time on. I never dreamed that she could bring me fresh news of that rare spirit whom I have so wished to see, and for one week in the woods with whom I would give any year of my life. Are they possibly the Henderson family to whom Audubon intrusted the box of his original drawings during his absence in Philadelphia, and who let a pair of Norway rats rear a family in it, and cut to pieces nearly a thousand inhabitants of the air?

There are two more days of June. Since the talk with Sylvia I have called twice more upon the elder Miss Cobb. Upon reflection, it is misleading to refer to this young lady in terms so dry, stiff, and denuded; and I shall drop into Sylvia's form, and call her simply Georgiana. That looks better—Georgiana! It sounds well, too—Georgiana!

Georgiana, then, is a rather elusive character. The more I see of her the less I understand her. If your nature draws near hers, it retreats. If you pursue, it flies—a little frightened perhaps. If then you keep still and look perfectly safe, she will return, but remain at a fixed distance, like a bird that will stay in your yard, but not enter your house. It is hardly shyness, for she is not shy, but more like some strain of wild nature in her that refuses to be domesticated. One's faith is strained to accept Sylvia's estimate that Georgiana is deep—she is so light, so airy, so playful. Sylvia is a demure little dove that has pulled over itself an owl's skin, and is much prouder of its wicked old feathers than of its innocent heart; but Georgiana—what is she? Secretly an owl with the buoyancy of a humming-bird? However, it's nothing to me. She hovers around her mother and Sylvia with a fondness that is rather beautiful. I did not mention the subject of Audubon and her father, for it is never well to let an elder sister know that a younger one has been talking about her. I merely gave her several chances to speak of birds, but she ignored them. As for me and my love of birds, such trifles are beneath her notice. I don't like her, and it will not be worth while to call again soon, though it would be pleasant to see those drawings.

This morning as I was accidentally passing under her window I saw her at it and lifted my hat. She leaned over with her cheek in her palm, and said, smiling,

"You mustn't spoil Sylvia!"

"What is my definite offence in that regard?"

"Too much arbour, too many flowers, too much fine treatment."

"Does fine treatment ever harm anybody? Is it not bad treatment that spoils people?"

"Good treatment may never spoil people who are old enough to know its rarity and value. But you say you are a student of nature; have you not observed that nature never lets the sugar get to things until they are ripe? Children must be kept tart."

"The next time that Miss Sylvia comes over, then, I am to give her a tremendous scolding and a big basket of green apples."

"Or, what is worse, suppose you encourage her to study the Greatest Common Divisor? I am trying to get her ready for school in the fall."

"Is she being educated for a teacher?"

"You know that Southern ladies never teach."

"Then she will never need the Greatest Common Divisor. I have known many thousands of human beings, and none but teachers ever has the least use for the Greatest Common Divisor."

"But she needs to do things that she dislikes. We all do."

I smiled at the memory of a self-willed little bare foot on a log years ago.

"I shall see that my grape arbour does not further interfere with Miss Sylvia's progress towards perfection."

"Why didn't you wish us to be your neighbours?"

"I didn't know that you were the right sort of people."

"Are we the right sort?"

"The value of my land has almost been doubled."

"It is a pleasure to know that you approve of us on those grounds. Will the value of our land rise also, do you think? And why do you suppose we objected to you as a neighbour?"

"I cannot imagine."

"The imagination can be cultivated, you know. Then tell me this: why do Kentuckians in this part of Kentucky think so much of themselves compared with the rest of the world?"

"Perhaps it's because they are Virginians. There may be various reasons."

"Do the people ever tell what the reasons are?"

"I have never heard one."

"And if we stayed here long enough, and imitated them closely, do you suppose we would get to feel the same way?"

"I am sure of it."

"It must be so pleasant to consider Kentucky the best part of the world, and your part of Kentucky the best of the State, and your family the best of all the best families in that best part, and yourself the best member of your family. Ought not that to make one perfectly happy?"

"I have often observed that it seems to do so."

"It is delightful to remember that you approve of us. And we should feel so glad to be able to return the compliment. Good-bye!"

Any one would have to admit, however, that there is no sharpness in Georgiana's pleasantry. The child-nature in her is so sunny, sportive, so

bent on harmless mischief. She still plays with life as a kitten with a ball of
yarn. Some day Kitty will fall asleep with the Ball poised in the cup of one
foot. Then, waking, when her dream is over, she will find that her plaything has become a rocky, thorny, storm-swept, immeasurable world, and
that she, a woman, stands holding out towards it her imploring arms, and
asking only for some littlest part in its infinite destinies.

After the last talk with Georgiana I felt renewed desire to see those
Audubon drawings. So yesterday morning I sent over to her some things written by a Northern man, whom I call the young Audubon of the Maine woods.
His name is Henry D. Thoreau, and it is, I believe, known only to me down
here. Everything that I can find of his is as pure and cold and lonely as a
wild cedar of the mountain rocks, standing far above its smokeless valley
and hushed white river. She returned them to-day, with word that she
would thank me in person, and to-night I went over in a state of rather
senseless eagerness.

Her mother and sister had gone out, and she sat on the dark porch
alone. The things of Thoreau's have interested her, and she asked me to tell
her all I knew of him, which was little enough. Then of her own accord she
began to speak of her father and Audubon—of the one with the worship of
love, of the other with the worship of greatness. I felt as though I were in a
moonlit cathedral; for her voice, the whole revelation of her nature, made
the spot so impressive and so sacred. She scarcely addressed me; she was
communing with them. Nothing that her father told her regarding Audubon
appears to have been forgotten; and, brought nearer than ever before to
that lofty, tireless spirit in its wanderings through the Kentucky forests, I
almost forgot her to whom I was listening. But in the midst of it she
stopped, and it was again kitten and yarn. I left quite as abruptly. Upon
my soul I believe that Georgiana doesn't think me worth talking to
seriously.

VII

July has dragged like a log across a wet field.

There was the Fourth, which is always the grandest occasion of the
year with us. Society has taken up Sylvia and rejected Georgiana; and so
with its great gallantry, and to her boundless delight, Sylvia was invited to
sit with a bevy of girls in a large furniture wagon covered with flags and
bunting. The girls were to be dressed in white, carry flowers and flags, and
sing "The Star-Spangled Banner" in the procession, just before the fire-
engine. I wrote a note to Georgiana, asking whether it would interfere with
Sylvia's Greatest Common Divisor if I presented her with a profusion of
elegant flowers on that occasion. Georgiana herself had equipped Sylvia

with a truly exquisite silken flag on a silver staff; and as Sylvia both sang
and waved with all her might, not only to keep up the Green River reputation in such matters, but with a mediæval determination to attract a young
man on the fire-engine behind, she quite eclipsed every other miss in the
wagon, and was not even hoarse when persuaded at last to stop. So that several of the representatives of the other States voted afterwards in a special
congress that she was loud, and in no way as nice as they had fancied, and
that they ought never to recognize her again except in church and at
funerals.

And then the month brought down from West Point the son of the
family, who cut *off*—or cut *at*—Georgiana's toes, I remember. With him a
sort of cousin, who lives in New York State; and after a few days of top-
loftical strutting around town, and a pusillanimous crack or two over the
back-garden fence at my birds, they went away again, to the home of this
New York cousin, carrying Georgiana with them to spend the summer.

Nothing has happened since. Only Sylvia and I have been making hay
while the sun shines—or does not shine, if one chooses to regard Georgiana's
absence in that cloudy fashion. Sylvia's ordinary armour consists of a
slate-pencil for a spear, a slate for a shield, and a volume of Sir Walter for
a bludgeon. Now and then I have found her sitting alone in the arbour with
the drooping air of Lucy Ashton beside the fountain; and she would be
better pleased if I met her clandestinely there in cloak and plume with the
deadly complexion of Ravenswood.

The other day I caught her toiling at something, and she admitted
being at work on a poem which would be about half as long as the "Lay of
the Last Minstrel." She read me the opening lines, after that bland habit
of young writers; and as nearly as I recollect, they began as follows:

> "I love to see gardens and arbours and plants;
> I love the fine air, but not my fine aunts."

When not under the spell of mediæval chivalry she prattles needlessly
of Georgiana, early life, and their old home in Henderson. Although I have
pointed out to her the gross impropriety of her conduct, she has persisted
in reading me some of Georgiana's letters written from the home of that
New York cousin, whose mother they are now visiting. I didn't like *him*
particularly. Sylvia relates that he was a favourite of her father's.

The dull month passes to-day. One thing I have secretly wished to
learn: did her brother cut Georgiana's toes entirely off?

VIII

In August the pale and delicate poetry of the Kentucky land makes
itself felt as silence and repose. Still skies, still woods, still sheets of forest

water, still flocks and herds, long lanes winding without the sound of a
traveller through fields of the universal brooding stillness. The sun no longer
blazing, but muffled in a veil of palest blue. No more black clouds rumbling
and rushing up from the horizon, but a single white one brushing slowly
against the zenith like the lost wing of a swan. Far beneath it the silver-
breasted hawk, using the cloud as his lordly parasol. The eagerness of
spring gone, now all but incredible as having ever existed; the birds hushed
and hiding; the bee, so nimble once, fallen asleep over his own cider-press
in the shadow of the golden apple. From the depths of the woods may come
the notes of the cuckoo; but they strike the air more and more slowly, like
the *clack, clack, clack* of a distant wheel that is being stopped at the close
of harvest. The whirring wings of the locust let themselves go in one long
wave of sound, passing into silence. All nature is a vast sacred goblet,
filling drop by drop to the brim, and not to be shaken. But the stalks of the
later flowers begin to be stuffed with hurrying bloom lest they be too late;
and the nighthawk rapidly mounts his stairway of flight higher and higher,
higher and higher, as though he would rise above the warm white sea of
atmosphere and breathe in cold ether.

Always in August my nature will go its own way and seek its own
peace. I roam solitary, but never alone, over this rich pastoral land, crossing farm after farm, and keeping as best I can out of sight of the labouring
or loitering negroes. For the sight of them ruins every landscape, and I shall
never feel myself free till they are gone. What if they sing? The more is the
pity that any human being could be happy enough to sing so long as he
was a slave in any thought or fibre of his nature.

Sometimes it is through the aftermath of fat wheat-fields, where float
like myriad little nets of silver gauze the webs of the crafty weavers, and
where a whole world of winged small folk flit from tree-top to tree-top of
the low weeds. They are all mine—these Kentucky wheatfields. After the
owner has taken from them his last sheaf I come in and gather my harvest
also—one that he did not see, and doubtless would not begrudge me—the
harvest of beauty. Or I walk beside tufted aromatic hemp-fields, as along
the shores of softly foaming emerald seas; or past the rank and file of fields
of Indian-corn, which stand like armies that had gotten ready to march, but
been kept waiting for further orders, until at last the soldiers had grown
tired, as the gayest will, of their yellow plumes and green ribbons, and let
their big hands fall heavily down at their sides. There the white and the
purple morning-glories hang their long festoons and open to the soft midnight winds their elfin trumpets.

This year as never before I have felt the beauty of the world. And with
the new brightness in which every common scene has been apparelled
there has stirred within me a need of human companionship unknown in

the past. It is as if Nature had spread out her last loveliness and said: "See! You have before you now all that you can ever get from me! It is not enough. Realize this in time. I am your Mother. Love me as a child. But remember! such love can be only a little part of your life."

Therefore I have spent the month restless, on the eve of change, drawn to Nature, driven from her. In September it will be different, for then there are more things to do on my small farm, and I see people on account of my grapes and pears. My malady this August has been an idle mind—so idle that a letter from Georgiana seems its main event. This was written from the old home of Audubon on the Hudson, whither they had gone sight-seeing. It must have been to her much like a pilgrimage to a shrine. She wrote informally, telling me about the place and enclosing a sprig of cedar from one of the trees in the yard. Her mind was evidently overflowing on the subject. It was rather pleasant to have the overflow turned my way. I shall plant the cedar where it will stay always green.

I saw Georgiana once more before her leaving. The sudden appearance of her brother and cousin, and the news that she would return with them for the summer, spurred me up to make another attempt at those Audubon drawings.

How easy it was to get them! It is what a man thinks a woman will be willing to do that she seldom does. But she made a confession. When she first found that I was a smallish student of birds, she feared I would not like Audubon, since men so often sneer at those who do in a grand way what they can do only in a poor one. I had another revelation of Georgiana's more serious nature, which is always aroused by the memory of her father. There is something beautiful and steadfast in this girl's soul. In our hemisphere vines climb round from left to right; if Georgiana loved you she would, if bidden, reverse every law of her nature for you as completely as a vine that you had caused to twine from right to left.

Sylvia enters school the 1st of September, and Georgiana is to be at home then to see to that. How surely she drives this family before her—and with as gentle a touch as that of a slow south wind upon the clouds.

Those poor first drawings of Audubon! He succeeded; we study his early failings. The world never studies the failures of those who do not succeed in the end.

The birds are moulting. If man could only moult also—his mind once a year its errors, his heart once a year its useless passions! How fine we should all look if every August the old plumage of our natures would drop out and be blown away, and fresh quills take the vacant places! But we have one set of feathers to last us through our three-score years and ten— one set of spotless feathers, which we are told to keep spotless through all our lives in a dirty world. If one gets broken, broken it stays; if one gets blackened, nothing will cleanse it. No doubt we shall all fly home at last, like a flock of pigeons that were once turned loose snow-white from the sky, and made to descend and fight one another and fight everything else for a poor living amid soot and mire. If then the hand of the unseen Fancier is stretched forth to draw us in, how can he possibly smite any one of us, or cast us away, because we come back to him black and blue with bruises, and besmudged and bedraggled past recognition!

IX

To-day, the 7th of September, I made a discovery. The pair of red-birds that built in my cedar-trees last winter got duly away with the brood. Several times during summer rambles I cast my eye about, but they were not to be seen. Early this afternoon I struck out across the country towards a sink-hole in a field two miles away, some fifty yards in diameter, very deep, and enclosed by a fence. A series of these circular basins, at regular intervals apart, runs across the country over there, suggesting the remains of ancient earth-works. The bottom had dropped out of this one, probably communicating with the many caves that are characteristic of this blue limestone.

Within the fence everything is an impenetrable thicket of weeds and vines—blackberry, thistle, ironweed, pokeweed, elder, golden-rod. As I drew near, I saw two or three birds dive down, with the shy way they have at this season; and when I came to the edge, everything was quiet. But I threw a stone at a point where the tangle was deep, and there was a great fluttering and scattering of the pretenders. And then occurred more than I had looked for. The stone had hardly struck the brush when what looked like a tongue of vermilion flame leaped forth near by, and, darting across, struck itself out of sight in the green vines on the opposite slope. A male and a female cardinal flew up also, balancing themselves on sprays of the blackberry, and uttering excitedly their quick call-notes. I whistled to the male as I had been used, and he recognized me by shooting up his crest, and hopping to nearer twigs with louder inquiry. All at once, as if an idea had urged him, he sprang across to the spot where the first frightened male had disappeared. I could still hear him under the vines, and presently he reappeared and flew up into a locust-tree on the farther edge of the basin, followed by the other. What had taken place or took place then I do not know; but I wished he might be saying: "My son, that man over there is the one who was very good to your mother and me last winter, and who owns the tree you were born in. I have warned you, of course, never to trust Man; but I would advise you, when you have found your sweetheart, to give him a trial, and take her to his cedar-trees."

If he said anything like this, it certainly had a terrible effect on the son; for, having mounted rapidly to the tree-top, he clove the blue with his scarlet wings as though he were flying from death. I lost sight of him over a corn-field.

One fact pleased me: the father returned to his partner under the briers, for he is not of the lower sort who forget the mother when the children are reared. They hold faithfully together during the ever more silent, ever more shadowy autumn days; his warming breast is close to hers through frozen winter nights; and if they both live to see another May she is still all the world to him, and woe to any brilliant vagabond who should warble a wanton love-song under her holy windows.

Georgiana returned the last of August. The next morning she was at her window, looking across into my yard. I was obliged to pass that way, and welcomed her gayly, expressing my thanks for the letter.

"I had to come back, you see," she said, with calm simplicity. I lingered awkwardly, stripping upward the stalks of some weeds.

"Very few Kentucky birds are migratory," I replied at length, with desperate brilliancy and an overwhelming grimace.

"I shall go back some time—to stay," she said, and turned away with a parting faintest smile.

Is that West Point brother giving trouble? If so, the sooner a war breaks out and he gets killed, the better. One thing is certain: if, for the next month, fruit and flowers will give Georgiana any pleasure, she shall have a good deal of pleasure. She is so changed! But why need I take on about it?

They have been cleaning out a drain under the streets along the Town Fork of Elkhorn, and several people are down with fever.

X

New-year's night again, and bitter cold.

When I forced myself away from my fire before dark, and ran down to the stable to see about feeding and bedding the horses and cows, every beast had its head drawn in towards its shoulders, and looked at me with the dismal air of saying, "Who is tempering the wind now?" The dogs in the kennel, with their noses between their hind-legs, were shivering under their blankets and straw like a nest of chilled young birds. The fowls on the roost were mere white and blue puffs of feathers. Nature alone has the keeping of her creatures; why doesn't she make them comfortable?

After supper old Jack and Dilsy came in, and standing against the wall with their arms folded, told me more of what happened after I got sick. That was about the middle of September, and it is only two weeks since I became well enough to go in and out through all sorts of weather.

It was the middle of September then, my servants said, and as within a week after taking the fever I was very ill, a great many people came out to inquire for me. Some of these, walking around the garden, declared it was a pity for such fruit and flowers to be wasted, and so helped themselves freely every time. The old doctor, who always fears for my health at this season, stopped by nearly every day to repeat how he had warned me, and always walked back to his gig in a roundabout way, which required him to pass a favourite tree; and once he was so indignant to find several other persons gathered there, and mournfully enjoying the last of the fruit as they predicted I would never get well, that he came back to the house—with two pears in each duster pocket and one in his mouth—and told Jack it was an outrage. The preacher, likewise, who appears in the spring-time, one afternoon knocked reproachfully at the front door and inquired whether I was in a condition to be reasoned with. In his hand he carried a nice little work-basket, which may have been brought along to catch his prayers; but he took it home piled with grapes.

And then they told me, also, how many a good and kind soul came with hushed footsteps and low inquiries, turning away sometimes with brightened faces, sometimes with rising tears—often people whom I had done no kindness or whom I did not know; how others whom I had quarrelled with or did not like, forgot the poor puny quarrels and the dislike, and begged to do for me whatever they could; how friends went softly around the garden, caring for a flower, putting a prop under a too-heavily laden limb, or climbing on step-ladders to tie sacks around the finest bunches of grapes, with the hope that I might be well in time to eat them—touching nothing themselves, having no heart to eat; how dear, dear ones would never leave me day or night; how a good doctor wore himself out with watching, and a good pastor sent up for me his spotless prayers; and at last, when I began to mend, how from far and near there poured in flowers and jellies and wines, until, had I been the multitude by the Sea of Galilee, there must have been baskets to spare. God bless them! God bless them all! And God forgive us all the blindness, the weakness, and the cruelty with which we judge each other when we are in health.

This and more my beloved old negroes told me a few hours ago, as I sat in deep comfort and bright health again before my blazing hickories; and one moment we were in laughter and the next in tears—as is the strange life we live. This is a gay household now, and Dilsy cannot face me without a fleshy earthquake of laughter that I have become such a high-tempered tiger about punctual meals.

In particular, my two nearest neighbours were much at odds as to which had better claim to nurse me; so that one day Mrs. Walters, able to endure it no longer, thrust Mrs. Cobb out of the house by the shoulder-blades, locked the door on her, and then opened the shutters and scolded her out of the window.

One thing I miss. My servants have never called the name of Georgiana. The omission is unnatural, and must be intentional. Of course I have not asked whether she showed any concern; but that little spot of silence affects me as the sight of a tree remaining leafless in the woods where everything else is turning green.

XI

To-day I was standing at a window, looking out at the aged row of cedars, now laden with snow, and thinking of Horace and Soracte. Suddenly, beneath a jutting pinnacle of white boughs which left under themselves one little spot of green, I saw a cardinal hop out and sit full-breasted towards me. The idea flashed through my mind that this might be that shyest, most beautiful fellow whom I had found in September, and whom I tried to make out as the son of my last winter's pensioner. At least he has never lived in my yard before; for when, to test his shyness, I started to raise the window-sash, at the first noise of it he was gone. My birds are not so afraid of me. I must get on better terms with this stranger.

Mrs. Walters over for a while afterwards. I told her of my fancy that this bird was one of last summer's brood, and that he appeared a trifle larger than any male I had ever seen. She said of course. Had I not fed the parents all last winter? When she fed her hens, did they not lay bigger eggs? Did not bigger eggs contain bigger chicks? Did not bigger chicks become bigger hens, again? According to Mrs. Walters, a single winter's feeding of hot corn-meal, scraps of bacon, and pods of red pepper will all but bring about a variation of species; and so if the assumed rate at which I am now going were kept up a hundred years, my cedar-trees might be full of a race of red-birds as large and as fat as geese.

Standing towards sundown at another window, I saw Georgiana sewing at hers, as I have seen her every day since I got out of bed. Why should she sew so much? There is a servant also; and they sew, sew, sew, as if eternal sewing were eternal happiness, eternal salvation. The first day she sprang up, letting her work roll off her lap, and waved her handkerchief inside the panes, and smiled with what looked to me like radiant pleasure that I was well again. I was weak and began to tremble, and, going back to the fireside, lay back in my chair with a beating of the heart that was a warning. Since then she has recognized me only by a quiet, kindly smile. Why has no one ever called her name? I believe Mrs. Walters knows. She comes nowadays as if to tell me something, and goes away with a struggle that she has not told it. But a secret can no more stay in the depths of Mrs. Walters's mind than cork at the bottom of water; some day I shall see this mystery riding on the surface.

XII

Yes, she knew; while unconscious I talked of Georgiana, of being in love with her. Mrs. Walters added, sadly, that Georgiana came home in the fall engaged to that New York cousin. Hence the sewing—he was to marry her in June.

I am *not* in love with her. It is now four weeks since hearing this conventional fiction and every day I have been perfectly able to repeat: "I am *not* in love with Georgiana!" There was one question which I put severely to Mrs. Walters: Had she told Georgiana of my foolish talk? She shook her head violently, and pressed her lips closely together, suggesting how impossible it would be for the smallest monosyllable in the language to escape by that channel; but she kept her eyes wide open, and the truth issued from them, as smoke in a hollow tree, if stopped in at a lower hole, simply rises and comes out at a higher one. "You should have shut your eyes also," I said. "You have told her every word of it, and the Lord only knows how much more."

This February has let loose its whole pack of grizzly sky-hounds. Unbroken severe weather. Health has not returned as rapidly as was promised, and I have not ventured outside the yard. But it is a pleasure to chronicle the beginning of an acquaintanceship between his proud eminence the young cardinal and myself. For a long time he would have naught to do with me, fled as I approached, abandoned the evergreens altogether and sat on the naked tree-tops, as much as threatening to quit the place altogether if I did not leave him in peace. Surely he is the shyest of his kind, and to my fancy, the most beautiful; and therefore Nature seems to have stored him with extra caution towards his arch-enemy.

But in the old human way I have taken advantage of his necessities. The north wind has been my friend against him. I have called in the aid of sleets and snows, have besieged him in his white castle behind the glittering array of his icicles with threats of starvation. So one day, dropping like a glowing coal down among the other birds, he snatched a desperate hasty meal from the public poor-house table that I had spread under the trees.

It is the first surrender that decides. Since then some progress has been made in winning his confidence, but the struggle going on in his nature is plain enough still. At times he will rush away from me in utter terror; at others he lets me draw a little nearer, without moving from a limb; and now, after a month of persuasion, he begins to discredit the experience which he has inherited from centuries upon centuries of ancestors. In all that I have done I have tried to say to him: "Don't judge me by mankind in general. With me you are safe. I pledge myself to defend you from enemies, high and low."

This has not escaped the notice of Georgiana at the window, and more than once she has let her work drop to watch my patient progress and to bestow upon me a rewarding smile. Is there nearly always sadness in it, or is the sadness in my eyes? If Georgiana's brother is giving her trouble, I'd like to take a hand-axe to *his* feet. I suppose I shall never know whether he cut her foot in two. She carries the left one a little peculiarly; but so many women do that.

Sometimes, when the day's work is over and the servant is gone, Georgiana comes to the window and looks away towards the sunsets of winter, her hands clasped behind her back, her motionless figure in relief against the darkness within, her face white and still. Being in the shadow of my own room, so that she could not see me, and knowing that I ought not to do it, but unable to resist, I have softly taken up the spy-glass which I use in the study of birds, and have drawn Georgiana's face nearer to me, holding it there till she turns away. I have noted the traces of pain, and once the tears which she could not keep back and was too proud to shed. Then I have sat before my flickering embers, with I know not what all but ungovernable yearning to be over there in the shadowy room with her, and, whether she would or not, to fold my arms around her, and, drawing her face against mine, whisper: "What is it, Georgiana? And why must it be?"

XIII

The fountains of the great deep opened. A new heaven, a new earth. Georgiana has broken her engagement with her cousin. Mrs. Cobb let it out in the strictest confidence to Mrs. Walters. Mrs. Walters, with stricter confidence still, has told me only.

The West-Pointer had been writing for some months in regard to the wild behaviour of his cousin. This grew worse, and the crisis came. Georgiana snapped her thread and put up her needle. He travelled all the way down here to implore. I met him at the gate as he left the house—a fine, straight, manly, handsome young fellow, his face pale with pain, and his eyes flashing with anger—and bade him a long, affectionate, inward Godspeed as he hurried away. It was her father's influence. He had always wished for this union. Ah, the evils that come to the living from the wrongful wishes of the dead! Georgiana is so happy now, since she has been forced to free herself, that spring in this part of the United States seems to have advanced about half a month.

"What on earth will she do with all those clothes?" inquired Mrs. Walters the other night, eyeing me with curious impressiveness.

"Let them be hanged," I said, promptly.

There is a young scapegrace who passes my house morning and eve-

ning with his cows. He has the predatory instincts of that being who loves
to call himself the image of his Maker, and more than once has given annoyance, especially last year, when he robbed a damson-tree of a brood of
Baltimore orioles. This winter and spring his friendly interest in my birds
has increased, and several times I have caught him skulking among the
pines. Last night what should I stumble on but a trap, baited and sprung,
under the cedar-tree in which the cardinal roosts. I was up before daybreak
this morning. Awhile after the waking of the birds here comes my young
bird-thief, creeping rapidly to his trap. As he stooped I had him by the collar, and within the next five minutes I must have set up in his nervous
system a negative disposition to the caging of red-birds that will descend as
a positive tendency to all the generations of his offspring.

All day this meditated outrage has kept my blood up. Think of this
beautiful cardinal beating his heart out against maddening bars, or caged
for life in some dark city street, lonely, sick, and silent, bidden to sing
joyously of that high world of light and liberty where once he sported!
Think of the exquisite refinement of cruelty in wishing to take him on the
eve of May!

It is hardly a fancy that something as loyal as friendship has sprung
up between this bird and me. I accept his original shyness as a mark of his
finer instincts; but, like the nobler natures, when once he found it possible
to give his confidence, how frankly and fearlessly has it been given. The
other day, brilliant, warm, windless, I was tramping across the fields a mile
from home, when I heard him on the summit of a dead sycamore, cleaving
the air with stroke after stroke of his long melodious whistle, as with the
swing of a silken lash. When I drew near he dropped down from bough to
bough till he reached the lowest, a few feet from where I stood, and showed
by every movement how glad he was to see me. We really have reached the
understanding that the immemorial persecution of his race by mine is ended;
and now more than ever my fondness settles about him, since I have found
his happiness plotted against, and have perhaps saved his very life. It
would be easy to trap him. His eye should be made to distrust every well-
arranged pile of sticks under which lurks a morsel.

To-night I called upon Georgiana and sketched the arrested tragedy
of the morning. She watched me curiously, and then dashed into a little
treatise on the celebrated friendships of man for the lower creatures, in fact
and fiction, from camels down to white mice. Her father must have been a
remarkably learned man. I didn't like this. It made me somehow feel as
though I were one of Æsop's Fables, or were being translated into English
as that old school-room horror of Androclus and the Lion. In the bottom of
my soul I don't believe that Georgiana cares for birds, or knows the difference between a blackbird and a crow. I am going to send her a little story,

"The Passion of the Desert." Mrs. Walters is now confident that Georgiana regrets having broken off her engagement. But then Mrs. Walters can be a great fool when she puts her whole mind to it.

XIV

In April I commence to scratch and dig in my garden.

To-day as I was raking off my strawberry bed, Georgiana, whom I have not seen since the night when she satirized me, called from the window:

"What are you going to plant this year?"

"Oh, a little of everything," I answered, under my hat. "What are *you* going to plant this year?"

"Are you going to have many strawberries?"

"It's too soon to tell: they haven't bloomed yet. It's too soon to tell when they *do* bloom. Sometimes strawberries are like women: Whole beds full of showy blossoms; but when the time comes to be ripe and luscious, you can't find them."

"Indeed."

" 'Tis true, 'tis pity."

"I had always supposed that to a Southern gentleman woman was not a berry, but a rose. What does he hunt for in woman as much as bloom and fragrance? But I do not belong to the rose-order of Southern women myself. Sylvia does. Why did you send me that story?"

"Didn't you like it?"

"No. A woman couldn't care for a story about a man and a tigress. Either she would feel that she was too much left out, or suspect that she was too much put in. The same sort of story about a lion and a woman— that would be better."

I raked in silence for a minute, and when I looked up Georgiana was gone. I remember her saying once that children should be kept tart; but now and then I fancy that she would like to keep even a middle-aged man in brine. Who knows but that in the end I shall sell my place to the Cobbs and move away.

Five more days of April, and then May! For the last half of this light-and-shadow month, when the clouds, like schools of changeable lovely creatures, seem to be playing and rushing away through the waters of the sun, life to me has narrowed more and more to the red-bird, who gets tamer and tamer with habit, and to Georgiana, who gets wilder and wilder with happiness. The bird fills the yard with brilliant singing; she fills her room with her low, clear songs, hidden behind the window-curtains, which are now so much oftener and so needlessly closed. I work myself nearly to death in my garden, but she does not open them. The other day the red-bird sat in a tree near by, and his notes floated out on the air like scarlet streamers. Georgiana was singing, so low that I was making no noise with my rake in order to hear; and when he began, before I realized what I was doing, I had seized a brickbat and hurled it, barely missing him, and driving him away. He did not know what to make of it; neither did I; but as I raised my eyes I saw that Georgiana had opened the curtains to listen to him, and was closing them with her eyes on my face, and a look on hers that has haunted me ever since.

April the 26th. It's of no use. To-morrow night I will go to see Georgiana, and ask her to marry me.

April 28th. Man that is born of woman is of few days and full of trouble. I am not the least sick, but I am not feeling at all well. So have made a will, and left everything to Mrs. Walters. She has been over five times to-day, and this evening sat by me a long time, holding my hand and smoothing my forehead, and urging me to try a cream poultice—a mustard-plaster—a bowl of gruel—a broiled chicken.

I believe Georgiana thinks I'll ask her again. Not if I lived by her through eternity! Thy rod and Thy staff—*they* comfort me.

XV

A poor devil will ask a woman to marry him. She will refuse him. The day after she will meet him as serenely as if he had asked her for a pin.

It is now May 15th, and I have not spoken to Georgiana when I've had a chance. She has been entirely too happy, to judge from her singing, for me to get along with under the circumstances. But this morning, as I was planting a hedge inside my fence under her window, she leaned over and said, as though nothing were wrong between us, "What are you planting?"

I have sometimes thought that Georgiana can ask more questions than Socrates.

"A hedge."

"What for?"

"To grow."

"What do you want it to grow for?"

"My garden is too public. I wish to be protected from outsiders."

"Would it be the same thing if I were to nail up this window? That would be so much quicker. It will be ten years before your hedge is high enough to keep me from seeing you. And even then, you know, I could move upstairs. But I am so sorry to be an outsider."

"I merely remarked that I was planting a hedge."

When Georgiana spoke again her voice was lowered: "Would you open a gateway for me into your garden, to be always mine, so that I might go out and come in, and never another human soul enter it?"

Now Jacob had often begged me to cut him a private gateway on that side of the garden, so that only he might come in and go out; and I had refused, since I did not wish him to get to me so easily with his complaints. Besides, a gate once opened, who may not use it? and I was indignant that Georgiana should lightly ask anything at my hands; therefore I looked quickly and sternly up at her and said, "I will not."

Afterwards the thought rushed over me that she had not spoken of any gateway through my garden fence, but of another one, mystical, hidden, infinitely more sacred. For her voice descended almost in a whisper, and her face, as she bent down towards me, had on it I know not what angelic expression. She seemed floating to me from heaven.

May 17. To-day I put a little private gate through my fence under Georgiana's window, as a sign to her. Balaam's beast that I am! Yes, seven times more than the inspired ass.

As I passed to-day, I noticed Georgiana looking down at the gate that I made yesterday. She held a flower to her nose and eyes, but behind the leaves I detected that she was laughing.

"Good-morning!" she called to me. "What did you cut that ugly hole in your fence for?"

"That's not an ugly hole. That's a little private gateway."

"But what's the little private gateway *for?*"

"Oh, well! You don't understand these matters. I'll tell your mother."

"My mother is too old. She no longer stoops to such things. Tell *me!*"

"Impossible!"

"I'm dying to know."

"What will you give me?"

"Anything—this flower!"

"But what would the flower stand for in that case? A little pri—"

"Nothing. Take it!" and she dropped it lightly on my face and disappeared. As I stood twirling it ecstatically under my nose, and wondering how I could get her to come back to the window, the edge of a curtain was lifted, and a white hand stole out and softly closed the shutters.

In the evening Sylvia went in to a concert of the school, which was to be held at the Courthouse, a chorus of girls being impanelled in the jury-box, and the principal, who wears a little wig, taking her seat on the woolsack. I promised to have the very pick of the garden ready, and told

Sylvia to come to the arbour the last thing before starting. She wore big blue rosettes in her hair, and at that twilight hour looked as lovely, soft, and pure as moonshine; so that I lost control of myself and kissed her twice— once for Georgiana and once for myself. Surely it must have been Sylvia's first experience. I hope so. Yet she passed through it with the composure of a graduate of several years' standing. But, then, women inherit a great stock of fortitude from their mothers in this regard, and perpetually add to it by their own dispositions. Ought I to warn Georgiana—good heavens! in a general way, of course—that Sylvia should be kept away from sugar, and well under the influence of vulgar fractions?

It made me feel uncomfortable to see her go tripping out of her front gate on the arm of a youth. Can it be possible that *he* would try to do what *I* did? Men differ so in their virtues, and are so alike in their transgressions. This forward gosling displayed white duck pantaloons, brandished pumps on his feet, which looked flat enough to have been webbed, and was scented as to his marital locks with a far-reaching pestilence of bergamot and cinnamon.

After they were gone I strolled back to my arbour and sat down amid the ruins of Sylvia's flowers. The night was mystically beautiful. The moon seemed to me to be softly stealing down the sky to kiss Endymion. I looked across towards Georgiana's window. She was there, and I slipped over and stood under it.

"Georgiana," I whispered, "were you, too, looking at the moon?"

"Part of the time," she said, sourly. "Isn't it permitted?"

"Sylvia left her scissors in the arbour, and I can't find them."

"She'll find them to-morrow."

"If they get wet, you know, they'll rust."

"I keep something to take rust off."

"Georgiana, I've got something to tell you about Sylvia."

"What? That you kissed her?"

"N—o! Not *that*, exactly!"

"Good-night!"

May 21st. Again I asked Georgiana to be mine. I am a perfect fool about her. But she's coming my way at last—God bless her!

May 24th. I renewed my suit to Georgiana.

May 27th. I besought Georgiana to hear me.

May 28th. For the last time I offered my hand in marriage to the elder Miss Cobb. Now I am done with her forever. I am no fool.

May 29th. Oh, *damn* Mrs. Walters.

XVI

This morning, the 3d of June, I went out to pick the first dish of strawberries for my breakfast. As I was stooping down I heard a timid, playful voice at the window like the echo of a year ago: "Are you the gardener?"

Since Georgiana will not marry me, if she would only let me alone!

"Old man, are you the gardener?"

"Yes, I'm the gardener. I know what you are."

"How much do you ask for your strawberries?"

"They come high. Nothing of mine is to be as cheap hereafter as it has been."

"I am so glad—for your sake. I should like to possess something of yours, but I suppose everything is too high now."

"Entirely too high!"

"If I only could have foreseen that there would be an increase of value! As for me, I have felt that I am getting cheaper lately. I may have to *give* myself away soon. If I only knew of some one who loved the lower animals."

"The fox, for instance?"

"Yes; do you know of any one who would accept the present of a fox?"

"Ahem! I wouldn't mind having a *tame* fox. I don't care much for wild foxes."

"Oh, this one would get tame—in time."

"I don't believe I know of any one just at present."

"Very well. Sylvia will get the highest mark in arithmetic. And Joe is distinguishing himself at West Point. That's what I wanted to tell you. I'll send over the cream and sugar, and hope you will enjoy all your berries. We shall buy some in the market-house next week."

Later in the forenoon I sent the strawberries over to Georgiana. I have a variety that is the shape of the human heart, and when ripe it matches in colour that brighter current of the heart through which runs the hidden history of our passions. All over the top of the dish I carefully laid these heart-shaped berries, and under the biggest one, at the very top, I slipped this little note: "Look at the shape of them, Georgiana! I send them all to you. They are perishable."

This afternoon Georgiana sent back the empty dish, and inside the napkin was this note: "They are exactly the shape and colour of my emery needle-bag. I have been polishing my needles in it for many years."

Later, as I was walking to town, I met Georgiana and her mother coming out. No explanation had ever been made to the mother of that goose of a gate in our division fence; and as Georgiana had declined to accept the sign, I determined to show her that the gate could now stand for something else. So I said: "Mrs. Cobb, when you send your servants over for green corn, you can let them come through that little gate. It will be more convenient."

Only, I was so angry and confused that I called her Mrs. Corn, and said that when she sent her little Cobbs over . . . etc., etc.

After Georgiana's last treatment of me I resolved not to let her talk to me out of her window. So about nine o'clock this morning I took a negro boy and set him to picking the berries, while I stood by, directing him in a deep, manly voice as to the best way of managing that intricate business. Presently I heard Georgiana begin to sing to herself behind the curtains.

"Hurry up and fill that cup," I said to him, savagely. "And that will do this morning. You can go to the mill. The meal's nearly out."

When he was gone I called, in an undertone: "Georgiana! Come to the window! Please! Oh, Georgiana!"

But the song went on. What was the matter? I could not endure it. There was one way by which perhaps she could be brought. I whistled long and loud again and again. The curtains parted a little space.

"I was merely whistling to the bird," I said.

"I knew it," she answered, looking as I had never seen her. "Whenever you speak to him your voice is full of confidence and of love. I believe in it and like to hear it."

"What do you mean, Georgiana?" I cried, imploringly.

"Ah, Adam!" she said, with a rush of feeling. It was the first time she had ever called me by name. She bent her face down. Over it there passed a look of sweetness and sadness indescribably blended. "Ah, Adam! you have asked me many times to *marry* you! Make me believe once that you *love* me! Make me feel that I could trust myself to you for life!"

"What else can I do?" I answered, stirred to the deepest that was in me, throwing my arms backward, and standing with an open breast into which she might gaze.

And she did search my eyes and face in silence.

"What more?" I cried again, "in God's name?"

She rested her face on her palm, looking thoughtfully across the yard. Over there the red-bird was singing. Suddenly she leaned down towards me. Love was on her face now. But her eyes held mine with determination to wrest from them the last truth they might contain, and her voice trembled with doubt:

"Would you put the red-bird in a cage for me? Would you be willing to do that for me, Adam?"

At those whimsical, cruel words I shall never be able to reveal all that I felt—the surprise, the sorrow, the pain. Scenes of boyhood flashed through my memory. A conscience built up through years of experience stood close

by me with admonition. I saw the love on her face, the hope with which she
hung upon my reply, as though it would decide everything between us. I
did not hesitate; my hands dropped to my side, the warmth died out of my
heart as out of spent ashes, and I answered her, with cold reproach:

"I—will—not!"

The colour died out of her face also. Her eyes still rested on mine, but
now with pitying sadness.

"I feared it," she murmured, audibly, but to herself, and the curtains
fell together.

Four days have passed. Georgiana has cast me off. Her curtains are
closed except when she is not there. I have tried to see her; she excuses
herself. I have written; my letters come back unread. I have lain in wait for
her on the streets; she will not talk with me. The tie between us has been
severed. With her it could never have been affection.

And for what? I ask myself over and over and over and over—for
what? Was she jealous of the bird, and did she require that I should put it
out of the way? Sometimes women do that. Did she take that means of
forcing me to a test? Women do that. Did she wish to show her power over
me, demanding the one thing she knew would be the hardest for me to
grant? Women do that. Did she crave the pleasure of seeing me do wrong
to humour her caprice? Women do that. But not one of these things can I
even associate with the thought of Georgiana. I have sought in every way
to have her explain, to explain myself. She will neither give nor receive an
explanation.

I had supposed that her unnatural request would have been the end of
my love, but it has not; that her treatment since would have fatally stung
my pride, but it has not. I understand neither; forgive both; love her now
with that added pain which comes from a man's discovering that the woman
dearest to him must be pardoned—pardoned as long as he shall live.

Never since have I been able to look at the red-bird with the old glad-
ness. He is the reminder of my loss. Reminder? Do I ever forget? Am I not
thinking of that before his notes lash my memory at dawn? All day can
they do more than furrow deeper the channel of unforgetfulness? Little
does he dream what my friendship for him has cost me. But this solace I
have at heart—that I was not even tempted to betray him.

Three days more have passed. No sign yet that Georgiana will relent
soon or ever. Each day the strain becomes harder to bear. My mind has
dwelt upon my last meeting with her, until the truth about it wavers upon
my memory like vague, uncertain shadows. She doubted my love for her.
What proof was it she demanded? I must stop looking at the red-bird, lying here and there under the trees, and listening to him as he sings above
me. My eyes devour him whenever he crosses my path with an uncompre-

hended fascination that is pain. How gentle he has become, and how, without intending it, I have deepened the perils of his life by the very gentleness that I have brought upon him. Twice already the fate of his species has struck at him, but I have pledged myself to be his friend. This is his happiest season; a few days now, and he will hear the call of his young in the nest.

I shut myself in my workshop in the yard this morning. I did not wish my servants to know. In there I made a bird-trap such as I had often used when a boy. And late this afternoon I went to town and bought a bird-cage. I was afraid the merchant would misjudge me, and explained. He scanned my face silently. To-morrow I will snare the red-bird down behind the pines long enough to impress on his memory a life-long suspicion of every such artifice, and then I will set him free again in his wide world of light. Above all things, I must see to it that he does not wound himself or have the least feather broken.

It is far past midnight now, and I have not slept or wished for slumber.

Constantly since darkness came on I have been watching Georgiana's window for the light of her candle, but there has been no kindly glimmer yet. The only radiance shed upon the gloom outside comes from the heavens. Great cage-shaped white clouds are swung up to the firmament, and within these pale, gentle, imprisoned lightnings flutter feebly to escape, fall back, rise, and try again and again, and fail.

. . . A little after dark this evening I carried the red-bird over to Georgiana. . . .

I have seen her so little of late that I did not know she had been away from home for days. But she was expected to-night, or, at furthest, to-morrow morning. I left the bird with the servant at the door, who could hardly believe what he saw. As I passed out of my front gate on my way there, the boy who returns about that time from the pasture for his cows joined me as I hurried along, attracted by the fluttering of the bird in the cage.

"Is it the red-bird? *I* tried to catch him once," he said, with entire forgiveness of me, as having served him right, "but I caught something else. I'll never forget that whipping. Oh, but wouldn't I like to have him! Mr. Moss, you wouldn't mind my trying to catch one of those little bits o' brown fellows, would you, that hop around under the pine-trees? They aren't any account to anybody. Oh my! but wouldn't I like to have *him!* May I bring my trap some time, and will you help me to catch one o' those little bits o' brown ones? You can't beat *me* catching them!"

Several times to-night I have gone across and listened under Georgiana's window. The servant must have set the cage in her room, for, as I listened, I am sure I heard the red-bird beating his head and breast against the wires. A while ago I went again, and did not hear him. I waited a long time. . . . He may be quieted. . . .

Ah, if any one had said to me that I would ever do what I have done, with what full, deep joy could I have throttled the lie in his throat! I put the trap under one of the trees where I have been used to feed him. When it fell he was not greatly frightened. He clutched the side of it, and looked out at me. My own mind supplied his words: "Help! I'm caught! Take me out! You promised!" When I transferred him to the cage, for a moment his confidence lasted still. He mounted the perch, shook his plumage, and spoke out bravely and cheerily. Then all at once came on the terror.

The dawn came on this morning with its old splendour. The birds in my yard, as of old, poured forth their songs. But those loud, long, clear, melodious, deep-hearted, passionate, best-loved notes! As the chorus swelled from shadowy shrubs and vines to the sparkling tree-tops I listened for some sound from Georgiana's room, but over there I saw only the soft, slow flapping of the white curtains like signals of distress.

Towards ten o'clock, wandering restless, I snatched up a book which I had no wish to read, and went to the arbour where I had so often discoursed to Sylvia about children's cruelty to birds. Through the fluttering leaves the sunlight dripped as a weightless shower of gold, and the long pendants of young fruit swayed gently in their cool waxen greenness. Where some rotting planks crossed the top of the arbour a blue-jay sat on her coarse nest; and presently the mate flew to her with a worm, and then talked to her in a low voice, as much as saying that they must now leave the place forever. I was thinking how love softens even the voice of this file-throated screamer, when along the garden walk came the rustle of a woman's clothes, and, springing up, I stood face to face with Georgiana.

"What have you done?" she implored.

"What have *you* done?" I answered as quickly.

"Oh, Adam, *Adam!* You have killed it! How could you? How could you?"

". . . Is he dead, Georgiana? Is he dead? . . ."

I forgot everything else, and pulling my hat down over my eyes, turned from her in the helpless shock of silence that came with those irreparable words.

Then, in ungovernable anger, suffering remorse, I turned upon her where she sat: "It is *you* who killed him! Why do you come here to blame me? And now you pretend to be sorry. You felt no pity when pity would have done some good. Trifler! Hypocrite!"

"It is false!" she cried, her words flashing from her whole countenance, her form drawn up to repel the shock of the blow.

"Did you not ask for him?"

"No!"

"Oh, deny it all! It is a falsehood—invented by me on the spot. You know nothing of it! You did not ask me to do this! And when I have yielded, you have not run to reproach me here and to cry, 'How could you? How could you?'"

"No! No! Every word of it—"

"Untruth added to it all! Oh, that I should have been so deceived, blinded, taken in!"

"*Adam!*"

"Lovely innocence! It is too much! Go away!"

"I will not stand this any longer!" she cried. "I will go away; but not till I have told you why I have acted as I have."

"It is too late for that! I do not care to hear!"

"Then you *shall* hear!" she replied. "You shall know that it is because I have believed you capable of speaking to me as you have just spoken: believed you at heart unsparing and unjust. You think I asked you to do what you have done? No! I asked you whether you would be willing to do it; and when you said you would not, I saw then—by your voice, your eyes, your whole face and manner—that you would. Saw it as plainly at that moment, in spite of your denial, as I see it now—the cruelty in you, the unfaithfulness, the willingness to betray. It was for this reason—not because I heard you refuse, but because I saw you consent—that I could not forgive you."

She paused abruptly and looked across into my face. What she may now have read in it I do not know. Then anger swept her on:

"How often had I not heard you bitter and contemptuous towards people because they are treacherous, cruel! How often have you talked of your love of nature, of our inhumanity towards lower creatures! But what have you done?

"You set your fancy upon one of these creatures, lie in wait for it, beset it with kindness, persevere in overcoming its wildness. You are amused, delighted, proud of your success. One day—you remember?—it sang as you had always wished to hear it. It annoyed you, and you threw a stone at it. With a little less angry aim you would have killed it. I have never seen anything more inhuman. How do I know that some day you would not be tired of me, and throw a stone at *me?* When a woman submits to this once, she will have them thrown at her whenever she sings at the wrong time, and she will never know when the right time is.

"Then you thought you were asked to sacrifice it, and now you have done that. How do I know that some day you might not be tempted to sacrifice me?" She paused, her voice breaking, and remained silent, as if unable to get beyond that thought.

"If you have finished," I said, very quietly, "I have something to say to you, and we need not meet after this.

"I trapped the bird; you trapped me. I understood you to ask something of me, to cast me off when I refused it. Such was my faith in you that beneath your words I did not look for a snare. How hard it was for me to forgive you what you asked is my own affair now; but forgive you I did. How hard it was to grant it that also is now, and will always be, my own secret. I beg you merely to believe this: knowing it to be all that you have described—and far more than you can ever understand—still, I did it. Had you demanded of me something worse, I should have granted that. If you think a man will not do wrong for a woman, you are mistaken. If you think men always love the wrong that they do for the women whom they love, you are mistaken again.

"You have held up my faults to me. I knew them before. I have not loved them. Do not think that I am trying to make a virtue out of anything I say; but in all my thoughts of you there has been no fault of yours that I have not hidden from my sight, and have not resolved as best I could never to see. Yet do not dream that I have found you faultless.

"You fear I might sacrifice you to something else. It is possible. Every man resists temptation only to a certain point; every man has his price. It is a risk you will run with any.

"If you doubt that a man is capable of sacrificing one thing that he loves to another that he loves more, tempt him, lie in wait for his weakness, ensnare him in the toils of his greater passion, and learn the truth.

"I make no defence—believe all that you say. But had you loved me, I might have been all this, and it would have been nothing."

With this I walked slowly out of the arbour, but Georgiana stood beside me. Her light touch was on my arm.

"Let me see things clearly!"

"You have a lifetime in which to see things clearly," I answered. "How can that concern me now?" And I passed on into the house.

During the morning I wandered restless. For a while I lay on the grass down behind the pines. How deep and clear are the covered springs of memory! All at once it was a morning in my boyhood on my father's farm. I, a little Saul of Tarsus among the birds, was on my way to the hedgerows and woods, as to Damascus, breathing out threatenings and slaughter. Then suddenly the childish miracle, which no doubt had been preparing silently within my nature, wrought itself out; for from the distant forest trees, from the old orchard, from thicket and fence, from the wide green meadows, and down out of the depths of the blue sky itself, a vast chorus of innocent creatures sang to my newly opened ears the same words: "Why persecutest thou me?" One sang it with indignation; another with remonstrance; still another with resignation; others yet with ethereal sadness or wild elusive pain. Once more the house-wren met me at the rotting gate-post, and cried aloud, "*per-se-cu-test—per-se-cu-test—per-se-cu-test—per-se-cu-test!*" And as I peeped into the brush-pile, again the brown thrush, building within, said, "*thou—thou—thou!*"

Through all the years since I had thought myself changed, and craved no greater glory than to be accounted the chief of their apostles. But now I was stained once more with the old guilt, and once more I could hear the birds in my yard singing that old, old chorus against man's inhumanity.

Towards the middle of the afternoon I went away across the country —by any direction; I cared not what. On my way back I passed through a large rear lot belonging to my neighbour, and adjoining my own, in which is my stable. There has lately been imported into this part of Kentucky from England the much-prized breed of the beautiful white Berkshire. As I crossed the lot, near the milk-trough, ash-heap, and parings of fruit and vegetables thrown from my neighbour's kitchen, I saw a litter of these pigs having their awkward sport over some strange red plaything, which one after another of them would shake with all its might, root and tear at, or tread into greater shapelessness. It was all there was left of him. If I could have been spared the sight of that!

I entered my long yard. The sun was setting. Around me was the last peace and beauty of the world. Through a narrow avenue of trees I could see my house, and on its clustering vines fell the angry red of the sun darting across the cool green fields.

The last hour of light touches the birds as it touches us. When they sing in the morning, it is with the happiness of the earth; but as the shadows fall strangely about them, and the helplessness of the night comes on, their voices seem to be lifted up like the loftiest poetry of the human spirit, with sympathy for realities and mysteries past all understanding.

A great choir was hymning now. On the tops of the sweet old honeysuckles the cat-birds; robins in the low boughs of maples; on the high limb of the elm the silvery-throated lark, who had stopped as he passed from meadow to meadow; on a fence rail of the distant wheatfield the quail— and many another. I walked to and fro, receiving the voice of each as a spear hurled at my body. The sun sank. The shadows rushed on and deepened. Suddenly, as I turned once more in my path, I caught sight of the figure of Georgiana moving straight towards me from the direction of the garden. She was bare-headed, dressed in white; and she advanced over the smooth lawn, through evergreens and shrubs, with a gentle grace and dignity of movement such as I had never beheld. I kept my weary pace, and when she came up I did not lift my eyes.

"Adam!" she said, with gentle reproach. I stood still then, but with my face turned away.

"Forgive me!" All girlishness was gone out of her voice. It was the woman at last.

I turned my face farther from her, and we stood in silence.

"I have suffered enough, Adam," she pleaded.

I answered quietly, doggedly, for there was nothing left in me to appeal to:

"I am glad we can part kindly. . . . Neither of us may care much for the kindness now, but we will not be sorry hereafter. . . . The quarrels, the mistakes, the right and the wrong of our lives, the misunderstandings— they are so strange, so pitiful, so full of pain, and come so soon to nothing." And I lifted my hat, and took the path towards my house.

There was a point ahead where it divided, the other branch leading towards the little private gate through which Georgiana had come. Just before reaching the porch I looked that way, with the idea that I should see Georgiana's white figure moving across the lawn; but I discovered that she was following me. Mounting my door-steps, I turned. She had paused on the threshold. I waited. At length she said, in a voice low and sorrowful:

"Are you not going to forgive me, Adam?"

"I do forgive you!" The silence fell and lasted. I no longer saw her face. At last her despairing voice barely reached me again:

"And—is—*that*—all?"

I had no answer to make, and sternly waited for her to go.

A moment longer she lingered, then turned slowly away; and I watched her figure growing fainter and fainter till it was lost. I sprang after her, my voice rang out hollow, and broke with terror and pain and longing:

"Georgiana! Georgiana!"

"Oh, Adam, *Adam!*" I heard her cry, with low, piercing tenderness, as she ran back to me through the darkness.

When we separated we lighted fresh candles and set them in our windows, to burn a pure pathway of flame across the intervening void. Henceforth we are like poor little foolish children, sick and lonesome in the night without one another. Happy, happy night to come when one short candle will do for us both!

. . . Ah, but the long, long silence of the trees! . . .

William Alexander Caruthers
(1802-1846)

William Alexander Caruthers was born in Lexington, Virginia, of Presbyterian Scotch-Irish stock. He attended Washington College in Lexington from 1817 to 1820 but left without taking a degree. He received a strong classical education there and evinced some literary interest. Enrolling in the medical school at the University of Pennsylvania, he took his M.D. degree in 1823. He returned to his home town to practice medicine for six years, during which time he married Louisa Gibson of Savannah, Georgia.

In 1830 Caruthers transferred his family and his practice to New York City, where he spent the seven years of his greatest literary activity. He contributed to the *Knickerbocker Magazine*; in June, 1834, Harper & Brothers brought out his first novel, *The Kentuckian in New-York,* and the following January published his second novel, *The Cavaliers of Virginia.* His third and best novel, *The Knights of the Horse-Shoe,* was begun in New York.

He left New York in 1837, probably because of financial strain, and settled in his wife's home town of Savannah, where he spent the remaining nine years of his life. He had completed *Knights of the Horse-Shoe* by 1838, though he had to re-write it after his manuscript was destroyed by fire. It first appeared in serial form in the Savannah periodical, the *Magnolia,* in 1841, and was brought out in book form in 1845. It is unfortunate that this, Caruthers' best novel, was published by a small Alabama publisher who was unable to provide the publicity and distribution that Harper & Brothers had given his two earlier novels. As a result, *Knights of the Horse-Shoe* received only one known review and attracted little attention. It has been reprinted several times since his death, however. The only important work in his last years was the story "Love and Consumption," published in three installments in the *Magnolia* in 1842 under the heading, "Excerpts from the Port Folio of a Physician." In the summer of 1846 he went to Marietta in northern Georgia in the vain search for improved health. He died there of tuberculosis on August 29 in his forty-fourth year.

Caruthers' literary mentor was Scott, and he hoped to do for his native South what Scott had done for Scotland in the Waverley novels. He began writing historical romances earlier than either Simms or Kennedy. While Caruthers was a loyal Virginian, he had no liking for slavery and frankly admitted its abuses. After he moved to Savannah, however, he refrained from making statements opposed to slavery as he had done earlier in his career.

Textual note

Copy-text is the *Magnolia; or Southern Apalachian,* n.s., I (July, 1842), 35-38; (August, 1842), 103-108; (September, 1842), 177-182. Quotation marks have been regularized and obvious typographical errors corrected.

Love and Consumption

Eliza Parker, at fifteen, was a beautiful creature,—a fair, gentle thing, almost too fragile for this rough world of ours. Her skin was so delicate and transparent, that the blood could almost be seen coursing along her fair temples beneath her blonde ringlets. She was rather a *petite* figure, but of such fairy-like and perfect proportions, as to more than compensate for any deficiency on this head. I became acquainted with her at the boarding-school of L—— village, a charming and romantic place, just under the shadows of the Blue Ridge. She was the intimate friend of a girl of her own age, to whom my own first boyish passion led me to pay particular devotions. I was also very intimate with the youth who imagined himself deeply enamoured of Eliza, and was the confidant of all his most secret thoughts and feelings. We were permitted (having relations in the school,) to meet the young ladies every Saturday, and to accompany them to church on Sunday. Divine service was sometimes performed in the village, and sometimes three miles off. These three miles were often walked by the whole bevy of charming young things, fluttering among the gay flowers and romantic hills, and attended by their brothers and cousins, and such chance beaux, like ourselves, who, under the pretext of relationship, smuggled themselves into the goodly company.

I will call my young friend by the name of Fauquier. Fred. was an ardent, sanguine, impetuous creature, and often led away to do things from the impulse of the moment, which would afterwards bring repentance of a much longer duration. Truth to say, however, even his repentance was none of the longest. It is not my intention to dwell long upon these boyish loves. Suffice it to say, that Fred. was desperately in for it,—he was maddened, frantic, furious. He would walk half the night under the trees which shaded the windows where he knew the loved one slept; and the groves around he made vocal with an old cracked flute upon which he was learning to play. If any other lad dared to make himself agreeable to his Eliza, especially during the three mile Sunday walk, he was frantic with rage and jealousy. This state of things could not last long, and I saw, even before the denouement, that there was not the least cause for apprehension on the part of my friend. They were mutually enamoured, and their tell-tale faces betrayed their secret to all those who chose to read.

One night, I was called for by Fred. in breathless haste; he had something of the "last importance" to communicate. It was Sabbath evening, and we had just had one of those charming three mile walks into the country. I saw at once that he was brim-full. He told me that he had broken the ice,—that he had told Eliza how much he loved her, and that she had acknowledged a reciprocal affection. It is of no use now to dwell upon the violation of the rules of the school, and all that; he was deaf just then, particularly, to every thing but the fact that he was *"miserably happy."* I use his own expression. He could not give vent to his ecstacy. He was the maddest boy in the universe. He wanted to run, to halloo,—and did skip and play along the path, like some young setter free from leash; and finally, in the exuberance of boyish phrenzy, he proposed that we should go and shave old sly-boots' tail. This was a favorite old horse, belonging to the President of the College where we were both pupils, and shaving the poor old beast's tail was usually considered tip-top fun. What connection there was between the feelings of an accepted lover, and those of one who desires to shave a horse's tail, we must leave our readers to find out for themselves. Enough to say, that I got Fred. home that night about three quarters drunk, and put him to bed hiccuping the most loving things of Eliza, and lamenting pathetically that I had prevented him from the double enjoyment of shaving the horse, and shooting the old *swivel* under the President's portico—another favorite amusement. Fred's happiness was quite extravagant for a week. In two, it had become tamed down to a more rational cast; and in three, one would have supposed that he was actually married, so demure had he become. It appeared to me, that if the term had held out, his love would have burnt out before its termination; but, unluckily, (as I must now think it,) came the Commencement, with fathers and guardians and friends, from a distance, to remove (despitefully) young lovers from each other. Eliza's father was among the number. She was to leave the seminary not to return. Whether the excellent Principal had given her father a hint touching their young loves, (Fred. was seventeen, and Eliza fifteen,) I know not, but they were to be sundered:—"the course of true love," you know,—and now that this was certain, both parties thought it dreadful. This cruel event roused up the slumbering passion, in all its original power, in our hero's bosom. The close of the term, and the presence of the lassie's father, relaxed the vigilance of all the argus eyes about the establishment, and Fred. almost lived at the seminary, and would scarcely suffer her own father to escort her into the streets. At length the parting came, and such tears and protestations of eternal love on the part of Fred., and such plaintive and sad looks from Eliza's blue eyes, just ready to run over with tears! Fred. tore himself from the carriage wheels, and hurrying me into the woods, kept me all day as a special audience to witness that he enacted the part of a disconsolate lover to the life; and truth to say, he not only tore the passion to tatters, but along with it no small number of tufts from his own head and—the sward. I was not experienced enough, then, to let him alone, and suffer his maudlin fury to work itself out, but I worked and worried with him,—pleaded the constancy of his lady-love, and the perfect smoothness with which the current of his affairs promised to run, until we were both pretty nigh exhausted.

Years passed away, and I had become a practising physician; and amidst the pains and privations of an all-engrossing profession, had almost forgotten that such beings as Fred. and Eliza had ever lived. I had received occasional letters from him during the first two years from our separation, but after that they came like "angels' visits," and then ceased to come altogether.

To seek relaxation from the fatigues of my laborious calling, I had resorted to the Salt Sulphur Springs of Virginia to spend the summer. I was not allowed, however, wholly "to sink the shop." Every few days I was called upon to visit some poor, helpless and hopeless case of disease, the subject of which had been dragged from home only to die in a strange land; or I was called to be a witness to the incipient stages of that fell destroyer, which lays low so many lovely heads,—I mean consumption.

As I was reclining in my cabin one day, (the visiters dwell in miniature cottages at the Virginia Springs, called cabins,) poring over some recent production, a servant entered with the usual message: "a sick lady at No.—, Alabama row, who wishes to see you." After doffing my dressing-gown, and brushing up the outward man a little, I repaired to the designated number in the high stone range of buildings before-mentioned, and was ushered into the presence of a lady, who was reclining at the moment with her back towards me, in a large cushioned chair. An old grey-headed gentleman was standing ready to receive me, near by, and the misery expressed in his countenance, quickly told me that he was some nearly interested connection of the invalid. He thanked me for my prompt attendance, and then introduced me to his daughter, Mrs. Means! "Means," said I to myself, "Means! I have never known any body by that name," and yet I was satisfied, at the first glance, that I had seen both father and daughter before; and this was more than confirmed by the painful and embarrassed manner in which the lady received me.

Though her checks, before raising her eyes to mine, were as pale as the flower of the night-blooming cereus, and almost as beautifully delicate, yet she blushed to her very temples, and was immediately after seized with a fit of coughing. During its continuance, I was perplexing myself in trying to remember when and where before I had seen that beautiful and delicate creature. My dilemma was solved in a moment by my happening just then to turn my head toward the table, and seeing the direction on a letter of the old gentleman's. Some faint glimpse of the truth had already, more than once, flashed across my mind, but I was not prepared for the changes which time and sorrow had made on my quondam pretty little friend. As soon as she was sufficiently composed after her paroxysm of coughing, I again moved my chair near to her own, and at one glance she saw that I now remembered her, and burst into tears. I was inexpressibly embarrassed, for I knew not whether to allude to by-gone days, or not, and whether, if I did, I should not make matters worse. Upon a hasty reflection given to the whole subject, I resolved to be governed by her in that matter, and if she did not allude to *old times* herself, to take it as a conclusive hint that she did not wish me to do so.

Her father hastened to soothe her, and to assure me that this sensitive-ness and melancholy at leaving home, as he called it, would soon wear away. In my own mind, I resolved to seek an early opportunity to see my pa-tient, without the presence of her father, and satisfy myself whether she wished to unburthen herself to me. I determined upon this course, from the unutterable things which I saw in her pale and gentle blue eyes.

As to her symptoms, (detailed to me by the old gentleman,) they were very unpromising. Dry, hacking cough, with some expectoration in the morning, on first awaking,—burning on the soles of the feet and palms of the hands, with *constant* pain in the breast, attended with more or less of general fever every afternoon, followed by copious, clammy perspiration at night. This is a sad catalogue of symptoms now, alas! too well known even to unprofessional readers, but the old man did not seem to consider her case by any means a hopeless one.

As we walked towards "the Pavilion," I endeavoured gently and gradually to prepare his mind for what I felt it would, hereafter, be my duty to tell him, namely, that I considered his daughter's case almost hope-less; but I found him very obtuse,—perhaps wilfully so: of this I know no more than I state. I seized this opportunity, also, to inquire if the lady's husband was alive? (I had heard her called *Mrs.* Means.) "Oh, yes!" said the old gentleman, "he has gone with some friends over to the White Sulphur for the day." So, so, thought I, I shall see this Adonis who has proved such a formidable rival to my poor friend, Fred. Poor Fred!—I could not help mentally ejaculating half a dozen times in half an hour, while I made these inquiries of Eliza's father.

I advised them to remove to the Red Sulphur, as soon as the fair invalid could bear the half-day's journey. At this time, Eliza (for she was still the Eliza of my memory,) was yet very lovely. The deceitful and insidious disease had made few inroads upon her beauty. Indeed, in some respects it was heightened. The bright crimson spot which burnt in each cheek, and the vivid fire of her eye when roused up by fever or excitement, gave her fair and beautiful face an expression of almost angelic loveliness. Her hand, too,—what a study it would have been for a painter or a sculptor. Such perfect fingers,—so delicately tapering, and the skin so purely white, like some transparent water flower. Oh! it was sad, sad to look upon all these deceitful appearances, as I looked upon them, only to recognise the harbingers of an early grave. Yet, strange to say, from the glimpse which I had of her, she seemed to smile with inward satisfaction at the gloomy auguries which I detected her reading in my tell-tale countenance.

I had appointed six in the afternoon to visit her again, that being the hour of the accession of her fever. I was impatient for the hour to arrive, that I might satisfy my longing desire to learn more of the history of my interesting patient, and to solve the question, whether the disease lay in the heart, (as I suspected,) or in the lungs:—its primitive seat, I mean. I had a faint hope, also, that I might see this Mr. Means, of whom, on account of my old friend, I was already jealous.

At length the appointed hour arrived, and I hastened to keep my appointment. I found my patient alone,—her maid excepted,—and she withdrew soon after my entrance into the chamber. My patient was reclining upon the bed, wrapped in a *robe de chamber*. She held out her hand to me, as soon as I was seated at her side. "Oh, Doctor," she said, "I knew you *too well* the moment that I saw you."

"Indeed," I replied, "I did not recognise you upon the instant, but I knew that I had seen both you and your father at some past period."

"No wonder you did not know me! I have sadly changed, no doubt, and the very least part of that change is visible to you. I am dying, doctor; —I know it, and rejoice to know it,—but my poor father's affection blinds him to the truth."

All this while, there was no mention of her husband, or of poor Fred. What did it mean? Her father's deep interest in her case was alluded to, but no mention of the nearer and usually dearer relationship,—and his opinions concerning its probable termination.

"Your husband," said I, suddenly, and with my finger upon her pulse; "is he prepared for such a result?"

Her blood bounded beneath my finger, and then gradually subsided away almost to an imperceptible trill, while her changing countenance exactly corresponded with these changes: first the blush, and then the deadly pallor. But these all might arise from excess of affection, or the reverse. I was no wiser than before;—the failure to return any answer, however, shed some light upon the mystery. Why should she not answer? At length she did answer,—she was compelled to relieve the painful embarrassment into which we were thrown by my unfortunate question. That answer was a flood of tears, and a convulsive heaving of the throat and chest, which determined me to be more cautious in the future, how I pushed my inquiries as to the seat of her disease.

I was sufficiently answered, nevertheless, by two or three words of apology for her husband, which she added to her flood of tears. *"Mr. Means is gay and fashionable, and loves not the sick room!"* The whole story was now told, so far as her expectations of matrimonial happiness were concerned; but how came he to supplant poor Fred? This, though longing to know, I had no right to seek after, through my professional position. After heaving a profound sigh, and as if in answer more to her own thoughts than addressed to me, she murmured the first line of a sweet poem by one of our Southern poets,—

"My life is like the summer rose!"

Suddenly checking herself, she placed her hand upon her heart, and said emphatically, "Here, doctor,—here is the seat of my disease. I will relieve your perplexity, and tell you at once that it is beyond your skill.

Thou can'st not minister to a mind diseased,
Nor pluck from memory its rooted sorrow.' "

She seemed to have divined my very thoughts, and replied to them; and this was introduction enough for me to follow up the subject of my poor friend. "Do you ever hear now," said I, "of our old friend, Fauquier?" To the day of my death, I shall never cease to remember the despairing,—the imploring look which she threw into her face. It was full two minutes before she could speak, though evidently labouring to do so. At length she gasped out, "Pray, doctor, never breathe that name in my presence again!" and she covered her face with her hands. At that moment a young gentleman entered the room, whom, from his free and familiar way with the servants, and the absence of all ceremony on entering, I knew at once to be her husband. She faintly articulated, "Mr. Means, this is Doctor ——." He bowed coldly and distantly, and then seated himself in a remote part of the room, without once inquiring as to the state of his wife's health, though he had been absent all day. A cup of tea and a muffin were brought to him, and he deliberately discussed them, while inquiring carelessly of the servants, who had arrived, and who departed; who were their new neighbours whose trunks he saw in the entry? &c. All this while I was bowed down over his wife's pulse, and more bowed down with the consciousness that the fair creature whose hand I held, was lost equally to happiness and hope in this world. After I had prescribed, I left the room, glad enough to escape from the overpowering weight of infectious misery.

Mr. Means was a middle-sized young gentleman, fashionably and rather ostentatiously dressed, with sandy-coloured hair, and whiskers meeting under his chin, and a cold, searching grey eye, of rather sinister expression. There was a keenness and shrewdness about this expression, which I could not at that time understand. It was by no means that sort of intelligence induced either by high breeding, or extensive intellectual culture.

The problem was solved for me the next morning, when I happened to meet him at the stables, where he was descanting to some of his friends upon the virtues of his horses. *He was a fashionable jockey,*—boasted of his dogs and horses, and could drive four in hand, and talked technically of handling the ribbons. Instead of believing that "the proper study of mankind is man," he seemed to believe that the proper study of mankind is horse-flesh, and his shrewdness and sagacity had been developed upon the race path. "Heavens!" thought I, after listening to his discourse for a quarter of an hour, "what a husband for the gentle and lovely Eliza Parker, the belle of L—— seminary."*

My repeated visits to my unfortunate patient—unfortunate in every sense of the word—only served to confirm my first impressions of her case. She declined so rapidly that I began to fear that her friends would not be able to remove her at all to the Red Sulphur, and though, at this time, I had little hopes of a beneficial result even from the effects of that far famed fountain, in pulmonary diseases, yet hope still pointed them in that direction, and I was doing nothing, and could do nothing to compensate them even for the loss of that solitary hope.

Poor Eliza! she did not again allude to my quondam class-mate in words, but often, even when her father was present, she would, in dumb show, communicate to me secretly the seat of her disease, by laying her hand upon her heart. Sometimes, when performing this pantomime, which I too well understood, she would elevate her eyes and gaze out of the window at the blue sky, until the tears would stream down her cheeks;— lost for the time—as it seemed—in her own aspirations after a higher and a purer state of existence.

It seemed strange to me that she never once alluded to the village of L——, nor to her old instructors, to whom she was devotedly attached —nor to any of her associates—especially to the one, my intimacy with

---

*The first installment ended here.

whom had just made me acquainted with her. Nothing of the kind ever escaped her lips;—and what seemed still more strange, her father was equally cautious, although he must, long ere this, have recognised me, and seen also that I was recognised by the daughter. This evinced to me that the secret dread of even poor Fred's name, was well understood, by the two at least: and this understanding could not readily have been brought about without some painful *ecclaircissement*, long past, but not to be forgotten. As time progressed and my visits became more frequent, I farther learned that this little mystery was not enacted for my benefit alone— there was another who seemed to be kept equally in the dark concerning the painful memories of by gone days. This was her husband. Mr. Means was by no means a troublesome or inquisitive husband, and it required no great effort to conceal any thing from him, which concerned his wife;— but my presence rendered it much more difficult to manage the affair. The old gentleman, it seemed to me, was constantly on the tenter-hooks of apprehension, lest I should make some unhappy revelation in presence of his son-in-law. Poor old man, he knew not how well his daughter and myself understood each other. Yet this understanding did not go far enough to satisfy me.—I had been let into the secret of this interesting little family, just far enough to perplex and worry me. I could not conceive that Fred. had been false, and I longed to learn by what means the old gentleman had broken off the match, in order to promote one with a suitor of greater wealth and worldly pretensions; for upon his shoulders I cast the whole burden of the iniquity, without supposing it possible, for a single moment, that either of the young hearts whom I had known so devotedly attached to each other, could prove false. Time will show whether my surmises were correct or not.

Sometimes the invalid would walk, supported by two of us, to the long double portico of the stone building, and there, propt up with pillows, would drink in the sweet fragrance forever exhaling from the lovely valley below. She had no children, and her only desire now seemed for flowers and fresh air. She complained of very little acute pain, and looked as calm, seated in her easy chair, and trifling with her *bouquets*, as a summer evening. It was not exactly happiness expressed in her countenance, but it was an enviable resignation, and, as it seemed to me, a steady looking forward, with hope, to that fatal catastrophe which every one else contemplated with so much dread. She seldom, indeed, alluded to that sad event, but one accustomed to read the countenance, could there discern that she constantly communed with the invisible world. She would shut her eyes for several minutes together, and then open them, looking so sweetly hopeful, that I could almost envy her those trances, which had evidently brought such happy reveries to her soul. She did not speak of religion, in public or to indifferent persons, and very seldom indeed alluded to it in my presence. Once or twice I surprised her with her Bible in her hand, and then she quickly laid it aside; not that she was ashamed to acknowledge her Lord and Master before men, but because she had such a nice and almost intuitive sense of the holy privacy which should belong to such a communion. Truth was she a most holy and a most lovely creature.

Though so studious of the feelings of others, as never to intrude even those things upon their attention which evidently were all in all to her, yet she never avoided the topic, when introduced by others. At first she seemed to consider me as one of those worldly minded persons to whom any serious subject is in the last degree disagreeable, or in fashionable *parlance,* a bore; but I would occasionally suffer the conversation to glide into that channel, and then she would pour forth the sweet fervour of her soul. The constitution of her mind was eminently poetical and, of course, over all engrossing themes, it would cast its own colour of fancy and imagination. At other times, our discourse would take a philosophical turn, and that fair and gentle thing would wander into unknown worlds with a reach and masculine vigor of thought which really astonished me. Often did I exclaim to myself, "Oh Fred! what a treasure you have lost or thrown away!"

One evening, I happened, in a merely casual conversation, to say something of the deceitfulness of the world. She immediately sat forward in her chair and bent a smiling glance upon me, and then asked, "Do you use those words in their mere common-place sense or are you too aware of the great truth which they express?"

"I don't know," replied I, "whether my views on the subject are common-place or not. I have always thought that my profession gave me uncommon opportunities to verify the trite assertion."

"It was exactly that which made me push the enquiry," said she. "You seemed to enforce your views with such heart-felt ardour, that I thought, for the moment, that the whole magnitude of this world's deception, had been laid bare to you too." She fell back rather disappointed at my replies. The fact was, that the ardour of my manner, to which she alluded, had reference entirely to her own case. She did not seem disposed to drop the subject entirely, but, after closing her eyes, in one of her sweet little reveries, she roused up again, and pointing her attenuated, wax-like finger, by way of emphasis, resumed:—"The deceitfulness of the world to which I alluded, is not the mere every day cheating, which takes place in the senseless scramble of men after money—nor even in the more delicate, and therefore cruel, and refined deception practised between the sexes," (here there was a perceptible flush upon her cheek,) "but it is upon a grand scale, co-extensive with the world. Look at that sweet valley, and that meadow, and all those lovely summer flowers, and that pretty little bubbling brook meandering its whole length among rocks and green leaves and brilliant pebbles, and then the dark and forest crowned hills beyond—the whole surmounted by sky, which makes one long for wings to soar beyond the reach of sight. Is not all this now calculated to make one imagine this a beautiful world—a little paradise?"

"Certainly," said I, "and I think it is a very lovely world—so much so that I have often heard men say that they would surrender up every chance of another, only that they might live here forever, in perpetual youth."

She clasped her hand, and exclaimed fervently,—"Oh what a thought. All the luxury of this world refined into an earthly elysium, and all the beauty of it—gorgeous and lovely as it is—concentrated into one lovely little *home*, (a woman's thought,) surrounded with all the friends that I could name, and, over the whole, throw all the poetry and romance that genius ever conceived—would not bribe me, Doctor, for one moment, to surrender my hopes of heaven?"

"What," said I, "is your heaven so much more lovely than the picture you have drawn? Would not such a scene and such friends be a heaven on earth?"

"All a mere optical or mental illusion, Doctor—insidious disease is creeping through the veins of those nearest and dearest to you; every exhibition of worth only excites regrets for the last struggle—if beauty has any claims for you, it is ever on the wing and is like some charming flower, nearest to death when it is most fully blown. Oh! Doctor, what a grave-yard is this whole round world we live in. It is but one vast charnel house, and every step we take is upon the bones of our predecessors—we seem to swarm most plenteously where death has been most busy—as the trees of the forest grow most vigorously where the decay of former ages is most rank and manifest. Decay and reproduction is the great probationary law of our being. Can there be any happiness where every thing is so evanescent?"

"As to my Heaven," she continued, just stopping long enough to catch her breath;—"the first great difference between it and the earthly one of my dreaming, with which you have chosen to be pleased, is, that, in the former, there is no death. *That* is the first love of Heaven and the cornerstone (so to speak) of all our ultimate hopes, we cannot tell in what our employments will consist; but we have good reasons from analogy for believing that they will be in the highest degree intellectual, because, even in the preparatory state here, the intellectual predominates, in our notices, over the earthly—dreadfully corrupt as we are. It would be almost impossible to suppose (with my notions of God) that our natures hereafter could be less so. Why should they be? Can Heaven be inferior to earth in any thing that produces happiness and promotes good? The supposition is absurd on its very face. Taking it for granted, then, that we grow in knowledge as we grow in grace, oh! how illimitable may our aspirations after Heaven be? It is a Heaven for the mind as well as the body; for the profound as well as the simple minded."

"And yet," said I, "the book of books says that not many wise, not many great are chosen."

"True, true, too true;" she said; "but that is because their worldly pride unfits them for Heaven, not because Heaven is not fit for them."

Just at this moment there was a great stir at the farther end of the long portico in which we were sitting;—servants bearing the usual paraphernalia of a new arrival, viz: band-boxes—trunks—carpet-bags, *et cetera*. I was sitting with my back rather to the entry, and had to turn my head in order to ascertain the cause of the commotion. Having done so, I prepared to resume our interesting dialogue; not so, however, with my interesting patient.

The pupils of her eyes gradually dilated, and her whole countenance wore a startled expression, which arrested my undivided attention; and so rapid was her changing colour, and so fearful was I that she would pitch forward from her chair, that I could scarcely turn my head to see who it was that thus alarmed her. I did, however, steal one furtive glance in that direction. That was enough! The next moment she was in my arms, as lifeless, to all appearance, as a corpse! A few moments repose, in her own room, in the recumbent position, with the usual restoratives, sufficed to restore her languid pulsations; but oh, how different was the expression of her always sad countenance. Before, there had been something inexpressibly melancholy in her appearance.—Now! there was a fixed look of despair. What could I say! what do, but look on and sympathise with her as I did in my inmost heart. How forcibly her own words of quotation recurred to me: "Canst thou minister to a mind diseased, pluck from the memory a rooted sorrow!" &c. I felt powerless—my lips were sealed by herself upon the only subject, upon which I saw and knew that her thoughts dwelt with a lingering agony. As soon as her father returned, in answer to the summons which had been despatched for him, I hastily left the room, and made my way with rapid strides to the main hotel where the list of arrivals was kept, and there satisfied myself, by reading in full "Frederick Faquier, Esq., family and servants;" and as I walked over the lawn to my cabin,—sad and dispirited, and dreading to meet my old chum,—*his* chariot and four, with numberless horses and attendants, passed by me on their return from the hill, where I had seen them depositing their baggage.

So—thought I, poor Fred. has married a fortune too—and if I am to judge by the glimpse which I caught of him, with as little hope of its ministering to his real happiness, as it has been to the poor girl whom he has deserted, or who has jilted him. I was satisfied that a great wrong had been done somewhere, and by one of these parties; but, by which, I had yet to learn. Of one thing I felt satisfied, *that Providence was visiting, with retributive justice, the evil upon the head of the guilty one,* and the other was innocently suffering from the same cause. I was very much inclined to think my poor patient the latter; there was something so pure and heavenly-minded in all her thoughts, words and actions.

The next morning, at the *table d'hôte,* my eyes were fastened upon the lower end of the long line of heads, to catch the first look of Fred. and his wife, before they could perceive me. I wanted to take a look at them *incog.* and see what sort of a person she was for whom he had deserted (if deserted he had) that sweet creature on the hill. Luckily, Mrs. Means did not come to the public table often, and never to breakfast, so that there was little danger of a premature *denouément.* I was disappointed, Fred. did not come to the table. Was it possible that he had recognised us? I thought not.

About eleven o'clock in the day, I sauntered, as usual, towards the Pavilion, to quaff the health-giving waters, and there I beheld the object of my search. Poor Fred., how he had altered. He was standing over the fountain, leaning on his wife's arms, rather than the reverse; and well might he seek such support, for he was attenuated almost to a shadow of his former self, and very sallow and sickly looking: and she, Heavens!— what an Amazon! What a bold front and eagle eye, and such a majestic figure, and withal so beautiful. I approached slowly to give him time to recognise me, for, as I had surmised, he had not done so on the previous evening. He rivetted his eyes upon my face, as if he were lost in a dream, then, slowly disengaging himself from his wife's arms, he approached and held out his hand. "Can I be mistaken?" said he. "Is it possible?"

When satisfied that he was not mistaken, I was really afraid that he would burst into tears and make a scene in the public place, he was so overcome. I had to apologise to his wife and introduce myself, she frowned so terribly upon poor Fred. Nor did my good offices appear to mollify her very much. Of course, she was magnificently polite to me, but cold and distant. His health was excuse enough to drag off the poor invalid out of my dreaded clutches. I did not understand all this, at the time, but I grew wiser as I grew older. A gentleman with whom I had formed a watering-place acquaintance, stepped up to me after they were gone, and asked me if I knew the gentleman who had just gone?

"When he was a boy," was my reply.

"He is but the wreck of the most promising man I have ever known," said he. "Indeed! did he bid so fair for eminence? He was not very re-markable at College for abilities—he was rather more distinguished for the qualities of his heart, than those of his head."

"Wait till you hear him talk, even now;" said he, and added, in a sarcastic tone and *sotto voice*, "but his wife must not be near." (I ascer-tained soon afterwards, that *he* was an old bachelor.) I walked to my cabin with my head down upon my chest, sadly ruminating upon these things, and perplexing myself with the vain endeavours to account for all this double wretchedness, which was plain enough to be perceived, and which, I knew, had been produced by a false step somewhere—now, alas! irre-vocable.

I was scarcely seated, before a servant entered and handed me a slip of paper, on which was written these words:

"Dear C——, I will try and *steal away* and see you during the morning."

"Yours as ever,　　　　　　Fred."

(The italics are mine.) What could this mean? Was my poor *chum* a prisoner?

Again I sauntered forth to find my acquaintance, before mentioned, and learn from him, if possible, what Fred's. exact position was. I could see, for myself, that he was in wretched health, and, perhaps, his stealing away alluded to some rigid routine prescribed by his physician. My ac-quaintance, it appeared, was a near neighbour of Fred., and knew all about him.

He informed me that Fauquier had come to the bar with the brightest prospects of any young man he had ever known; that he was universally beloved and respected, and not less distinguished for great native abilities, and great acquirements, than for estimable qualities of the heart: that he was quite an orator, especially promising great things before a popular assembly, or, in the language of the country, "on the stump." There had been a gradual progression in all these bright prospects, up to the day of his marriage with a great heiress, but, from that day, or soon after, he began to neglect his business—deserted his old acquaintance—ceased to cultivate the popular favour, and had actually withdrawn his name from before the people as a candidate for the Legislature, that very spring. Since that time, he had become retired—sour and morose at times, and for months together would confine himself to his own house, until at length his health began to fail him, and it was now commonly believed that he was far gone in con-sumption. "I have given you," said this gentleman, "the common rumor of the country. If you wish to know my own private opinion," said he, "I will give it to you in all frankness."

I begged him to do so, and told him our former relations, and that I thought it very probable I should be called upon for professional advice upon his disease—in which case it was very important that I should know as much of his history as possible, from the time of his leaving College, up to the present moment.

"Tut, tut," said my crusty bachelor, "I'm not going into any history about it, when I can explain the whole matter to you in five words. *He is henpecked to death.*"

"Can it be possible?"

"Possible! aye, it is very possible,—it is every word true! Did you not observe his wife. The very wife for a Petruchio?" With these words, he walked off, not deigning to enlighten me farther on the subject.

Two o'clock, and dinner came, and yet no Fred. Again, I anxiously watched the position at the table occupied by those who have recently arrived, and this time not in vain. He came in, leaning, as before, upon the arm of that magnificent creature, his wife, and I could not but think of the five words of the old bachelor, though I had determined to make great allowances for them, on account of the peculiar prejudices supposed to exist in his class; and I must say they received nothing but confirmation from what I saw. The dinner having disappeared, and such gentlemen as drank wine having collected their little cliques around their bottles and segars— I lingered over mine, "solitary and alone," watching the proceedings at the other end of the table. Of course, I was only *solus* in my own thoughts, for every five feet of that immense table was occupied with some little knot of politicians, philosophers, quidnuns, &c. &c. It was not long before I began to perceive some of the grounds upon which Fred's. reputation for eloquence was founded. My old bachelor was sitting opposite to him, and evidently drawing him out. His wife had been compelled to retire, of course, with the appearance of the wine and nuts; and the crusty old fellow seemed to enjoy a malicious pleasure in showing me what my old friend could be when cut loose from her apron strings. It was not long before he sent up a servant to ask the pleasure of a glass of wine with me. This attracted Fred's attention, and the servant soon returned, begging me, in the name of the two, to join their party.

Never did I hear such conversational eloquence. I could almost imagine the pale, emaciated, boyish-looking youth before me, inspired. I could not well realise, in the person speaking, the old playmate and school-fellow, over whom I had exercised such unbounded control. Oh, how false are the collegiate estimates of talent and character, not less among professors than

pupils. Fred. had always been a great reader, but he was far from distinguished in his classes, and I, who had known him most intimately of all,
had as little understood him as any of them.

One thing struck me peculiarly during our social afternoon—that he
received several little scraps of paper during the sitting, which he crumpled
up and thrust into his pocket, as it seemed to me, with manifest chagrin—
while his bachelor neighbor took no pains to conceal from me, on such occasions, a malicious smile of pregnant meaning. Another thing, too, struck me
in a lesser degree—namely, that Fred's cheeks were becoming very much
flushed, and his tongue going at a prodigious rate. Notwithstanding the
little billets, he continued to pour forth sometimes a torrent of indignant
eloquence—and then again a current of more smooth, but still keen and
polished remark.

I began really to fear that the lion of the evening would become in-
toxicated; and this, in the present state of his health, I felt was, of all
things, to be avoided. I began to surmise, that this, too, might be the subject of those mysterious miseries. At length, our sitting was adjourned;
Fred. was assisted to his quarters by a servant under each arm. This surprised me a little at first, but then I thought it possible that his state of
health might account for it on other grounds, than those of my first suspicion.

After he was out of "ear shot," the bachelor, (whom I may as well
name) Mr. Patten, laughed outright. "Oh! love! oh! matrimony!" exclaimed he, with elevated hands, "in the language of Madame Roland, when
she spoke of liberty, what crimes have been perpetrated in thy name."

"You are severe," said I, "upon my poor friend." "You mistake;" was
his response—"It is upon your friend's wife. The only thing I blame him
for, is that he is such a giant in intellectual stature, and such a mere baby in
his dealings with the other sex."

"You do not know his early history as I do," said I; "perhaps, if our
knowledge were united, the whole mystery would be solved."

"Oh, as to that," he replied, "you will soon know all that I do, and a
great deal more. Take my word for it, you will see sights before your friends
depart; and now, let me tell you upon the threshold,—that you are the very
man, of all the world, to emancipate him from this wretched thraldom."

It was now time to see Eliza, and as her image passed through my
mental vision—in all its subdued gentleness and unrepining submission—I
could not but clear her of all blame in the double *mesalliance,* which had
been brought about. However crooked may have run the current of their
young loves, she, at least, was not the guilty party. My readers, I am sure,
will think me but a poor judge, thus to suffer my judicial functions to be
bribed by a sweet face, plaintive voice and subdued manner. I plead guilty

to the charge, and promise as the only compensation in my power, a true report of the facts and evidence, so that they can themselves occupy my judicial seat.

I found Eliza alone, and, contrary to my expectation, very calm and resigned to whatever might be in store for her. She was lying down, and motioned for me to be seated. "Doctor," said she, "I want you to explain to those around me, that it is worse than useless for me to go on to the Red Sulphur. Your skill, I am sure, has revealed the truth to you long ago, that I am dying, and not of ordinary consumption. Why then must I go there to die among the wild mountains. Do persuade them to let me stay here, if they will not carry me home where I may take my last farewell of the scenes of my childhood." Here she clasped her hands and exclaimed fervently, "Oh, I have but one wish left, and that is to return at once to the house of my fathers, and there die amidst the scenes with which the sweetest associations of my young life are blended."

"Then it is not to *your own* home to which you wish to return?" I saw her shudder, as she covered her face for a moment, and then answered, "Oh, no! no! no! It is cruel of you, Doctor, to be so wilfully obtuse. I am sure, I am not mistaken in your countenance, when I think I see there that you understand my whole case, without the pain and humiliation of a verbal confession. Spare me, spare me, Doctor. Spare me not only the bitter tale, but spare me this dreaded journey."

I promised her to do all that I could, and assured her, at the same time, that I agreed with her fully in opinion as to the nature of her case, and that *home* would do her more good than the springs. Poor child! (for child she was, in innocence, in experience and almost in age) she saw from the glance which she had caught of Fred. that he too was bound to that bourne from whence no traveller returns—by the way of the Red Sulphur perhaps. She though *this* latter more than probable, and this was what she dreaded. I will not say that her imagination had not ventured upon the idea that they might meet hereafter—the great hereafter—but she dreaded, doubtless, to meet him again on earth.

After some exertion, I managed to get the husband and father together, and opened the subject to them. Of course, I had to skirmish round the real truth. I could not say to them,—"Eliza's first love is here, and, like her, the victim of what is called consumption; and like her bound to the Red Sulphur. She dreads, of all things, to meet him." I could not say this, but I did express, most truly, my opinion that the springs would do her no good. "Why," said the old gentleman, "she has very little cough and expectorates scarcely any. True, she is greatly reduced, but not so much, I think, as when we set out. Indeed, Doctor, she has improved more under your own treatment, than that of all her other physicians put together, (it was all the effect of my sympathy—she was really declining) and you are the only one that she has been satisfied with, and against whom she has not taken prejudices and sneered and scoffed at."

I felt my cheeks tingle at the false tribute to my skill, for my readers must know, I had administered nothing of any moment in the shape of medicine. But I understood her history and case, and felt for her,—having this knowledge—and that, to her, was much. The husband was even more blind than the father to her real condition. He had supposed, and still thought, that her complaint was little else but the *vapors*. Poor ass and fool —he had more vapors *in* his head, and even *outside* of his huge locks and whiskers, than his wife ever had in her whole life. And this is the *thing*, I could not help thinking, for whom the happiness of two noble creatures has been sacrificed! What would I give if I only had the power to meta-morphose Fred's wife into the position occupied by poor Eliza, and, *vice versa*—it would have been a capital arrangement all round. Then the ama-zon might have combed the long flowing locks of the fashionable fool before me; and Fred. go on to the high destiny for which his talents and attain-ments so nobly fitted him; while that sweet and gentle sufferer might still breathe out her life sweetly, upon the bosom of him whom still she loved.*

I was too much dejected at the failure of my mission, to the father and husband, and with the gloomy reflections to which the interview gave rise, to visit Eliza in person, to communicate the result. I wrote her a short note, softening the matter as much as possible, and endeavoring to reconcile her to the measure, by directing her thoughts to the pleasure her ready and cheerful acquiescence would give to her friends. I knew that she loved her father, with all his coldness of heart,—and desired to do her duty to her hus-band in all things. This note I sealed up and left on my table, ready to be despatched by a servant next morning.

I had been in bed, I suppose about an hour, when a thundering rap, at my cabin door, roused me up. "What's the matter?" said I, half asleep, and forgetting, for the time, that I was even at the Spring. "Masta want see you, sir, quick as possible, at No. — Alabama row—Misses taken very ill?" "And who's your master, boy?" "Mass Fred. Fauquiere, sir." "Ah! I remember —tell him I will be with him immediately."

It will be seen by my readers, how successful I was in obtaining that, at the Springs, which I had gone there in part to run away from—"prac-tice." I hurried to the place designated by the servant, and, after a slight knock at the door, was admitted to such a scene as, in all my professional experience, I had scarcely ever fancied before. There were two beds in the room, upon one of which poor Fred. was stretched, while one servant held a basin to his head, and another supported it, as he paid the penalty for

---

*The second installment ended here.

his excesses of the day. I approached him, of course, supposing that the servant had been mistaken, and that it was his master instead of his mistress, who wanted my services. He motioned me away and pointed in the direction of the other bed; at the same instant I heard a clatter upon the floor, similar to that of an urchin drumming with his heels upon a box. I walked round towards a sort of recess, in which the other bed stood, and there beheld his magnificent wife, not laid up in state and dignity upon the bed, but lying upon the floor, "in all the wild distraction of grief" *apparently*. She was wrapped in an elegant *robe,* but her hair was dishevelled, and she was beating an awful *reveillé* with her *bare* heels upon the floor, while, with clenched fists, she tossed her arms wildly about, in every conceivable attitude. At one moment writhing, as if in mortal agony, and the next every muscle as rigid as death. Her teeth were clenched as tightly as a smith's vice, —the froth gathered upon her lips, and her eyes rolled in any thing but a fine frenzy, through their blood-red sockets. Heavens! what a transformation for a fashionable beauty? Truth to say, however, she was beautiful still—but not in such a way as to excite very ardent admiration in a fastidious taste. I spoke to her—no answer! I felt her pulse—no indication of consciousness, except, occasionally, a renewal of the spasmodic writhing. These symptoms were as familiar to me as my horn-book, and would scarcely have excited me as much as a pang in her tooth, but from the circumstances attending the case.—Fred. cried out to me in great distress to know if she was in imminent danger? "No more," said I, with great emphasis, "than you are!" I saw at once that this was one of her woman's weapons, by which, in the last resort, she ruled his master-mind—and I was resolved to break the charm.

Though not often resorting to the lancet in such cases, I resolved to try its efficacy upon her, and, accordingly, rapidly rolled up her sleeve, and opened a vein, before she could be aware of it. She writhed and twisted terribly, and made a bloody figure of her beruffled *robe,* but I let the stream flow on most plenteously. Her maid pleaded piteously in her behalf, and even poor Fred. began to think I had designs upon her life; but I persisted until she was as gentle as a lamb. When she gave in, or, rather, when her disease gave in—(for hysteria is a real physical disease, whatever may be the popular opinion,) I gave in, also, and, bandaging up the arm, administered a soothing potion, and then left her for the other side of the room.

"Will she die, Doctor?" whispered Fred.—I could not tell whether he was in terror *of* her or *for* her.

"Not this time!" said I, slyly smiling in his woe-begone face. "I wish to God," I continued, as I sat myself down, and bent my head towards his, "that I could cure you as easily as I can her."

He started from his momentary repose, and raising his face beseechingly, almost touching mine, asked earnestly—"Can you cure her, Doctor, *permanently?*"

"I cannot say as to that, but I shall certainly cure her for this time."

"What!" said he, "for the whole journey?"

"Why," said I, Yankee fashion, asking a question instead of answering his own,—"is she so very subject to these attacks?"

"Oh! Doctor," whispered he, "they are the bane of my life, as well as her own!"

"Well, well, be calm, Fred.; we will see what can be done for you both." I gave him a little pounded ice, which soon arrested his troublesome symptoms, and then left them for the night.

My readers may well imagine that there was but little sleep for me that night. I tossed on a bed of restlessness, wondering at the mysterious ways of providence, in thus dealing with these poor creatures, so apparently at cross purposes. I thought that if some marplot of an internal fiend could have mixed the bitter cup for these parties, so as completely to thwart their happiness, and reverse those positions in which they would now choose to be, the purpose could not have been more completely answered. That fiend was mammon!—the love of gold for its own sake! Oh! how much happiness has been wrecked in this world, by an unrighteous pursuit of wealth!

Above all things the unholy passion should have been excluded from the sacred altar, before which the vows of love are offered up; but there, in the very temple of the living God, has the insane worship been most ardently carried on. There the golden calf has been erected, and thousands daily bend at its altars, in some of the worst forms of a beastly worship.

In the morning I despatched my note to Eliza, and was just congratulating myself that I had got that part of the business off my hands, when I received a summons to attend her in person. I went, of course, dreading, all the way, lest she might have heard the noise and confusion during the night. The moment I entered her chamber, I saw, or thought I saw, in her speaking countenance, that she had already gathered from some source or other the whole story. I endeavored to wear a calm and unconcerned exterior, and led the way at once to the message with which she had charged me. It was all to no purpose. She replied with wonderful calmness—"You know, very well, Doctor, that it is now cruelty to carry me farther. Indeed, I ought not to go. You know I ought not."

I told her that I had done every thing in my power to induce her father and husband to forego the farther prosecution of the journey.—"Well," she said, "their course only condemns me for life to my apartments, and if it must be, the sooner we go the better."

I understood the motives of her haste, and did not oppose her. No allusion was made, directly, to the disturbance of the night; this satisfied me that she knew all about it;—else, why should she not enquire about so remarkable an occurrence, in the same building—remarkable, I mean for that quiet and secluded place?

Fred. was up bright and early. I met him at the Spring. He seemed to suffer little from the excesses of the previous day—that is, little except his usual languor and debility. He took my arm and dismissed his servant, and we sauntered through the green meadows as in days of yore. But, oh! how altered was my poor friend, as he hung, almost like a lifeless weight, upon my arm—how different from the buoyant youth with whom some of the pleasantest hours of my life had been spent.

For a while he gave the rein to his romantic imagination, and descanted upon the beauties of the wild scene around us; occasionally stooping from his grander flight to cull a beautiful meadow flower. At length, however, all these novelties were exhausted, and we had, by this time, left the meadows and ascended that lofty parade commanding the whole vale, in which the fountain is situated. This feat was not accomplished by him, without many stoppages and much assistance from me. When we were seated, and he had recovered his breath, he looked round with self-complacency, and remarked —"Here, at least, we cannot be interrupted."

"Why, who are you afraid of, Fred.?" said I, with well affected surprise.

"Of my wife, to be sure!"

I laughed long and loudly, and, this time, in right good earnest; at first struggling with other feelings, but bursting out at length into an unrestrained paroxysm, as I saw his comico-serious countenance, suffused with a crimson flush, and, at the same time, looking like that of a school-boy just escaped from his master. He waited patiently for some time, but at length interrupted my pleasant amusement, by exclaiming, petulantly—

"It may be all very amusing to you, Doctor; but, I assure you, it is one of the most serious things to me in the world. My life is about to become the sacrifice in the hopeless struggle." Here, I saw his large, bright eye suffused.—Another unfeeling burst from me would cause it to run over. I was all attention and seriousness at once. He resumed: "I have often, Doctor, been on the point of sending for you, under the pretence of professional aid, in order that I might have the benefit of your *friendly*, instead of your professional, counsel. I see now that I ought to have availed myself of both; but it is all too late. Feel that pulse, Doctor, and tell me if I have not postponed consulting you too long."

I placed my finger upon the artery, which was going then at a rate considerably over a hundred to the minute—somewhat excited, no doubt, by the exertion of climbing the hill. I had seen enough, and heard enough about him, however, to be satisfied that he was right, and that the dread disease was even then making inroads upon his lungs. I manifested, by a look, that he was right, and he continued—"I am glad that you are satisfied upon that point, because it must, in part, be my excuse for making any mortal man acquainted with those delicate domestic troubles, which are making such sad ravages upon this miserable frame. You have seen my wife, and, that too, in the two opposite extremes of her moods. I shall therefore have the less to tell."

"Stop," said I, "and before you go upon that branch of your story, tell me by what fatal accident you were estranged from the charming girl to whom you were *engaged* (the American word) when I last saw you."

Poor Fred.! he seemed as if he could sink into the earth with shame and mortification.—He struggled manfully, and at length succeeded in bracing himself for the painful confession.

"My old, my earliest friend," said he, "I will not now shrink from the whole truth. I have come here to make a frank and honest confession to you, and it shall be done without reserve. In few words, then, I behaved like a scoundrel to poor Eliza; but I had this excuse—I thought I was acting for the best even then. You know my impulsive mercurial temperament? Well, it cheated me into that step which has wrecked all my happiness. After I left the College at L——, I kept up my correspondence with Eliza for some time, and felt myself as secure, (as indeed I was) in her affections,—as I believed myself firm in my devotion to her. In an evil hour, at a public assembly, I saw the most brilliant creature which had ever then flashed across my secluded path. You know me, my old friend,—or, rather, you know what I then was,—a mere impulsive boy. I fell desperately in love, as I supposed, with this brilliant, fashionable beauty. Her beauty—her fortune—her position in society—were all superior to those of Eliza. All that first night of my infatuation, I bemoaned my cruel fate, in having thus engaged myself to an unknown country girl, and that, before my mind was sufficiently matured, and my experience enlarged, to know my own mind. I had then been called to the bar, and was not only making considerable advances in my profession, but in popular favour.

"The gay butterfly by which my imagination was captivated, did not suffer the advantage which she had gained to go unimproved.—Others united with her in the conspiracy. We were thrown together on all occasions. Parties were given for the express purpose (as I now believe) of promoting, what every one said was the most suitable match in the country. As the passion grew upon me—or, rather, upon my imagination—my distress, at my former entanglement, became proportioned to it. I had, at that time, a friend, rather older than myself—an old bachelor—in short, the very gentleman who dined with us yesterday. He was known to be cynical in all matters concerning the other sex: and I supposed that he would give me the most sage and disinterested advice. I accordingly consulted him. He laughed immoderately at my youthful vows, and swore that I was an antediluvian to pay the least regard to such flimsy things; and he offered to wager that the object of my former passion was, at that moment, married to another. He said that returning a ring or two,—a lock of hair, and a few letters, and the whole thing was cancelled in half the time, and twice as neatly, as some of our State Legislatures divorce the actually married. He treated the whole affair very lightly. If I had known then, as I know now, that he had been jilted in his youth, after having been engaged just as I was, I should have known how to understand him; but I took it all seriously, and went straight home and wrote a letter to Eliza, acknowledging, frankly, to her, that I had ceased to love her, and returning such favours as I had received from her. In due course of mail I received her answer. There was not a complaint or reproach of any sort in it, but cold and dignified as possible, and very respectful. She did not return my letters, but said that they should be destroyed—at all events they should never appear against me in this world. I saw there had been tears upon the paper, and that gave me a few compunctious visitings then, and, oh! how many since.

"I was now free, as I supposed, to prosecute my new suit—which I did with ardour, and, as you may surmise, from what I have before said, with success. I need not dwell upon the preliminaries. I was married to a fashionable belle, and made what the world unanimously called 'an excellent match!' I thought so too, for the first month of the honey-moon. While we were whirled through a continued round of gaiety with the same meretricious attractions surrounding my wife as before, the scales did not absolutely fall from my eyes, but I had some painful misgivings, even thus early. When, however, we were removed to my own paternal home—to the sweets of country life—Heavens! what a falling off was there! She had not one single resource in the world. I found her as ignorant as a parrot, and nearly as noisy. She not only disliked books, but took my devotion to them as so many slights to herself. If I rode to the neighbouring village to attend to my necessary professional business, a messenger was sure to be despatched after me. My wife was taken suddenly sick, &c. &c. It made no difference how important the case in which I was engaged,—in the midst of a jury speech—I would receive messages from home of a sort which instantly unmanned me. As I was not forced, from necessity, to pursue my profession, of course I abandoned it, and with it all hope of political preferment. I confined myself at home for six months, in my dressing-gown and slippers, and became chief nurse, and wholly a slave to my wife. If I rode out, the finger on every side would point out the hen-pecked husband—at least I imagined it—and that was pretty much the same thing. I undertook to travel, for the health of all parties; but I soon found that I was only publishing to a wider circle, the pitiful and contemptible state into which I had fallen. My wife quarrelled with all the village doctors in succession, but still took more villainous compounds in a month, than would have set up a village apothecary—at least they were sent home, and I had to pay for them. Still, she preserved her good looks, and when my house happened to be filled with company,—from a distance especially,—it was really wonderful what a charming creature she appeared, so that those persons who had heard of our unhappiness, uniformly laid all the blame at my door, because I looked gloomy and miserable, and could not shake off such feelings, even at the approach of my dearest friends.

"At length, my own health began to sink under this accumulated pressure. My mind preyed upon my body. I had no better resources, under the new order of things in my house, than my wife, herself; and we just moped each other to death, or, rather, the concentrated tyranny of this Kingdom of Boredom, fell, with destructive weight, upon my more delicate organization."

"But, why did you not make a bold move to relieve yourself from the wretched thraldom?"

"I did, Doctor, make more than a hundred, and if nothing had intervened but storm and passion, and even tears, I could have fought out the battle bravely, but those dreadful fits, one of which you so lately witnessed, was sure to wind up the performance of the evening."

"Good Heavens!" said I, "and have you sacrificed your health and prospects to so poor a fetch as that? Why, they are nothing! Do you not perceive that they do not affect her health permanently, and not even her good looks for any length of time?"

"Too late, Doctor—too late!" exclaimed poor Fred. in the deepest despondency; and then rousing himself up again, continued: "But I do not consult you now, Doctor, with any hopes of retrieving the things which I have lost. I know that my fortunes, my health, my happiness in this world, are totally shipwrecked. I only want to find some quiet spot where I may die in peace and seclusion. Now, tell me how I can accomplish this? Can't you advise me to go to Europe; that the voyage would benefit mine, but injure my wife's nerves; or can't you counsel the Red Sulphur, and insist upon some one,—I care not which—of the other springs for her?"

"Against your last proposition, Fred." said I, "there is one objection which you little know of." I watched his countenance while I continued: "Eliza, is here, on her way to the Red—even in feebler health than yourself; and I expect her husband is as anxious to get clear of her, and her sick room, as you are to get clear of yours."

His face became moved by strange contortions, as I gave him this painful intelligence. His soul was harrowed up—the feeling of his first and *true love*, was once more in the ascendant, and the struggles of the poor fellow were frightful to behold. I became alarmed at his condition. The muscles of his mouth quivered in such irresistible wretchedness, that I was under some apprehension of a paralysis on the spot. But, at length, he threw himself upon the green sward and wept like a child.

When restored to something like composure, he made me sit down and tell him the most minute particulars about her—how she looked—what she said, &c. When he had got every thing out of me which I knew about her,—he again fell into a paroxysm of remorse and grief, and bemoaned the consequences of his own acts, in such exclamations as these:—"Oh, God, how just is thy retribution! How have I reaped as I have sown!" &c. And he declared to me, that could he be near Eliza, and just die with her, he would now consider it the greatest earthly boon which could be conferred upon him.

I pointed to Eliza's happy religious experience, and recommended him to seek the same heavenly source of consolation; but he replied that "she was pure and bright, and that heaven was a fit place for a spirit purified like hers, but for him—he was an outcast upon earth and doomed for eternity." I could not but feel how inadequate I was to administer to him ghostly comfort, and therefore I did not push the subject home, as I should have done. I suggested to him, however, that his ardent desire to spend his last days on earth near Eliza, did not seem to me so wholly impossible, as he appeared to think. He bounded at the suggestion, and I began to fear that I had gone too far, and perhaps was betraying him into a greater degree of misery. The result will show whether I was too fast or not.

In furtherance of the views above alluded to, I suggested that any intercourse between them now,—in their present state of health,—and their blighted prospects in this world, must necessarily be entirely free from passion.

This was an after thought, for, until Fred. had unbosomed himself entirely to me, the feasibility of the plan had never occurred to my mind. It appeared to me that there was very little that was selfish in the poor fellow's desire, to spend his last moments near one whom he had now ceased to look upon in any other light, than as an already purified spirit. I foresaw that all this would end in another piece of unpleasant diplomacy, on my part; and so it proved, but I did not shrink from it. I promised to see Eliza that afternoon, and, in violation of her charge, once more mention the dreaded name, and even request an interview for him;—of course, in my presence.

When we returned to the green and beautiful vale below, he seemed improved by having unburthened himself to me, and appeared altogether more cheerful than I had of late seen him. Before separating for the day, it was arranged that, after visiting his wife, I was to call for him in the afternoon, and should the coast be clear, and should I succeed in my mission, I was to introduce him at once.

My readers will perceive how completely I had got myself into business, in the midst of their tangled meshes. A good deal of it was extra-professional, no doubt, but into this I was in some measure forced, by my former relation to the parties.

I entered Mrs. Fauquiere's room in my usual cool and subdued manner. The curtains were drawn—the room darkened—and the most profound quiet reigned throughout the whole suit of apartments. The servant who ushered me in, threw up one of the curtains to give us light, and then the storm commenced. Preserve me from an enraged woman's tongue—especially one of those "upon the high pressure principle." Such a torrent of words as fell from those beautiful lips, I certainly shall never forget. She said she "had often been threatened with me before"—that she "had no idea that she was to be brought from home on purpose to be murdered by me"—that I had "bled her to death"—that she "did not believe there was any thing more the matter with Mr. Fauquiere's lungs than with hers," (hers were sound enough in all conscience)—that if she "were dead and buried, he would soon be well enough"—(a little sooner, and this might have been true perhaps)—that I "had poisoned the whole atmosphere of her room and her wardrobe with villainous drugs"—(assafoetida) that "all the Cologne in France could not wash out the plague spot"—that I "had purposely prevented her from going to the assembly rooms that night"—that I was "in a conspiracy with her husband"—that she "had thrown all my boxes and phials out of the window"—and that "if she was a man she would throw me after them"—that I "should not feel her pulse"—that she "would take no more medicine"—that she "would die a thousand deaths first." She called me, "Pill-garlic," and sundry other not very flattering names;—all the while foaming at the mouth and fanning herself, with one of those rapid motions which seem to me habitual to bad tempered ladies. I saw how all this would end—I had for some time apprehended that she would go off into another paroxysm, and I coolly drew forth my lancet case (as a mere device) and called for a bowl and bandage. At this she set up a scream that might have waked all the slumberers on the premises. It brought poor Fred. to the rescue, but I coolly put him out of the door, and persevered until I had completely subdued my grand-lady patient, principally by letting her see, that I was made of different metal from her husband. The victory once gained—she ever afterwards looked upon me with the same dread with which a poor maniac looks upon his keeper. Often have I gone into her room and just raised my finger, and she would fall back as if spell bound. There was no *charlatanerie* in this. Every experienced physician has met with similar cases, and it does not militate against the position before assumed, that hysteria is a physical as well as a mental disease. It simply illustrates the controlling influence which the latter has over the former.

I found Fred. sitting upon the step leading from his wife's apartments, an anxious husband, certainly; but my readers may form some idea, by this time, what sort of anxiety it was.

When informed that I had succeeded—he exclaimed, "Well Doctor you may turn hen-tamer next;" and he then launched out in regrets that he had not sent for me before, when he had first contemplated it, and a great deal more of the like, which it is needless to repeat.

At the appointed time I waited upon the gentle being who was such a perfect contrast to my last patient. She was unusually calm and benignant, and free from any distressing symptom of her disease; but still supported in her pillowed chair.

In common *parlance*, I beat about the bush for some time before I dared to broach the forbidden subject, and at last I had to begin as formally as if I had entered upon it, at the first moment of entrance. "Mrs. Means," said I, "you have solemnly enjoined upon me never to mention the name of a certain person in your presence;" (here she raised her hand in prohibition, but I begged her to hear me out;) "since that time, he has arrived here himself, in a similar state of health to your own. He has unfolded to me the whole story of his wrongs to you, and is very repentant and is anxious to receive forgiveness from your own lips. Will you not see him for half an hour?" Until I came to his self-condemnation, she looked as stern as a criminal judge, and very dignified, but, at that point, the woman triumphed, and she burst into a flood of tears. Seizing the moment, I stole to the door and brought Fred. in from the long portico, where he had been walking ever since my entrance.   *   *   *   *   *   *

It would have melted a hard heart to have seen those two young creatures, thus reconciled to each other upon the eve of the final close of all their interests in this world. They both saw the remnants of the storm which wrecked all their worldly fortunes—but neither alluded to it again, after Fred. had made his first hurried confession. He was forgiven of course. Her reply was in these words, as near as I can recollect. "Frederic—all that is now left to us is the memory of a troubled dream—let us only cherish among those recollections what is agreeable,—at all events only such as are useful. Let us remember that we were playmates in our youthful days, and promise to be friends for the future. Since I have seen you (and oh, how altered you are!) I am sure that I can look upon you as a brother—'let by-gones be by-gones.' I may perhaps be useful to you, as I have approached nearer than you to the commencement of our last journey." *I* was forgiven, as a matter of course.   *   *   *   *   *   *

Nearly two months had passed away, and the leaves of the forest trees began to be tinged, here and there, with their russet dress. The long table at the Salt Sulphur, had been shorn of its huge proportions; and those of us who still lingered among the mountains, gathered round, and clung together, like a single family. We were trifling over our tea one evening, thus huddled together, and recounting the adventures of "the season," when a horseman was perceived coming down the winding road from the Red Sulphur, *post-haste*. He dashed over the creek and soon stood in our presence. I saw one of the servants point to me as he entered the room. He presented me with two letters. One was for me in Fred's hand-writing, and the other for Mr. Means, who was supposed to be with us also. Alas! no one could tell where *he* was. He had followed the sportsmen of the faro table, a few days before, to the White Sulphur—but he might be at the Sweet—(in all probability he was, as that usually wound up the season) or he might be at the Blue, or the Grey, or the Warm, or the Hot Springs. My letter contained but a few lines.

RED SULPHUR SPRINGS.

Dear Doctor,—Poor Eliza is almost gone, and her father desires that you will come over immediately. He knows, and we all know, that you can do nothing towards her ultimate recovery, but you may afford momentary relief. *We* know that you will not weigh a night ride one moment against the hope even of this temporary relief.

Your's, ever truly and sincerely,

FRED. FAUQUIERE.

I procured a fleet horse, and soon entered upon my solitary mountain ride. I arrived at the Red Sulphur about three o'clock in the morning; and as I wound down the long descending road, which leads the traveller to that sweet, secluded valley, I could see the solitary light as it twinkled from Eliza's lonely cabin-chamber. It was a fit scene for the departure of a spirit like hers. Shut out from the noise of all the world by the high blue mountains on every side,—a profound silence reigning uninterruptedly for miles and miles around,—it seemed as one of the holiest temples of the living God. If a plaintive note struck upon the ear, occasionally, from some melancholy bird, startled by the sound of my horse's feet,—or the bark of the watch-dog, roused by the same cause to a momentary growl,—they only served to render the succeeding silence more full of awe and solemnity. I hastened to follow the lead of the rays of light, which fell athwart the lawn from the window which had guided me for the last half hour. Tapping gently at the door, I was admitted by Frederick himself. He grasped my hand without uttering a word, and led me to the chair beside the bed, where he had been seated. Old Mr. Parker, worn out by long watching and fatigue, was sound asleep in his daughter's arm-chair. The sufferer was sitting, almost upright, against a mountain of pillows,—one hand resting upon an open prayer-book, with the foot of the page turned towards the seat which

Frederick had just resigned to me. He had been reading to her,—aye, and he had been on his knees, too; for the cushion of the chair yet remained upon the floor, where he had left it. She extended to me the other hand, and whispered in an infantile voice, "that she was so rejoiced I had come." I saw her eye fastened upon the door after I had entered, in evident expectation of some one else. I knew full well who it was, but I could say nothing. She did not ask for the absent one, possibly, because she was too weak,—possibly, because she may have feared the answer!

After I had felt her pulse, listened to her breathing, and prescribed such simples, for her relief, as were at hand, she said to me, "Now, we are all here, just as in days of yore,—yet, what a contrast to many of the scenes of our youth!—and how little did either of us foresee that we should be here, and thus,—two of us to die in the midst of these lone mountains. Not that I regret the solitude and quiet of the place, since the visitors have all gone,—far from it. It seems to me that this grand solitariness of place, realizes to my mind the sublime idea of God's own presence, in his own temple. Here, now, with the human world almost shut out, I feel, that the Lord is in his holy temple, and how proper that the whole earth should keep silence before him! I, who am about to leave the world for another, feel the present loneliness as but properly preparatory to my departure,—and am grateful that the noise and confusion of the one life, should seem awe-struck and hushed before the opening glories of the other!"

Soon after, she fell into a sweet sleep, which lasted for some hours,—Frederick sitting, all the while, with her hand clasped in his. As the sun began to peep through the curtains he touched me, and motioned me to draw near, when he placed her hand in mine and whispered, *"it is very cold."* Cold, indeed, it was—for death had already chilled the whole vital current in that beautiful tenement,—beautiful was it, exceedingly, even in death!

* * * * * *

The next evening, the corse was followed to its last home, in the bosom of the mountains, by Mr. Parker, as chief mourner, and Frederick and myself, as pall-bearers. Pall, indeed, there was none, but we walked alongside of the coffin, which was borne by four neatly-dressed servants, and followed by twice as many more. I read the funeral service over the remains of my late gentle friend, and that evening Frederick spent in gathering the beautiful wild flowers, which she loved so well in life, and strewing them over her grave.

We spent the night together—the last I ever spent with him on earth; and he shewed me a bundle of letters which she had given him. They were his own, which she had preserved till a little time before her death, and had then returned to him.

Frederick lived to return home, but died the following winter. He had a great desire to be laid alongside of her whom he had loved so truly in life, but I suppose no one felt interest enough in the matter, of those about him, to see it accomplished,—and he sleeps, therefore, among his fathers. His widow, when I last chanced to hear from her, was a dashing lady of fortune; and I did hope, might, somehow or other, captivate Mr. Means,—but this, it seems, was rather too great a manifestation of providential or poetical justice to happen in reality.

Edgar Allan Poe
(1809-1849)

In his monumental study, *The South in American Literature, 1607–1900* (1954), Professor Jay B. Hubbell pointed out the irony that the "greatest of all Southern writers," Edgar Allan Poe, was born, of all places, in Boston—on January 19, 1809, the son of Maryland actor David Poe and English actress Elizabeth Arnold Poe. When, however, apparently deserted by her husband, Mrs. Poe died (after a lingering illness) in Richmond on December 8, 1811, young Poe was taken into the home of a Richmond merchant and his wife and became thenceforth "a Virginian," as the author later was to write in 1841: "at least I call myself one, for I have resided all my life, until the last few years, in Richmond."

Though the John Allans had wealth and a certain amount of social status, the homeless child was not fortunate in coming under their conflicting influences. John Allan was a narrow-minded, wayward husband intent upon providing for his illegitimate children, while at the same time cutting off his artistic foster-son (with whom he had little sympathy); Frances Valentine Allan was a weak, self-centered woman who at times pampered the beautiful orphan boy but failed to provide what he needed most—discipline, guidance, and stability. As a youth Poe attended good academies in Richmond, and when the Allans were in England he was enrolled from 1818 to 1820 at an excellent English school, John Bransby's, at Stoke Newington. His experiences in England helped to rid Poe of provinciality and to develop in him the cosmopolitan views he maintained throughout his literary career.

Poe's alienation from his foster-father was widened during 1826 when the unfortunate youth, sent to the University of Virginia without sufficient funds to meet expenses, in desperation ran up gambling debts which Allan refused to honor. Poe then struck out on his own, going to Boston, where in

1827 he published anonymously and at his own expense his first volume, *Tamberlane, and Other Poems,* which met with no success. Under financial necessity Poe enlisted in the United States Army and was stationed at Fort Moultrie, on Sullivan's Island, near Charleston, from 1827 to 1829, during which time he rose to the rank of sergeant major and recorded impressions of the South Carolina coastal region that led to the writing of "The Gold-Bug" years later. In 1830 Poe won an ill-fated appointment to West Point, but soon decided against a military career and, unable to get the written permission from his adamant foster-father which would have released him honorably, proceeded to get himself dismissed in 1831 by gross neglect of duty.

Poe now fully committed himself to the literary life, first briefly in New York, where he published *Poems* (1831); then in Baltimore (1831–1835), where he attracted attention by winning a Baltimore *Saturday Visiter* contest with his short-story "MS. Found in a Bottle"; and once again in Richmond, where he took an editorial position with the *Southern Literary Messenger* (1835–1837) and continued to write—poems, stories, essays, reviews—at a killing pace. Returning to New York in 1837 with his child-bride of scarcely a year, Virginia Clemm Poe, and his mother-in-law, Mrs. Maria Clemm, Poe worked desperately to make a living by writing, issuing the *The Narrative of Arthur Gordon Pym* (1838) and doing much energy-consuming work. As co-editor of *Burton's Gentleman's Magazine* in Philadelphia in 1839–1840 Poe did some of his best work, including "The Fall of the House of Usher," "William Wilson," and "Morella." During this time he also published his first collection of fiction, *Tales of the Grotesque and Arabesque* (1840). After leaving *Burton's* with the hope of establishing in Philadelphia a literary magazine of his own, he was forced to drop these plans because of lack of financing, but secured the literary editorship of *Graham's Magazine* (1841–1842), for which journal he did such distinguished writing, both in fiction and in criticism, that his reputation rose to a new zenith. In 1843 he won first prize in the *Dollar Newspaper* contest with "The Gold-Bug," published in the numbers for June 21 and 28. Nevertheless Poe continued to struggle financially, and to become embroiled in controversies with other literary figures, ill-advisedly wasting much of his creative energy. He moved back to New York in 1844, becoming associated with the *New-York Mirror* and in 1845 with the *Broadway Journal,* of which he became sole owner some three months before its collapse around the end of the year. But 1845 was probably the most remarkable year in Poe's career: during it he published not only the most famous collection of his fiction, simply entitled *Tales,* but also the first collected edition of his poetry in book form since 1831, *The Raven and Other Poems.*

After the death of his wife in 1847 Poe rapidly declined in mental and physical health, though he continued to write feverishly until his own tragic death, of not fully determined causes, in Baltimore on October 7, 1849.

Textual note

The text of "The Gold-Bug" is that of the first impression, first edition of *Tales* (New York: Wiley and Putnam, 1845), pp. [1]–36.

The Gold-Bug

What ho! what ho! this fellow is dancing mad!
He hath been bitten by the Tarantula.
All in the Wrong.

Many years ago, I contracted an intimacy with a Mr. William Legrand.
He was of an ancient Huguenot family, and had once been wealthy; but a
series of misfortunes had reduced him to want. To avoid the mortification
consequent upon his disasters, he left New Orleans, the city of his forefathers, and took up his residence at Sullivan's Island, near Charleston,
South Carolina.

This Island is a very singular one. It consists of little else than the
sea sand, and is about three miles long. Its breadth at no point exceeds a
quarter of a mile. It is separated from the main land by a scarcely perceptible creek, oozing its way through a wilderness of reeds and slime, a favorite
resort of the marsh-hen. The vegetation, as might be supposed, is scant, or
at least dwarfish. No trees of any magnitude are to be seen. Near the western extremity, where Fort Moultrie stands, and where are some miserable
frame buildings, tenanted, during summer, by the fugitives from Charleston
dust and fever, may be found, indeed, the bristly palmetto; but the whole
island, with the exception of this western point, and a line of hard, white
beach on the sea-coast, is covered with a dense undergrowth of the sweet
myrtle, so much prized by the horticulturists of England. The shrub here
often attains the height of fifteen or twenty feet, and forms an almost impenetrable coppice, burthening the air with its fragrance.

In the inmost recesses of this coppice, not far from the eastern or more
remote end of the island, Legrand had built himself a small hut, which he
occupied when I first, by mere accident, made his acquaintance. This soon
ripened into friendship—for there was much in the recluse to excite interest and esteem. I found him well educated, with unusual powers of mind,

but infected with misanthropy, and subject to perverse moods of alternate enthusiasm and melancholy. He had with him many books, but rarely employed them. His chief amusements were gunning and fishing, or sauntering along the beach and through the myrtles, in quest of shells or entomological specimens;—his collection of the latter might have been envied by a Swammerdamm. In these excursions he was usually accompanied by an old negro, called Jupiter, who had been manumitted before the reverses of the family, but who could be induced, neither by threats nor by promises, to abandon what he considered his right of attendance upon the footsteps of his young "Massa Will." It is not improbable that the relatives of Legrand, conceiving him to be somewhat unsettled in intellect, had contrived to instil this obstinacy into Jupiter, with a view to the supervision and guardianship of the wanderer.

The winters in the latitude of Sullivan's Island are seldom very severe, and in the fall of the year it is a rare event indeed when a fire is considered necessary. About the middle of October, 18—, there occurred, however, a day of remarkable chilliness. Just before sunset I scrambled my way through the evergreens to the hut of my friend, whom I had not visited for several weeks—my residence being, at that time, in Charleston, a distance of nine miles from the Island, while the facilities of passage and re-passage were very far behind those of the present day. Upon reaching the hut I rapped, as was my custom, and getting no reply, sought for the key where I knew it was secreted, unlocked the door and went in. A fine fire was blazing upon the hearth. It was a novelty, and by no means an ungrateful one. I threw off an overcoat, took an arm-chair by the crackling logs, and awaited patiently the arrival of my hosts.

Soon after dark they arrived, and gave me a most cordial welcome. Jupiter, grinning from ear to ear, bustled about to prepare some marsh-hens for supper. Legrand was in one of his fits—how else shall I term them?— of enthusiasm. He had found an unknown bivalve, forming a new genus, and, more than this, he had hunted down and secured, with Jupiter's assistance, a *scarabæus* which he believed to be totally new, but in respect to which he wished to have my opinion on the morrow.

"And why not to-night?" I asked, rubbing my hands over the blaze, and wishing the whole tribe of *scarabæi* at the devil.

"Ah, if I had only known you were here!" said Legrand, "but it's so long since I saw you; and how could I foresee that you would pay me a visit this very night of all others? As I was coming home I met Lieutenant G——, from the fort, and, very foolishly, I lent him the bug; so it will be impossible for you to see it until the morning. Stay here to-night, and I will send Jup down for it at sunrise. It is the loveliest thing in creation!"

"What?—sunrise?"

"Nonsense! no!—the bug. It is of a brilliant gold color—about the size of a large hickory-nut—with two jet black spots near one extremity of the back, and another, somewhat longer, at the other. The *antennæ* are—"

"Dey aint *no* tin in him, Massa Will, I keep a tellin on you," here interrupted Jupiter; "de bug is a goole bug, solid, ebery bit of him, inside and all, sep him wing—neber feel half so hebby a bug in my life."

"Well, suppose it is, Jup," replied Legrand, somewhat more earnestly, it seemed to me, than the case demanded, "is that any reason for your letting the birds burn? The color"—here he turned to me—"is really almost enough to warrant Jupiter's idea. You never saw a more brilliant metallic lustre than the scales emit—but of this you cannot judge till to-morrow. In the mean time I can give you some idea of the shape." Saying this, he seated himself at a small table, on which were a pen and ink, but no paper. He looked for some in a drawer, but found none.

"Never mind," said he at length, "this will answer;" and he drew from his waistcoat pocket a scrap of what I took to be very dirty foolscap, and made upon it a rough drawing with the pen. While he did this, I retained my seat by the fire, for I was still chilly. When the design was complete, he handed it to me without rising. As I received it, a loud growl was heard, succeeded by a scratching at the door. Jupiter opened it, and a large Newfoundland, belonging to Legrand, rushed in, leaped upon my shoulders, and loaded me with caresses; for I had shown him much attention during previous visits. When his gambols were over, I looked at the paper, and, to speak the truth, found myself not a little puzzled at what my friend had depicted.

"Well!" I said, after contemplating it for some minutes, "this *is* a strange *scarabæus*, I must confess: new to me: never saw anything like it before—unless it was a skull, or a death's-head—which it more nearly resembles than anything else that has come under *my* observation."

"A death's-head!" echoed Legrand—"Oh—yes—well, it has something of that appearance upon paper, no doubt. The two upper black spots look like eyes, eh? and the longer one at the bottom like a mouth—and then the shape of the whole is oval."

"Perhaps so," said I; "but, Legrand, I fear you are no artist. I must wait until I see the beetle itself, if I am to form any idea of its personal appearance."

"Well, I don't know," said he, a little nettled, "I draw tolerably—*should* do it at least—have had good masters, and flatter myself that I am not quite a blockhead."

"But, my dear fellow, you are joking then," said I, "this is a very passable *skull*—indeed, I may say that it is a very *excellent* skull, according to the vulgar notions about such specimens of physiology—and your *scarabæus* must be the queerest *scarabæus* in the world if it resembles it. Why, we may get up a very thrilling bit of superstition upon this hint. I presume you will call the bug *scarabæus caput hominis,* or something of that kind—there are many similar titles in the Natural Histories. But where are the *antennæ* you spoke of?"

"The *antennæ!*" said Legrand, who seemed to be getting unaccountably warm upon the subject; "I am sure you must see the *antennæ.* I made them as distinct as they are in the original insect, and I presume that is sufficient."

"Well, well," I said, "perhaps you have—still I don't see them;" and I handed him the paper without additional remark, not wishing to ruffle his temper; but I was much surprised at the turn affairs had taken; his ill humor puzzled me—and, as for the drawing of the beetle, there were positively *no antennæ* visible, and the whole *did* bear a very close resemblance to the ordinary cuts of a death's-head.

He received the paper very peevishly, and was about to crumple it, apparently to throw it in the fire, when a casual glance at the design seemed suddenly to rivet his attention. In an instant his face grew violently red—in another as excessively pale. For some minutes he continued to scrutinize the drawing minutely where he sat. At length he arose, took a candle from the table, and proceeded to seat himself upon a sea-chest in the farthest corner of the room. Here again he made an anxious examination of the paper; turning it in all directions. He said nothing, however, and his conduct greatly astonished me; yet I thought it prudent not to exacerbate the growing moodiness of his temper by any comment. Presently he took from his coat pocket a wallet, placed the paper carefully in it, and deposited both in a writing-desk, which he locked. He now grew more composed in his demeanor; but his original air of enthusiasm had quite disappeared. Yet he seemed not so much sulky as abstracted. As the evening wore away he became more and more absorbed in reverie, from which no sallies of mine could arouse him. It had been my intention to pass the night at the hut, as I had frequently done before, but, seeing my host in this mood, I deemed it proper to take leave. He did not press me to remain, but, as I departed, he shook my hand with even more than his usual cordiality.

It was about a month after this (and during the interval I had seen nothing of Legrand) when I received a visit, at Charleston, from his man, Jupiter. I had never seen the good old negro look so dispirited, and I feared that some serious disaster had befallen my friend.

"Well, Jup," said I, "what is the matter now?—how is your master?"

"Why, to speak de troof, massa, him not so berry well as mought be."

"Not well! I am truly sorry to hear it. What does he complain of?"

"Dar! dat's it!—him neber plain of notin—but him berry sick for all dat."

"*Very* sick, Jupiter!—why didn't you say so at once? Is he confined to bed?"

"No, dat he aint!—he aint find nowhar—dat's just whar de shoe pinch—my mind is got to be berry hebby bout poor Massa Will."

"Jupiter, I should like to understand what it is you are talking about. You say your master is sick. Hasn't he told you what ails him?"

"Why, massa, taint worf while for to git mad about de matter—Massa Will say noffin at all aint de matter wid him—but den what make him go about looking dis here way, wid he head down and he soldiers up, and as white as a goose? And den he keep a syphon all de time—"

"Keeps a what, Jupiter?"

"Keeps a syphon wid de figgurs on de slate—de queerest figgurs I ebber did see. Ise gittin to be skeered, I tell you. Hab for to keep mighty tight eye pon him noovers. Todder day he gib me slip fore de sun up and was gone de whole ob de blessed day. I had a big stick ready cut for to gib him deuced good beating when he did come—but Ise sich a fool dat I hadn't de heart arter all—he look so berry poorly."

"Eh?—what?—ah yes!—upon the whole I think you had better not be too severe with the poor fellow—don't flog him, Jupiter—he can't very well stand it—but can you form no idea of what has occasioned this illness, or rather this change of conduct? Has anything unpleasant happened since I saw you?"

"No, massa, dey aint bin noffin onpleasant *since* den—'twas *fore* den I'm feared—'twas de berry day you was dare."

"How? what do you mean?"

"Why, massa, I mean de bug—dare now."

"The what?"

"De bug—I'm berry sartain dat Massa Will bin bit somewhere bout de head by dat goole-bug."

"And what cause have you, Jupiter, for such a supposition?"

"Claws enuff, massa, and mouff too. I nebber did see sich a deuced bug—he kick and he bite ebery ting what cum near him. Massa Will cotch him fuss, but had for to let him go gin mighty quick, I tell you—den was de time he must ha got de bite. I did n't like de look ob de bug mouff, myself, no how, so I would n't take hold ob him wid my finger, but I cotch him wid a piece ob paper dat I found. I rap him up in de paper and stuff piece ob it in he mouff—dat was de way."

"And you think, then, that your master was really bitten by the beetle, and that the bite made him sick?"

"I do n't tink noffin about it—I nose it. What make him dream bout de goole so much, if taint cause he bit by de goole-bug? Ise heerd bout dem goole-bugs fore dis.

"But how do you know he dreams about gold?"

"How I know? why cause he talk about it in he sleep—dat's how I nose."

"Well, Jup, perhaps you are right; but to what fortunate circumstance am I to attribute the honor of a visit from you to-day?"

"What de matter, massa?"

"Did you bring any message from Mr. Legrand?"

"No, massa, I bring dis here pissel;" and here Jupiter handed me a note which ran thus:

MY DEAR——

Why have I not seen you for so long a time? I hope you have not been so foolish as to take offence at any little *brusquerie* of mine; but no, that is improbable.

Since I saw you I have had great cause for anxiety. I have something to tell you, yet scarcely know how to tell it, or whether I should tell it at all.

I have not been quite well for some days past, and poor old Jup annoys me, almost beyond endurance, by his well-meant attentions. Would you believe it?—he had prepared a huge stick, the other day, with which to chastise me for giving him the slip, and spending the day, *solus,* among the hills on the main land. I verily believe that my ill looks alone saved me a flogging.

I have made no addition to my cabinet since we met.

If you can, in any way, make it convenient, come over with Jupiter. *Do* come. I wish to see you *to-night,* upon business of importance. I assure you that it is of the *highest* importance.

Ever yours,   WILLIAM LEGRAND.

There was something in the tone of this note which gave me great uneasiness. Its whole style differed materially from that of Legrand. What could he be dreaming of? What new crotchet possessed his excitable brain? What "business of the highest importance" could *he* possibly have to transact? Jupiter's account of him boded no good. I dreaded lest the continued pressure of misfortune had, at length, fairly unsettled the reason of my friend. Without a moment's hesitation, therefore, I prepared to accompany the negro.

Upon reaching the wharf, I noticed a scythe and three spades, all apparently new, lying in the bottom of the boat in which we were to embark.

"What is the meaning of all this, Jup?" I inquired.

"Him syfe, massa, and spade."

"Very true; but what are they doing here?"

"Him de syfe and de spade what Massa Will sis pon my buying for him in de town, and de debbils own lot of money I had to gib for em."

"But what, in the name of all that is mysterious, is your 'Massa Will' going to do with scythes and spades?"

"Dat's more dan *I* know, and debbil take me if I don't blieve 'tis more dan he know, too. But it's all cum ob de bug."

Finding that no satisfaction was to be obtained of Jupiter, whose whole intellect seemed to be absorbed by "de bug," I now stepped into the boat and made sail. With a fair and strong breeze we soon ran into the little cove to the northward of Fort Moultrie, and a walk of some two miles brought us to the hut. It was about three in the afternoon when we arrived. Legrand had been awaiting us in eager expectation. He grasped my hand with a nervous *empressement* which alarmed me and strengthened the suspicions already entertained. His countenance was pale even to ghastliness, and his deep-set eyes glared with unnatural lustre. After some inquiries respecting his health, I asked him, not knowing what better to say, if he had yet obtained the *scarabœus* from Lieutenant G——.

"Oh, yes," he replied, coloring violently, "I got it from him the next morning. Nothing should tempt me to part with that *scarabœus*. Do you know that Jupiter is quite right about it?"

"In what way?" I asked, with a sad foreboding at heart.

"In supposing it to be a bug of *real gold*." He said this with an air of profound seriousness, and I felt inexpressibly shocked.

"This bug is to make my fortune," he continued, with a triumphant smile, "to reinstate me in my family possessions. Is it any wonder, then, that I prize it? Since Fortune has thought fit to bestow it upon me, I have only to use it properly and I shall arrive at the gold of which it is the index. Jupiter, bring me that *scarabœus!*"

"What! de bug, massa? I'd rudder not go fer trubble dat bug—you mus git him for your own self." Hereupon Legrand arose, with a grave and stately air, and brought me the beetle from a glass case in which it was enclosed. It was a beautiful *scarabœus*, and, at that time, unknown to naturalists—of course a great prize in a scientific point of view. There were two round, black spots near one extremity of the back, and a long one near the other. The scales were exceedingly hard and glossy, with all the appearance of burnished gold. The weight of the insect was very remarkable, and, taking all things into consideration, I could hardly blame Jupiter for his opinion respecting it; but what to make of Legrand's concordance with that opinion, I could not, for the life of me, tell.

"I sent for you," said he, in a grandiloquent tone, when I had completed my examination of the beetle, "I sent for you, that I might have your counsel and assistance in furthering the views of Fate and of the bug"—

"My dear Legrand," I cried, interrupting him, "you are certainly unwell, and had better use some little precautions. You shall go to bed, and I will remain with you a few days, until you get over this. You are feverish and"—

"Feel my pulse," said he.

I felt it, and, to say the truth, found not the slightest indication of fever.

"But you may be ill and yet have no fever. Allow me this once to prescribe for you. In the first place, go to bed. In the next"—

"You are mistaken," he interposed, "I am as well as I can expect to be under the excitement which I suffer. If you really wish me well, you will relieve this excitement."

"And how is this to be done?"

"Very easily. Jupiter and myself are going upon an expedition into the hills, upon the main land, and, in this expedition, we shall need the aid of some person in whom we can confide. You are the only one we can trust. Whether we succeed or fail, the excitement which you now perceive in me will be equally allayed."

"I am anxious to oblige you in any way," I replied; "but do you mean to say that this infernal beetle has any connection with your expedition into the hills?"

"It has."

"Then, Legrand, I can become a party to no such absurd proceeding."

"I am sorry—very sorry—for we shall have to try it by ourselves."

"Try it by yourselves! The man is surely mad!—but stay!—how long do you propose to be absent?"

"Probably all night. We shall start immediately, and be back, at all events, by sunrise."

"And will you promise me, upon your honor, that when this freak of yours is over, and the bug business (good God!) settled to your satisfaction, you will then return home and follow my advice implicitly, as that of your physician?"

"Yes; I promise; and now let us be off, for we have no time to lose."

With a heavy heart I accompanied my friend. We started about four o'clock—Legrand, Jupiter, the dog, and myself. Jupiter had with him the scythe and spades—the whole of which he insisted upon carrying—more through fear, it seemed to me, of trusting either of the implements within reach of his master, than from any excess of industry or complaisance. His demeanor was dogged in the extreme, and "dat deuced bug" were the sole words which escaped his lips during the journey. For my own part, I had charge of a couple of dark lanterns, while Legrand contented himself with the *scarabæus*, which he carried attached to the end of a bit of whip-cord; twirling it to and fro, with the air of a conjuror, as he went. When I observed this last, plain evidence of my friend's aberration of mind, I could scarcely refrain from tears. I thought it best, however, to humor his fancy, at least for the present, or until I could adopt some more energetic measures with a chance of success. In the mean time I endeavored, but all in vain, to sound him in regard to the object of the expedition. Having succeeded in inducing me to accompany him, he seemed unwilling to hold conversation upon any topic of minor importance, and to all my questions vouchsafed no other reply than "we shall see!"

We crossed the creek at the head of the island by means of a skiff, and, ascending the high grounds on the shore of the main land, proceeded in a northwesterly direction, through a tract of country excessively wild and desolate, where no trace of a human footstep was to be seen. Legrand led the way with decision; pausing only for an instant, here and there, to consult what appeared to be certain landmarks of his own contrivance upon a former occasion.

In this manner we journeyed for about two hours, and the sun was just setting when we entered a region infinitely more dreary than any yet seen. It was a species of table land, near the summit of an almost inaccessible hill, densely wooded from base to pinnacle, and interspersed with huge crags that appeared to lie loosely upon the soil, and in many cases were prevented from precipitating themselves into the valleys below, merely by the support of the trees against which they reclined. Deep ravines, in various directions, gave an air of still sterner solemnity to the scene.

The natural platform to which we had clambered was thickly overgrown with brambles, through which we soon discovered that it would have been impossible to force our way but for the scythe; and Jupiter, by direction of his master, proceeded to clear for us a path to the foot of an enormously tall tulip-tree, which stood, with some eight or ten oaks, upon the level, and far surpassed them all, and all other trees which I had then ever seen, in the beauty of its foliage and form, in the wide spread of its branches, and in the general majesty of its appearance. When we reached this tree, Legrand turned to Jupiter, and asked him if he thought he could climb it. The old man seemed a little staggered by the question, and for some moments made no reply. At length he approached the huge trunk, walked slowly around it, and examined it with minute attention. When he had completed his scrutiny, he merely said,

"Yes, massa, Jup climb any tree he ebber see in he life."

"Then up with you as soon as possible, for it will soon be too dark to see what we are about."

"How far mus go up, massa?" inquired Jupiter.

"Get up the main trunk first, and then I will tell you which way to go —and here—stop! take this beetle with you."

"De bug, Massa Will!—de goole bug!" cried the negro, drawing back in dismay—"what for mus tote de bug way up de tree?—d—n if I do!"

"If you are afraid, Jup, a great big negro like you, to take hold of a harmless little dead beetle, why you can carry it up by this string—but, if you do not take it up with you in some way, I shall be under the necessity of breaking your head with this shovel."

"What de matter now, massa?" said Jup, evidently shamed into compliance; "always want for to raise fuss wid old nigger. Was only funnin any how. *Me* feered de bug! what I keer for de bug?" Here he took cautiously hold of the extreme end of the string, and, maintaining the insect as far from his person as circumstances would permit, prepared to ascend the tree.

In youth, the tulip-tree, or *Liriodendron Tulipiferum,* the most magnificent of American foresters, has a trunk peculiarly smooth, and often rises to a great height without lateral branches; but, in its riper age, the bark becomes gnarled and uneven, while many short limbs make their appearance on the stem. Thus the difficulty of ascension, in the present case, lay more in semblance than in reality. Embracing the huge cylinder, as closely as possible, with his arms and knees, seizing with his hands some projections, and resting his naked toes upon others, Jupiter, after one or two narrow escapes from falling, at length wriggled himself into the first great fork, and seemed to consider the whole business as virtually accomplished. The *risk* of the achievement was, in fact, now over, although the climber was some sixty or seventy feet from the ground.

"Which way mus go now, Massa Will?" he asked.

"Keep up the largest branch—the one on this side," said Legrand. The negro obeyed him promptly, and apparently with but little trouble; ascending higher and higher, until no glimpse of his squat figure could be obtained through the dense foliage which enveloped it. Presently his voice was heard in a sort of halloo.

"How much fudder is got for go?"

"How high up are you?" asked Legrand.

"Ebber so fur," replied the negro; "can see de sky fru de top ob de tree."

"Never mind the sky, but attend to what I say. Look down the trunk and count the limbs below you on this side. How many limbs have you passed?"

"One, two, tree, four, fibe—I done pass fibe big limb, massa, pon dis side."

"Then go one limb higher."

In a few minutes the voice was heard again, announcing that the seventh limb was attained.

"Now, Jup," cried Legrand, evidently much excited, "I want you to work your way out upon that limb as far as you can. If you see anything strange, let me know."

By this time what little doubt I might have entertained of my poor friend's insanity, was put finally at rest. I had no alternative but to conclude him stricken with lunacy, and I became seriously anxious about getting him home. While I was pondering upon what was best to be done, Jupiter's voice was again heard.

"Mos feerd for to ventur pon dis limb berry far—tis dead limb putty much all de way."

"Did you say it was a *dead* limb, Jupiter?" cried Legrand in a quavering voice.

"Yes, massa, him dead as de door-nail—done up for sartain—done departed dis here life."

"What in the name of heaven shall I do?" asked Legrand, seemingly in the greatest distress.

"Do!" said I, glad of an opportunity to interpose a word, "why come home and go to bed. Come now!—that's a fine fellow. It's getting late, and, besides, you remember your promise."

"Jupiter," cried he, without heeding me in the least, "do you hear me?"

"Yes, Massa Will, hear you ebber so plain."

"Try the wood well, then, with your knife, and see if you think it *very* rotten."

"Him rotten, massa, sure nuff," replied the negro in a few moments, "but not so berry rotten as mought be. Mought ventur out leetle way pon de limb by myself, dat's true."

"By yourself!—what do you mean?"

"Why I mean de bug. 'Tis *berry* hebby bug. Spose I drop him down fuss, and den de limb won't break wid just de weight ob one nigger."

"You infernal scoundrel!" cried Legrand, apparently much relieved, "what do you mean by telling me such nonsense as that? As sure as you drop that beetle I'll break your neck. Look here, Jupiter, do you hear me?"

"Yes, massa, needn't hollo at poor nigger dat style."

"Well! now listen!—if you will venture out on the limb as far as you think safe, and not let go the beetle, I'll make you a present of a silver dollar as soon as you get down."

"I'm gwine, Massa Will—deed I is," replied the negro very promptly —"mos out to the eend now."

"*Out to the end!*" here fairly screamed Legrand, "do you say you are out to the end of that limb?"

"Soon be to de eend, massa,—o-o-o-o-oh! Lor-gol-a-marcy! what *is* dis here pon de tree?"

"Well!" cried Legrand, highly delighted, "what is it?"

"Why taint noffin but a skull—somebody bin lef him head up de tree, and de crows done gobble ebery bit ob de meat off."

"A skull, you say!—very well!—how is it fastened to the limb?—what holds it on?"

"Sure nuff, massa; mus look. Why dis berry curous sarcumstance, pon my word—dare's a great big nail in de skull, what fastens ob it on to de tree."

"Well now, Jupiter, do exactly as I tell you—do you hear?"

"Yes, massa."

"Pay attention, then!—find the left eye of the skull."

"Hum! hoo! dat's good! why dare aint no eye left at all."

"Curse your stupidity! do you know your right hand from your left?"

"Yes, I nose dat—nose all bout dat—tis my lef hand what I chops de wood wid."

"To be sure! you are left-handed; and your left eye is on the same side as your left hand. Now, I suppose, you can find the left eye of the skull, or the place where the left eye has been. Have you found it?"

Here was a long pause. At length the negro asked,

"Is de lef eye of de skull pon de same side as de lef hand of de skull, too?—cause de skull aint got not a bit ob a hand at all—nebber mind! I got de lef eye now—here de lef eye! what mus do wid it?"

"Let the beetle drop through it, as far as the string will reach—but be careful and not let go your hold of the string."

"All dat done, Massa Will; mighty easy ting for to put de bug fru de hole—look out for him dare below!"

During this colloquy no portion of Jupiter's person could be seen; but the beetle, which he had suffered to descend, was now visible at the end of the string, and glistened, like a globe of burnished gold, in the last rays of the setting sun, some of which still faintly illumined the eminence upon which we stood. The *scarabæus* hung quite clear of any branches, and, if allowed to fall, would have fallen at our feet. Legrand immediately took the scythe, and cleared with it a circular space, three or four yards in diameter, just beneath the insect, and, having accomplished this, ordered Jupiter to let go the string and come down from the tree.

Driving a peg, with great nicety, into the ground, at the precise spot where the beetle fell, my friend now produced from his pocket a tape-measure. Fastening one end of this at that point of the trunk of the tree which was nearest the peg, he unrolled it till it reached the peg, and thence farther unrolled it, in the direction already established by the two points of the tree and the peg, for the distance of fifty feet—Jupiter clearing away the brambles with the scythe. At the spot thus attained a second peg was driven, and about this, as a centre, a rude circle, about four feet in diameter, described. Taking now a spade himself, and giving one to Jupiter and one to me, Legrand begged us to set about digging as quickly as possible.

To speak the truth, I had no especial relish for such amusement at any time, and, at that particular moment, would most willingly have declined it; for the night was coming on, and I felt much fatigued with the exercise already taken; but I saw no mode of escape, and was fearful of disturbing my poor friend's equanimity by a refusal. Could I have depended, indeed, upon Jupiter's aid, I would have had no hesitation in attempting to get the lunatic home by force; but I was too well assured of the old negro's disposition, to hope that he would assist me, under any circumstances, in a personal contest with his master. I made no doubt that the latter had been infected with some of the innumerable Southern superstitions about money buried, and that his phantasy had received confirmation by the finding of the *scarabæus*, or, perhaps, by Jupiter's obstinacy in maintaining it to be "a bug of real gold." A mind disposed to lunacy would readily be led away by such suggestions—especially if chiming in with favorite preconceived ideas —and then I called to mind the poor fellow's speech about the beetle's being "the index of his fortune." Upon the whole, I was sadly vexed and puzzled, but, at length, I concluded to make a virtue of necessity—to dig with a good will, and thus the sooner to convince the visionary, by ocular demonstration, of the fallacy of the opinions he entertained.

The lanterns having been lit, we all fell to work with a zeal worthy a more rational cause; and, as the glare fell upon our persons and implements, I could not help thinking how picturesque a group we composed, and how strange and suspicious our labors must have appeared to any interloper who, by chance, might have stumbled upon our whereabouts.

We dug very steadily for two hours. Little was said; and our chief embarrassment lay in the yelpings of the dog, who took exceeding interest in our proceedings. He, at length, became so obstreperous that we grew fearful of his giving the alarm to some stragglers in the vicinity;—or, rather, this was the apprehension of Legrand;—for myself, I should have rejoiced at any interruption which might have enabled me to get the wanderer home. The noise was, at length, very effectually silenced by Jupiter, who, getting out of the hole with a dogged air of deliberation, tied the brute's mouth up with one of his suspenders, and then returned, with a grave chuckle, to his task.

When the time mentioned had expired, we had reached a depth of five feet, and yet no signs of any treasure became manifest. A general pause ensued, and I began to hope that the farce was at an end. Legrand, however, although evidently much disconcerted, wiped his brow thoughtfully and recommenced. We had excavated the entire circle of four feet diameter, and now we slightly enlarged the limit, and went to the farther depth of two feet. Still nothing appeared. The gold-seeker, whom I sincerely pitied, at length clambered from the pit, with the bitterest disappointment imprinted upon every feature, and proceeded, slowly and reluctantly, to put on his coat, which he had thrown off at the beginning of his labor. In the mean time I made no remark. Jupiter, at a signal from his master, began to gather up his tools. This done, and the dog having been unmuzzled, we turned in profound silence towards home.

We had taken, perhaps, a dozen steps in this direction, when, with a loud oath, Legrand strode up to Jupiter, and seized him by the collar. The astonished negro opened his eyes and mouth to the fullest extent, let fall the spades, and fell upon his knees.

"You scoundrel," said Legrand, hissing out the syllables from between his clenched teeth—"you infernal black villain!—speak, I tell you!—answer me this instant, without prevarication!—which—which is your left eye?"

"Oh, my golly, Massa Will! aint dis here my lef eye for sartain?" roared the terrified Jupiter, placing his hand upon his *right* organ of vision, and holding it there with a desperate pertinacity, as if in immediate dread of his master's attempt at a gouge.

"I thought so!—I knew it! hurrah!" vociferated Legrand, letting the negro go, and executing a series of curvets and caracols, much to the astonishment of his valet, who, arising from his knees, looked, mutely, from his master to myself, and then from myself to his master.

"Come! we must go back," said the latter, "the game 's not up yet;" and he again led the way to the tulip-tree.

"Jupiter," said he, when we reached its foot, "come here! was the skull nailed to the limb with the face outwards, or with the face to the limb?"

"De face was out, massa, so dat de crows could get at de eyes good, widout any trouble."

"Well, then, was it this eye or that through which you dropped the beetle?"—here Legrand touched each of Jupiter's eyes.

"Twas dis eye, massa—de lef eye—jis as you tell me," and here it was his right eye that the negro indicated.

"That will do—we must try it again."

Here my friend, about whose madness I now saw, or fancied that I saw, certain indications of method, removed the peg which marked the spot where the beetle fell, to a spot about three inches to the westward of its former position. Taking, now, the tape-measure from the nearest point of the trunk to the peg, as before, and continuing the extension in a straight line to the distance of fifty feet, a spot was indicated, removed, by several yards, from the point at which we had been digging.

Around the new position a circle, somewhat larger than in the former instance, was now described, and we again set to work with the spades. I was dreadfully weary, but, scarcely understanding what had occasioned the change in my thoughts, I felt no longer any great aversion from the labor imposed. I had become most unaccountably interested—nay, even excited. Perhaps there was something, amid all the extravagant demeanor of Legrand—some air of forethought, or of deliberation, which impressed me. I dug eagerly, and now and then caught myself actually looking, with something that very much resembled expectation, for the fancied treasure, the vision of which had demented my unfortunate companion. At a period when such vagaries of thought most fully possessed me, and when we had been at work perhaps an hour and a half, we were again interrupted by the violent howlings of the dog. His uneasiness, in the first instance, had been, evidently, but the result of playfulness or caprice, but he now assumed a bitter and serious tone. Upon Jupiter's again attempting to muzzle him, he made furious resistance, and, leaping into the hole, tore up the mould frantically with his claws. In a few seconds he had uncovered a mass of human bones, forming two complete skeletons, intermingled with several buttons of metal, and what appeared to be the dust of decayed woollen. One or two strokes of a spade upturned the blade of a large Spanish knife, and, as we dug farther, three or four loose pieces of gold and silver coin came to light.

At sight of these the joy of Jupiter could scarcely be restrained, but the countenance of his master wore an air of extreme disappointment. He urged us, however, to continue our exertions, and the words were hardly uttered when I stumbled and fell forward, having caught the toe of my boot in a large ring of iron that lay half buried in the loose earth.

We now worked in earnest, and never did I pass ten minutes of more intense excitement. During this interval we had fairly unearthed an oblong chest of wood, which, from its perfect preservation and wonderful hardness, had plainly been subjected to some mineralizing process—perhaps that of the Bi-chloride of Mercury. This box was three feet and a half long, three feet broad, and two and a half feet deep. It was firmly secured by bands of wrought iron, riveted, and forming a kind of open trellis-work over the whole. On each side of the chest, near the top, were three rings of iron—six in all—by means of which a firm hold could be obtained by six persons. Our utmost united endeavors served only to disturb the coffer very slightly in its bed. We at once saw the impossibility of removing so great a weight. Luckily, the sole fastenings of the lid consisted of two sliding bolts. These we drew back—trembling and panting with anxiety. In an instant, a treasure of incalculable value lay gleaming before us. As the rays of the lanterns fell within the pit, there flashed upwards a glow and a glare, from a confused heap of gold and of jewels, that absolutely dazzled our eyes.

I shall not pretend to describe the feelings with which I gazed. Amazement was, of course, predominant. Legrand appeared exhausted with excitement, and spoke very few words. Jupiter's countenance wore, for some minutes, as deadly a pallor as it is possible, in the nature of things, for any negro's visage to assume. He seemed stupified—thunderstricken. Presently he fell upon his knees in the pit, and, burying his naked arms up to the elbows in gold, let them there remain, as if enjoying the luxury of a bath. At length, with a deep sigh, he exclaimed, as if in a soliloquy,

"And dis all cum ob de goole-bug! de putty goole-bug! de poor little goole-bug, what I boosed in dat sabage kind ob style! Aint you shamed ob yourself, nigger?—answer me dat!"

It became necessary, at last, that I should arouse both master and valet to the expediency of removing the treasure. It was growing late, and it behooved us to make exertion, that we might get every thing housed before daylight. It was difficult to say what should be done, and much time was spent in deliberation—so confused were the ideas of all. We, finally, lightened the box by removing two thirds of its contents, when we were enabled, with some trouble, to raise it from the hole. The articles taken out were deposited among the brambles, and the dog left to guard them, with strict orders from Jupiter neither, upon any pretence, to stir from the spot, nor to open his mouth until our return. We then hurriedly made for home with the chest; reaching the hut in safety, but after excessive toil, at one o'clock in the morning. Worn out as we were, it was not in human nature to do more immediately. We rested until two, and had supper; starting for the hills immediately afterwards, armed with three stout sacks, which, by good luck, were upon the premises. A little before four we arrived at the pit, divided the remainder of the booty, as equally as might be, among us, and, leaving the holes unfilled, again set out for the hut, at which, for the second time, we deposited our golden burthens, just as the first faint streaks of the dawn gleamed from over the tree-tops in the East.

We were now thoroughly broken down; but the intense excitement of the time denied us repose. After an unquiet slumber of some three or four hours' duration, we arose, as if by preconcert, to make examination of our treasure.

The chest had been full to the brim, and we spent the whole day, and the greater part of the next night, in a scrutiny of its contents. There had been nothing like order or arrangement. Every thing had been heaped in promiscuously. Having assorted all with care, we found ourselves possessed of even vaster wealth than we had at first supposed. In coin there was rather more than four hundred and fifty thousand dollars—estimating the value of the pieces, as accurately as we could, by the tables of the period. There was not a particle of silver. All was gold of antique date and of great variety

—French, Spanish, and German money, with a few English guineas, and some counters, of which we had never seen specimens before. There were several very large and heavy coins, so worn that we could make nothing of their inscriptions. There was no American money. The value of the jewels we found more difficulty in estimating. There were diamonds—some of them exceedingly large and fine—a hundred and ten in all, and not one of them small; eighteen rubies of remarkable brilliancy;—three hundred and ten emeralds, all very beautiful; and twenty-one sapphires, with an opal. These stones had all been broken from their settings and thrown loose in the chest. The settings themselves, which we picked out from among the other gold, appeared to have been beaten up with hammers, as if to prevent identification. Besides all this, there was a vast quantity of solid gold ornaments;—nearly two hundred massive finger and ear rings;—rich chains —thirty of these, if I remember;—eighty-three very large and heavy crucifixes;—five gold censers of great value;—a prodigious golden punch-bowl, ornamented with richly chased vine-leaves and Bacchanalian figures; with two sword-handles exquisitely embossed, and many other smaller articles which I cannot recollect. The weight of these valuables exceeded three hundred and fifty pounds avoirdupois; and in this estimate I have not included one hundred and ninety-seven superb gold watches; three of the number being worth each five hundred dollars, if one. Many of them were very old, and as time keepers valueless; the works having suffered, more or less, from corrosion—but all were richly jewelled and in cases of great worth. We estimated the entire contents of the chest, that night, at a million and a half of dollars; and, upon the subsequent disposal of the trinkets and jewels (a few being retained for our own use), it was found that we had greatly undervalued the treasure.

When, at length, we had concluded our examination, and the intense excitement of the time had, in some measure, subsided, Legrand, who saw that I was dying with impatience for a solution of this most extraordinary riddle, entered into a full detail of all the circumstances connected with it.

"You remember," said he, "the night when I handed you the rough sketch I had made of the *scarabæus*. You recollect also, that I became quite vexed at you for insisting that my drawing resembled a death's-head. When you first made this assertion I thought you were jesting; but afterwards I called to mind the peculiar spots on the back of the insect, and admitted to myself that your remark had some little foundation in fact. Still, the sneer at my graphic powers irritated me—for I am considered a good artist—and, therefore, when you handed me the scrap of parchment, I was about to crumple it up and throw it angrily into the fire."

"The scrap of paper, you mean," said I.

"No; it had much of the appearance of paper, and at first I supposed it to be such, but when I came to draw upon it, I discovered it, at once, to be a piece of very thin parchment. It was quite dirty, you remember. Well, as I was in the very act of crumpling it up, my glance fell upon the sketch at which you had been looking, and you may imagine my astonishment when I perceived, in fact, the figure of a death's-head just where, it seemed to me, I had made the drawing of the beetle. For a moment I was too much amazed to think with accuracy. I knew that my design was very different in detail from this—although there was a certain similarity in general outline. Presently I took a candle, and seating myself at the other end of the room, proceeded to scrutinize the parchment more closely. Upon turning it over, I saw my own sketch upon the reverse, just as I had made it. My first idea, now, was mere surprise at the really remarkable similarity of outline— at the singular coincidence involved in the fact, that unknown to me, there should have been a skull upon the other side of the parchment, immediately beneath my figure of the *scarabæus,* and that this skull, not only in outline, but in size, should so closely resemble my drawing. I say the singularity of this coincidence absolutely stupified me for a time. This is the usual effect of such coincidences. The mind struggles to establish a connexion—a sequence of cause and effect—and, being unable to do so, suffers a species of temporary paralysis. But, when I recovered from this stupor, there dawned upon me gradually a conviction which startled me even far more than the coincidence. I began distinctly, positively, to remember that there had been *no* drawing upon the parchment when I made my sketch of the *scarabæus.* I became perfectly certain of this; for I recollected turning up first one side and then the other, in search of the cleanest spot. Had the skull been then there, of course I could not have failed to notice it. Here was indeed a mystery which I felt it impossible to explain; but, even at that early moment, there seemed to glimmer, faintly, within the most remote and secret chambers of my intellect, a glow-worm-like conception of that truth which last night's adventure brought to so magnificent a demonstration. I arose at once, and putting the parchment securely away, dismissed all farther reflection until I should be alone.

"When you had gone, and when Jupiter was fast asleep, I betook myself to a more methodical investigation of the affair. In the first place I considered the manner in which the parchment had come into my possession. The spot where we discovered the *scarabæus* was on the coast of the main land, about a mile eastward of the island, and but a short distance above high water mark. Upon my taking hold of it, it gave me a sharp bite, which caused me to let it drop. Jupiter, with his accustomed caution, before seizing the insect, which had flown towards him, looked about him

for a leaf, or something of that nature, by which to take hold of it. It was
at this moment that his eyes, and mine also, fell upon the scrap of parchment, which I then supposed to be paper. It was lying half buried in the
sand, a corner sticking up. Near the spot where we found it, I observed the
remnants of the hull of what appeared to have been a ship's long boat. The
wreck seemed to have been there for a very great while; for the resemblance to boat timbers could scarcely be traced.

"Well, Jupiter picked up the parchment, wrapped the beetle in it, and
gave it to me. Soon afterwards we turned to go home, and on the way met
Lieutenant G——. I showed him the insect, and he begged me to let him
take it to the fort. Upon my consenting, he thrust it forthwith into his
waistcoat pocket, without the parchment in which it had been wrapped,
and which I had continued to hold in my hand during his inspection. Perhaps
he dreaded my changing my mind, and thought it best to make sure of
the prize at once—you know how enthusiastic he is on all subjects connected with Natural History. At the same time, without being conscious
of it, I must have deposited the parchment in my own pocket.

"You remember that when I went to the table, for the purpose of
making a sketch of the beetle, I found no paper where it was usually kept.
I looked in the drawer, and found none there. I searched my pockets, hoping to find an old letter, when my hand fell upon the parchment. I thus
detail the precise mode in which it came into my possession; for the circumstances impressed me with peculiar force.

"No doubt you will think me fanciful—but I had already established
a kind of *connexion,* I had put together two links of a great chain. There
was a boat lying upon a sea-coast, and not far from the boat was a parchment—*not a paper*—with a skull depicted upon it. You will, of course,
ask 'where is the connection?' I reply that the skull, or death's-head, is
the well-known emblem of the pirate. The flag of the death's-head is hoisted
in all engagements.

"I have said that the scrap was parchment, and not paper. Parchment
is durable—almost imperishable. Matters of little moment are rarely consigned to parchment; since, for the mere ordinary purposes of drawing or
writing, it is not nearly so well adapted as paper. This reflection suggested
some meaning—some relevancy—in the death's-head. I did not fail to
observe, also, the *form* of the parchment. Although one of its corners had
been, by some accident, destroyed, it could be seen that the original form
was oblong. It was just such a slip, indeed, as might have been chosen
for a memorandum—for a record of something to be long remembered and
carefully preserved."

"But," I interposed, "you say that the skull was *not* upon the parchment when you made the drawing of the beetle. How then do you trace

any connexion between the boat and the skull—since this latter, according to your own admission, must have been designed (God only knows how or by whom) at some period subsequent to your sketching the *scarabœus?*"

"Ah, hereupon turns the whole mystery; although the secret, at this point, I had comparatively little difficulty in solving. My steps were sure, and could afford but a single result. I reasoned, for example, thus: When I drew the *scarabœus*, there was no skull apparent upon the parchment. When I had completed the drawing 1 gave it to you, and observed you narrowly until you returned it. *You,* therefore, did not design the skull, and no one else was present to do it. Then it was not done by human agency. And nevertheless it was done.

"At this stage of my reflections I endeavored to remember, and *did* remember, with entire distinctness, every incident which occurred about the period in question. The weather was chilly (oh rare and happy accident!), and a fire was blazing upon the hearth. I was heated with exercise and sat near the table. You, however, had drawn a chair close to the chimney. Just as I placed the parchment in your hand, and as you were in the act of inspecting it, Wolf, the Newfoundland, entered, and leaped upon your shoulders. With your left hand you caressed him and kept him off, while your right, holding the parchment, was permitted to fall listlessly between your knees, and in close proximity to the fire. At one moment I thought the blaze had caught it, and was about to caution you, but, before I could speak, you had withdrawn it, and were engaged in its examination. When I considered all these particulars, I doubted not for a moment that *heat* had been the agent in bringing to light, upon the parchment, the skull which I saw designed upon it. You are well aware that chemical preparations exist, and have existed time out of mind, by means of which it is possible to write upon either paper or vellum, so that the characters shall become visible only when subjected to the action of fire. Zaffre, digested in *aqua regia*, and diluted with four times its weight of water, is sometimes employed; a green tint results. The regulus of cobalt, dissolved in spirit of nitre, gives a red. These colors disappear at longer or shorter intervals after the material written upon cools, but again become apparent upon the reapplication of heat.

"I now scrutinized the death's-head with care. Its outer edges—the edges of the drawing nearest the edge of the vellum—were far more *distinct* than the others. It was clear that the action of the caloric had been imperfect or unequal. I immediately kindled a fire, and subjected every portion of the parchment to a glowing heat. At first, the only effect was the strengthening of the faint lines in the skull; but, upon persevering in the experiment, there became visible, at the corner of the slip, diagonally opposite to the spot in which the death's-head was delineated, the figure of what I at first supposed to be a goat. A closer scrutiny, however, satisfied me that it was intended for a kid."

"Ha! ha!" said I, "to be sure I have no right to laugh at you—a million and a half of money is too serious a matter for mirth—but you are not about to establish a third link in your chain—you will not find any especial connexion between your pirates and a goat—pirates, you know, have nothing to do with goats; they appertain to the farming interest."

"But I have just said that the figure was *not* that of a goat."

"Well, a kid then—pretty much the same thing."

"Pretty much, but not altogether," said Legrand. "You may have heard of one *Captain* Kidd. I at once looked upon the figure of the animal as a kind of punning or hieroglyphical signature. I say signature; because its position upon the vellum suggested this idea. The death's-head at the corner diagonally opposite, had, in the same manner, the air of a stamp, or seal. But I was sorely put out by the absence of all else—of the body to my imagined instrument—of the text for my context."

"I presume you expected to find a letter between the stamp and the signature."

"Something of that kind. The fact is, I felt irresistibly impressed with a presentiment of some vast good fortune impending. I can scarcely say why. Perhaps, after all, it was rather a desire than an actual belief;—but do you know that Jupiter's silly words, about the bug being of solid gold, had a remarkable effect upon my fancy? And then the series of accidents and coincidences—these were so *very* extraordinary. Do you observe how mere an accident it was that these events should have occurred upon the *sole* day of all the year on which it has been, or may be, sufficiently cool for fire, and that without the fire, or without the intervention of the dog at the precise moment in which he appeared, I should never have become aware of the death's-head, and so never the possessor of the treasure?"

"But proceed—I am all impatience."

"Well; you have heard, of course, the many stories current—the thousand vague rumors afloat about money buried, somewhere upon the Atlantic coast, by Kidd and his associates. These rumors must have had some foundation in fact. And that the rumors have existed so long and so continuous, could have resulted, it appeared to me, only from the circumstance of the buried treasure still *remaining* entombed. Had Kidd concealed his plunder for a time, and afterwards reclaimed it, the rumors would scarcely have reached us in their present unvarying form. You will observe that the stories told are all about money-seekers, not about money-finders. Had the pirate recovered his money, there the affair would have dropped. It seemed to me that some accident—say the loss of a memorandum indicating its locality— had deprived him of the means of recovering it, and that this accident had become known to his followers, who otherwise might never have heard that treasure had been concealed at all, and who, busying themselves in vain, because unguided attempts, to regain it, had given first birth, and then universal currency, to the reports which are now so common. Have you ever heard of any important treasure being unearthed along the coast?"

"Never."

"But that Kidd's accumulations were immense, is well known. I took it for granted, therefore, that the earth still held them; and you will scarcely be surprised when I tell you that I felt a hope, nearly amounting to certainty, that the parchment so strangely found, involved a lost record of the place of deposit."

"But how did you proceed?"

"I held the vellum again to the fire, after increasing the heat; but nothing appeared. I now thought it possible that the coating of dirt might have something to do with the failure; so I carefully rinsed the parchment by pouring warm water over it, and, having done this, I placed it in a tin pan, with the skull downwards, and put the pan upon a furnace of lighted charcoal. In a few minutes, the pan having become thoroughly heated, I removed the slip, and, to my inexpressible joy, found it spotted, in several places, with what appeared to be figures arranged in lines. Again I placed it in the pan, and suffered it to remain another minute. Upon taking it off, the whole was just as you see it now."

Here Legrand, having re-heated the parchment, submitted it to my inspection. The following characters were rudely traced, in a red tint, between the death's-head and the goat:

53‡‡†305))6*;4826)4‡.)4‡);806*;48†8¶60))85;1‡(;:‡*8†83(88)5*†; 46(;88*96*?;8)*‡(;485);5*†2:*‡(;4956*2(5*—4)8¶8*;4069285);)6†8) 4‡‡;1(‡9;48081;8:8‡1;48†85;4)485†528806*81(‡9;48;(88;4(‡?34;48)4 ‡;161;:188;‡?;

"But," said I, returning him the slip, "I am as much in the dark as ever. Were all the jewels of Golconda awaiting me upon my solution of this enigma, I am quite sure that I should be unable to earn them."

"And yet," said Legrand, "the solution is by no means so difficult as you might be led to imagine from the first hasty inspection of the characters. These characters, as any one might readily guess, form a cipher—that is to say, they convey a meaning; but then, from what is known of Kidd, I could not suppose him capable of constructing any of the more abstruse cryptographs. I made up my mind, at once, that this was of a simple species —such, however, as would appear, to the crude intellect of the sailor, absolutely insoluble without the key."

"And you really solved it?"

"Readily; I have solved others of an abstruseness ten thousand times greater. Circumstances, and a certain bias of mind, have led me to take interest in such riddles, and it may well be doubted whether human ingenuity can construct an enigma of the kind which human ingenuity may not, by proper application, resolve. In fact, having once established connected and legible characters, I scarcely gave a thought to the mere difficulty of developing their import.

"In the present case—indeed in all cases of secret writing—the first question regards the *language* of the cipher; for the principles of solution, so far, especially, as the more simple ciphers are concerned, depend upon, and are varied by, the genius of the particular idiom. In general, there is no alternative but experiment (directed by probabilities) of every tongue known to him who attempts the solution, until the true one be attained. But, with the cipher now before us, all difficulty was removed by the signature. The pun upon the word 'Kidd' is appreciable in no other language than the English. But for this consideration I should have begun my attempts with the Spanish and French, as the tongues in which a secret of this kind would most naturally have been written by a pirate of the Spanish main. As it was, I assumed the cryptograph to be English.

"You observe there are no divisions between the words. Had there been divisions, the task would have been comparatively easy. In such case I should have commenced with a collation and analysis of the shorter words, and, had a word of a single letter occurred, as is most likely, (*a* or *I*, for example,) I should have considered the solution as assured. But, there being no division, my first step was to ascertain the predominant letters, as well as the least frequent. Counting all, I constructed a table, thus:

Of the character 8 there are 33.

;	"	26.
4	"	19.
‡)	"	16.
*	"	13.
5	"	12.
6	"	11.
†1	"	8.
0	"	6.
9 2	"	5.
:3	"	4.
?	"	3.
¶	"	2.
—.	"	1.

"Now, in English, the letter which most frequently occurs is *e*. Afterwards, the succession runs thus: *a o i d h n r s t u y c f g l m w b k p q x z*.

E predominates so remarkably that an individual sentence of any length is rarely seen, in which it is not the prevailing character.

"Here, then, we have, in the very beginning, the groundwork for something more than a mere guess. The general use which may be made of the table is obvious—but, in this particular cipher, we shall only very partially require its aid. As our predominant character is 8, we will commence by assuming it as the *e* of the natural alphabet. To verify the supposition, let us observe if the 8 be seen often in couples—for *e* is doubled with great frequency in English—in such words, for example, as 'meet,' 'fleet,' 'speed,' 'seen,' 'been,' 'agree,' &c. In the present instance we see it doubled no less than five times, although the cryptograph is brief.

"Let us assume 8, then, as *e*. Now, of all *words* in the language, 'the' is most usual; let us see, therefore, whether there are not repetitions of any three characters, in the same order of collocation, the last of them being 8. If we discover repetitions of such letters, so arranged, they will most probably represent the word 'the.' Upon inspection, we find no less than seven such arrangements, the characters being ;18. We may, therefore, assume that ; represents *t*, 4 represents *h*, and 8 represents *e*—the last being now well confirmed. Thus a great step has been taken.

"But, having established a single word, we are enabled to establish a vastly important point; that is to say, several commencements and terminations of other words. Let us refer, for example, to the last instance but one, in which the combination ;48 occurs—not far from the end of the cipher. We know that the ; immediately ensuing is the commencement of a word, and, of the six characters succeeding this 'the,' we are cognizant of no less than five. Let us set these characters down, thus, by the letters we know them to represent, leaving a space for the unknown—

t eeth.

"Here we are enabled, at once, to discard the *'th,'* as forming no portion of the word commencing with the first *t;* since, by experiment of the entire alphabet for a letter adapted to the vacancy, we perceive that no word can be formed of which this *th* can be a part. We are thus narrowed into

t ee,

and, going through the alphabet, if necessary, as before, we arrive at the word 'tree,' as the sole possible reading. We thus gain another letter, *r*, represented by (, with the words 'the tree' in juxtaposition.

"Looking beyond these words, for a short distance, we again see the combination ;48, and employ it by way of *termination* to what immediately precedes. We have thus this arrangement:

the tree ;4(‡?34 the,

or, substituting the natural letters, where known, it reads thus:

the tree thr‡?3h the.

"Now, if, in place of the unknown characters, we leave blank spaces, or substitute dots, we read thus:

the tree thr. . . h the,

when the word *'through'* makes itself evident at once. But this discovery gives us three new letters, *o, u* and *g,* represented by ‡ ? and 3.

"Looking now, narrowly, through the cipher for combinations of known characters, we find, not very far from the beginning, this arrangement,

83(88, or egree,

which, plainly, is the conclusion of the word 'degree,' and gives us another letter, *d,* represented by †.

"Four letters beyond the word 'degree,' we perceive the combination

;48(;88.

"Translating the known characters, and representing the unknown by dots, as before, we read thus:

th rtee.

an arrangement immediately suggestive of the word 'thirteen,' and again furnishing us with two new characters, *i* and *n,* represented by 6 and *.

"Referring, now, to the beginning of the cryptograph, we find the combination,

53‡‡†.

"Translating, as before, we obtain

. good,

which assures us that the first letter is *A,* and that the first two words are 'A good.'

"It is now time that we arrange our key, as far as discovered, in a tabular form, to avoid confusion. It will stand thus:

5	represents	a
†	"	d
8	"	e
3	"	g
4	"	h
6	"	i
*	"	n
‡	"	o
(	"	r
;	"	t

"We have, therefore, no less than ten of the most important letters represented, and it will be unnecessary to proceed with the details of the solution. I have said enough to convince you that ciphers of this nature are readily soluble, and to give you some insight into the *rationale* of their development. But be assured that the specimen before us appertains to the very simplest species of cryptograph. It now only remains to give you the full translation of the characters upon the parchment, as unriddled. Here it is:

'A good glass in the bishop's hostel in the devil's seat forty-one degrees and thirteen minutes northeast and by north main branch seventh limb east side shoot from the left eye of the death's-head a bee line from the tree through the shot fifty feet out.' "

"But," said I, "the enigma seems still in as bad a condition as ever. How is it possible to extort a meaning from all this jargon about 'devil's seats,' 'death's-heads,' and 'bishop's hotels?' "

"I confess," replied Legrand, "that the matter still wears a serious aspect, when regarded with a casual glance. My first endeavor was to divide the sentence into the natural division intended by the cryptographist."

"You mean, to punctuate it?"

"Something of that kind."

"But how was it possible to effect this?"

"I reflected that it had been a *point* with the writer to run his words together without division, so as to increase the difficulty of solution. Now, a not over-acute man, in pursuing such an object, would be nearly certain to overdo the matter. When, in the course of his composition, he arrived at a break in his subject which would naturally require a pause, or a point, he would be exceedingly apt to run his characters, at this place, more than usually close together. If you will observe the MS., in the present instance, you will easily detect five such cases of unusual crowding. Acting upon this hint, I made the division thus:

'A good glass in the Bishop's hostel in the Devil's seat—forty-one degrees and thirteen minutes—northeast and by north—main branch seventh limb east side—shoot from the left eye of the death's-head—a bee-line from the tree through the shot fifty feet out.' "

"Even this division," said I, "leaves me still in the dark."

"It left me also in the dark," replied Legrand, "for a few days; during which I made diligent inquiry, in the neighborhood of Sullivan's Island, for any building which went by the name of the 'Bishop's Hotel;' for, of course, I dropped the obsolete word 'hostel.' Gaining no information on the subject, I was on the point of extending my sphere of search, and proceeding in a more systematic manner, when, one morning, it entered into my head, quite suddenly, that this 'Bishop's Hostel' might have some reference to an old family, of the name of Bessop, which, time out of mind, had held possession of an ancient manor-house, about four miles to the northward of the Island. I accordingly went over to the plantation, and reinstituted my inquiries among the older negroes of the place. At length one of the most aged of the women said that she had heard of such a place as *Bessop's Castle,* and thought that she could guide me to it, but that it was not a castle, nor a tavern, but a high rock.

"I offered to pay her well for her trouble, and, after some demur, she consented to accompany me to the spot. We found it without much difficulty, when, dismissing her, I proceeded to examine the place. The 'castle' consisted of an irregular assemblage of cliffs and rocks—one of the latter being quite remarkable for its height as well as for its insulated and artificial appearance. I clambered to its apex, and then felt much at a loss as to what should be next done.

"While I was busied in reflection, my eyes fell upon a narrow ledge in the eastern face of the rock, perhaps a yard below the summit upon which I stood. This ledge projected about eighteen inches, and was not more than a foot wide, while a niche in the cliff just above it, gave it a rude resemblance to one of the hollow-backed chairs used by our ancestors. I made no doubt that here was the 'devil's-seat' alluded to in the MS., and now I seemed to grasp the full secret of the riddle.

"The 'good glass,' I knew, could have reference to nothing but a telescope; for the word 'glass' is rarely employed in any other sense by seamen. Now here, I at once saw, was a telescope to be used, and a definite point of view, *admitting no variation,* from which to use it. Nor did I hesitate to believe that the phrases, 'forty-one degrees and thirteen minutes,' and 'northeast and by north,' were intended as directions for the levelling of the glass. Greatly excited by these discoveries, I hurried home, procured a telescope, and returned to the rock.

"I let myself down to the ledge, and found that it was impossible to retain a seat upon it except in one particular position. This fact confirmed my preconceived idea. I proceeded to use the glass. Of course, the 'forty-one degrees and thirteen minutes' could allude to nothing but elevation above the visible horizon, since the horizontal direction was clearly indicated by the words, 'northeast and by north.' This latter direction I at once established by means of a pocket-compass; then, pointing the glass as nearly at an angle of forty-one degrees of elevation as I could do it by guess, I moved it cautiously up or down, until my attention was arrested by a circular rift or opening in the foliage of a large tree that overtopped its fellows in the distance. In the centre of this rift I perceived a white spot, but could not, at first, distinguish what it was. Adjusting the focus of the telescope, I again looked, and now made it out to be a human skull.

"Upon this discovery I was so sanguine as to consider the enigma solved; for the phrase 'main branch, seventh limb, east side,' could refer only to the position of the skull upon the tree, while 'shoot from the left eye of the death's-head' admitted, also, of but one interpretation, in regard to a search for buried treasure. I perceived that the design was to drop a bullet from the left eye of the skull, and that a bee-line, or, in other words, a straight line, drawn from the nearest point of the trunk through 'the shot,' (or the spot where the bullet fell,) and thence extended to a distance of fifty feet, would indicate a definite point—and beneath this point I thought it at least *possible* that a deposit of value lay concealed."

"All this," I said, "is exceedingly clear, and, although ingenious, still simple and explicit. When you left the Bishop's Hotel, what then?"

"Why, having carefully taken the bearings of the tree, I turned homewards. The instant that I left 'the devil's seat,' however, the circular rift vanished; nor could I get a glimpse of it afterwards, turn as I would. What seems to me the chief ingenuity in this whole business, is the fact (for repeated experiment has convinced me it *is* a fact) that the circular opening in question is visible from no other attainable point of view than that afforded by the narrow ledge upon the face of the rock.

"In this expedition to the 'Bishop's Hotel' I had been attended by Jupiter, who had, no doubt, observed, for some weeks past, the abstraction of my demeanor, and took especial care not to leave me alone. But, on the next day, getting up very early, I contrived to give him the slip, and went into the hills in search of the tree. After much toil I found it. When I came home at night my valet proposed to give me a flogging. With the rest of the adventure I believe you are as well acquainted as myself."

"I suppose," said I, "you missed the spot, in the first attempt at digging, through Jupiter's stupidity in letting the bug fall through the right instead of through the left eye of the skull."

"Precisely. This mistake made a difference of about two inches and a half in the 'shot'—that is to say, in the position of the peg nearest the tree; and had the treasure been *beneath* the 'shot,' the error would have been of little moment; but 'the shot,' together with the nearest point of the tree, were merely two points for the establishment of a line of direction; of course the error, however trivial in the beginning, increased as we proceeded with the line, and by the time we had gone fifty feet, threw us quite off the scent. But for my deep-seated impressions that treasure was here somewhere actually buried, we might have had all our labor in vain."

"But your grandiloquence, and your conduct in swinging the beetle—how excessively odd! I was sure you were mad. And why did you insist upon letting fall the bug, instead of a bullet, from the skull?"

"Why, to be frank, I felt somewhat annoyed by your evident suspicions touching my sanity, and so resolved to punish you quietly, in my own way, by a little bit of sober mystification. For this reason I swung the beetle, and for this reason I let it fall from the tree. An observation of yours about its great weight suggested the latter idea."

"Yes, I perceive; and now there is only one point which puzzles me. What are we to make of the skeletons found in the hole?"

"That is a question I am no more able to answer than yourself. There seems, however, only one plausible way of accounting for them—and yet it is dreadful to believe in such atrocity as my suggestion would imply. It is clear that Kidd—if Kidd indeed secreted this treasure, which I doubt not —it is clear that he must have had assistance in the labor. But this labor concluded, he may have thought it expedient to remove all participants in his secret. Perhaps a couple of blows with a mattock were sufficient, while his coadjutors were busy in the pit; perhaps it required a dozen—who shall tell?"

Augustus Baldwin Longstreet
(1790-1870)

Augustus Baldwin Longstreet was born September 22, 1790, in Augusta, Georgia—then a bustling frontier village. His father, William Longstreet, was a businessman and inventor, whom tradition says invented both a steamboat and a cotton gin, though unfortunately slightly later than their noted creators. Young Longstreet was sent to the prominent Augusta preparatory school, Richmond Academy, where his classroom antics caused the master to declare him "mad." As a result of this opprobrium, William Longstreet removed his family to a farm in South Carolina for several years. Young Longstreet never learned to like the Academy's methods or curriculum, but a boyhood friendship with an eager and intelligent young scholar —George McDuffie—kindled a love of learning and promoted assiduous study.

When Longstreet was eighteen years old he entered the school of the Reverend Dr. Moses Waddel at Willington, South Carolina, and, like many other young scholars, thrived under the tutelage of Dr. Waddel, years later recording his experiences at the rather unconventional school in his book *William Mitten*. Following the lead of his friend John C. Calhoun, Longstreet entered Yale College in 1811, and upon graduation two years later he enrolled in the Law School of Reeves and Gould at Litchfield, Connecticut. He returned to Georgia late in 1814 and began a successful law practice. Seven years after being admitted to the bar, he was made a judge of the state superior court. In 1817 Longstreet married Frances Eliza Parke from Greensboro, Georgia, where the couple resided for several years after their marriage.

It was during his years as a young lawyer riding the circuit into the more primitive areas of the state that Longstreet observed many of the events later recorded in *Georgia Scenes*. He began publishing some of these sketches of frontier life in the Milledgeville *Southern Recorder* in 1833, and then transferred the series to his own newspaper, the Augusta *State Rights*

Sentinel, of which he was editor from 1834 to 1836. In 1835 he brought the sketches together in book form—*Georgia Scenes, Characters, Incidents, &c. in the First Half Century of the Republic . . . By a Native Georgian*—issued from the press of the *State Rights Sentinel.* The book was an immediate popular success, was republished by Harper & Brothers in 1840, and enjoyed a great vogue in the North as well as in the South. It was hailed by critics for its authenticity of character and dialect and its genuine humor.

Two years after the publication of *Georgia Scenes* Longstreet was converted to Methodism and in 1838 became a Methodist minister. Perhaps because of his sense of position, from this time on he tried to emphasize the moral nature of his sketches and the fact that the book filled a gap in the state's history. In later years, Longstreet was president of colleges and universities of four Southern states, serving successively at Emory College in Georgia, Centenary College in Louisiana, the University of Mississippi, the University of South Carolina, and again at the University of Mississippi. He died in Oxford, Mississippi, on July 9, 1870.

Textual note

In the preface to the first edition of *Georgia Scenes* (Augusta, 1835), Longstreet states, "I commenced the publication of [the sketches], in one of the gazettes of the State, rather more than a year ago; and I was not more pleased than astonished, to find that they were well received by readers generally. For the last six months, I have been importuned by persons from all quarters of the State to give them to the public in the present form." Of even more textual significance is the comment he later adds: "I have not had it in my power to superintend the publication of them, though they issue from a press in the immediate vicinity of my residence. I discovered, that if the work was delayed until I could have an opportunity of examining the proof sheets, it would linger in the press, until the expenses (already large) would become intolerable. Consequently there may be many typographical errors among them, for which I must crave the reader's indulgence" ("Preface," pp. [iii]–IV).

Copy-text for "The Horse Swap" is the first periodical printing, in the Milledgeville *Southern Recorder,* November 13, 1833. Despite Longstreet's disclaimer of authority for the text of *Georgia Scenes,* there are substantive variants between its text of "The Horse Swap" and the one here made readily available for the first time.

The Horse Swap

During the session of the Superior Court, in the village of ——, about three weeks ago, when a number of people were collected in the principal street of the village, I observed a young man riding up and down the street, as I supposed, in a violent passion. He galloped this way, then that, and then the other—spurred his horse to one group of citizens, then to another —then dashed off at half speed, as if fleeing from danger, and suddenly checking his horse, returned—now in a pace, now in a trot, and again in a canter. While he was performing these various evolutions, he cursed, swore, whooped, screamed, and tossed himself in every attitude which man could assume on horse-back.—In short, he *cavorted* most magnanimously, (a term which, in the Georgia dialect, expresses all that I have described, and a little more) and seemed to be setting all creation at defiance. As I like to see all that is passing, I determined to take a position a little nearer to him, and to ascertain, if possible, what it was that affected him so sensibly. Accordingly I approached a crowd before which he had stopt for a moment, and examined it with the strictest scrutiny. But I could see nothing in it, that seemed to have any thing to do with the cavorter. Every man appeared to be in a good humor, and all minding their own business. Not one so much as noticed the principal figure. Still he went on. After a semicolon pause, which my appearance seemed to produce, (for he eyed me closely as I approached) he fetched a whoop, and swore that "he could out-swap any live man, woman or child, that ever walked these hills, or that ever straddled horse flesh since the days of old daddy Adam." "Stranger," said he to me, "did you ever see the *Yallow* Blossom from Jasper?" "No," said I, "but I have often heard of him." "I'm the boy," continued he; "perhaps a *leetle*—jist a *leetle* of the best man, at a horse swap, that ever trod shoe-leather."

I began to feel my situation a little awkward, when I was relieved by a man somewhat advanced in years, who stept up and began to survey the "*Yallow Blossom's*" horse with much apparent interest. This drew the rider's attention, and he turned the conversation from me to the stranger. "Well, my old coon," said he, "do you want to swap *hosses!*" "Why, I don't know," replied the stranger; "I believe I've got a beast I'd trade with you for that one, if you like him." "Well, fetch up your nag, my old cock; you're jist the lark I wanted to get hold of. I am perhaps a *leetle*, jist a *leetle*, of the best man at a horse swap, that ever stole *cracklins* out of his mammy's fat gourd. Where's your *hoss?*" "I'll bring him presently; but I want to examine your horse a little."

"Oh! look at him," said the Blossom, alighting and hitting him a cut— "look at him. He's the best piece of *hoss* flesh in the thirteen united universal worlds. There's no sort o' mistake in little Bullet. He can pick up miles on his feet and fling 'em behind him as fast as the next man's *hoss*, I don't care where he comes from. And he can keep at it as long as the Sun can shine without resting."

During this harangue, little Bullet looked as if he understood it all, and believed it, and was ready at any moment to make it all good. He was a horse of goodly countenance, rather expressive of vigilance than fire; though an unnatural appearance of fierceness was thrown into it, by the loss of his ears, which had been cropt pretty close to his head and neck; but he managed, in a great measure, to hide their defects, by bowing perpetually. He had obviously suffered severely for corn; but if his ribs and hip bones had not disclosed the fact, *he* never would have done it; for he was in all respects, as cheerful and happy, as if he commanded all the corn-cribs and fodder stacks in Georgia. His height was about twelve hands; but as his shape partook somewhat of that of the Giraffe, his rump stood much lower. This was short, strait, peaked, and concave on both sides. Bullet's tail, however, made amends for all his defects. All that the artist could do to beautify it, had been done; and all that horse could do to compliment the artist, Bullet did. His tail was nicked in superior style, and exhibited the line of beauty in so many directions, that it could not fail to hit the most fastidious taste in some of them. From the root it dropt into a graceful festoon; then rose in a handsome curve; then resumed its first direction; and then mounted suddenly upwards like a cypress knee to a perpendicular of about two and a half inches. The whole had a careless and bewitching inclination to the right. Bullet obviously knew where his beauty lay, and took all occasions to display it to the best advantage. If a stick cracked, or if any one moved suddenly about him, or coughed, or hawked, or spoke a little louder than common, up went Bullet's tail like lightning; and if the going up did not please, the coming down must of necessity, for it was as different from the other movement as was its direction. The first was a bold and rapid flight upward, usually to an angle of forty-five degrees. In this position he kept his interesting appendage until he satisfied himself that nothing in particular was to be done, when he commenced dropping it by half inches, in second beats—then in triple time—then faster and shorter, and faster and shorter still, until it finally died away imperceptibly into its natural position. If I might compare sights to sounds, I should say its *settling* was more like the note of a locust than any thing else in nature.

Either from native sprightliness of disposition, from uncontrolable activity, or from an unconquerable habit of removing flies by the stamping of the feet, Bullet never stood still; but always kept up a gentle fly-scaring movement of his limbs, which was peculiarly interesting.

"I tell you, man," proceeded the Yellow Blossom, "he's the best live hoss that ever trod the grit of Georgia. Bob Smart knows the hoss. Come here, Bob, and mount this hoss and show Bullet's motions." Here, Bullet bristled up, and looked as if he had been hunting for Bob all day long, and had just found him. Bob sprang on his back—"Boo-oo-oo," said Bob, with a fluttering noise of the lips; and away went Bullet, as if in a quarter race, with all his beauties spread in handsome style.

"Now fetch him back," said Blossom. Bullet turned and came in pretty much as he went out.

"Now trot him by." Bullet reduced his tail to *"customary"*—sidled to the right and left airily, and exhibited at least three variations of trot in the short space of fifty yards.

"Make him pace." Bob commenced twitching the bridle and kicking at the same time. These inconsistent movements obviously (and most naturally) disconcerted Bullet; for it was impossible for him to learn, from them, whether he was to proceed or stand still.—He started to trot—and was told that wouldn't do. He attempted a canter—and was checked again. He stopt —and was urged to go on. Bullet now rushed into the wide field of experiment, and struck out a gait of his own, that completely turned the tables upon his rider, and certainly deserved a patent. It seemed to have derived its elements from the jig, the minuet and the cotillon. If it was not a pace, it certainly had *pace* in it; and no man would venture to call it any thing else; so it passed off to the satisfaction of the owner.

"Walk him." Bullet was now at home again; and he walked as if money was staked on him.

The stranger, whose name I afterwards learned was Peter Ketch, having examined Bullet to his heart's content, ordered his son Neddy to go and bring up Kit.—Neddy soon appeared upon Kit—a well formed sorrel, of the middle size, and in good order. His *tout ensemble* threw Bullet entirely in the shade, though a glance was sufficient to satisfy any one, that Bullet had the decided advantage of him in point of intellect.

"Why man," said Blossom, "do you bring such a hoss as that to trade for Bullet? Oh! I see you're no notion of trading."

"Ride him off, Neddy," said Peter. Kit put off at a handsome lope.

"Trot him back." Kit came in at a long, sweeping trot, and stopt suddenly at the crowd.

"Well," said Blossom, "let me look at him; may be he'll do to plough."

"Examine him," said Peter, taking hold of the bridle close to the mouth; "he's nothing but a tacky. He an't as pretty a horse as Bullet, I know; but he'll do. Start 'em together for a hundred and fifty mile; and if Kit an't twenty mile ahead of him at the coming out, any man may take Kit for nothing. But he's a monstrous mean horse, gentlemen: any man may see that. He's the scariest horse, too, you ever saw. He won't do to hunt on, no how. Stranger, will you let Neddy have your rifle to shoot off him? Lay the rifle between his ears, Neddy, and shoot at the blaze in that stump. Tell me when his head is high enough."

Ned fired, and hit the blaze; and Kit did not move a hair's breadth.

"Neddy, take a couple of sticks and beat on that hogshead at Kit's tail."

Ned made a tremendous rattling, at which *Bullet* took fright, broke his bridle and dashed off in grand style; and would have stopt all farther negotiations, by going home in disgust, had not a traveller arrested him and brought him back; but Kit never moved.

"I tell you, gentlemen," continued Peter, "he's the scariest horse you ever saw. He an't as gentle as Bullet; but he won't do any harm if you watch him.—Shall I put him in a cart, gig, or wagon for you, stranger? He'll cut the same capers there he does here.—He's a monstrous mean horse."

During all this time, Blossom was examining him with the nicest scrutiny. Having examined his frame and limbs, he now looked at his eyes.

"He's got a curious look out of his eyes," said Blossom.

"Oh yes, sir," said Peter—"just as blind as a bat.—Blind horses always have clear eyes. Make a motion at his eyes, if you please, sir."

Blossom did so, and Kit threw up his head rather as if something pricked him under the chin, than as fearing a blow. Blossom repeated the experiment, and Kit jerked back in considerable astonishment.

"Stone blind, you see, gentlemen," proceeded Peter; "but he's just as good to travel of a dark night as if he had eyes."

"Blame my buttons," said Blossom, "if I like them eyes."

"No," said Peter, "nor I neither. I'd rather have 'em made of diamonds; but they'll do, if they don't show as much white as Bullet's."

"Well," said Blossom, "make a pass at me."

"No," said Peter; "you made the banter—now make your pass."

"Well I'm never afraid to price my hosses. You must give me twenty-five dollars boot."

"Oh certainly; say fifty, and my saddle and bridle in. Here, Neddy, my son, take away daddy's horse."

"Well," said Blossom, "I've made my pass; now you make yours."

"I'm for short talk in a horse swap; and therefore always tell a gentleman, at once, what I mean to do. You must give me ten dollars."

Blossom swore absolutely, roundly and profanely, that he never would give boot.

"Well," said Peter, "I didn't care about trading; but you cut such high shines, that I thought I'd like to back you out; and I've done it. Gentlemen, you see I've brought him to a hack."

"Come, old man," said Blossom, "I've been joking with you. I begin to think you do want to trade; therefore, give me five dollars and take Bullet. I'd rather lose ten dollars, any time, than not make a trade; though I hate to fling away a good hoss."

"Well," said Peter, "I'll be as clever as you are.—Just put the five dollars on Bullet's back and hand him over—it's a trade."

Blossom swore again, as roundly as before, that he would not give boot; and, said he, "Bullet wouldn't hold five dollars on his back, no how. But as I bantered you, if you say an even swap, here's at you."

"I told you," said Peter, "I'd be as clever as you; therefore, here goes two dollars more, just for trade sake. Give me three dollars, and it's a bargain."

Blossom repeated his former assertion; and here the parties stood for a long time, and the by-standers (for many were now collected,) began to taunt both parties. After some time, however, it was pretty unanimously decided that the old man had backed Blossom out.

At length Blossom swore he "never would be backed out, after bantering a man, for three dollars;" and accordingly they closed the trade.

"Now," said Blossom, as he handed Peter the three dollars, "I'm a man, that when he makes a bad trade, makes the most of it until he can make a better. I'm for no rues and after-claps."

"That's just my way," said Peter; "I never goes to law to mend my bargains."

"Ah, you're the kind of boy I love to trade with.—Here's your hoss, old man: Take the saddle and bridle off him, and I'll strip yours; but lift up the blanket easy from Bullet's back, for he's a mighty tender backed hoss."

The old man removed the saddle, but the blanket stuck fast. He attempted to raise it, and Bullet bowed himself, switched his tail, danced a little, and gave signs of biting.

"Don't hurt him, old man," said Blossom archly—"take it off easy. I am, perhaps, a leetle of the best man at a horse-swap that ever catched a coon."

Peter continued to pull at the blanket more and more roughly; and Bullet became more and more *cavortish*—in so much, that when the blanket came off, he had reached the kicking point in good earnest.

The removal of the blanket, disclosed a sore on Bullet's back-bone, that seemed to have defied all medical skill. It measured six full inches in length, and four in breadth; and had as many features as Bullet had motions. My heart sickened at the sight; and I felt that the brute who had been riding him in that situation, deserved the halter.

The prevailing feeling, however, was that of mirth. The laugh became loud and general, at the old man's expense; and rustic witticisms were liberally bestowed upon him and his late purchase. These, Blossom continued to provoke by various remarks. He asked the old man, "if he thought Bullet would let five dollars lie on his back." He declared most seriously, that he had owned that horse three months, and had never discovered before, that he had a sore back, "or he never should have thought of trading him," &c. &c.

The old man bore it all with the most philosophic composure. He evinced no astonishment at his late discovery, and made no replies. But his son, Neddy, had not disciplined his feelings quite so well. His eyes opened, wider and wider, from the first to the last pull of the blanket; and when the whole sore burst upon his view, astonishment and fright seemed to contend for the mastery of his countenance. As the blanket disappeared, he stuck his hands in his breeches pockets, heaved a deep sigh, and lapsed into a profound reverie; from which he was only roused by the cuts at his father. He bore them as long as he could; and when he could contain himself no longer, he began, with a certain wildness of expression, which gave a peculiar interest to what he uttered: "His back's mighty bad off; but dod drot my soul, if he's put it to daddy as bad as he thinks he has, for old Kit's both blind and *deef*, any how." "The devil he is," said Blossom. "Yes, dod drot my soul if he *eint*. You walk him and see if he *eint*. His eyes don't look like it; but he *jist as live go agin* the house with you, or in a ditch, as any how.—Now you go try him." The laugh was now turned on Blossom; and many rushed to test the fidelity of the little boy's report. A few experiments established the truth, beyond controversy. "Neddy," said the old man, "you oughtn't to try and make people discontented with their things." "Stranger, don't mind what the little boy says: if you can only get Kit rid of them little failings, you'll find him all sorts of a horse. You are a *leetle* the best man, at a horse swap, that ever I got hold of; but don't fool away Kit. Come, Neddy, my son, let's be moving; the stranger seems to be getting snappish."

William Elliott
(1788-1863)

William Elliott was born at Beaufort, South Carolina, into a prominent Low Country family of the planter aristocracy. He attended Harvard College, where he was at the head of his class when poor health forced him to leave at the end of his junior year. In his young manhood he began a career in politics, following the traditions of his family and class. He served in both houses of the state legislature and one term in the United States House of Representatives. Although a plantation owner and a slave-holder, Elliott opposed Nullification and secession. It was his refusal to support Nullification policies which led him to resign his seat in the state senate in 1832.

Elliott never considered literature as anything other than an avocation, appropriate to the accomplishments of a gentleman farmer but not to be pursued as a profession. His reviews show him to be a perceptive and well-read critic. Declining to give his name to anything so frivolous as poetic tragedy, he had printed anonymously in 1850 a verse drama, *Fiesco*. He did, however, acknowledge his authorship of a collection of sketches of hunting and fishing experiences brought together under the title *Carolina Sports, by Land and Water* (1846). An avid hunter and fisherman himself, Elliott captures in these sketches much of the zest and color of game pursuit. Among the *Carolina Sports* selections which had not been published previously is "The Fire Hunter," the only sketch which can properly be called a short story and one of the best pieces in the collection. Before his death in Charleston on February 3, 1863, Elliott had published one other book, *The Letters of Agricola* (1852).

Textual note

The text used here is the first edition of *Carolina Sports, by Land and Water* published by Burges and James of Charleston, South Carolina, in 1846. In his preface to the volume Elliott states that "Several of the

Sketches, which go to compose the present volume, have already been published under the signatures of 'Piscator' and 'Venator.' Their reception has been so flattering, that the author has been induced to re-publish them, and to enlarge the collection by the addition of other Sketches, now for the first time given to the public." "The Fire Hunter" is not one of the sketches signed "Piscator" or "Venator."

The Fire Hunter

It was on a fine evening in October, when the coolness of the air gave promise of an approaching frost, that a man in the common country garb might be observed pacing with hurried step the piazza of his humble dwelling, in lower Carolina. He was short, of sinewy frame, with high shoulders, lank whitish hair, sallow skin, and vulgar features; redeemed from their common-place expression, only, by a squint in one eye, and a mouth extending from ear to ear. A crumpled letter was in his hand, and he cast looks of indignation, from time to time, towards a negro boy, who had posted himself without the paling that enclosed the house,—as if he feared a nearer approach might expose him to proofs of his displeasure, yet more decisive. The man in homespun garb, was an overseer; the letter, was from his employer; and the boy, was the plantation messenger, who had just delivered him the letter which provoked his spleen.

"How dared you, sir, tell your master about them bucks that lie in the pea-field?" said the man, while a scowl settled on his weather-beaten face.

"Ei, obshaa! you tink I tell?—I know better dan dat; maussa can't tek off de lick, ater you stick um on me! I *got more sense*, I tell you!"

"How, then, could he know any thing about them? Who could have told him, if you did'nt,—tell me that?"

"No me! by gosh! somebody must be see the track where he feed in de pea-patch, and gone tell maussa—if he know bout um as you say."

"Clear yourself, you young villain; I'll find it out, if you did tell, and pay you for it too! Off with you, and send Pompey to me."

The messenger quickly disappeared; and presently the field-minder made his appearance, and touched his cap to the overseer.

"Where are them bucks that live in the pea-field?"

"Enty dey come dere ebery night?" said Pompey.

"Go to the pine barren, get me some of the fattest pine knots, prepare the pan,—I mean to go fire hunting to night."

"But, obshaa!" rejoined Pompey,—"maussa count pun dem buck for heself. Frost cum, you see maussa; den cum de question, 'Pompey, whey dem buck?' What Pompey guine say? dey fat for tru."

"Fat or no fat, I have one of them to night—I'll do it, by jingo, if I have to walk for it. Here he's been writing to me, as if I was a nigger; telling me to keep them bucks, till he comes over with his friends to hunt them. Dang me, if I do. Who gave them to him? were they born in his cattle pen? have they got his mark and brand upon them? all that have white tails are in my mark, and I'll shoot them as I please, and ask no odds."

"Dey fatten on maussa peas, any how," said Pompey.

"How do you know they're fat?" said the independent overseer.

"Case I see deir tracks, and de print deep in the eart, where dey walk."

"I've seen them, too," said Slouch, "and more besides than you think for. Who was it, pray, that took off the rider from the fence, and slipped away one rail, that they might jump that pannel? and who set the stakes, to snag them, when they were used to the path? And no thanks to you, that you did not kill them, for I found the hair on the point of your stake where it just grazed them in their leap."

Pompey cast down his eyes, convicted of having been poaching, on his own hook; and finding further remonstrance vain, said, with a shrug "Well, den, I 'spose I must git the lightwood."

"Certainly; and when the buck is shot, you get a fore-quarter; but mum! it needn't be known,—tho' I'd do it any how!"

In three hours time, Pompey re-appeared at the house, with tinder-box, lightwood and frying-pan; while Slouch had caparisoned his raw-boned steed, and stood ready for service. A sheep-skin, spread upon his back, was surmounted by a large saddle, from the croup of which dangled a small rope, with pulley and tackle attached,—so that, sitting on his horse, he might draw up his deer, when once fastened to the cord, without the trouble of dismounting.

Stealthily they took their way towards the field; making a circuit to avoid the watch, whose notice they were not anxious to attract. The night was still and clear; the winds hushed; and the dews lay thick and heavy on the foliage. They passed onward silently, until they approached the spot in which the deer were accustomed to feed.

"The moon is down," said Slouch; "in a half hour they will begin to feed. I'll hitch my horse to this hickory, and we'll raise a fire and go into the field. Let me see!—which way is the wind! D'rat me if it blows at all! That's bad; for if he noses me, he'll snort and be off in a jiffy."

"Eh, eh!" said Pompey, "how he guine nose you, when you mout and you jacket smell so strong of 'bacca?"

"Damme! if you aint spelling for a chew!" said Slouch, handing him over a quid. "Now, strike fire, and let's be off."

It was soon done: the blazing chips of lightwood were placed in the frying-pan, and the handle passed over the shoulder of the negro, who swayed it backward and forward, horizontally, with a knowing look, illuminating all objects far and near, except the space kept in shadow by the intervention of the head. It is in this shaded space, that the eyes of the deer become visible to the fire-hunter, appearing like globes of greenish flame.

"Got, Mass Slouch, dat 'ill do!" said Pompey,—his love of sport overcoming his hitherto reluctant acquiescence. "Spose you gee me de gun,—I'll slam um ober, I tell you!"

"When did you larn, pray?" said Slouch, eyeing him keenly and not over-kindly. "How do you know the distance?—you'd fire before you had got close enough, or scare him by getting too near!"

Pompey looked as if he knew more on the subject than he would readily confess to,—while Slouch continued,—

"I'll hardly let you scare off this one, I tell you! I know the distance by the size of the eyes; and it took me fifty shots to know that, as I know it now. You'd be for sneaking up till you could see their horns; but an old buck aint a-going to let you get that close, I tell you. He's the almightiest cunning creature to get round. But, quiet now; for we are getting near. Don't speak a word, but follow me; for I'll keep in the shade made by your body,—so throw the shadow right on me."

They now entered the pea-field, nightly visited by the deer; and had advanced but fifty yards, when, at a sudden turn, they came unexpectedly upon a fine antlered buck, feeding upon the tempting vines. He saw—*the men, as well as the fire,*—and stamping with his feet, and snuffing the air, which seemed to him fraught with danger, bounded off so suddenly, that Slouch lost the chance to fire. In truth, he was only prepared for a standing shot; and the suddenness of the movement disconcerted him.

"Confound the fellow," said the fire-hunter, "he has cleared himself; but there's two of 'em,—and we must keep a better look-out for the second!"

They now moved through the field more warily than before,—Slouch in the lead, and Pompey following him close, with a sort of lock-step, so that they cast but one shadow. Presently, by a sign from Slouch, they slackened their pace. He had caught glimpses of a deer's eyes, though yet at a distance; and they continued advancing, but with increased circumspection.

"He's a whacker, I know," said Slouch, "by the distance between his eyes. Don't let's scare him!"

They had now approached within fifty yards, when the deer suddenly lifted his head, and stared directly at the light. Slouch stopped at the instant, drew his gun to his shoulder, and fired. The sound of the gun,—the louder, as it seemed, from the stillness of the air,—came echoing back from the thick woodland, that enclosed the field like a wall; and the owls, frighted by the reverberation, flapped their wings about the unwelcome light, and hooted to each other in solemn concert.

"He's done for," said Slouch, after a moment's pause. "I don't hear him break."

And the hunters moved to the spot, where a noble buck lay weltering in his blood. They soon turned him over on his back,—dragged him by the horns to the fence, which stood at no great distance,—and proceeded to clean and divide him. They showed great expertness; and the process did not last long. When they had separated the deer into two divisions, it was bestowed in a long valise-like bag; and, bound with the cord before mentioned, was slung up in a most business-like way behind the saddle of the hunter. And now they were moving from the ground, when a noise attracted the quick ear of Slouch.

"I hear a deer," said he. "He'll stop to look at the light. I'll take the fire, and try if he will stand. You, Pompey, stand by my horse till I fire."

Onward, with noiseless step, on tiptoe, Slouch advanced in the direction of the sound: the ground (as they were now outside of the field) was not so open as before,—some shrubs occasionally intervening to obstruct the view; but he looked eagerly forward,—and catching sight of an eye that glared from the midst of the shrubbery, fired the barrel which he had in reserve. Pompey moved quickly up, to give his help; and came just in time to find Slouch in great confusion, standing over *a fine colt*, that he had shot down by mistake!

"The devil!" said the fire-hunter, in dismay; "had it been clear ground, I should never have done that. Pompey, man,—see where he's shot."

"Wha use!—he dead as door-nail," said Pompey.

"What's to be done?" said Slouch, in a tone of despondency. "I shouldn't like to pay for it out of my wages, that's a fact. None but a fool would inform against himself!"

"You far from fool, Mass Slouch?" said Pompey, slily.

"I reckon I am," said Slouch; and flinging off the top rail from the fence, he drove the sharp point of it into the side of the colt, e'er it had well ceased to breathe; and, tickled at the idea of so ingeniously covering his trail, thus continued aloud,—"He'll be a smart chap, now, that'll find out you aint died of a snag!—the pea-field is so inviting,—and it's so nat'ral for a young colt to leap the fence after the green fodder! Pompey! keep this close, and I'll make it up to you! You needn't know any thing about it, nor miss the colt, till day after to-morrow; and, by then, I reckon, my shot-holes will tell no tales!" And he chuckled, as he thought, how the harpies (his allies) would, long before that time, whet their beaks in the carcase of his victim, and obliterate by their loathesome orgies all traces by which his participation in the death might be detected:

"Contactuque omnia fœdant—
Immundo."

In a few minutes, the worthies are on their way home; and Pompey war preparing for an expedition, better suited to the darkness that encompassed them; than to the too searching glance of the mid-day sun. They approached the settlement unperceived; for the watch, as in duty bound, was, by this time, fast asleep!—and the haunches and loin of the buck, were carefully bestowed in a sack; while the fore-quarters were reserved for the fire-hunter and his associate.

"Now, Pompey! start off with this venison, and carry it to the stage-house, and give it to Snug the driver; and tell him to take it to town, and leave it, he knows where. Tell him to keep back his part of the money, and send me the things I spoke for, out of the balance."

"Leetle 'bacca for me, Mass Slouch?"

"Certainly, Pompey."

"An mus I tek your hoss?"

"No! day-light may catch you on the road; and I don't wish my horse seen there. Take the old mare; that will keep her from whickering after her colt. And, do you hear, Pompey,—when you're coming back, just turn into Softhead's field, and let the creetur go inside. If they knock her brains out, I don't care; and she'll be out of sight for one day, any how! So off, Pompey, and make no stay."

We shall now leave the faithful Slouch, after having acquitted himself thus honorably of his trusts, to retire to his rest; which, we may assure the reader, was disturbed by no qualms of conscience,—while we follow Pompey on his mission to the stage-house.

Every thing went according to his wish,—the mare was lashed into a brisk gallop; Snug received the venison; and Pompey, rewarded by a dram and a slice of cavendish, set out on his return. When he had now got near his home, he turned off the mare within the fence of Softhead, as he had been directed; and took a cut-off path through the woods, to save himself the trouble of a longer walk by the road. And now, when he had well nigh completed his journey, he was brought to a pause by observing the remains of a fire near the path, of which the embers were yet burning.

"What's dis," says Pompey; "here's been somebody fire hunting to-night, besides we. Ah! ha! here 'tis! dey tro out de lightwood down here! wonder what dey kill!" and he kindled the fire with the splintered pine, which blazed like gunpowder. "Here's de frying-pan, by jing!" said Pompey, as the rising flame illuminated every thing around; "dey must hab kill someting, or dey wouldn't throw away de pan!—hog mabe!—mabe calf!—for calf eye, when meat scarce, shine so like deer, ee tek a bery honest man to know de difference! Ecod, I look out; mabe I ketch someting wot while!"—and flinging the blazing faggots into the pan, he proceeded on his way, examining the road for some signs, by which to guide him to what he sought. "Ho! ho! I on the right course now; for here de horse track,—and here de blood!—ee point for home! Mass Slouch may be, double behind my back, and gone out gen; one buck! one colt! he want more meat,—dese buckra man greedy for tru! Well, I on the trail now, and I find um 'fore long!"

The negro's attention was soon arrested by the distinct sounds of a horse's tread, which seemed to proceed from the path directly ahead, and which, indicating at first but a slow pace,—came suddenly to mark the movement of a horse at speed.

"He run from de light," said Pompey; "you at some debiltry, is you?" and he hastened forward to reconnoitre the spot, from which the horseman had so hurriedly sped.

The spectacle that met his eye, was any thing but what he expected! Lying across the path, and turned over upon his face, was the body of a man, whose suppressed groans, and writhing limbs, gave token of the agony that tortured him. Pompey set down the light, and turning over the fallen man, had no sooner looked into his ghastly face, than he screamed out, "My God! my brudder!—oh, who has done dis ting? Tell me, Toney; as God is me judge, I'll kill um! Dat dam Slouch done it, aint he?"

Toney shook his head.

"Who den?"

The wounded man made signs to Pompey, to raise him up to a sitting posture. His shirt and jacket were soaked in blood, and his hand was pressed upon his breast, which had been pierced by shot. The lung had been wounded, for the blood flowed from his mouth as he essayed to speak, and threatened immediate suffocation.

"Tell me," said Pompey, as he supported his head on his shoulder, and bathed his face with his tears, that fell like rain; "how dis cum?—who done this?—who kill my brudder?"

Toney pointed to the neighboring plantation. "He done it, but not on purpose!!"—and with many interruptions, the dying man communicated to his brother, the particulars of his misfortune, which were briefly these: His wife was sick, and he wanted to buy some sugar for her, but the distance to the store was great, and he thought it would be no harm to take the mule, from the stable, and ride there to make his purchase. Having placed his sack of corn on the mule, and exchanged it for the sugar, he was, on his return home, attracted by a light in a field which lay on the route, and supposing no danger, and led by curiosity alone, he rode up to the fence, and was looking towards the light, when he received the shot in his breast, which struck him to the ground. On recovering, he found —— standing over him, and lamenting himself for having killed him. He begged his forgiveness; and told him he had mistaken the eyes of the mule for those of a deer! Toney had begged to be taken home to die, but the fire hunter, selfish to the last, and fearing that his agency in the matter, would thus be exposed; had refused to do so, until he had exacted a solemn pledge from him that he would not divulge who had done it. The pledge given, he placed him on the back of the mule, and was thus leading him home, when, startled by the approach of the torch, he suffered the wounded man to fall from the mule, and mounting him himself, rode off to escape detection.

The story of the poor fellow's misfortune was rather gathered from hints and broken sentences, uttered in the intervals of pain, than from any connected narrative, which, from his failing strength, he was incapable of giving.

"Bless God, me brudder, dat you find me here! 'Tis berry hard to die alone, in dese dark woods! Life is sweet, me brudder. Oh! dat God would let me stay here longer! But, I see how 'tis!—I must go,—I feel it at me heart! Maussa musn't say I die like a tief!—tell um all bout it! If he bin here; de fire-hunter neber bin shoot me! Feel in me pocket, brudder,—take out de paper wid de sugar. Oh! me blood upon it! Neber mind!—gib it to me poor wife: tell um to 'member me!—tell um, for him sake I get me death! I'm cold,—draw me to the fire."

And the poor fellow stretched himself out,—his head sunk upon his brother's breast,—and he was a corpse.

NOTE.—The practice of fire-hunting, forbidden by the laws, is nevertheless but too much pursued in certain parts of the country. It is the author's aim, in this narrative, to expose the dangers to property, and to life, attendant on this illicit practice. It is nearer akin to poaching, than to legitimate hunting; and he professes no personal acquaintance with it. The sketch here given, unlike those that precede it, must be considered as illustrative of life,—rather than as "a sketch from life." The melancholy incident with which the narrative concludes, is nevertheless true; and came within the range of his personal observation.

Thomas Bangs Thorpe
(1815-1878)

Thomas Bangs Thorpe, the first son of Thomas and Rebecca Farnham Thorpe, was born March 1, 1815, at Westfield, Massachusetts. The elder Thorpe, a Methodist minister, died of tuberculosis when his son was not yet four years old. Thorpe's childhood after his father's death was spent in Albany, New York, at the home of his maternal grandparents, and there he began his formal education in the public school. Later, however, his mother moved the family back to New York City, where he finished his secondary education. Young Thorpe decided to become a painter; and in preparation for his chosen profession studied under the figure painter John Quidor. In 1833 he first exhibited a picture, a genre piece inspired by the writings of Washington Irving, at the American Academy of Fine Arts. Thorpe continued to paint all his life, though he never achieved the financial success as a painter he had hoped for. His most noted works as an artist are his scenes of American life and landscape and his portraits of notables such as Zachary Taylor.

From 1834 to 1836 Thorpe attended Wesleyan University, the Methodist college at Middletown, Connecticut. Poor health forced him to leave the college at the end of his second year, but years later after he had gained recognition as a writer, painter, and editor, Wesleyan awarded him the Master of Arts degree. While at Wesleyan, Thorpe made a number of friends among the sons of Southern planters, and at their insistence decided to move to the milder climate of the South in an effort to improve his health and avert the threat of tuberculosis. Consequently, in late 1836 and early 1837, he made the grueling trip to Louisiana by overland stage. For several years, Thorpe lived in various parts of Louisiana, attempting to make a living as a portrait painter among the wealthy planter class. It was during this period that he observed much of the life of the river and backwoods, especially the hunting culture of the Southwest, which he employed with great success in his tales and sketches. The first of these sketches, and the one which actually started him on his writing career, was published in 1839 in William Trotter Porter's magazine, the New York *Spirit of the Times*. Entitled "Tom Owen, the Bee Hunter," it recounted an actual character and event witnessed by Thorpe in the Louisiana backwoods. The piece was an immediate favorite with readers of the *Spirit* and was reprinted many times at home and abroad. Its popularity gave Thorpe the impetus he needed to continue writing, and it afforded him a subject matter, a style, and a pseudonym—"the Author of 'Tom Owen the Bee-Hunter.' "

From 1840 to 1842 Thorpe did the writing for which he is largely remembered. He contributed sporting sketches to the *Spirit of the Times* and romantic essays of nature description to the *Knickerbocker Magazine*. His best known and finest piece of writing, "The Big Bear of Arkansas," was published in the *Spirit of the Times*, March 27, 1841. It combines frontier humor, realistic dialogue, and a memorable character to create a kind of genre of its own. Its inclusion of a legendary animal which symbolizes primitive forces and compels the hunter to pursue it incorporates a motif that recurs in American literature from Melville to Faulkner. After "The Big Bear of Arkansas," Thorpe continued to write hunting sketches and nature descriptions. He also contributed more humorous tales to the *Spirit*—"A Piano in Arkansas," "The Disgraced Scalp Lock," and "The Devil's Summer Retreat in Arkansaw."

In 1843 Thorpe launched on a career as a newspaper editor which lasted nearly twenty years. During this time, he published and edited a number of newspapers, such as the Vidalia, Louisiana, *Concordia Intelligencer,* the New Orleans *Daily Tropic,* and the Baton Rouge *Conservator.* In 1846 his first volume, *Mysteries of the Backwoods,* a collection of essays and sketches depicting the scenery and life of the Southwest, was published by Carey and Hart of Philadelphia. When the Mexican War broke out, Thorpe traveled to Mexico as a correspondent for his newspaper. Out of his experiences at the front came three volumes, *Our Army on the Rio Grande* (1846), *Our Army at Monterey* (1847), and *The Taylor Anecdote Book* (1848). In 1854 he published *The Hive of "the Bee-Hunter,"* a "Repository of Sketches" of frontier material including "Tom Owen, the Bee-Hunter" and "The Big Bear of Arkansas," which he revised for this edition.

Thorpe continued to write, to paint, and to edit and publish periodicals for the remainder of his life. He also became increasingly active in politics, especially in campaigning for Zachary Taylor. Thorpe was married twice— to Anne Marie Hinckley in 1838 and to Jane Fosdick in 1857, after his first wife's death—and was the father of four children. He died in New York on September 20, 1878, of Bright's disease.

Textual note

The text used here is *The Hive of "the Bee-Hunter," A Repository of Sketches, Including Peculiar American Character, Scenery, and Rural Sports* (New York: D. Appleton and Company, 1854), pp. 72–93.

The Big Bear of Arkansas

A steamboat on the Mississippi, frequently, in making her regular trips, carries between places varying from one to two thousand miles apart; and, as these boats advertise to land passengers and freight at "all intermediate landings," the heterogeneous character of the passengers of one of these up-country boats can scarcely be imagined by one who has never seen it with his own eyes.

Starting from New Orleans in one of these boats, you will find yourself associated with men from every State in the Union, and from every portion of the globe; and a man of observation need not lack for amusement or instruction in such a crowd, if he will take the trouble to read the great book of character so favorably opened before him.

Here may be seen, jostling together, the wealthy Southern planter and the pedler of tin-ware from New England—the Northern merchant and the Southern jockey—a venerable bishop, and a desperate gambler—the land speculator, and the honest farmer—professional men of all creeds and characters—Wolvereens, Suckers, Hoosiers, Buckeyes, and Corncrackers, beside a "plentiful sprinkling" of the half-horse and half-alligator species of men, who are peculiar to "old Mississippi," and who appear to gain a livelihood by simply going up and down the river. In the pursuit of pleasure or business, I have frequently found myself in such a crowd.

On one occasion, when in New Orleans, I had occasion to take a trip of a few miles up the Mississippi, and I hurried on board the well-known "high-pressure-and-beat-every-thing" steamboat "Invincible," just as the last note of the last bell was sounding; and when the confusion and bustle that is natural to a boat's getting under way had subsided, I discovered that I was associated in as heterogeneous a crowd as was ever got together. As my trip was to be of a few hours' duration only, I made no endeavors to become acquainted with my fellow-passengers, most of whom would be together many days. Instead of this, I took out of my pocket the "latest paper," and more critically than usual examined its contents; my fellow-passengers, at the same time, disposed of themselves in little groups.

While I was thus busily employed in reading, and my companions were more busily still employed, in discussing such subjects as suited their humors best, we were most unexpectedly startled by a loud Indian whoop, uttered in the "social hall," that part of the cabin fitted off for a bar; then was to be heard a loud crowing, which would not have continued to interest us—such sounds being quite common in that *place of spirits*—had not the hero of these windy accomplishments stuck his head into the cabin, and hallooed out, "Hurra for the Big Bear of Arkansaw!"

Then might be heard a confused hum of voices, unintelligible, save in such broken sentences as "horse," "screamer," "lightning is slow," &c.

As might have been expected, this continued interruption, attracted the attention of every one in the cabin; all conversation ceased, and in the midst of this surprise, the "Big Bear" walked into the cabin, took a chair, put his feet on the stove, and looking back over his shoulder, passed the general and familiar salute—"Strangers, how are you?"

He then expressed himself as much at home as if he had been at "the Forks of Cypress," and "prehaps a little more so."

Some of the company at this familiarity looked a little angry, and some astonished; but in a moment every face was wreathed in a smile. There was something about the intruder that won the heart on sight. He appeared to be a man enjoying perfect health and contentment; his eyes were as sparkling as diamonds, and good-natured to simplicity. Then his perfect confidence in himself was irresistibly droll.

"Prehaps," said he, "gentlemen," running on without a person interrupting, "prehaps you have been to New Orleans often; I never made *the first visit before,* and I don't intend to make another in a crow's life. I am thrown away in that ar place, and useless, that ar a fact. Some of the gentlemen thar called me *green*—well, prehaps I am, said I, *but I arn't so at home;* and if I aint off my trail much, the heads of them perlite chaps themselves wern't much the hardest; for according to my notion, they were *real know-nothings,* green as a pumpkin-vine—couldn't, in farming, I'll bet, raise a crop of turnips; and as for shooting, they'd miss a barn if the door was swinging, and that, too, with the best rifle in the country. And then they talked to me 'bout hunting, and laughed at my calling the principal game in Arkansaw poker, and high-low-jack.

" 'Prehaps,' said I, 'you prefer checkers and roulette;' at this they laughed harder than ever, and asked me if I lived in the woods, and didn't know what *game* was?

"At this, I rather think *I* laughed.

" 'Yes,' I roared, and says I, 'Strangers, if you'd asked me *how we got our meat* in Arkansaw, I'd a told you at once, and given you a list of varmints that would make a caravan, beginning with the bar, and ending off with the cat; that's *meat* though, not game.

"Game, indeed,—that's what city folks call it; and with them it means chippen-birds and shite-pokes; may be such trash live in my diggins, but I arn't noticed them yet: a bird anyway is too trifling. I never did shoot at but one, and I'd never forgiven myself for that, had it weighed less than forty pounds. I wouldn't draw a rifle on any thing less heavy than that; and when I meet with another wild turkey of the same size, I will drap him."

"A wild turkey weighing forty pounds!" exclaimed twenty voices in the cabin at once.

"Yes, strangers, and wasn't it a whopper? You see, the thing was so fat that it couldn't fly far; and when he fell out of the tree, after I shot him, on striking the ground he bust open behind, and the way the pound gobs of tallow rolled out of the opening was perfectly beautiful."

"Where did all that happen?" asked a cynical-looking Hoosier.

"Happen! happened in Arkansaw: where else could it have happened, but in the creation State, the finishing-up country—a State where the *sile* runs down to the centre of the 'arth, and government gives you a title to every inch of it? Then its airs—just breathe them, and they will make you snort like a horse. It's a State without a fault, it is."

"Excepting mosquitoes," cried the Hoosier.

"Well, stranger, except them; for it ar a fact that they are rather *enormous,* and do push themselves in somewhat troublesome. But, stranger, they never stick twice in the same place; and give them a fair chance for a few months, and you will get as much above noticing them as an alligator. They can't hurt my feelings, for they lay under the skin; and I never knew but one case of injury resulting from them, and that was to a Yankee: and they take worse to foreigners, any how, than they do to natives. But the way they used that fellow up! first they punched him until he swelled up and busted; then he sup-per-a-ted, as the doctor called it, until he was as raw as beef; then, owing to the warm weather, he tuck the ager, and finally he tuck a steamboat and left the country. He was the only man that ever tuck mosquitoes at heart that I knowd of.

"But mosquitoes is natur, and I never find fault with her. If they ar large, Arkansaw is large, her varmints ar large, her trees ar large, her rivers ar large, and a small mosquito would be of no more use in Arkansaw than preaching in a cane-brake."

This knock-down argument in favor of big mosquitoes used the Hoosier up, and the logician started on a new track, to explain how numerous bear were in his "diggins," where he represented them to be "about as plenty as blackberries, and a little plentifuller."

Upon the utterance of this assertion, a timid little man near me inquired, if the bear in Arkansaw ever attacked the settlers in numbers?

"No," said our hero, warming with the subject, "no, stranger, for you see it ain't the natur of bear to go in droves; but the way they squander about in pairs and single ones is edifying.

"And then the way I hunt them—the old black rascals know the crack of my gun as well as they know a pig's squealing. They grow thin in our parts, it frightens them so, and they do take the noise dreadfully, poor things. That gun of mine is a perfect *epidemic among bear:* if not watched closely, it will go off as quick on a warm scent as my dog Bowieknife will: and then that dog—whew! why the fellow thinks that the world is full of bear, he finds them so easy. It's lucky he don't talk as well as think; for with his natural modesty, if he should suddenly learn how much he is acknowledged to be ahead of all other dogs in the universe, he would be astonished to death in two minutes.

"Strangers, that dog knows a bear's way as well as a horse-jockey knows a woman's: he always barks at the right time, bites at the exact place, and whips without getting a scratch.

"I never could tell whether he was made expressly to hunt bear, or whether bear was made expressly for him to hunt; any way, I believe they were ordained to go together as naturally as Squire Jones says a man and woman is, when he moralizes in marrying a couple. In fact, Jones once said, said he, 'Marriage according to law is a civil contract of divine origin; it's common to all countries as well as Arkansaw, and people take to it as naturally as Jim Doggett's Bowieknife takes to bear.' "

"What season of the year do your hunts take place?" inquired a gentlemanly foreigner, who, from some peculiarities of his baggage, I suspected to be an Englishman, on some hunting expedition, probably at the foot of the Rocky Mountains.

"The season for bear hunting, stranger," said the man of Arkansaw, "is generally all the year round, and the hunts take place about as regular. I read in history that varmints have their fat season, and their lean season. That is not the case in Arkansaw, feeding as they do upon the *spontenacious* productions of the sile, they have one continued fat season the year round; though in winter things in this way is rather more greasy than in summer, I must admit. For that reason bear with us run in warm weather, but in winter they only waddle.

"Fat, fat! its an enemy to speed; it tames every thing that has plenty of it. I have seen wild turkeys, from its influence, as gentle as chickens. Run a bear in this fat condition, and the way it improves the critter for eating is amazing; it sort of mixes the ile up with the meat, until you can't tell t'other from which. I've done this often.

"I recollect one perty morning in particular, of putting an old he fellow on the stretch, and considering the weight he carried, he run well. But the dogs soon tired him down, and when I came up with him wasn't he in a beautiful sweat—I might say fever; and then to see his tongue sticking out of his mouth a feet, and his sides sinking and opening like a bellows, and his cheeks so fat that he couldn't look cross. In this fix I blazed at him, and pitch me naked into a briar patch, if the steam didn't come out of the bullet-hole ten foot in a straight line. The fellow, I reckon, was made on the high-pressure system, and the lead sort of bust his biler."

"That column of steam was rather curious, or else the bear must have been very *warm*," observed the foreigner, with a laugh.

"Stranger, as you observe, that bear was WARM, and the blowing off of the steam show'd it, and also how hard the varmint had been run. I have no doubt if he had kept on two miles farther his insides would have been stewed; and I expect to meet with a varmint yet of extra bottom, that will run himself into a skinfull of bear's grease: it is possible; much onlikelier things have happened."

"Whereabouts are these bears so abundant?" inquired the foreigner, with increasing interest.

"Why, stranger, they inhabit the neighborhood of my settlement, one of the prettiest places on old Mississipp—a perfect location, and no mistake; a place that had some defects until the river made the 'cut-off' at 'Shirt-tail bend,' and that remedied the evil, as it brought my cabin on the edge of the river—a great advantage in wet weather, I assure you, as you can now roll a barrel of whiskey into my yard in high water from a boat, as easy as falling off a log. It's a great improvement, as toting it by land in a jug, as I used to do, *evaporated* it too fast, and it became expensive.

"Just stop with me, stranger, a month or two, or a year, if you like, and you will appreciate my place. I can give you plenty to eat; for beside hog and hominy, you can have bear-ham, and bear-sausages, and a mattrass of bear-skins to sleep on, and a wildcat-skin, pulled off hull, stuffed with corn-shucks, for a pillow. That bed would put you to sleep if you had the rheumatics in every joint in your body. I call that ar bed, a *quietus*.

"Then look at my 'pre-emption'—the government aint got another like it to dispose of. Such timber, and such bottom land,—why you can't preserve any thing natural you plant in it unless you pick it young, things thar will grow out of shape so quick.

"I once planted in those diggins a few potatoes and beets; they took a fine start, and after that, an ox team couldn't have kept them from growing. About that time I went off to old Kaintuck on business, and did not hear from them things in three months, when I accidentally stumbled on a fellow who had drapped in at my place, with an idea of buying me out.

" 'How did you like things?' said I.

" 'Pretty well,' said he; 'the cabin is convenient, and the timber land is good; but that bottom land aint worth the first red cent.' "

" 'Why?' said I.

" ' 'Cause,' said he.

" ' 'Cause what?' said I.

" ' 'Cause it's full of cedar stumps and Indian mounds, and *can't be cleared.'*

" 'Lord,' said I, 'them ar "cedar stumps" is beets, and them ar "Indian mounds" tater hills.'

"As I had expected, the crop was overgrown and useless: the sile is too rich, *and planting in Arkansaw is dangerous.*

"I had a good-sized sow killed in that same bottomland. The old thief stole an ear of corn, and took it down to eat where she slept at night. Well, she left a grain or two on the ground, and lay down on them: before morning the corn shot up, and the percussion killed her dead. I don't plant any more: natur intended Arkansaw for a hunting ground, and I go according to natur."

The questioner, who had thus elicited the description of our hero's settlement, seemed to be perfectly satisfied, and said no more; but the "Big Bear of Arkansaw" rambled on from one thing to another with a volubility perfectly astonishing, occasionally disputing with those around him, particularly with a "live Sucker" from Illinois, who had the daring to say that our Arkansaw friend's stories "smelt rather tall."

The evening was nearly spent by the incidents we have detailed; and conscious that my own association with so singular a personage would probably end before morning, I asked him if he would not give me a description of some particular bear hunt; adding, that I took great interest in such things, though I was no sportsman. The desire seemed to please him, and he squared himself round towards me, saying, that he could give me an idea of a bear hunt that was never beat in this world, or in any other. His manner was so singular, that half of his story consisted in his excellent way of telling it, the great peculiarity of which was, the happy manner he had of emphasizing the prominent parts of his conversation. As near as I can recollect, I have italicized the words, and given the story in his own way.

"Stranger," said he, "in bear hunts *I am numerous,* and which particular one, as you say, I shall tell, puzzles me.

"There was the old she devil I shot at the Hurricane last fall—then there was the old hog thief I popped over at the Bloody Crossing, and then —Yes, I have it! I will give you an idea of a hunt, in which the greatest bear was killed that ever lived, *none excepted;* about an old fellow that I hunted, more or less, for two or three years; and if that aint a *particular bear hunt,* I ain't got one to tell.

"But in the first place, stranger, let me say, I am pleased with you, because you aint ashamed to gain information by asking and listening; and that's what I say to Countess's pups every day when I'm home; and I have got great hopes of them ar pups, because they are continually *nosing* about; and though they stick it sometimes in the wrong place, they gain experience any how, and may learn something useful to boot.

"Well, as I was saying about this big bear, you see when I and some more first settled in our region, we were drivin to hunting naturally; we soon liked it, and after that we found it an easy matter to make the thing our business. One old chap who had pioneered 'afore us, gave us to understand that we had settled in the right place. He dwelt upon its merits until it was affecting, and showed us, to prove his assertions, more scratches on the bark of the sassafras trees, than I ever saw chalk marks on a tavern door 'lection time.

" 'Who keeps that ar reckoning?' said I.

" 'The bear,' said he.

" 'What for?' said I.

" 'Can't tell,' said he; 'but so it is: the bear bite the bark and wood too, at the highest point from the ground they can reach, and you can tell, by the marks,' said he, 'the length of the bear to an inch.'

" 'Enough,' said I; 'I've learned something here a'ready, and I'll put it in practice.'

"Well, stranger, just one month from that time I killed a bar, and told its exact length before I measured it, by those very marks; and when I did that, I swelled up considerably—I've been a prouder man ever since.

"So I went on, larning something every day, until I was reckoned a buster, and allowed to be decidedly the best bear hunter in my district; and that is a reputation as much harder to earn than to be reckoned first man in Congress, as an iron ramrod is harder than a toadstool.

"Do the varmints grow over-cunning by being fooled with by greenhorn hunters, and by this means get troublesome, they send for me, as a matter of course; and thus I do my own hunting, and most of my neighbors'. I walk into the varmints though, and it has become about as much the same to me as drinking. It is told in two sentences—

"A bear is started, and he is killed.

"The thing is somewhat monotonous now—I know just how much they will run, where they will tire, how much they will growl, and what a thundering time I will have in getting their meat home. I could give you the history of the chase with all the particulars at the commencement, I know the signs so well—*Stranger, I'm certain*. Once I met with a match, though, and I will tell you about it; for a common hunt would not be worth relating.

"On a fine fall day, long time ago, I was trailing about for bear, and what should I see but fresh marks on the sassafras trees, about eight inches above any in the forests that I knew of. Says I, 'Them marks is a hoax, or it indicates the d——t bear that was ever grown.' In fact, stranger, I couldn't believe it was real, and I went on. Again I saw the same marks, at the same height, and *I knew the thing lived*. That conviction came home to my soul like an earthquake.

"Says I, 'Here is something a-purpose for me: that bear is mine, or I give up the hunting business.' The very next morning, what should I see but a number of buzzards hovering over my corn-field. 'The rascal has been there,' said I, 'for that sign is certain:' and, sure enough, on examining, I found the bones of what had been as beautiful a hog the day before, as was ever raised by a Buckeye. Then I tracked the critter out of the field to the woods, and all the marks he left behind, showed me that he was *the bear*.

"Well, stranger, the first fair chase I ever had with that big critter, I saw him no less than three distinct times at a distance: the dogs run him over eighteen miles and broke down, my horse gave out, and I was as nearly used up as a man can be, made on *my* principle, *which is patent*.

"Before this adventure, such things were unknown to me as possible; but, strange as it was, that bear got me used to it before I was done with him; for he got so at last, that he would leave me on a long chase *quite easy*. How he did it, I never could understand.

"That a bear runs at all, is puzzling; but how this one could tire down and bust up a pack of hounds and a horse, that were used to overhauling every thing they started after in no time, was past my understanding. Well, stranger, that bear finally got so sassy, that he used to help himself to a hog off my premises whenever he wanted one; the buzzards followed after what he left, and so, between *bear and buzzard*, I rather think I got *out of pork*.

"Well, missing that bear so often took hold of my vitals, and I wasted away. The thing had been carried too far, and it reduced me in flesh faster than an ager. I would see that bear in every thing I did: *he hunted me*, and that, too, like a devil, which I began to think he was.

"While in this shaky fix, I made preparations to give him a last brush, and be done with it. Having completed every thing to my satisfaction, I started at sunrise, and to my great joy, I discovered from the way the dogs run, that they were near him. Finding his trail was nothing, for that had become as plain to the pack as a turnpike road.

"On we went, and coming to an open country, what should I see but the bear very leisurely ascending a hill, and the dogs close at his heels, either a match for him this time in speed, or else he did not care to get out of their way—I don't know which. But wasn't he a beauty, though! I loved him like a brother.

"On he went, until he came to a tree, the limbs of which formed a crotch about six feet from the ground. Into this crotch he got and seated himself, the dogs yelling all around it; and there he sat eyeing them as quiet as a pond in low water.

"A greenhorn friend of mine, in company, reached shooting distance before me, and blazed away, hitting the critter in the centre of his forehead. The bear shook his head as the ball struck it, and then walked down from that tree, as gently as a lady would from a carriage.

" 'Twas a beautiful sight to see him do that—he was in such a rage, that he seemed to be as little afraid of the dogs as if they had been sucking pigs; and the dogs warn't slow in making a ring around him at a respectful distance, I tell you; even Bowieknife himself, stood off. Then the way his eyes flashed!—why the fire of them would have singed a cat's hair; in fact, that bear was in a *wrath all over*. Only one pup came near him, and he was brushed out so totally with the bear's left paw, that he entirely disappeared; and that made the old dogs more cautious still. In the mean time, I came up, and taking deliberate aim, as a man should do, at his side, just back of his foreleg, *if my gun did not snap*, call me a coward, and I won't take it personal.

"Yes, stranger, *it snapped*, and I could not find a cap about my person. While in this predicament, I turned round to my fool friend—'Bill,' says I, 'you're an ass—you're a fool—you might as well have tried to kill that bear by barking the tree under his belly, as to have done it by hitting him in the head. Your shot has made a tiger of him; and blast me, if a dog gets killed or wounded when they come to blows, I will stick my knife into your liver, I will ——.' My wrath was up. I had lost my caps, my gun had snapped, the fellow with me had fired at the bear's head, and I expected every moment to see him close in with the dogs and kill a dozen of them at least. In this thing I was mistaken; for the bear leaped over the ring formed by the dogs, and giving a fierce growl, was off—the pack, of course, in full cry after him. The run this time was short, for coming to the edge of a lake, the varmint jumped in, and swam to a little island in the lake, which it reached, just a moment before the dogs.

" 'I'll have him now,' said I, for I had found my caps in the *lining of my coat*—so, rolling a log into the lake, I paddled myself across to the island, just as the dogs had cornered the bear in a thicket. I rushed up and fired—at the same time the critter leaped over the dogs and came within three feet of me, running like mad; he jumped into the lake, and tried to mount the log I had just deserted, but every time he got half his body on it, it would roll over and send him under; the dogs, too, got around him, and pulled him about, and finally Bowieknife clenched with him, and they sunk into the lake together.

"Stranger, about this time I was excited, and I stripped off my coat, drew my knife, and intended to have taken a part with Bowieknife myself, when the bear rose to the surface. But the varmint staid under—Bowieknife came up alone, more dead than alive, and with the pack came ashore.

" 'Thank God!' said I, 'the old villain has got his deserts at last.'

"Determined to have the body, I cut a grape-vine for a rope, and dove down where I could see the bear in the water, fastened my rope to his leg, and fished him, with great difficulty, ashore. Stranger, may I be chawed to death by young alligators, if the thing I looked at wasn't a *she bear, and not the old critter after all.*

"The way matters got mixed on that island was onaccountably curious, and thinking of it made me more than ever convinced that I was hunting the devil himself. I went home that night and took to my bed—the thing was killing me. The entire team of Arkansaw in bear-hunting acknowledged himself used up, and the fact sunk into my feelings as a snagged boat will in the Mississippi. I grew as cross as a bear with two cubs and a sore tail. The thing got out 'mong my neighbors, and I was asked how come on that individ-u-al that never lost a bear when once started? and if that same individ-u-al didn't wear telescopes when he turned a she-bear, of ordinary size, into an old he one, a little larger than a horse?

" 'Prehaps,' said I, 'friends'—getting wrathy—'prehaps you want to call somebody a liar?'

" 'Oh, no,' said they, 'we only heard of such things being *rather common* of late, but we don't believe one word of it; oh, no,'—and then they would ride off, and laugh like so many hyenas over a dead nigger.

"It was too much, and I determined to catch that bear, go to Texas, or die,—and I made my preparations accordin'.

"I had the pack shut up and rested. I took my rifle to pieces, and iled it.

"I put caps in every pocket about my person, *for fear of the lining.*

"I then told my neighbors, that on Monday morning—naming the day —I would start THAT B(E)AR, and bring him home with me, or they might divide my settlement among them, the owner having disappeared.

"Well, stranger, on the morning previous to the great day of my hunting expedition, I went into the woods near my house, taking my gun and Bowieknife along, just *from habit,* and there sitting down, also from habit, what should I see, getting over my fence, but *the bear!* Yes, the old varmint was within a hundred yards of me, and the way he walked *over that fence—* stranger; he loomed up like a *black mist,* he seemed so large, and he walked right towards me.

"I raised myself, took deliberate aim, and fired. Instantly the varmint wheeled, gave a yell, and *walked through the fence*, as easy as a falling tree would through a cobweb.

"I started after, but was tripped up by my inexpressibles, which, either from habit or the excitement of the moment, were about my heels, and before I had really gathered myself up, I heard the old varmint groaning, like a thousand sinners, in a thicket near by, and, by the time I reached him, he was a corpse.

"Stranger, it took five niggers and myself to put that carcass on a mule's back, and old long-ears waddled under his load, as if he was foundered in every leg of his body; and with a common whopper of a bear, he would have trotted off, and enjoyed himself.

" 'Twould astonish you to know how big he was: I made a *bed-spread of his skin,* and the way it used to cover my bear mattress, and leave several feet on each side to tuck up, would have delighted you. It was, in fact, a creation bear, and if it had lived in Samson's time, and had met him in a fair fight, he would have licked him in the twinkling of a dice-box.

"But, stranger, I never liked the way I hunted him, *and missed him.* There is something curious about it, that I never could understand,—and I never was satisfied at his giving in so *easy at last.* Prehaps he had heard of my preparations to hunt him the next day, so he jist guv up, like Captain Scott's coon, to save his wind to grunt with in dying; but that ain't likely. My private opinion is, that that bear was an *unhuntable bear, and died when his time come.*"

When this story was ended, our hero sat some minutes with his auditors, in a grave silence; I saw there was a mystery to him connected with the bear whose death he had just related, that had evidently made a strong impression on his mind. It was also evident that there was some superstitious awe connected with the affair,—a feeling common with all "children of the wood," when they meet with any thing out of their every-day experience.

He was the first one, however, to break the silence, and, jumping up, he asked all present to "liquor" before going to bed,—a thing which he did, with a number of companions, evidently to his heart's content.

Long before day, I was put ashore at my place of destination, and I can only follow with the reader, in imagination, our Arkansas friend, in his adventures at the "Forks of Cypress," on the Mississippi.

William Gilmore Simms
(1806-1870)

William Gilmore Simms was born in Charleston, South Carolina, on April 17, 1806, the son of William Gilmore and Harriet Ann Augusta Singleton Simms. The elder Simms, an emigrant from Ireland, left Charleston in 1808, after the death of his wife and financial losses in business struck him severe blows, to seek his fortune in Mississippi; his young son, left in the custody of his maternal grandmother, Mrs. Jacob Gates, grew up to love the city of his birth and the only "mother" he ever knew. Thus, in 1816 when his father sent for him to come to Mississippi, young Simms balked; and, when the matter was taken to court, the judge allowed the ten-year-old youth to choose his own destiny. It was probably the most important decision of his life, for it committed Simms to Charleston, to the polite professions, and ultimately to literature, rather than to the Southwest with its emphasis upon rugged frontier life.

Simms did not have an easy avenue to success in Charleston. Mrs. Gates gave her grandson the best education she could afford but lacked the money to send him to college in the North or abroad, as wealthy Charlestonians traditionally did for their sons. Though Simms's formal education ended at twelve and he was apprenticed to a druggist, he later undertook the study of law in the office of Charles Rivers Carroll and was admitted to the Charleston bar in 1827 on his twenty-first birthday. A few months earlier Simms had married Anna Malcolm Giles of Charleston, on October 19, 1826.

Simms's literary talents had become manifest even before his marriage. At nineteen he had edited (and written extensively for) a short-lived literary journal, the *Album* (1825), and two years later he published his first two volumes of verse, *Lyrical and Other Poems* (1827) and *Early Lays* (1827). Simms's career continued to advance steadily despite the shock of his first wife's death and the failure of the Charleston *City Gazette*, which he edited—both in 1832. In 1833 he published *Martin Faber*, rapidly followed by *Guy Rivers* (1834), *The Yemassee* (1835), and *The Partisan* (1835). A bright new star had emerged on America's literary horizon.

In 1836 Simms, one of Charleston's most eligible bachelors as a young widower who had won national literary honors, was married to Chevilette

Eliza Roach, daughter of a wealthy plantation owner. As proprietor of Woodlands, a lovely 7,000-acre plantation on the banks of the Edisto River, Simms became a member of South Carolina's landed aristocracy and, as years passed, he became increasingly embroiled in political affairs as a widely recognized spokesman for the Southern point of view. But apart from the responsibilities of managing Woodlands, Simms after his second marriage had more time than ever before for writing books, for he no longer had to depend upon magazine or newspaper editing for his chief income. Thus between 1836 and 1842 he produced eight novels, another volume of poetry, a history of South Carolina, and two collections of short stories.

Amazing productivity continued to earmark Simms's career, and although he spread his abundant talent thin by refusing to limit himself to his best genre, prose fiction, he nevertheless produced two major series of novels and some of the best short stories in nineteenth-century America. His Revolutionary Romances, begun with *The Partisan,* also include *Mellichampe* (1836); *The Kinsmen* (1841), revised as *The Scout* (1854); *Katharine Walton* (1851); *The Sword and the Distaff* (1853), revised as *Woodcraft* (1854); *The Foragers* (1855); *Eutaw* (1856); and *Joscelyn* (1867). In addition to *Guy Rivers,* Simms's Border Romances include *Richard Hurdis* (1838), *Border Beagles* (1840), *Beauchampe* (1842), *Helen Halsey* (1845), *Charlement* (1856), *Voltmeier* (1869), and *The Cub of the Panther* (1869). Even better are Simms's best short stories, some of them collected in *Martin Faber and other Tales* (1837), *Carl Werner* (1838), and *The Wigwam and the Cabin* (1845), but including also such uncollected items as "How Sharp Snaffles Got His Capital and Wife," published after the author's death in *Harper's* for May, 1870, and two stories left in manuscript, "Bald-Head Bill Bauldy" and "The Humours of the Manager," published for the first time one hundred years later in *The Centennial Edition of the Writings of William Gilmore Simms.*

Ruined by the Civil War—Woodlands was set on fire by stragglers of Sherman's Army, with the resulting loss of its ten thousand-volume library —Simms lived the final years of his life amidst tragedy and poverty, continuing to write until the bitter end, which came in Charleston on June 11, 1870.

Textual note

"How Sharp Snaffles Got His Capital and His Wife" was published in *Harper's Magazine,* XLI (October 1870), 667–687. The text used here is that in John C. Guilds, General Editor, *The Centennial Edition of the Writings of William Gilmore Simms,* II (Columbia, South Carolina, 1971), 421–465. Reprinted by permission of the University of South Carolina Press.

How Sharp Snaffles Got His Capital and Wife

I

The day's work was done, and a good day's work it was. We had bagged
a couple of fine bucks and a fat doe; and now we lay camped at the foot
of the "Balsam Range" of mountains in North Carolina, preparing for
our supper. We were a right merry group of seven; four professional hunters, and three amateurs—myself among the latter. There was Jim Fisher,
Aleck Wood, Sam or Sharp Snaffles, *alias* "Yaou," and Nathan Langford,
alias the "Pious."

These were our *professional* hunters. Our *amateurs* may well continue
nameless, as their achievements do not call for any present record. Enough
that we had gotten up the "camp hunt," and provided all the creature
comforts except the fresh meat. For this we were to look to the mountain
ranges and the skill of our hunters.

These were all famous fellows with the rifle—moving at a trot along
the hill-sides, and with noses quite as keen of scent as those of their hounds
in rousing deer and bear from their deep recesses among the mountain
laurels.

A week had passed with us among these mountain ranges, some sixty
miles beyond what the conceited world calls "civilization."

Saturday night had come; and, this Saturday night closing a week of
exciting labors, we were to carouse.

We were prepared for it. There stood our tent pitched at the foot of
the mountains, with a beautiful cascade leaping headlong toward us, and
subsiding into a mountain runnel, and finally into a little lakelet, the waters
of which, edged with perpetual foam, were as clear as crystal.

Our baggage wagon, which had been sent round to meet us by trail
routes through the gorges, stood near the tent, which was of stout army
canvas.

That baggage wagon held a variety of luxuries. There was a barrel of the best bolted wheat flour. There were a dozen choice hams, a sack of coffee, a keg of sugar, a few thousand of cigars, and last, not least, a corpulent barrel of Western uisquebaugh,* vulgarly, "whisky;" to say nothing of a pair of demijohns of equal dimensions, one containing peach brandy of mountain manufacture, the other the luscious honey from the mountain hives.

Well, we had reached Saturday night. We had hunted day by day from the preceding Monday with considerable success—bagging some game daily, and camping nightly at the foot of the mountains. The season was a fine one. It was early winter, October, and the long ascent to the top of the mountains was through vast fields of green, the bushes still hanging heavy with their huckleberries.

From the summits we had looked over into Tennessee, Virginia, Georgia, North and South Carolina. In brief, to use the language of Natty Bumpo, we beheld "Creation." We had crossed the "Blue Ridge;" and the descending water-courses, no longer seeking the Atlantic, were now gushing headlong down the western slopes, and hurrying to lose themselves in the Gulf Stream and the Mississippi.

From the eyes of fountains within a few feet of each other we had blended our *eau de vie* with limpid waters which were about to part company forever—the one leaping to the rising, the other to the setting of the sun.

And buoyant, full of fun, with hearts of ease, limbs of health and strength, plenty of venison, and a wagon full of good things, we welcomed the coming of Saturday night as a season not simply of rest, but of a royal carouse. We were decreed to make a night of it.

But first let us see after our venison.

The deer, once slain, is, as soon after as possible, clapped upon the fire. All the professional hunters are good butchers and admirable cooks—of bear and deer meat at least. I doubt if they could spread a table to satisfy Delmonico; but even Delmonico might take some lessons from them in the preparation for the table of the peculiar game which they pursue, and the meats on which they feed. We, at least, rejoice at the supper prospect before us. Great collops hiss in the frying-pan, and finely cut steaks redden beautifully upon the flaming coals. Other portions of the meat are subdued to the stew, and make a very delightful dish. The head of the deer, including the brains, is put upon a flat rock in place of gridiron, and thus baked be-

---

* "Uisquebaugh," or the "water of life," is Irish. From the word we have dropped the last syllable. Hence we have "uisque," or, as it is commonly written, "whisky"— a very able-bodied man-servant, but terrible as a mistress or housekeeper. [Simm's note]

fore the fire—being carefully watched and turned until every portion has
duly imbibed the necessary heat, and assumed the essential hue which it
should take to satisfy the eye of appetite. This portion of the deer is greatly
esteemed by the hunters themselves; and the epicure of genuine stomach
for the *haut gout* takes to it as an eagle to a fat mutton, and a hawk to a
young turkey.

The rest of the deer—such portions of it as are not presently consumed
or needed for immediate use—is cured for future sale or consumption; being
smoked upon a scaffolding raised about four feet above the ground, under
which, for ten or twelve hours, a moderate fire will be kept up.

Meanwhile the hounds are sniffing and snuffing around, or crouched
in groups, with noses pointed at the roast and broil and bake; while their
great liquid eyes dilate momently while watching for the huge gobbets
which they expect to be thrown to them from time to time from the hands
of the hunters.

Supper over, and it is Saturday night. It is the night dedicated among
the professional hunters to what is called "The Lying Camp!"

"The Lying Camp!" quoth Columbus Mills, one of our party, a
wealthy mountaineer, of large estates, of whom I have been for some time
the guest.

"What do you mean by the 'Lying Camp,' Columbus?"

The explanation soon followed.

Saturday night is devoted by the mountaineers engaged in a camp
hunt, which sometimes contemplates a course of several weeks, to stories of
their adventures—"long yarns"—chiefly relating to the objects of their
chase, and the wild experiences of their professional life. The hunter who
actually inclines to exaggeration is, at such a period, privileged to deal in all
the extravagances of invention; nay, he is *required* to do so! To be literal,
or confine himself to the bald and naked truth, is not only discreditable, but
a *finable* offense! He is, in such a case, made to swallow a long, strong, and
difficult potation! He can not be too extravagant in his incidents; but he is
also required to exhibit a certain degree of *art,* in their use; and he thus frequently rises into a certain realm of fiction, the ingenuities of which are
made to compensate for the exaggerations, as they do in the "Arabian
Nights," and other Oriental romances.

This will suffice for explanation.

Nearly all our professional hunters assembled on the present occasion
were tolerable *raconteurs.* They complimented Jim Fisher, by throwing the
raw deer-skin over his shoulders; tying the antlers of the buck with a red
handkerchief over his forehead; seating him on the biggest boulder which
lay at hand; and, sprinkling him with a stoup of whisky, they christened

him "The Big Lie," for the occasion. And in this character he complacently presided during the rest of the evening, till the company prepared for sleep, which was not till midnight. He was king of the feast.

It was the duty of the "Big Lie" to regulate proceedings, keep order, appoint the *raconteurs* severally, and admonish them when he found them foregoing their privileges, and narrating bald, naked, and uninteresting truth. They must deal in fiction.

Jim Fisher was seventy years old, and a veteran hunter, the most famous in all the country. He *looked* authority, and promptly began to assert it, which he did in a single word:

"Yaou!"

II

"Yaou" was the *nom de nique* of one of the hunters, whose proper name was Sam Snaffles, but who, from his special smartness, had obtained the farther sobriquet of "*Sharp* Snaffles."

Columbus Mills whispered me that he was called "Yaou" from his frequent use of that word, which, in the Choctaw dialect, simply means "Yes." Snaffles had rambled considerably among the Choctaws, and picked up a variety of their words, which he was fond of using in preference to the vulgar English; and his common use of "*Yaou*," for the affirmative, had prompted the substitution of it for his own name. He answered to the name.

"Ay—yee, Yaou," was the response of Sam. "I was *afeard*, 'Big Lie,' that you'd be hitching me up the very first in your team."

"And what was you afeard of? You knows as well how to take up a crooked trail as the very best man among us; so you go ahead and spin your thread a'ter the best fashion."

"What shill it be?" asked Snaffles, as he mixed a calabash full of peach and honey, preparing evidently for a long yarn.

"Give 's the history of how you got your capital, Yaou!" was the cry from two or more.

"O Lawd! I've tell'd that so often, fellows, that I'm afeard you'll sleep on it; and then agin, I've tell'd it so often I've clean forgot how it goes. Somehow it changes a leetle every time I tells it."

"Never you mind! The Jedge never haird it, I reckon, for one; and I'm not sure that Columbus Mills ever did."

So the "Big Lie."

The "Jedge" was the *nom de guerre* which the hunters had conferred upon me; looking, no doubt, to my venerable aspect—for I had traveled considerably beyond my teens—and the general dignity of my bearing.

"Yaou," like other bashful beauties in oratory and singing, was disposed to hem and haw, and affect modesty and indifference, when he was brought up suddenly by the stern command of the "Big Lie," who cried out:

"Don't make yourself an etarnal fool, Sam Snaffles, by twisting your mouth out of shape, making all sorts of redickilous ixcuses. Open upon the trail at onst and give tongue, or, dern your digestion, but I'll fine you to hafe a gallon at a single swallow!"

Nearly equivalent to what Hamlet says to the conceited player:

"Leave off your damnable faces and begin."

Thus adjured with a threat, Sam Snaffles swallowed his peach and honey at a gulp, hemmed thrice lustily, put himself into an attitude, and began as follows. I shall adopt his language as closely as possible; but it is not possible, in any degree, to convey any adequate idea of his *manner,* which was admirably appropriate to the subject matter. Indeed, the fellow was a born actor.

III

"You see, Jedge," addressing me especially as the distinguished stranger, "I'm a telling this hyar history of mine jest to please *you,* and I'll try to please you ef I kin. These fellows hyar have hearn it so often that they knows all about it jest as well as I do my own self, and they knows the truth of it all, and would swear to it afore any hunters' court in all the county, ef so be the affidavy was to be tooken in camp and on a Saturday night.

"You see then, Jedge, it's about a dozen or fourteen years ago, when I was a young fellow without much beard on my chin, though I was full grown as I am now—strong as a horse, ef not quite so big as a buffalo. I was then jest a-beginning my 'prenticeship to the hunting business, and looking to sich persons as the 'Big Lie' thar to show me how to take the track of b'ar, buck, and painther.

"But I confess I weren't a-doing much. I hed a great deal to l'arn, and I reckon I miss'd many more bucks than I ever hit—that is, jest up to that time—"

"Look you, Yaou," said "Big Lie," interrupting him, "you're gitting too close upon the etarnal stupid truth! All you've been a-saying is jest nothing but the naked truth as I knows it. Jest crook your trail!"

"And how's a man to lie decently onless you lets him hev a bit of truth to go upon? The truth's nothing but a peg in the wall that I hangs the lie upon. A'ter a while I promise that you sha'n't see the peg."

"Worm along, Yaou!"

"Well, Jedge, I warn't a-doing much among the *bucks* yit—jest for the reason that I was quite too eager in the scent a'ter a sartin *doe!* Now, Jedge, you never seed my wife—my Merry Ann, as I calls her; and ef you was to see her *now*—though she's prime grit yit—you would never believe that, of all the womankind in all these mountains, she was the very yaller flower of the forest; with the reddest rose cheeks you ever did see, and sich a mouth, and sich bright curly hair, and so tall, and so slender, and so all over beautiful! O Lawd! when I thinks of it and them times, I don't see how 'twas possible to think of buck-hunting when thar was sich a doe, with sich eyes shining me on!

"Well, Jedge, Merry Ann was the only da'ter of Jeff Hopson and Keziah Hopson, his wife, who was the da'ter of Squire Claypole, whose wife was Margery Clough, that lived down upon Pacolet River—"

"Look you, Yaou, ain't you gitting into them derned facts agin, eh?"

"I reckon I em, 'Big Lie!' Scuse me: I'll kiver the pegs *direct-lie,* one a'ter t'other. Whar was I? Ah! Oh! Well, Jedge, poor hunter and poor man—jest, you see, a squatter on the side of a leetle bit of a mountain close on to Columbus Mills, at Mount Tyron, I was all the time on a hot trail a'ter Merry Ann Hopson. I went thar to see her a'most every night; and sometimes I carried a buck for the old people, and sometimes a doe-skin for the gal, and I do think, bad hunter as I then was, I pretty much kept the fambly in deer meat through the whole winter."

"Good for you, Yaou! You're a-coming to it! That's the only fair trail of a lie that you've struck yit!"

So the ""Big Lie," from the chair.

"Glad to hyar you say so," was the answer. "I'll git on in time! Well, Jedge, though Jeff Hopson was glad enough to git my meat always, he didn't affection me, as I did his da'ter. He was a sharp, close, money-loving old fellow, who was always considerate of the main chaince; and the old lady, his wife, who hairdly dare say her soul was her own, she jest looked both ways, as I may say, for Sunday, never giving a fair look to me or my chainces, when his eyes were sot on *her.* But 'twa'n't so with my Merry Ann. She hed the eyes for me from the beginning, and soon she hed the feelings; and, you see, Jedge, we sometimes did git a chaince, when old Jeff was gone from home, to come to a sort of onderstanding about our feelings; and the long and the short of it was that Merry Ann confessed to me that she'd like nothing better than to be my wife. She liked no other man but me. Now, Jedge, a'ter that, what was a young fellow to do? That, I say, was the proper kind of incouragement. So I said, 'I'll ax your daddy.' Then she got scary, and said, 'Oh, don't; for somehow, Sam, I'm a-thinking daddy don't like you enough *yit.* Jest hold on a bit, and come often, and bring him venison, and try to make him laugh, which you kin do, you know, and a'ter a time you kin try him.' And so I did—or rether I didn't. I put off the axing. I come constant. I brought venison all the time, and b'ar meat a plenty, a'most three days in every week."

"That's it, Yaou. You're on trail. That's as derned a lie as you've tell'd yit; for all your hunting, in them days, didn't git more meat than you could eat your one self."

"Thank you, 'Big Lie.' I hopes I'll come up in time to the right measure of the camp.

"Well, Jedge, this went on for a long time, a'most the whole winter, and spring, and summer, till the winter begun to come in agin. I carried 'em the venison, and Merry Ann meets me in the woods, and we hes sich a pleasant time when we meets on them little odd chainces that I gits hot as thunder to bring the business to a sweet honey finish.

"But Merry Ann keeps on scary, and she puts me off; ontil, one day, one a'ternoon, about sundown, she meets me in the woods, and she's all in a flusteration. And she ups and tells me how old John Grimstead, the old bachelor (a fellow about forty years old, and the dear gal not yet twenty), how he's a'ter her, and bekaise he's got a good fairm, and mules and horses, how her daddy's giving him the open mouth incouragement.

"Then I says to Merry Ann:

" 'You sees, I kain't put off no longer. I must out with it, and ax your daddy at onst.' And then her scary fit come on again, and she begs me not to—not *jist yit*. But I swears by all the Hokies that I won't put off another day; and so, as I haird the old man was in the house that very hour, I left Merry Ann in the woods, all in a trimbling, and I jist went ahead, detarmined to have the figure made straight, whether odd or even.

"And Merry Ann, poor gal, she wrings her hainds, and cries a smart bit, and she wouldn't go to the house, but said she'd wait for me out thar. So I gin her a kiss into her very mouth—and did it over more than onst—and I left her, and pushed headlong for the house.

"I was jubous; I was mighty oncertain, and a leetle bit scary myself; for, you see, old Jeff was a fellow of tough grit, and with big grinders; but I was so oneasy, and so tired out waiting, and so desperate, and so fearsome that old bachelor Grimstead would get the start on me, that nothing could stop me now, and I jist bolted into the house, as free and easy and bold as ef I was the very best customer that the old man wanted to see."

Here Yaou paused to renew his draught of peach and honey.

IV

"Well, Jedge, as I tell you, I put a bold face on the business, though my hairt was gitting up into my throat, and I was almost a-gasping for my breath, when I was fairly in the big room, and standing up before the old

Squaire. He was a-setting in his big squar hide-bottom'd arm-chair, looking like a jedge upon the bench, jist about to send a poor fellow to the gallows. As he seed me come in, looking queer enough, I reckon, his mouth put on a sort of grin, which showed all his grinders, and he looked for all the world as ef he guessed the business I come about. But he said, good-natured enough:

" 'Well, Sam Snaffles, how goes it?'

"Says I:

" 'Pretty squar, considerin'. The winter's coming on fast, and I reckon the mountains will be full of meat before long.'

"Then says he, with another ugly grin, 'Ef 'twas your smoke-house that had it all, Sam Snaffles, 'stead of the mountains, 'twould be better for you, I reckon.'

" 'I 'grees with you,' says I. 'But I rether reckon I'll git my full shar' of it afore the spring of the leaf agin.'

" 'Well, Sam,' says he, 'I hopes, for your sake, 'twill be a big shar'. I'm afeard you're not the pusson to go for a big shar', Sam Snaffles. Seems to me you're too easy satisfied with a small shar'; sich as the fence-squarrel carries onder his two airms, calkilating only on a small corn-crib in the chestnut-tree.'

" 'Don't you be afeard, Squaire. I'll come out right. My cabin sha'n't want for nothing that a strong man with a stout hairt kin git, with good working—enough and more for himself, and perhaps another pusson.'

" 'What other pusson?' says he, with another of his great grins, and showing of his grinders.

" 'Well,' says I, "Squaire Hopson, that's jest what I come to talk to you about this blessed Friday night.'

"You see '*twas* Friday!

"Well,' says he, 'go ahead, Sam Snaffles, and empty your brain-basket as soon as you kin, and I'll light my pipe while I'm a-hearing you.'

"So he lighted his pipe, and laid himself back in his chair, shet his eyes, and begin to puff like blazes.

"By this time my blood was beginning to bile in all my veins, for I seed that he was jest in the humor to tread on all my toes, and then ax a'ter my feelings. I said to myself:

" 'It's jest as well to git the worst at onst, and then thar'll be an eend of the oneasiness.' So I up and told him, in pretty soft, smooth sort of speechifying, as how I was mighty fond of Merry Ann, and she, I was a-thinking, of me; and that I jest come to ax ef I might hev Merry Ann for my wife.

"Then he opened his eyes wide, as ef he never ixpected to hear sich a proposal from me.

" 'What!' says he. 'You?'

" 'Jest so, Squaire,' says I. 'Ef it pleases you to believe me, and to consider it reasonable, the axing.'

"He sot quiet for a minit or more, then he gits up, knocks all the fire out of his pipe on the chimney, fills it, and lights it agin, and then comes straight up to me, whar I was a-setting on the chair in front of him, and without a word he takes the collar of my coat betwixt the thumb and fore-finger of his left hand, and he says:

" 'Git up, Sam Snaffles. Git up, ef you please.'

"Well, I gits up, and he says:

" 'Hyar! Come! Hyar!'

"And with that he leads me right across the room to a big looking-glass that hung agin the partition wall, and thar he stops before the glass, facing it and holding me by the collar all the time.

"Now that looking-glass, Jedge, was about the biggest I ever did see! It was a'most three feet high, and a'most two feet wide, and it had a bright, broad frame, shiny like gold, with a heap of leetle figgers worked all round it. I reckon thar's no sich glass now in all the mountain country. I 'member when first that glass come home. It was a great thing, and the old Squaire was mighty proud of it. He bought it at the sale of some rich man's furni-ter, down at Greenville, and he was jest as fond of looking into it as a young gal, and whenever he lighted his pipe, he'd walk up and down the room, seeing himself in the glass.

"Well, thar he hed me up, both on us standing in front of this glass, whar we could a'most see the whole of our full figgers, from head to foot.

"And when we hed stood thar for a minit or so, he says, quite solemn like:

" 'Look in the glass, Sam Snaffles.'

"So I looked.

" 'Well,' says I. 'I sees you, Squaire Hopson, and myself, Sam Snaffles.'

" 'Look good,' says he, '*obzarve* well.'

" 'Well,' says I, 'I'm a-looking with all my eyes. I only sees what I tells you.'

" 'But you don't *obzarve*,' says he. 'Looking and seeing's one thing,' says he, 'but obzarving's another. Now *obzarve*.'

"By this time, Jedge, I was getting sort o' riled, for I could see that somehow he was jest a-trying to make me feel redickilous. So I says:

" 'Look you, Squaire Hopson, ef you thinks I never seed myself in a glass afore this, you're mighty mistaken. I've got my own glass at home, and though it's but a leetle sort of a small, mean consarn, it shows me as much of my own face and figger as I cares to see at any time. I never cares to look in it 'cept when I'm brushing, and combing, and clipping off the straggling beard when it's too long for my eating.'

" 'Very well,' says he; 'now obzarve! You sees your own figger, and your face, and you air obzarving as well as you know how. Now, Mr. Sam Snaffles—now that you've hed a fair look at yourself—jest now answer me, from your honest conscience, a'ter all you've seed, ef you honestly thinks you're the sort of pusson to hev *my* da'ter!'

"And with that he gin me a twist, and when I wheeled round he hed wheeled round too, and thar we stood, full facing one another.

"Lawd! how I was riled! But I answered, quick:

"And why not, I'd like to know, Squaire Hopson? I ain't the handsomest man in the world, but I'm not the ugliest; and folks don't generally consider me at all among the uglies. I'm as tall a man as you, and as stout and strong, and as good a man o' my inches as ever stepped in shoe-leather. And it's enough to tell you, Squaire, whatever *you* may think, that Merry Ann believes in me, and she's a way of thinking that I'm jest about the very pusson that ought to hev her.'

" 'Merry Ann's thinking,' says he, 'don't run all fours with her fayther's thinking. I axed you, Sam Snaffles, to *obzarve* yourself in the glass. I telled you that seeing warn't edzactly obzarving. You seed only the inches; you seed that you hed eyes and mouth and nose and the airms and legs of the man. But eyes and mouth and legs and airms don't make a man!'

" 'Oh, they don't!' says I.

" 'No, indeed,' says he. 'I seed that you hed all them; but then I seed thar was one thing that you hedn't got.'

" 'Jimini!' says I, mighty conflustered. 'What thing's a-wanting to me to make me a man?'

" '*Capital!*' says he, and he lifted himself up and looked mighty grand.

" 'Capital!' says I; 'and what's that?'

" 'Thar air many kinds of capital,' says he. 'Money's capital, for it kin buy every thing. House and lands is capital; cattle and horses and sheep—when thar's enough on 'em—is capital. And as I obzarved you in the glass, Sam Snaffles, I seed that *capital* was the very thing that you wanted to make a man of you! Now I don't mean that any da'ter of mine shall marry a pusson that's not a *parfect* man. I obzarved you long ago, and seed whar you was wanting. I axed about you. I axed your horse.'

" 'Axed my horse!' says I, pretty nigh dumfoundered.

" 'Yes; I axed your horse, and he said to me: "Look at me! I hain't got an ounce of spar' flesh on my bones. You kin count all my ribs. You kin lay the whole length of your airm betwixt any two on 'em, and it'll lie thar as snug as a black snake betwixt two poles of a log-house." Says he,

"Sam's got *no capital!* He ain't got, any time, five bushels of corn in his crib; and he's such a monstrous feeder himself that he'll eat out four bushels, and think it mighty hard upon him to give *me* the other one." Thar, now, was your horse's testimony, Sam, agin you. Then I axed about your cabin, and your way of living. I was curious, and went to see you one day when I knowed you waur at home. You hed but one chair, which you gin me to set on, and you sot on the eend of a barrel for yourself. You gin me a rasher of bacon what hedn't a streak of fat in it. You hed a poor quarter of a poor doe hanging from the rafters—a poor beast that somebody hed disabled—'

" 'I shot it myself,' says I.

" 'Well, it was a-dying when you shot it; and all the hunters say you was a poor shooter at any thing. You cooked our dinner yourself, and the hoe-cake was all dough, not hafe done, and the meat was all done as tough as ef you had dried it for a month of Sundays in a Flurriday sun! Your cabin had but one room, and that you slept in and ate in; and the floor was six inches deep in dirt! Then, when I looked into your garden, I found seven stalks of long collards only, every one seven foot high, with all the leaves stript off it, as ef you wanted 'em for broth; till thar waur only three top leaves left on every stalk. You hedn't a stalk of corn growing, and when I scratched at your turnip-bed I found nothing bigger that a chestnut. Then, Sam, I begun to ask about your fairm, and I found that you was nothing but a squatter on land of Columbus Mills, who let you have an old nigger pole-house, and an acre or two of land. Says I to myself, says I, "This poor fellow's got *no capital;* and he hasn't the head to git *capital;*" and from that moment, Sam Snaffles, the more I obzarved you, the more sartin 'twas that you never could be a man, ef you waur to live a thousand years. You may think, in your vanity, that you air a man; but you ain't, and never will be, onless you kin find a way to git *capital;* and I loves my gal child too much to let her marry any pusson whom I don't altogether consider a man!'

"A'ter that long speechifying, Jedge, you might ha' ground me up in a mill, biled me down in a pot, and scattered me over a manure heap, and I wouldn't ha' been able to say a word!

"I cotched up my hat, and was a-gwine, when he said to me, with his derned infernal big grin:

" 'Take another look in the glass, Sam Snaffles, and obzarve well, and you'll see jest whar it is I thinks that you're wanting.'

"I didn't stop for any more. I jest bolted, like a hot shot out of a shovel, and didn't know my own self, or whatever steps I tuk, tell I got into the thick and met Merry Ann coming towards me.

"I must liquor now!"

V

"Well, Jedge, it was a hard meeting betwixt me and Merry Ann. The poor gal come to me in a sort of run, and hairdly drawing her breath, she cried out:

"Oh, Sam! What does he say?'

"What could I say? How tell her? I jest wrapped her up in my airms, and I cries out, making some violent remarks about the old Squaire.

"Then she screamed, and I hed to squeeze her up, more close than ever, and kiss her, I reckon, more than a dozen times, jest to keep her from gwine into historical fits. I telled her all, from beginning to eend.

"I telled her that thar waur some truth in what the old man said: that I hedn't been keerful to do the thing as I ought; that the house *was* mean and dirty; that the horse was mean and poor; that I hed been thinking too much about her own self to think about other things; but that I would do better, would see to things, put things right, git corn in the crib, git 'capital,' ef I could, and make a good, comfortable home for *her*.

" 'Look at me,' says I, 'Merry Ann. Does I look like a man?'

" 'You're are all the man I wants,' says she.

" 'That's enough,' says I. 'You shall see what I kin do, and what I *will* do! That's ef you air true to me.'

" 'I'll be true to you, Sam,' says she.

" 'And you won't think of nobody else?'

" 'Never,' says she.

" 'Well, you'll see what I kin do, and what I *will* do. You'll see that I *em* a man; and ef thar's capital to be got in all the country, by working and hunting, and fighting, ef that's needful, we shill hev it. Only you be true to me, Merry Ann.'

"And she throwed herself upon my buzzom, and cried out:

" 'I'll be true to you, Sam. I loves nobody in all the world so much as I loves you.'

" 'And you won't marry any other man, Merry Ann, no matter what your daddy says?'

" 'Never,' she says.

" 'And you won't listen to this old bachelor fellow, Grimstead, that's got the "capital" already, no matter how they spurs you?'

" 'Never!' she says.

" 'Sw'ar it!' says I—'sw'ar it, Merry Ann—that you will be my wife, and never marry Grimstead!'

" 'I sw'ars it,' she says, kissing *me*, bekaize we had no book.

" 'Now,' says I, 'Merry Ann, that's not enough. Cuss him for my sake, and to make it sartin. Cuss that fellow Grimstead.'

" 'Oh, Sam, I kain't cuss,' says she; 'that's wicked.'

" 'Cuss him on my account,' says I—'to my credit.'

" 'Oh,' says she, 'don't ax me. I kain't do that.'

"Says I, 'Merry Ann, if you don't cuss that fellow, some way, I do believe you'll go over to him a'ter all. Jest you cuss him, now. Any small cuss will do, ef you're in airnest.'

" 'Well,' says she, 'ef that's your idee, then I says, "*Drot his skin,** and drot *my* skin, too, ef ever I marries any body but Sam Snaffles." '

" 'That'll do, Merry Ann,' says I. 'And now I'm easy in my soul and conscience. And now, Merry Ann, I'm gwine off to try my best, and git the "capital." Ef it's the "capital" that's needful to make a man of me, I'll git it, by all the Holy Hokies, if I kin.'

"And so, after a million of squeezes and kisses, we parted; and she slipt along through the woods, the back way to the house, and I mounted my horse to go to my cabin. But, afore I mounted the beast, I gin him a dozen kicks in his ribs, jest for bearing his testimony agin me, and telling the old Squaire that I hedn't 'capital' enough for a corn crib."

VI

"I was mightily let down, as you may think, by old Squaire Hopson; but I was mightily lifted up by Merry Ann.

"But when I got to my cabin, and seed how mean every thing was there, and thought how true it was, all that old Squaire Hopson had said, I felt overkim, and I said to myself, 'It's all true! How kin I bring that beautiful yaller flower of the forest to live in sich a mean cabin, and with sich poor accommydations? She that had every thing comforting and nice about her.'

"Then I considered all about 'capital;' and it growed on me, ontil I begin to see that a man might hev good legs and arms and thighs, and a good face of his own, and yit not be a parfect and proper man a'ter all! I hed lived, you see, Jedge, to be twenty-three years of age, and was living no better than a three old-year b'ar, in a sort of cave, sleeping on shuck and straw, and never looking after to-morrow.

---

*"Drot," or "Drat," has been called an American vulgarism, but it is genuine old English, as ancient as the days of Ben Jonson. Originally the oath was, "God rot it;" but Puritanism, which was unwilling to take the name of God in vain, was yet not prepared to abandon the oath, so the pious preserved it in an abridged form, omitting the G from God, and using "Od rot it." It reached its final contraction, "Drot," before it came to America. "Drot it," "Drat it," "Drot your eyes," or "Drot his skin," are so many modes of using it among the uneducated classes. [Simm's note]

"I couldn't sleep all that night for the thinking, and obzarvations. That impudent talking of old Hopson put me on a new track. I couldn't give up hunting. I knowed no other business, and I didn't hafe know that.

"I thought to myself, 'I must l'arn my business so as to work like a master.'

"But then, when I considered how hard it was, how slow I was to git the deers and the b'ar, and what a small chaince of money it brought me, I said to myself:

" 'Whar's the "capital" to come from?'

"Lawd save us! I ate up the meat pretty much as fast as I got it!

"Well, Jedge, as I said, I had a most miserable night of consideration and obzarvation and concatenation accordingly. I felt all over mean, 'cept now and then, when I thought of dear Merry Ann, and her felicities and cordialities and fidelities; and then, the cuss which she gin, onder the kiver of 'Drot,' to that dried up old bachelor Grimstead. But I got to sleep at last. And I hed a dream. And I thought I seed the prettiest woman critter in the world, next to Merry Ann, standing close by my bedside; and, at first, I thought 'twas Merry Ann, and I was gwine to kiss her agin; but she drawed back and said:

" 'Scuse me! I'm not Merry Ann; but I'm her friend and your friend; so don't you be down in the mouth, but keep a good hairt, and you'll hev help, and git the "capital" whar you don't look for it now. It's only needful that you be determined on good works and making a man of yourself.'

"A'ter that dream I slept like a top, woke at day-peep, took my rifle, called up my dog, mounted my horse, and put out for the laurel hollows.

"Well, I hunted all day, made several *starts*, but got nothing; my dog ran off, the rascally pup, and I reckon, ef Squaire Hopson had met him he'd ha' said 'twas bekaise I starved him! Fact is, we hedn't any on us much to eat that day, and the old mar's ribs stood out bigger than ever.

"All day I rode and followed the track and got nothing.

"Well, jest about sunset I come to a hollow of the hills that I hed never seed before; and in the middle of it was a great pond of water, what you call a lake; and it showed like so much purple glass in the sunset, and 'twas jest as smooth as the big looking-glass of Squaire Hopson's. Thar wa'n't a breath of wind stirring.

"I was mighty tired, so I eased down from the mar', tied up the bridle and check, and let her pick about, and laid myself down onder a tree, jest about twenty yards from the lake, and thought to rest myself ontil the moon riz, which I knowed would be about seven o'clock.

"I didn't mean to fall asleep, but I did it; and I reckon I must ha' slept a good hour, for when I woke the dark hed set in, and I could only see one or two bright stars hyar and thar, shooting out from the dark of the heavens. But, ef I seed nothing, I haird; and jest sich a sound and noise as I hed never haird before.

"Thar was a rushing and a roaring and a screaming and a plashing, in the air and in the water, as made you think the univarsal world was coming to an eend!

"All that set me up. I was waked up out of sleep and dream, and my eyes opened to every thing that eye could see; and sich another sight I never seed before! I tell you, Jedge, ef there was one wild-goose settling down in that lake, thar was one hundred thousand of 'em! I couldn't see the eend of 'em. They come every minit, swarm a'ter swarm, in tens and twenties and fifties and hundreds; and sich a fuss as they did make! sich a gabbling, sich a splashing, sich a confusion, that I was fairly conflusterated; and I jest lay whar I was, a-watching 'em.

"You never seed beasts so happy! How they flapped their wings; how they gabbled to one another; how they swam hyar and thar, to the very middle of the lake and to the very edge of it, jest a fifty yards from whar I lay squat, never moving leg or arm! It was wonderful to see! I wondered how they could find room, for I reckon thar waur forty thousand on 'em, all scuffling in that leetle lake together!

"Well, as I watched 'em, I said to myself:

" 'Now, if a fellow could only captivate all them wild-geese—fresh from Canniday, I reckon—what would they bring in the market at Spartanburg and Greenville? Walker, I knowed, would buy 'em up quick at fifty cents a head. Forty thousand geese at fifty cents a head. Thar was "capital!" ' '

"I could ha' fired in among 'em with my rifle, never taking aim, and killed a dozen or more, at a single shot; but what was a poor dozen geese, when thar waur forty thousand to captivate?

"What a haul 'twould be, ef a man could only get 'em all in one net! Kiver 'em all at a fling!

"The idee worked like so much fire in my brain.

"How kin it be done?

"That was the question!

" 'Kin it be done?' I axed myself.

" 'It kin,' I said to myself; 'and I'm the very man to do it!' Then I begun to work away in the thinking. I thought over all the traps and nets and snares that I hed ever seen or haird of; and the leetle eends of the idee begun to come together in my head; and, watching all the time how the geese flopped and splashed and played and swum, I said to myself:

" 'Oh! most beautiful critters! ef I don't make some "capital" out of you, then I'm not dezarving sich a beautiful yaller flower of the forest as my Merry Ann!'

"Well, I watched a long time, ontil dark night, and the stars begun to peep down upon me over the high hill-tops. Then I got up and tuk to my horse and rode home.

"And thar, when I hed swallowed my bit of hoe-cake and bacon and a good strong cup of coffee, and got into bed, I couldn't sleep for a long time, thinking how I was to git them geese.

"But I kept nearing the right idee every minit, and when I was fast asleep it come to me in my dream.

"I seed the same beautifulest young woman agin that hed given me the incouragement before to go ahead, and she helped me out with the idee.

"So, in the morning, I went to work. I rode off to Spartanburg, and bought all the twine and cord and hafe the plow-lines in town; and I got a lot of great fishhooks, all to help make the tanglement parfect; and I got lead for sinkers, and I got cork-wood for floaters; and I pushed for home jist as fast as my poor mar' could streak it.

"I was at work day and night, for nigh on to a week, making my net; and when 'twas done I borrowed a mule and cart from Columbus Mills, thar;—he'll tell you all about it—he kin make his affidavy to the truth of it.

"Well, off I driv with my great net, and got to the lake about noon-day. I knowed 'twould take me some hours to make my fixings parfect, and git the net fairly stretched across the lake, and jest deep enough to do the tangling of every leg of the birds in the very midst of their swimming and snorting and splashing and cavorting! When I hed fixed it all fine, and jest as I wanted it, I brought the eends of my plow-lines up to where I was gwine to hide myself. This was onder a strong sapling, and my calkilation was when I hed got the beasts all hooked, forty thousand, more or less— and I could tell how that was from feeling on the line—why, then, I'd whip the line round the sapling, hitch it fast, and draw in my birds at my own ease, without axing much about their comfort.

"'Twas a most beautiful and parfect plan, and all would ha' worked beautiful well but for one leetle oversight of mine. But I won't tell you about that part of the business yit, the more pretickilarly as it all turned out for the very best, as you'll see in the eend.

"I hedn't long finished my fixings when the sun suddenly tumbled down the heights, and the dark begun to creep in upon me, and a pretty cold dark it waur! I remember it well! My teeth begun to chatter in my head, though I was boiling over with inward heat, all jest coming out of my hot eagerness to be captivating the birds.

"Well, Jedge, I hedn't to wait overlong. Soon I haird them coming, screaming fur away, and then I seed them pouring, jest like so many white clouds, straight down, I reckon, from the snow mountains off in Canniday.

"Down they come, millions upon millions, till I was sartin thar waur already pretty nigh on to forty thousand in the lake. It waur always a nice calkilation of mine that the lake could hold fully forty thousand, though onst, when I went round to measure it, stepping it off, I was jubous whether it could hold over thirty-nine thousand; but, as I tuk the measure in hot weather and in a dry spell, I concluded that some of the water along the edges hed dried up, and 'twa'n't so full as when I made my first calkilation. So I hev stuck to that first calkilation ever since.

"Well, thar they waur, forty thousand, we'll say, with, it mout be, a few millions and hundreds over. And Lawd! how they played and splashed and screamed and dived! I calkilated on hooking a good many of them divers, in pretickilar, and so I watched and waited, ontil I thought I'd feel of my lines; and I begun, leetle by leetle, to haul in, when, Lawd love you, Jedge, sich a ripping and raging, and bouncing and flouncing, and flopping and splashing, and kicking and screaming, you never did hear in all your born days!

"By this I knowed that I hed captivated the captains of the host, and a pretty smart chaince, I reckoned, of the rigilar army, ef 'twa'n't edzactly forty thousand; for I calkilated that some few would git away—run off, jest as the cowards always does in the army, jest when the shooting and confusion begins; still, I reasonably calkilated on the main body of the rigiments; and so, gitting more and more hot and eager, and pulling and hauling, I made one big mistake, and, instid of wrapping the eends of my lines around the sapling that was standing jest behind me, what does I do but wraps 'em round my own thigh—the right thigh, you see—and some of the loops waur hitched round my left arm at the same time!

"All this come of my hurry and ixcitement, for it was burning like a hot fever in my brain, and I didn't know when or how I hed tied myself up, ontil suddenly, with an all-fired scream, all together, them forty thousand geese rose like a great black cloud in the air, all tied up, tangled up—hooked about the legs, hooked about the gills, hooked and fast in some way in the beautiful leetle twistings of my net!

"Yes, Judge, as I'm a living hunter to-night, hyar a-talking to you, they riz up all together, as ef they hed consulted upon it, like a mighty thunder-cloud, and off they went, screaming and flouncing, meaning, I reckon, to take the back track to Canniday, in spite of the freezing weather.

"Before I knowed whar I was, Jedge, I was twenty feet in the air, my right thigh up and my left arm, and the other thigh and arm a-dangling useless, and feeling every minit as ef they was gwine to drop off.

"You may be sure I pulled with all my might, but that waur mighty leetle in the fix I was in, and I jest hed to hold on, and see whar the infernal beasts would carry me. I couldn't loose myself, and ef I could I was by this time quite too fur up in the air, and darsn't do so, onless I was willing to hev my brains dashed out, and my whole body mashed to a mammock!

"Oh, Jedge, jest consider my sitivation! It's sich a ricollection, Jedge, that I must rest and liquor, in order to rekiver the necessary strength to tell you what happened next."

VII

"Yes, Jedge," said Yaou, resuming his narrative, "jest stop whar you air, and consider my sitivation!

"Thar I was dangling, like a dead weight, at the tail of that all-fired cloud of wild-geese, head downward, and gwine, the Lawd knows whar!— to Canniday, or Jericho, or some other heathen territory beyond the Massissipp, and it mout be, over the great etarnal ocean!

"When I thought of *that,* and thought of the plow-lines giving way, and that on a suddent I should come down plump into the big sea, jest in the middle of a great gathering of shirks and whales, to be dewoured and tore to bits by their bloody grinders, I was ready to die of skeer outright. I thought over all my sinnings in a moment, and I thought of my poor dear Merry Ann, and I called out her name, loud as I could, jest as ef the poor gal could hyar me or help me.

"And jest then I could see we waur a drawing nigh a great thundercloud. I could see the red tongues running out of its black jaws; and 'Lawd!' says I, 'ef these all-fired infarnal wild beasts of birds should carry me into that cloud to be burned to a coal, fried, and roasted, and biled alive by them tongues of red fire!'

"But the geese fought shy of the cloud, though we passed mighty nigh on to it, and I could see one red streak of lightning run out of the cloud and give us chase for a full hafe a mile; but we waur too fast for it, and, in a tearing passion bekaise it couldn't ketch us, the red streak struck its horns into a great tree jest behind us, that we hed passed over, and tore it into flinders, in the twink of a musquito.

"But by this time I was beginning to feel quite stupid. I knowed that I waur fast gitting onsensible, and it did seem to me as ef my hour waur come, and I was gwine to die—and die by rope, and dangling in the air, a thousand miles from the airth!

"But jest then I was roused up. I felt something brush agin me; then my face was scratched; and, on a suddent, thar was a stop put to my travels by that conveyance. The geese had stopped flying, and waur in a mighty great conflusteration, flopping their wings, as well as they could, and screaming with all the tongues in their jaws. It was clar to me now that we hed run agin something that brought us all up with a short hitch.

"I was shook roughly agin the obstruction, and I put out my right arm and cotched a hold of a long arm of an almighty big tree; then my legs waur cotched betwixt two other branches, and I rekivered myself, so as to set up a leetle and rest. The geese was a tumbling and flopping among the branches. The net was hooked hyar and thar; and the birds waur all about me, swinging and splurging, but onable to break loose and git away.

"By leetle and leetle I come to my clar senses, and begun to feel my sitivation. The stiffness was passing out of my limbs. I could draw up my legs, and after some hard work, I managed to onwrap the plow-lines from my right thigh and my left arm, and I hed the sense this time to tie the eends pretty tight to a great branch of the tree which stretched clar across and about a foot over my head.

"Then I begun to consider my sitivation. I hed hed a hard riding, that was sartin; and I felt sore enough. And I hed hed a horrid bad skear, enough to make a man's wool turn white afore the night was over. But now I felt easy, bekaise I considered myself safe. With day-peep I calkilated to let myself down from the tree by my plow-lines, and thar, below, tied fast, warn't thar my forty thousand captivated geese?

"Hurrah!' I sings out. 'Hurrah, Merry Ann; we'll hev the "capital" now, I reckon!'

"And singing out, I drawed up my legs and shifted my body so as to find an easier seat in the crutch of the tree, which was an almighty big chestnut oak, when, O Lawd! on a suddent the stump I hed been a-setting on give way onder me. 'Twas a rotten jint of the tree. It give way, Jedge, as I tell you, and down I went, my legs first and then my whole body—slipping down not on the outside, but into a great hollow of the tree, all the hairt of it being eat out by the rot; and afore I knowed whar I waur, I waur some twenty foot down, I reckon; and by the time I touched bottom, I was up to my neck in honey!

"It was an almighty big honey-tree, full of the sweet treacle; and the bees all gone and left it, I reckon, for a hundred years. And I in it up to my neck.

"I could smell it strong. I could taste it sweet. But I could see nothing.

"Lawd! Lawd! From bad to worse; buried alive in a hollow tree with never a chaince to git out! I would then ha' given all the world ef I was only sailing away with them bloody wild-geese to Canniday, and Jericho, even across the sea, with all its shirks and whales dewouring me.

"Buried alive! O Lawd! O Lawd! 'Lawd save me and help me!' I cried out from the depths. And 'Oh, my Merry Ann,' I cried, 'shill we never meet agin no more!' Scuse my weeping, Jedge, but I feels all over the sin-sation, fresh as ever, of being buried alive in a beehive tree and presarved in honey. I must liquor, Jedge."

VIII

Yaou, after a great swallow of peach and honey, and a formidable groan after it, resumed his narrative as follows:

"Only think of me, Jedge, in my sitivation! Buried alive in the hollow of a mountain chestnut oak! Up to my neck in honey, with never no more an appetite to eat than ef it waur the very gall of bitterness that we reads of in the Holy Scripters!

"All dark, all silent as the grave; 'cept for the gabbling and the cack-ling of the wild-geese outside, that every now and then would make a great splurging and cavorting, trying to break away from their hitch, which was jist as fast fixed as my own.

"Who would git them geese that hed cost me so much to captivate? Who would inherit my 'capital?' and who would hev Merry Ann? and what will become of the mule and cart of Mills fastened in the woods by the leetle lake?

"I cussed the leetle lake, and the geese, and all the 'capital.'

"I cussed. I couldn't help it. I cussed from the bottom of my hairt, when I ought to ha' bin saying my prayers. And thar was my poor mar' in the stable with never a morsel of feed. She had told tales upon me to Squaire Hopson, it's true, but I forgin her, and thought of her feed, and nobody to give her none. Thar waur corn in the crib and fodder, but it warn't in the stable; and onless Columbus Mills should come looking a'ter me at the cabin, thar waur no hope for me or the mar.'

"Oh, Jedge, you couldn't jedge of my sitivation in that deep hollow, that cave, I may say, of mountain oak! My head waur jest above the honey, and ef I backed it to look up, my long ha'r at the back of the neck a'most stuck fast, so thick was the honey.

"But I couldn't help looking up. The hollow was a wide one at the top, and I could see when a star was passing over. Thar they shined, bright and beautiful, as ef they waur the very eyes of the angels; and, as I seed them come and go, looking smiling in upon me as they come, I cried out to 'em, one by one:

" 'Oh, sweet sperrits, blessed angels! ef so be thar's an angel sperrit, as they say, living in all them stars, come down and extricate me from this fix; for, so fur as I kin see, I've got no chaince of help from mortal man or woman. Hairdly onst a year does a human come this way; and ef they did come, how would they know I'm hyar? How could I make them hyar me?

O Lawd! O blessed, beautiful angels in them stars! O give me help! Help me out!' I knowed I prayed like a heathen sinner, but I prayed as well as I knowed how; and thar warn't a star passing over me that I didn't pray to, soon as I seed them shining over the opening of the hollow; and I prayed fast and faster as I seed them passing away and gitting out of sight.

"Well, Jedge, suddently, in the midst of my praying, and jest after one bright, big star hed gone over me without seeing my sitivation, I hed a fresh skeer.

"Suddent I haird a monstrous fluttering among my geese—my 'capital.' Then I haird a great scraping and scratching on the outside of the tree, and, suddent, as I looked up, the mouth of the hollow was shet up.

"All was dark. The stars and sky waur all gone. Something black kivered the hollow, and, in a minit a'ter, I haird something slipping down into the hollow right upon me.

"I could hairdly draw my breath. I begun to fear that I was to be siffocated alive; and as I haird the strange critter slipping down, I shoved out my hands and felt ha'r—coarse wool—and with one hand I cotched hold of the ha'ry leg of a beast, and with t'other hand I cotched hold of his tail.

" 'Twas a great b'ar, one of the biggest, come to git his honey. He knowed the tree, Jedge, you see, and ef any beast in the world loves honey, 'tis a b'ar beast. He'll go his death on honey, though the hounds are tearing at his very haunches.

"You may be sure, when I onst knowed what he was, and onst got a good gripe on his hindquarters, I warn't gwine to let go in a hurry. I knowed that was my only chaince for gitting out of the hollow, and I do believe them blessed angels in the stars sent the beast, jest at the right time, to give me human help and assistance.

"Now, yer see, Jedge, thar was no chaince for him turning round upon me. He pretty much filled up the hollow. He knowed his way, and slipped down, eend foremost—the latter eend, you know. He could stand up on his hind-legs and eat all he wanted. Then, with his great sharp claws and his mighty muscle, he could work up, holding on to the sides of the tree, and git out a'most as easy as when he come down.

"Now, you see, ef he weighed five hundred pounds, and could climb like a cat, he could easy carry up a young fellow that hed no flesh to spar', and only weighed a hundred and twenty-five. So I laid my weight on him, eased him off as well as I could, but held on to tail and leg as ef all life and etarnity depended upon it.

"Now I reckon, Jedge, that b'ar was pretty much more skeered than I was. He couldn't turn in his shoes, and with something fastened to his ankles, and, as he thought, I reckon, some strange beast fastened to his tail, you never seed beast more eager to git away, and git upwards. He knowed the way, and stuck his claws in the rough sides of the hollow, hand over hand, jest as a sailor pulls a rope, and up we went. We hed, howsomdever, more than one slip back; but, Lawd bless you! I never let go. Up we went, I say, at last, and I stuck jest as close to his haunches as death sticks to a dead nigger. Up we went. I felt myself moving. My neck was out of the honey. My airms were free. I could feel the sticky thing slipping off from me, and a'ter a good quarter of an hour the b'ar was on the great mouth of the hollow; and as I felt that I let go his tail, still keeping fast hold of his leg, and with one hand I cotched hold of the outside rim of the hollow; I found it fast, held on to it; and jest then the b'ar sat squat on the very edge of the hollow, taking a sort of rest a'ter his labor.

"I don't know what 'twas, Jedge, that made me do it. I warn't a-thinking at all. I was only feeling and drawing a long breath. Jest then the b'ar sort o'looked round, as ef to see what varmint it was a-troubling him, when I gin him a mighty push, strong as I could, and he lost his balance and went over outside down cl'ar to the airth, and I could hyar his neck crack, almost as loud as a pistol.

"I drawed a long breath a'ter that, and prayed a short prayer; and feeling my way all the time, so as to be sure agin rotten branches, I got a safe seat among the limbs of the tree, and sot myself down, determined to wait tell broad daylight before I tuk another step in the business."

IX

"And thar I sot. So fur as I could see, Jedge, I was safe. I hed got out of the tie of the flying geese, and thar they all waur, spread before me, flopping now and then and trying to ixtricate themselves; but they couldn't come it! Thar they waur, captivated, and so much 'capital' for Sam Snaffles.

"And I hed got out of the lion's den; that is, I hed got out of the honey-tree, and warn't in no present danger of being buried alive agin. Thanks to the b'ar, and to the blessed, beautiful angel sperrits in the stars, that hed sent him thar seeking honey, to be my deliverance from my captivation!

"And thar he lay, jest as quiet as ef he waur a-sleeping, though I knowed his neck was broke. And that b'ar, too, was so much 'capital.'

"And I sot in the tree making my calkilations. I could see now the meaning of that beautiful young critter that come to me in my dreams. I was to hev the 'capital,' but I was to git it through troubles and tribulations, and a mighty bad skeer for life. I never knowed the valley of 'capital' till now, and I seed the sense in all that Squaire Hopson told me, though he did tell it in a mighty spiteful sperrit.

"Well, I calkilated.

"It was cold weather, freezing, and though I had good warm clothes on, I felt monstrous like sleeping, from the cold only, though perhaps the tire and the skeer together hed something to do with it. But I was afeard to sleep. I didn't know what would happen, and a man has never his right courage ontil daylight. I fou't agin sleep by keeping on my calkilation.

"Forty thousand wild-geese!

"Thar wa'n't forty thousand, edzactly—very far from it—but thar they waur, pretty thick; and for every goose I could git from forty to sixty cents in all the villages in South Carolina.

"Thar was 'capital!'

"Then thar waur the b'ar.

"Jedging from his strength in pulling me up, and from his size and fat in filling up that great hollow in the tree, I calkilated that he couldn't weigh less than five hundred pounds. His hide, I knowed, was worth twenty dollars. Then thar was the fat and tallow, and the biled marrow out of his bones, what they makes b'ars grease out of, to make chicken whiskers grow big enough for game-cocks. Then thar waur the meat, skinned, cleaned, and all; thar couldn't be much onder four hundred and fifty pounds, and whether I sold him as fresh meat or cured, he'd bring me ten cents a pound at the least.

"Says I, 'Thar's capital!'

" 'Then,' says I, 'thar's my honey-tree! I reckon thar's a matter of ten thousand gallons in hyar same honey-tree; and if I kint git fifty to seventy cents a gallon for it thar's no alligators in Flurriday!'

"And so I calkilated through the night, fighting agin sleep, and thinking of my 'capital' and Merry Ann together.

"By morning I had calkilated all I hed to do and all I hed to make.

"Soon as I got a peep of day I was bright on the look-out.

"Thar all around me were the captivated geese critters. The b'ar laid down parfectly easy and waiting for the knife; and the geese, I reckon they waur much more tired than me, for they didn't seem to hev the hairt for a single flutter, even when they seed me swing down from the tree among 'em, holding on to my plow-lines and letting myself down easy.

"But first I must tell you, Jedge, when I seed the first signs of daylight and looked around me, Lawd bless me, what should I see but old Tryon Mountain, with his great head lifting itself up in the east! And beyant I could see the house and fairm of Columbus Mills; and as I turned to look a leetle south of that, thar was my own poor leetle log-cabin standing quiet, but with never a smoke streaming out from the chimbley.

" 'God bless them good angel sperrits,' I said, 'I ain't two miles from home!' Before I come down from the tree I knowed edzactly whar I waur. 'Twas only four miles off from the lake and whar I hitched the mule of

Columbus Mills close by the cart. Thar, too, I had left my rifle. Yit in my miserable fix, carried through the air by them wild-geese, I did think I hed gone a'most a thousand miles towards Canniday.

"Soon as I got down from the tree I pushed off at a trot to git the mule and cart. I was pretty sure of my b'ar and geese when I come back. The cart stood quiet enough. But the mule, having nothing to eat, was sharping her teeth upon a boulder, thinking she'd hev a bite or so before long.

"I hitched her up, brought her to my bee-tree, tumbled the b'ar into the cart, wrung the necks of all the geese that waur thar—many hed got away—and counted some twenty-seven hundred that I piled away atop of the b'ar."

"Twenty-seven hundred!" cried the "Big Lie" and all the hunters at a breath. "Twenty-seven hundred! Why, Yaou, whenever you telled of this thing before you always counted them at 3150!"

"Well, ef I did, I reckon I was right. I was sartinly right then, it being all fresh in my 'membrance; and I'm not the man to go back agin his own words. No, fellows, I sticks to first words and first principles. I scorns to eat my own words. Ef I said 3150, then 3150 it waur, never a goose less. But you'll see how to 'count for all. I reckon 'twas only 2700 I fotched to market. Thar was 200 I gin to Columbus Mills. Then thar was 200 more I carried to Merry Ann; and then thar waur 50 at least, I reckon, I kep for myself. Jest you count up, Jedge, and you'll see how to squar' it on all sides. When I said 2700 I only counted what I sold in the villages, every head of 'em at fifty cents a head; and a'ter putting the money in my pocket I felt all over that I hed the 'capital.'

"Well, Jedge, next about the b'ar. Sold the hide and tallow for a fine market-price; sold the meat, got ten cents a pound for it fresh—'twas most beautiful meat; biled down the bones for the marrow; melted down the grease; sold fourteen pounds of it to the barbers and apothecaries; got a dollar a pound for that; sold the hide for twenty dollars; and got the cash for every thing.

"Thar warn't a fambly in all Greenville and Spartanburg and Asheville that didn't git fresh, green wild-geese from me that season, at fifty cents a head, and glad to git, too; the cheapest fresh meat they could buy; and, I reckon, the finest. And all the people of them villages, ef they hed gone to heaven that week, in the flesh, would have carried nothing better than goose-flesh for the risurrection! Every body ate goose for a month, I reckon, as the weather was freezing cold all the time, and the beasts kept week after week, ontil they waur eaten. From the b'ar only I made a matter of full one hundred dollars. First, thar waur the hide, $20; then 450 pounds of meat, at 10 cents, was $45; then the grease, 14 pounds, $14; and the tallow, some $6 more; and the biled marrow, $11.

"Well, count up, Jedge; 2700 wild-geese, at 50 cents, you sees, must be more than $1350. I kin only say, that a'ter all the selling—and I driv at it day and night, with Columbus Mills's mule and cart, and went to every house in every street in all them villages. I hed a'most fifteen hundred dollars, safe stowed away onder the pillows of my bed, all in solid gould and silver.

"But I warn't done! Thar was my bee-tree. Don't you think I waur gwine to lose that honey! no, my darlint! I didn't beat the drum about nothing. I didn't let on to a soul what I was a-doing. They axed me about the wild-geese, but I sent 'em on a wild-goose chase; and 'twa'n't till I hed sold off all the b'ar meat and all the geese that I made ready to git at that honey. I reckon them bees must ha' been making that honey for a hundred years, and was then driv out by the b'ars.

"Columbus Mills will tell you; he axed me all about it; but, though he was always my good friend, I never even told it to him. But he lent me his mule and cart, good fellow as he is, and never said nothing more; and, quiet enough, without beat of drum, I bought up all the tight-bound barrels that ever brought whisky to Spartanburg and Greenville, whar they hes the taste for that article strong; and day by day I went off carrying as many barrels as the cart could hold and the mule could draw. I tapped the old tree —which was one of the oldest and biggest chestnut oaks I ever did see— close to the bottom, and drawed off the beautiful treacle. I was more than sixteen days about it, and got something over two thousand gallons of the purest, sweetest, yellowest honey you ever did see. I could hairdly git barrels and jimmyjohns enough to hold it; and I sold it out at seventy cents a gallon, which was mighty cheap. So I got from the honey a matter of fourteen hundred dollars.

"Now, Jedge, all this time, though it went very much agin the grain, I kept away from Merry Ann and the old Squaire, her daddy. I sent him two hundred head of geese—some fresh, say one hundred, and another hundred that I hed cleaned and put in salt—and I sent him three jimmyjohns of honey, five gallons each. But I kept away and said nothing, beat no drum, and hed never a thinking but how to git in the 'capital.' And I did git it in!

"When I carried the mule and cart home to Columbus Mills I axed him about a sartin farm of one hundred and sixty acres that he hed to sell. It hed a good house on it. He selled it to me cheap. I paid him down, and put the titles in my pocket. 'Thar's capital!' says I.

"*That* waur a fixed thing for ever and ever. And when I hed moved every thing from the old cabin to the new farm, Columbus let me hev a fine milch cow that gin eleven quarts a day, with a beautiful young caif. Jest about that time thar was a great sale of the furniter of the Ashmore family down at Spartanburg, and I remembered I hed no decent bedstead, or any thing rightly sarving for a young woman's chamber; so I went to the sale, and bought a fine strong mahogany bedstead, a dozen chairs, a chist of drawers, and some other things that ain't quite mentionable, Jedge, but all proper for a lady's chamber; and I soon hed the house fixed up ready for any thing. And up to this time I never let on to any body what I was a-thinking about or what I was a-doing, ontil I could stand up in my own doorway and look about me, and say to myself—this is my 'capital,' I reckon; and when I hed got all that I thought a needcessity to git, I took 'count of every thing.

"I spread the title-deeds of my fairm out on the table. I read 'em over three times to see ef 'twaur all right. Thar was my name several times in big letters, 'to hev and to hold.'

"Then I fixed the furniter. Then I brought out into the stable-yard the old mar'—you couldn't count her ribs *now*, and she was spry as ef she hed got a new conceit of herself.

"Then thar was my beautiful cow and caif, sealing fat, both on 'em, and sleek as a doe in autumn.

"Then thar waur a fine young mule that I bought in Spartanburg; my cart, and a strong second-hand buggy, that could carry two pussons convenient of two different sexes. And I felt big, like a man of consekence and capital.

"That warn't all.

"I had the shiners, Jedge, besides—all in gould and silver—none of your dirty rags and blotty spotty paper. That was the time of Old Hickory —General Jackson, you know—when he kicked over Nick Biddle's consarn, and gin us the beautiful Benton Mint Drops, in place of rotten paper. You could git the gould and silver jest for the axing, in them days, you know.

"I hed a grand count of my money, Jedge. I hed it in a dozen or twenty little bags of leather—the gould—and the silver I hed in shot-bags. It took me a whole morning to count it up and git the figgers right. Then I stuffed it in my pockets, hyar and thar, every whar, wherever I could stow a bag; and the silver I stuffed away in my saddle-bags, and clapped it on the mar'.

"Then I mounted myself, and sot the mar's nose straight in a bee-line for the fairm of Squaire Hopson.

"I was a-gwine, you see, to surprise him with my 'capital;' but, fust, I meant to give him a mighty grand skeer.

"You see, when I was a-trading with Columbus Mills about the fairm and cattle and other things, I ups and tells him about my courting of Merry Ann; and when I told him about Squaire Hopson's talk about 'capital,' he says:

" 'The old skunk! What right hes he to be talking big so, when he kain't pay his own debts. He's been owing me three hundred and fifty dollars now gwine on three years, and I kain't git even the *intrust* out of him. I've got a mortgage on his fairm for the whole, and ef he won't let you hev his da'ter, jest you come to me, and I'll clap the screws to him in short order.'

"Says I, 'Columbus, won't you sell me that mortgage?'

" 'You shill hev it for the face of the debt,' says he, 'not considerin' the intrust.'

"It's a bargin,' says I; and I paid him down the money, and he signed the mortgage over to me for a vallyable consideration.

"I hed that beautiful paper in my breast pocket, and felt strong to face the Squaire in his own house, knowing how I could turn him out of it! And I mustn't forget to tell you how I got myself a new rig of clothing, with a mighty fine over-coat, and a new fur cap; and as I looked in the glass I felt my consekence all over at every for'a'd step I tuk; and I felt my inches growing with every pace of the mar' on the high-road to Merry Ann and her beautiful daddy!' "

X

"Well, Jedge, before I quite got to the Squaire's farm, who should come out to meet me in the road but Merry Ann, her own self! She hed spied me, I reckon, as I crossed the bald ridge a quarter of a mile away. I do reckon the dear gal hed been looking out for me every day the whole eleven days in the week, counting in all the Sundays. In the mountains, you know, Jedge, that the weeks sometimes run to twelve, and even fourteen days, specially when we're on a long camp-hunt!

"Well, Merry Ann cried and laughed together, she was so tarnation glad to see me agin. Says she:

" 'Oh, Sam! I'm so glad to see you! I was afeard you had clean gin me up. And thar's that fusty old bachelor Grimstead, he's a-coming here a'most every day; and daddy, he sw'ars that I shill marry him, and nobody else; and mammy, she's at me too, all the time, telling me how fine a fairm he's got, and what a nice carriage, and all that; and mammy says as how daddy'll be sure to beat me ef I don't hev him. But I kain't bear to look at him, the old griesly!'

" 'Cuss him!' says I. 'Cuss him, Merry Ann!'

"And she did, but onder her breath—the old cuss.

" 'Drot him!' says she; and she said louder, 'and drot me, too, Sam, ef I ever marries any body but you.'

"By this time I hed got down and gin her a long strong hug, and a'most twenty or a dozen kisses, and I says:

" 'You sha'n't marry nobody but me, Merry Ann; and we'll hev the marriage this very night, ef you says so!'

" 'Oh! psho, Sam! How you does talk!'

" 'Ef I don't marry you to-night, Merry Ann, I'm a holy mortar, and a sinner not to be saved by any salting, though you puts the petre with the salt. I'm come for that very thing. Don't you see my new clothes?'

" 'Well, you hev got a beautiful coat, Sam; all so blue, and with sich shiny buttons.'

" 'Look at my waistcoat, Merry Ann! What do you think of that?'

" 'Why, it's a most beautiful blue welvet!'

" 'That's the very article,' says I. 'And see the breeches, Merry Ann; and the boots!'

" 'Well,' says she, 'I'm fair astonished, Sam! Why whar, Sam, did you find all the money for these fine things?'

" 'A beautiful young woman, a'most as beautiful as you, Merry Ann, come to me the very night of that day when your daddy driv me off with a flea in my ear. She come to me to my bed at midnight—'

" 'Oh, Sam! *ain't* you ashamed!'

" ' 'Twas in a dream, Merry Ann; and she tells me something to incourage me to go for'a'd, and I went for'a'd, bright and airly next morning, and I picked up three servants that hev been working for me ever sence.'

" 'What sarvants?' says she.

" 'One was a goose, one was a b'ar, and t'other was a bee!'

" 'Now you're a-fooling me, Sam.'

" 'You'll see! Only you git yourself ready, for, by the eternal Hokies, I marries you this very night, and takes you home to *my* fairm bright and airly to-morrow morning.'

" 'I do think, Sam, you must be downright crazy.'

" 'You'll see and believe! Do you go home and git yourself fixed up for the wedding. Old Parson Stovall lives only two miles from your daddy, and I'll hev him hyar by sundown. You'll see!'

" 'But ef I waur to b'lieve you, Sam—'

" 'I've got on my wedding-clothes o' purpose, Merry Ann.'

" 'But *I* hain't got no clothes fit for a gal to be married in,' says she.

" 'I'll marry you this very night, Merry Ann,' says I, 'though you hedn't a stitch of clothing at all!'

" 'Git out, you sassy Sam,' says she, slapping my face. Then I kissed her in her very mouth, and a'ter that we walked on together, I leading the mar.'

"Says she, as we neared the house, 'Sam, let me go before, or stay hyar in the thick, and you go in by yourself. Daddy's in the hall, smoking his pipe and reading the newspapers.'

" 'We'll walk in together,' says I, quite consekential.

"Says she, 'I'm so afeard.'

" 'Don't you be afeard, Merry Ann,' says I; 'you'll see that all will come out jest as I tells you. We'll be hitched to-night, ef Parson Stovall, or any other parson, kin be got to tie us up!'

"Says she, suddenly, 'Sam, you're a-walking lame, I'm a-thinking. What's the matter? Hev you hurt yourself any way?'

"Says I, 'It's only owing to my not balancing my accounts even in my pockets. You see I feel so much like flying in the air with the idee of marrying you to-night that I filled my pockets with rocks, jest to keep me down.'

" 'I do think, Sam, you're a leetle cracked in the upper story.'

" 'Well,' says I, 'ef so, the crack has let in a blessed chaince of the beautifulest sunlight! You'll see! Cracked, indeed! Ha, ha, ha! Wait till I've done with your daddy! I'm gwine to square accounts with *him*, and, I reckon, when I'm done with him, you'll guess that the crack's in *his* skull, and not in mine.'

" 'What! you wouldn't knock my father, Sam!' says she, drawing off from me and looking skeary.

" 'Don't you be afeard; but it's very sartin, ef our heads don't come together, Merry Ann, you won't hev me for your husband to-night. And that's what I've swore upon. Hyar we air!'

"When we got to the yard I led in the mar', and Merry Ann she ran away from me and dodged round the house. I hitched the mar' to the post, took off the saddle-bags, which was mighty heavy, and walked into the house stiff enough I tell you, though the gould in my pockets pretty much weighed me down as I walked.

"Well, in I walked, and thar sat the old Squire smoking his pipe and reading the newspaper. He looked at me through his specs over the newspaper, and when he seed who 'twas his mouth put on that same conceited sort of grin and smile that he ginerally hed when he spoke to me.

" 'Well,' says he, gruffly enough, 'it's you, Sam Snaffles, is it?' Then he seems to diskiver my new clothes and boots, and he sings out, 'Heigh! you're tip-toe fine to-day! What fool of a shop-keeper in Spartanburg have you tuk in this time, Sam?'

"Says I, cool enough, 'I'll answer all them illgant questions a'ter a while, Squaire; but would prefar to see to business fust.'

" 'Business!' says he; 'and what business kin you hev with me, I wants to know?'

" 'You shill know, Squaire, soon enough; and I only hopes it will be to your liking a'ter you l'arn it.'

"So I laid my saddle-bags down at my feet and tuk a chair quite at my ease; and I could see that he was all astare in wonderment at what he thought my sassiness. As I felt I had my hook in his gills, though he didn't know it yit, I felt in the humor to tickle him and play him as we does a trout.

"Says I, 'Squire Hopson, you owes a sartin amount of money, say $350, with intrust on it for now three years, to Dr. Columbus Mills.'

"At this he squares round, looks me full in the face, and says:

" 'What the old Harry's that to you?'

"Says I, gwine on cool and straight, 'You gin him a mortgage on this fairm for security.'

" 'What's that to you?' says he.

" 'The mortgage is over-due by two years, Squaire,' says I.

" 'What the old Harry's all that to you, I say?' he fairly roared out.

" 'Well, nothing much, I reckon. The $350, with three years' intrust at seven per cent., making it now—I've calkelated it all without compounding—something over $425—well, Squaire, that's not much to *you*, I reckon, with your large capital. But it's something to me.'

" 'But I ask you again, Sir,' he says, 'what is all this to you?'

" 'Jist about what I tells you—say $425; and I've come hyar this morning, bright and airly, in hope you'll be able to square up and satisfy the mortgage. Hyar's the dockyment.'

"And I drawed the paper from my breast pocket.

" 'And you tell me that Dr. Mills sent you hyar,' says he, 'to collect this money?'

" 'No; I come myself on my own hook.'

" 'Well,' says he, 'you shill hev your answer at onst. Take that paper back to Dr. Mills and tell him that I'll take an airly opportunity to call and arrange the business with him. You hev your answer, Sir,' he says, quite grand, 'and the sooner you makes yourself scarce the better.'

" 'Much obleeged to you, Squaire, for your ceveelity,' says I; 'but I ain't quite satisfied with that answer. I've come for the money due on this paper, and must hev it, Squaire, or thar will be what the lawyers call *four closures* upon it!'

" 'Enough! Tell Dr. Mills I will answer his demand in person.'

" 'You needn't trouble yourself, Squaire; for ef you'll jest look at the back of that paper, and read the 'signmeant, you'll see that you've got to settle with Sam Snaffles, and not with Columbus Mills!'

"Then he snatches up the dockyment, turns it over, and reads the rigilar 'signmeant, writ in Columbus Mills's own handwrite.

"Then the Squaire looks at me with a great stare, and he says, to himself like:

" 'It's a *bonny fodder* 'signmeant.'

" 'Yes,' says I, 'it's *bonny fodder*—rigilar in law—and the titles all made out complete to me, Sam Snaffles; signed, sealed, and delivered, as the lawyers says it.'

" 'And how the old Harry come you by this paper?' says he.

"I was gitting riled, and I was determined, this time, to gin my hook a pretty sharp jerk in his gills; so I says:

" 'What the old Harry's that to *you*, Squaire? Thar's but one question 'twixt us two—air you ready to pay that money down on the hub, at onst, to me, Sam Snaffles?'

" 'No, Sir, I am not.'

" 'How long a time will you ax from me, by way of marciful indulgence?'

" 'It must be some time yit,' says he, quite sulky; and then he goes on agin:

" 'I'd like to know how you come by that 'signmeant, Mr. Snaffles.'

"Mr. Snaffles! Ah! ha!

" 'I don't see any neecessity,' says I, 'for answering any questions. Thar's the dockyment to speak for itself. You see that Columbus Mills 'signs to me for full *con*sideration. That means I paid him!'

" 'And why did you buy this mortgage?'

" 'You might as well ax me how I come by the money to buy any thing,' says I.

" 'Well, I do ax you,' says he.

" 'And I answers you,' says I, 'in the very words from your own mouth, What the old Harry's that to you?'

" 'This is hardly 'spectful, Mr. Snaffles,' says he.

"Says I, ' 'Spectful gits only what 'spectful gives! Ef any man but you, Squaire, hed been so onrespectful in his talk to me as you hev been I'd ha' mashed his muzzle! But I don't wish to be onrespectful. All I axes is the civil answer. I wants to know when you kin pay this money?'

" 'I kain't say, Sir.'

" 'Well, you see, I thought as how you couldn't pay, spite of all your "capital," as you hedn't paid even the *intrust* on it for three years; and, to tell you the truth, I was in hopes you couldn't pay, as I hed a liking for this fairm always; and as I am jest about to git married, you see—'

" 'Who the old Harry air you gwine to marry?' says he.

" 'What the old Harry's that to you?' says I, giving him as good as he sent. But I went on:

" 'You may be sure it's one of the woman kind. I don't hanker a'ter a wife with a beard; and I expects—God willing, weather premitting, and the parson being sober—to be married this very night!'

" 'To-night!' says he, not knowing well what to say.

" 'Yes; you see I've got my wedding-breeches on. I'm to be married to-night, and I wants to take my wife to her own fairm as soon as I kin. Now, you see, Squaire, I all along set my hairt on this fairm of yourn, and I determined, ef ever I could git the "capital," to git hold of it; and that was the idee I hed when I bought the 'signmeant of the mortgage from Columbus Mills. So, you see, ef you kain't pay a'ter three years, you never kin pay, I reckon; and ef I don't git my money this day, why—I kain't help it— the lawyers will hev to see to the *four closures* to-morrow!'

" 'Great God, Sir!' says he, rising out of his chair, and crossing the room up and down, 'do you coolly propose to turn me and my family head-long out of my house?'

" 'Well now,' says I, 'Squaire, that's not edzactly the way to put it. As I reads this dockyment'—and I tuk up and put the mortgage in my pocket —'the house and fairm are *mine* by law. They onst was yourn; but it wants nothing now but the *four closures* to make 'em mine.'

" 'And would you force the sale of property worth $2000 and more for a miserable $400?'

" 'It must sell for what it'll bring, Squaire; and I stands ready to buy it for my wife, you see, ef it costs me twice as much as the mortgage.'

" 'Your wife!' says he; 'who the old Harry is she? You once pertended to have an affection for my da'ter.'

" 'So I hed; but you hedn't the proper affection for your da'ter that I hed. You prefar'd money to her affections, and you driv me off to git "capital!" Well, I tuk your advice, and I've got the capital.'

" 'And whar the old Harry,' said he, 'did you git it?'

" 'Well, I made good tairms with the old devil for a hundred years, and he found me in the money.'

" 'It must hev been so,' said he. 'You waur not the man to git capital in any other way.'

"Then he goes on: 'But what becomes of your pertended affection for my da'ter?'

" ' 'Twa'n't pertended; but you throwed yourself betwixt us with all your force, and broke the gal's hairt, and broke mine, so far as you could; and as I couldn't live without company, I hed to look out for myself and find a wife as I could. I tell you, as I'm to be married to-night, and as I've swore a most etarnal oath to hev this fairm, you'll hev to raise the wind to-day, and square off with me, or the lawyers will be at you with the *four closures,* to-morrow, bright and airly.'

" 'Dod dern you!' he cries out. 'Does you want to drive me mad!'

" 'By no manner of means,' says I, jest about as cool and quiet as a cowcumber.

"But he was at biling heat. He was all over in a stew and a fever. He filled his pipe and lighted it, and then smashed it over the chimbly. Then he crammed the newspaper in the fire, and crushed it into the blaze with his boot. Then he turned to me, suddent, and said:

" 'Yes, you pertended to love my da'ter, and now you are pushing her father to desperation. Now ef you ever did love Merry Ann, honestly, raally, truly, and *bonny fodder,* you couldn't help loving her yit. And yit, hyar you're gwine to marry another woman, that, prehaps, you don't affection at all.'

" 'It's quite a sensible view you takes of the subject,' says I; 'the only pity is that you didn't take the same squint at it long ago, when I axed you to let me hev Merry Ann. *Then* you didn't valley her affections or mine. You hed no thought of nothing but the "capital" then, and the affections might all go to Jericho, for what you keered! I'd ha' married Merry Ann, and she me, and we'd ha' got on for a spell in a log-cabin, for, though I was poor, I hed the genwine grit of a man, and would come to something, and we'd ha' got on; and yit, without any "capital" our own self, and kivered up with debt as with a winter over-coat, hyar, you waur positive that I shouldn't hev your da'ter, and you waur a-preparing to sell her hyar to an old sour-tempered bachelor, more than double her age. Dern the capital! A man's the best capital for any woman, ef so be he *is* a man. Bekaise, ef he be a man, he'll work out cl'ar, though he may hev a long straining for it through the sieve. Dern the capital! You've as good as sold that gal child to old Grimstead, jest from your love of money!'

" 'But she won't hev him,' says he.

" 'The wiser gal child,' says I. 'Ef you only hed onderstood me and that poor child, I hed it in me to make the "capital"—dern the capital!— and now you've ruined her, and yourself, and me, and all; and dern my buttons but I must be married to-night, and jest as soon a'ter as the lawyers kin fix it I must hev this fairm for my wife. My hairt's set on it, and I've swore it a dozen o' times on the Holy Hokies!'

"The poor old Squaire fairly sweated; but he couldn't say much. He'd come up to me and say:

" 'Ef you only did love Merry Ann!'

" 'Oh,' says I, 'what's the use of your talking that? Ef you only hed ha' loved your own da'ter!'

"Then the old chap begun to cry, and as I seed that I jest kicked over my saddle-bags lying at my feet, and the silver Mexicans rolled out—a bushel on 'em, I reckon—and, O Lawd! how the old fellow jumped, staring with all his eyes at me and the dollars!

" 'It's money!' says he.

"Yes,' says I, 'jest a few hundreds of thousands of *my* "capital." ' I didn't stop at the figgers, you see.

"Then he turns to me and says, 'Sam Snaffles, you're a most wonderful man. You're a mystery to me. Whar, in the name of God, hev you been? and what hev you been doing? and whar did you git all this power of capital?'

"I jest laughed, and went to the door and called Merry Ann. She come mighty quick. I reckon she was watching and waiting.

"Says I, 'Merry Ann, that's money. Pick it up and put it back in the saddle-bags, ef you please.'

"Then says I, turning to the old man, 'Thar's that whole bushel of Mexicans, I reckon. Thar monstrous heavy. My old mar'—ax her about her ribs now!—she fairly squelched onder the weight of me and that money. And I'm pretty heavy loaded myself. I must lighten; with your leave, Squaire.'

"And I pulled out a leetle doeskin bag of gould half eagles from my right-hand pocket and poured them out upon the table; then I emptied my left-hand pocket, then the side pockets of the coat, then the skairt pockets, and jist spread the shiners out upon the table.

"Merry Ann was fairly frightened, and run out of the room; then the old woman she come in, and as the old Squaire seed her, he tuk her by the shoulder and said:

" 'Jest you look at that thar.'

"And when she looked and seed, the poor old hypercritical scamp sinner turned round to me and flung her airms round my neck, and said:

" 'I always said you waur the only right man for Merry Ann.'

"The old spooney!

"Well, when I hed let 'em look enough, and wonder enough, I jest turned Merry Ann and her mother out of the room.

"The old Squaire, he waur a-setting down agin in his airm-chair, not edzactly knowing what to say or what to do, but watching all my motions, jest as sharp as a cat watches a mouse when she is hafe hungry.

"Thar was all the Mexicans put back in the saddle-bags, but he hed seen 'em, and thar was all the leetle bags of gould spread upon the table; the gould—hafe and quarter eagles—jest lying out of the mouths of the leetle bags as ef wanting to creep back agin.

"And thar sot the old Squaire, looking at 'em all as greedy as a fish-hawk down upon a pairch in the river. And, betwixt a whine and a cry and a talk, he says:

" 'Ah, Sam Snaffles, ef you ever did love my leetle Merry Ann, you would never marry any other woman.'

"Then you ought to ha' seed me. I felt myself sixteen feet high, and jest as solid as a chestnut oak. I walked up to the old man, and I tuk him quiet by the collar of his coat, with my thumb and forefinger, and I said:

" 'Git up, Squaire, for a bit.'

"And up he got.

"Then I marched him to the big glass agin the wall, and I said to him: 'Look, ef you please.'

"And he said, 'I'm looking.'

"And I said, 'What does you see?'

"He answered, 'I sees you and me.'

"I says, 'Look agin, and tell me what you *obzarves*.'

" 'Well,' says he, 'I obzarves.'

"And says I, 'What does your *obzarving* amount to? That's the how.'

"And says he, 'I sees a man alongside of me, as good-looking and handsome a young man as ever I seed in all my life.'

" 'Well,' says I, 'that's a correct obzarvation. But,' says I, 'what does you see of *your own self?*'

" 'Well, I kain't edzackly say.'

" 'Look good!' says I. 'Obzarve.'

"Says he, 'Don't ax me.'

" 'Now,' says I, 'that won't edzactly do. I tell you now, look good, and ax yourself ef you're the sawt of looking man that hes any right to be a feyther-in-law to a fine, young, handsome-looking fellow like me, what's got the "capital?" ' '

"Then he laughed out at the humor of the sitivation; and he says, 'Well, Sam Snaffles, you've got me dead this time. You're a different man from what I thought you. But, Sam, you'll confess, I reckon, that ef I hedn't sent you off with a flea in your ear when I hed you up afore the looking-glass, you'd never ha' gone to work to git in the "capital." ' '

" 'I don't know *that*, Squaire,' says I. 'Sarcumstances sarve to make a man take one road when he mout take another; but when you meets a man what has the hairt to love a woman strong as a lion, and to fight an inimy big as a buffalo, he's got the raal grit in him. You knowed I was young, and I was poor, and you knowed the business of a hunter is a mighty poor business ef the man ain't born to it. Well, I didn't do much at it jest bekaise my hairt was so full of Merry Ann; and you should ha' made a calkilation and allowed for *that*. But you poked your fun at me and riled me consumedly; but I was determined that you shouldn't break *my* hairt or the hairt of Merry Ann. Well, you hed your humors, and I've tried to take the change out of you. And now, ef you raally thinks, a'ter that obzarvation in the glass, that you kin make a respectable feyther-in-law to sich a fine-looking fellow as me, what's got the "capital," jest say the word, and we'll call Merry Ann into bind the bargin. And you must talk out quick, for the wedding's to take place this very night. I've swore it by the etarnal Hokies.'

" 'To-night!' says he.

" 'Look at the "capital" ' says I; and I pinted to the gould on the table and the silver in the saddle-bags.

" 'But, Lawd love you, Sam,' says he, 'it's so suddent, and we kain't make the preparations in time.'

"Says I, 'Look at the "capital," Squaire, and dern the preparations!'

" 'But,' says he, 'we hain't time to ax the company.'

" 'Dern the company!' says I; I don't b'lieve in company the very night a man gits married. His new wife's company enough for him ef he's sensible.'

" 'But, Sam,' says he, 'it's not possible to git up a supper by to-night.'

"Says I, 'Look you, Squaire, the very last thing a man wants on his wedding night is supper.'

"Then he said something about the old woman, his wife.

"Says I, 'Jest you call her in and show her the "capital." ' '

"So he called in the old woman, and then in come Merry Ann, and thar was great hemmings and hawings; and the old woman she said:

" 'I've only got the one da'ter, Sam, and we *must* hev a big wedding! We must spread ourselves. We've got a smart chaince of friends and ac-quaintances, you see, and 'twon't be decent onless we axes them, and they won't like it! We *must* make a big show for the honor and 'spectability of the family.'

"Says I, 'Look you, old lady! I've swore a most tremendous oath, by the Holy Hokies, that Merry Ann and me air to be married this very night, and I kain't break sich an oath as that! Merry Ann,' says I, 'you wouldn't hev me break sich a tremendous oath as that?'

"And, all in a trimble, she says, 'Never, Sam! No!'

" 'You hyar that, old lady!' says I. 'We marries to-night, by the Holy Hokies! and we'll hev no company but old Parson Stovall, to make the hitch; and Merry Ann and me go off by sunrise to-morrow morning—you hyar?—to my own fairm, whar thar's a great deal of furniter fixing for her to do. A'ter that you kin advertise the whole county to come in, ef you please, and eat all the supper you kin spread! Now hurry up,' says I, 'and git as ready as you kin, for I'm gwine to ride over to Parson Stovall's this minit. I'll be back to dinner in hafe an hour. Merry Ann, you gether up that gould and silver, and lock it up. It's *our* "capital!" As for you, Squaire, thar's the mortgage on your fairm, which Merry Ann shill give you, to do as you please wit it, as soon as the parson has done the hitch, and I kin call Merry Ann, Mrs. Snaffles—Madam Merry Ann Snaffles, and so forth, and aforesaid.'

"I laid down the law that time for all parties, and showed the old Squaire sich a picter of himself, and me standing aside him, looking seven foot high, at the least, that I jest worked the business 'cording to my own pleasure. When neither the daddy nor the mammy hed any thing more to say, I jumped on my mar' and rode over to old Parson Stovall.

"Says I, 'Parson, thar's to be a hitch to-night, and you're to see a'ter the right knot. You knows what I means. I wants you over at Squaire Hop-son's. Me and Merry Ann, his da'ter, mean to hop the twig to-night, and you're to see that we hop squar', and that all's even, 'cording to the law,

Moses, and the profits! I stand treat, Parson, and you won't be the worse for your riding. I pays in gould!'

"So he promised to come by dusk; and come he did. The old lady hed got some supper, and tried her best to do what she could at sich short notice. The vension ham was mighty fine, I reckon, for Parson Stovall played a great stick at it; and ef they hedn't cooked up four of my wild-geese, then the devil's an angel of light, and Sam Snaffles no better than a sinner! And thar was any quantity of jimmyjohns, peach and honey considered. Parson Stovall was a great feeder, and I begun to think he never would be done. But at last he wiped his mouth, swallowed his fifth cup of coffee, washed it down with a stiff dram of peach and honey, wiped his mouth agin, and pulled out his prayer-book, psalmody, and Holy Scrip—three volumes in all—and he hemmed three times, and begun to look out for the marriage text, but begun with giving out the 100th Psalm.

" 'With one consent, let's all unite—'

" 'No,' says I, 'Parson; not all! It's only Merry Ann and me what's to unite to-night!'

"Jest then, afore he could answer, who should pop in but old bachelor Grimstead! and he looked round 'bout him, specially upon me and the parson, as ef to say:

" 'What the old Harry's they doing hyar!'

"And I could see that the old Squaire was oneasy. But the blessed old Parson Stovall, he gin 'em no time for ixplanation or palaver; but he gits up, stands up squar', looks solemn as a meat-axe, and he says:

" 'Let the parties which I'm to bind together in the holy bonds of wedlock stand up before me!'

"And, Lawd bless you, as he says the words, what should that old skunk of a bachelor do, but he gits up, stately as an old buck in spring time, and he marches over to my Merry Ann! But I was too much and too spry for him. I puts in betwixt 'em, and I takes the old bachelor by his coat-collar, 'twixt my thumb and forefinger, and afore he knows whar he is, I marches him up to the big looking-glass, and I says:

" 'Look!'

" 'Well,' says he, 'what?'

" 'Look good,' says I.

" 'I'm looking,' says he. 'But what do you mean, Sir?'

"Says I, 'Obzarve! Do you see yourself? Obzarve!'

" 'I reckon I do,' says he.

" 'Then,' says I, 'ax yourself the question, ef you're the sawt of looking man to marry my Merry Ann.'

"Then the old Squaire burst out a-laughing. He couldn't help it.

" 'Capital!' says he.

" 'It's capital,' says I. 'But hyar we air, Parson. Put on the hitch, jest as quick as you kin clinch it; for thar's no telling how many slips thar may be 'twixt the cup and the lips when these hungry old bachelors air about.'

" 'Who gives away this young woman?' axes the parson; and the Squaire stands up and does the thing needful. I hed the ring ready, and before the parson had quite got through, old Grimstead vamoosed.

"He waur a leetle slow in onderstanding that he warn't wanted, and warn't, nohow, any party to the business. But he and the Squaire hed a mighty quarrel a'terwards, and ef 't hedn't been for me, he'd ha' licked the Squaire. He was able to do it; but I jest cocked my cap at him one day, and, says I, in the Injin language:

" 'Yaou!' And he didn't know what I meant; but I looked tomahawks at him, so he gin ground; and he's getting old so fast that you kin see him growing downwards all the time.

"All that, Jedge, is jest thirteen years ago; and me and Merry Ann git on famously, and thar's no eend to the capital! Gould breeds like the cows, and it's only needful to squeeze the bags now and then to make Merry Ann happy as a tomtit. Thirteen years of married life, and look at me! You see for yourself, Jedge, that I'm not much the worse for wear; and I kin answer for Merry Ann, too, though, Jedge, we hev had thirty-six children."

"What!" says I, "thirty-six children in thirteen years!"

The "Big Lie" roared aloud.

"Hurrah, Sharp! Go it! You're making it spread! That last shot will make the Jedge know that you're a right truthful sinner, of a Saturday night, and in the 'Lying Camp.'

"To be sure! You see, Merry Ann keeps on. But you've only got to do the ciphering for yourself. Here, now, Jedge, look at it. Count for yourself. First we had *three* gal children, you see. Very well! Put down three. Then we had *six* boys, one every year for four years; and then, the fifth year, Merry Ann throwed deuce. Now put down the six boys a'ter the three gals, and ef that don't make thirty-six, thar's no snakes in all Flurriday!

"Now, men," says Sam, "let's liquor all round, and drink the health of Mrs. Merry Ann Snaffles and the thirty-six children, all alive and kicking; and glad to see you, Jedge, and the rest of the company. We're doing right well; but I hes, every now and then, to put my thumb and forefinger on the Squaire's collar, and show him his face in the big glass, and call on him for an *obzarvation*—for he's mighty fond of *going shar's* in my 'capital.' "

George Washington Cable
(1844-1925)

George Washington Cable was born, brought up, and educated in Louisiana, although his father was a native of Virginia and his staunch Presbyterian mother, Rebecca Boardman, was a middle westerner whose ancestors were from New England. The elder Cable attempted various business ventures in New Orleans, and prospered for a while, though a combination of bad luck and bad risks finally caused him to fail. When he died in 1859, his son became the chief means of support for his mother and sisters and younger brother. The influence of his mother's stern religious teachings affected Cable most of his life, and he was often called a "Yankee" Puritan. Though he later came to oppose secession and slavery, he was an ardent and loyal Confederate, enlisted in the Confederate Army, was wounded, and served until the end of the war. Because he was forced to leave school when his father died, Cable was largely self-educated.

For many years Cable was an anathema to Southerners and especially to Creoles. He was denounced as a "Southern Yankee" because of his articles in Northern magazines in which he advocated "civil equality" for Negroes. To the proud Creoles he was even more distasteful because of his representation of their language, customs, and morals.

Cable wrote a column called "Drop Shot" for the New Orleans *Picayune* for a while and in 1871 tried unsuccessfully to interest Scribner, Armstrong and Company in publishing a collection of these articles. He finally managed to have one of his stories, " 'Sieur George,' " accepted by *Scribner's Monthly* in 1873. He published other stories in *Scribner's* during the seventies and finally in 1879 had his first book published, *Old Creole Days*, a collection of short stories, some of which had appeared earlier in magazines. The next year (1880) his first novel, *The Grandissimes*, was published. In 1881 he resigned his secretaryship in a cotton exchange in order to devote all of his time to writing.

The story "Madame Delphine" was first published as a serial in *Scribner's Monthly* in 1881 and afterwards included in the 1883 edition of *Old Creole Days*. Though generally considered to be one of his best stories, it particularly angered the Creoles because of the insinuation that they possessed Negro blood and incensed many other Southerners because they interpreted it to be an advocation of miscegenation. Cable himself considered it his best story and remarked of it in a preface written fifteen years after its initial publication, "I have a notion I shall always be glad I wrote it."

During the latter part of his career Cable deteriorated as an artist because he allowed art to become subservient to propaganda. His later writings were more tracts than literature. After he had given up his business interests in favor of literature he found lecturing to be a profitable means of supplementing his income. He joined with Mark Twain in 1884–1885 in a financially successful lecture tour.

In 1884 Cable left New Orleans and the South for New England, where he remained for the rest of his life. Though he never admitted that Southern hostility had anything to do with his leaving, it is possible that this was a contributing cause. Some critics feel that his decline as an artist was due to his removal from the region which he knew best.

Southern antipathy toward Cable was on the wane during the later years of his life, and when he read a story before the New Orleans Historical Club some five years before his death, he was enthusiastically received.

Textual note

First periodical publication, in *Scribner's Monthly*, XXII (May, June, July, 1881), 22–31, 191–199, 436–443, serves as copy-text.

Madame Delphine

Chapter I

An Old House

A few steps from the St. Charles Hotel, in New Orleans, brings you to
and across Canal street, the central avenue of the city, and to that corner
where the flower-women sit at the inner and outer edges of the arcaded sidewalk, and make the air sweet with their fragrant merchandise. The crowd—
and if it is near the time of the carnival it will be great—will follow Canal
street.

But you turn, instead, into the quiet, narrow way which a lover of
Creole antiquity, in fondness for a romantic past, is still prone to call the
Rue Royale. You will pass a few restaurants, a few auction rooms, a few
furniture warehouses, and will hardly realize that you have left behind you
the activity and clatter of a city of merchants before you find yourself in a
region of architectural decrepitude, where an ancient and foreign-seeming
domestic life, in second stories, overhangs the ruins of a former commercial
prosperity, and upon everything has settled down a long Sabbath of decay.
The vehicles in the street are few in number, and are merely passing through;
the stores are shrunken into shops; you see here and there, like a patch of
bright mold, the stall of that significant fungus, the Chinaman. Many great
doors are shut and clamped and grown gray with cobweb; many street
windows are nailed up; half the balconies are begrimed and rust-eaten, and
many of the humid arches and alleys which characterize the older Franco-
Spanish piles of stuccoed brick betray a squalor almost oriental.

Yet beauty lingers here. To say nothing of the picturesque, sometimes
you get sight of comfort, sometimes of opulence, through the unlatched
wicket in some *porte-cochère*—red-painted brick pavement, foliage of dark
palm or pale banana, marble or granite masonry and blooming parterres; or

through a chink between some pair of heavy batten window-shutters, opened with an almost reptile wariness, your eye gets a glimpse of lace and brocade upholstery, silver and bronze, and much similar rich antiquity.

The faces of the inmates are in keeping—a sad proportion of the passengers in the street are dingy and shabby; but just when these are putting you off your guard, there will pass you a woman—more likely two or three—of patrician beauty.

Now, if you will go far enough down this old street, you will see, as you approach its intersection with ——. Names in that region elude one like ghosts.

However, as you begin to find the way a trifle more open, you will not fail to notice on the right-hand side, about midway of the square, a small, low, brick house of a story and a half, set out upon the sidewalk, as weather-beaten and mute as an aged beggar fallen asleep. Its corrugated roof of dull red tiles, sloping down toward you with an inward curve, is overgrown with weeds, and in the fall of the year is gay with the yellow plumes of the golden-rod. You can almost touch with your cane the low edge of the broad, overhanging eaves. The batten shutters at door and window, with hinges like those of a postern, are shut with a grip that makes one's knuckles and nails feel lacerated. Save in the brick-work itself there is not a cranny. You would say the house has the lock-jaw. There are two doors, and to each a single chipped and battered marble step. Continuing on down the sidewalk, on a line with the house, is a garden masked from view by a high, close board-fence. You may see the tops of its fruit-trees—pomegranate, peach, banana, fig, pear, and particularly one large orange, close by the fence, that must be very old.

The residents over the narrow way, who live in a three-story house, originally of much pretension, but from whose front door hard times have removed almost all vestiges of paint, will tell you:

"Yass, de 'ouse is in'abit; 'tis live in."

And this is likely to be all the information you get—not that they would not tell, but they cannot grasp the idea that you wish to know—until, possibly, just as you are turning to depart, your informant, in a single word and with the most evident non-appreciation of its value, drops the simple key to the whole matter:

"Dey's quadroons."

He may then be aroused to mention the better appearance of the place in former years, when the houses of this region generally stood farther apart, and that garden comprised the whole square.

Here dwelt, sixty years ago and more, one Delphine Carraze; or, as she was commonly designated by the few who knew her, Madame Delphine. That she owned her home, and that it had been given her by the then deceased companion of her days of beauty, were facts so generally admitted as to be, even as far back as that sixty years ago, no longer a subject of gossip. She was never pointed out by the denizens of the quarter as a character, nor her house as a "feature." It would have passed all Creole powers of guessing to divine what you could find worthy of inquiry concerning a retired quadroon woman; and not the least puzzled of all would have been the timid and restive Madame Delphine herself.

Chapter II

Madame Delphine

During the first quarter of the present century, the free quadroon caste of New Orleans was in its golden age. Earlier generations—sprung, upon the one hand, from the merry gallants of a French colonial military service which had grown gross by affiliation with Spanish-American frontier life, and, upon the other hand, from comely Ethiopians culled out of the less negroidal types of African live goods, and bought at the ship's side with vestiges of quills and cowries and copper wire still in their head-dresses,— these earlier generations, with scars of battle or private rencontre still on the fathers, and of servitude on the manumitted mothers, afforded a mere hint of the splendor that was to result from a survival of the fairest through seventy-five years devoted to the elimination of the black pigment and the cultivation of hyperian excellence and nymphean grace and beauty. Nor, if we turn to the present, is the evidence much stronger which is offered by the *gens de couleur* whom you may see in the quadroon quarter this afternoon, with "Ichabod" legible on their murky foreheads through a vain smearing of toilet powder, dragging their chairs down to the narrow gate-way of their close-fenced gardens, and staring shrinkingly at you as you pass, like a nest of yellow kittens.

But as the present century was in its second and third decades, the *quadroones* (for we must contrive a feminine spelling to define the strict limits of the caste as then established) came forth in splendor. Old travelers spare no terms to tell their praises, their faultlessness of feature, their perfection of form, their varied styles of beauty,—for there were even pure Caucasian blondes among them,—their fascinating manners, their sparkling vivacity, their chaste and pretty wit, their grace in the dance, their modest propriety, their taste and elegance in dress. In the gentlest and most poetic sense they were indeed the syrens of this land, where it seemed "always afternoon"—a momentary triumph of an Arcadian over a Christian civilization, so beautiful and so seductive that it became the subject of special chapters by writers of the day more original than correct as social philosophers.

The balls that were got up for them by the male *sang-pur* were to that day what the carnival is to the present. Society balls given the same nights proved failures through the coincidence. The magnates of government,—municipal, state, federal,—those of the army, of the learned professions and of the clubs,—in short, the white male aristocracy in everything save the ecclesiastical desk,—were there. Tickets were high-priced to insure the exclusion of the vulgar. No distinguished stranger was allowed to miss them. They were beautiful! They were clad in silken extenuations from the throat to the feet, and wore, withal, a pathos in their charm that gave them a family likeness to innocence.

Madame Delphine, were you not a stranger, could have told you all about it; though hardly, I suppose, without tears.

But at the time of which we would speak (1821–22) her day of splendor was set, and her husband—let us call him so for her sake—was long dead. He was an American, and, if we take her word for it, a man of noble heart and extremely handsome; but this is knowledge which we can do without.

Even in those days the house was always shut, and Madame Delphine's chief occupation and end in life seemed to be to keep well locked up indoors. She was an excellent person, the neighbors said,—a very worthy person; and they were, may be, nearer correct than they knew. They rarely saw her save when she went to or returned from church; a small, rather tired-looking, dark quadroone of very good features and a gentle thoughtfulness of expression which it would take long to describe: call it a widow's look.

In speaking of Madame Delphine's house, mention should have been made of a gate in the fence on the Royal-street sidewalk. It is gone now, and was out of use then, being fastened once for all by an iron staple clasping the cross-bar and driven into the post.

Which leads us to speak of another person.

Chapter III

Capitaine Lemaitre

Capitaine Lemaitre was one of those men that might be any age,—thirty, forty, forty-five; there was no telling from his face what was years and what was only weather. His countenance was of a grave and quiet, but also luminous, sort, which was instantly admired and ever afterward remembered, as was also the fineness of his hair and the blueness of his eyes. Those pronounced him youngest who scrutinized his face the closest. But waiving the discussion of age, he was odd, though not with the oddness that he who reared him had striven to produce.

He had not been brought up by mother or father. He had lost both in infancy, and had fallen to the care of a rugged old military grandpapa of the colonial school, whose unceasing endeavor had been to make "his boy" as savage and ferocious a holder of unimpeachable social rank as it became a pure-blooded French Creole to be who could trace his pedigree back to the god Mars.

"Remember, my boy," was the adjuration received by him as regularly as his waking cup of black coffee, "that none of your family line ever kept the laws of any government or creed." And if it was well that he should bear this in mind, it was well to reiterate it persistently, for, from the nurse's arms, the boy wore a look, not of docility so much as of gentle, *judicial* benevolence. The domestics of the old man's house used to shed tears of laughter to see that look on the face of a babe. His rude guardian addressed himself to the modification of this facial expression; it had not enough of majesty in it, for instance, or of large dare-deviltry; but with care these could be made to come.

And, true enough, at twenty-one (in Ursin Lemaitre), the labors of his grandfather were an apparent success. He was not rugged, nor was he loud-spoken, as his venerable trainer would have liked to present him to society; but he was as serenely terrible as a well-aimed rifle, and the old man looked upon his results with pride. He had cultivated him up to that pitch where he scorned to practice any vice, or any virtue, that did not include the principle of self-assertion. A few touches only were wanting here and there to achieve perfection, when suddenly the old man died. Yet it was his proud satisfaction, before he finally lay down, to see Ursin a favored companion and the peer, both in courtesy and pride, of those polished gentlemen famous in history, the brothers Lafitte.

The two Lafittes were, at the time young Lemaitre reached his majority (say 1808 or 1812), only merchant blacksmiths, so to speak, a term intended to convey the idea of blacksmiths who never soiled their hands, who were men of capital, stood a little higher than the clergy, and moved in society among its autocrats. But they were full of possibilities, men of action, and men, too, of thought, with already a pronounced disbelief in the custom-house. In these days of big carnivals they would have been patented as the dukes of Little Manchac and Barrataria.

Young Ursin Lemaitre (in full the name was Lemaitre-Vignevielle) had not only the hearty friendship of these good people, but also a natural turn for accounts; and as his two friends were looking about them with an enterprising eye, it easily resulted that he presently connected himself with the blacksmithing profession. Not exactly at the forge in the Lafittes' famous smithy, among the African Samsons, who, with their shining black bodies bared to the waist, made the Rue St. Pierre ring with the stroke of their hammers; but as a—there was no occasion to mince the word in those days —smuggler.

Smuggler—patriot—where was the difference? Beyond the ken of a community to which the enforcement of the revenue laws had long been merely so much out of every man's pocket and dish, into the all-devouring treasury of Spain. At this date they had come under a kinder yoke, and to a treasury that at least echoed when the customs were dropped into it; but the change was still new. What could a man be more than Capitaine Lemaitre was—the soul of honor, the pink of courtesy, with the courage of the lion, and the magnanimity of the elephant; frank—the very exchequer of truth? Nay, go higher still: his paper was good in Toulouse street. To the gossips in the gaming-clubs he was the culminating proof that smuggling was one of the sublimer virtues.

Years went by. Events transpired which have their place in history. Under a government which the community by and by saw was conducted in their interest, smuggling began to lose its respectability and to grow disreputable, hazardous, and debased. In certain onslaughts made upon them by officers of the law, some of the smugglers became murderers. The business became unprofitable for a time until the enterprising Lafittes—thinkers— bethought them of a corrective,—"privateering."

Thereupon the United States Government set a price upon their heads. Later yet it became known that these outlawed pirates had been offered money and rank by Great Britain if they would join her standard, then hovering about the water-approaches to their native city, and that they had spurned the bribe; wherefore their heads were ruled out of the market, and, meeting and treating with Andrew Jackson, they were received as lovers of their country, and as compatriots fought in the battle of New Orleans at the head of their fearless men, and—here tradition takes up the tale—were never seen afterward.

Capitaine Lemaitre was not among the killed or wounded, but he was among the missing.

Chapter IV

Three Friends

The roundest and happiest-looking priest in the city of New Orleans was a little man fondly known among his people as Père Jerome. He was a Creole and a member of one of the city's leading families. His dwelling was a little frame cottage, standing on high pillars just inside a tall, close fence, and reached by a narrow out-door stair from the green batten gate. It was well surrounded by crape myrtles, and communicated behind by a descending stair and a plank-walk with the rear entrance of the chapel over whose worshipers he daily spread his hands in benediction. The name of the street —ah! there is where light is wanting. Save the Cathedral and the Ursulines, there is very little of record concerning churches at that time, though they were springing up here and there. All there is certainty of is that Père Jerome's frame chapel was some little new-born "downtown" thing, that may have survived the passage of years, or may have escaped "Paxton's Directory" "so as by fire." His parlor was dingy and carpetless; one could smell distinctly there the vow of poverty. His bed-chamber was bare and clean, and the bed in it narrow and hard, but between the two was a dining-room that would tempt a laugh to the lips of any who looked in. The table was small, but stout, and all the furniture of the room substantial, made of fine wood, and carved just enough to give the notion of wrinkling pleasantry. His mother's and sister's doing, Père Jerome would explain; they would not permit this apartment—or department—to suffer. Therein, as well as in the parlor, there was odor, but of a more epicurean sort, that explained interestingly the Père Jerome's rotundity and rosy smile.

In this room, and about this miniature round-table, used sometimes to sit with Père Jerome two friends to whom he was deeply attached—one, Evariste Varrillat, a playmate from early childhood, now his brother-in-law; the other, Jean Thompson, a companion from youngest manhood, and both, like the little priest himself, the regretful rememberers of a fourth comrade who was a comrade no more. Like Père Jerome, they had come, through years, to the thick of life's conflicts,—the priest's brother-in-law a physician, the other an attorney, and brother-in-law to the lonely wanderer,—yet they loved to huddle around this small board, and be boys again in heart while men in mind. Neither one nor another was leader. In earlier days they had always yielded to him who no longer met with them a certain chieftainship, and they still thought of him and talked of him, and, in their conjectures, groped after him, as one of whom they still continued to expect greater things than of themselves.

They sat one day drawn thus close together, sipping and theorizing, speculating upon the nature of things in an easy, bold, sophomoric way, the conversation for the most part being in French, the native tongue of the doctor and priest, and spoken with facility by Jean Thompson, the lawyer, who was half Américain; but running sometimes into English and sometimes into mild laughter. Mention had been made of the absentee.

Père Jerome advanced an idea something like this:

"It is impossible for any finite mind to fix the degree of criminality of any human act or of any human life. The Infinite One alone can know how much of our sin is chargeable to us, and how much to our brothers or our fathers. We all participate in one another's sins. There is a community of responsibility attaching to every misdeed. No human since Adam—nay, nor Adam himself—ever sinned entirely to himself. And so I never am called upon to contemplate a crime or a criminal but I feel my conscience pointing at me as one of the accessories."

"In a word," said Evariste Varrillat, the physician, "you think we are partly to blame for the omission of many of your Paternosters, eh?"

Father Jerome smiled.

"No; a man cannot plead so in his own defense; our first father tried that, but the plea was not allowed. But, now, there is our absent friend. I tell you truly this whole community ought to be recognized as partners in his moral errors. Among another people, reared under wiser care and with better companions, how different might he not have been! How can *we* speak of him as a law-breaker who might have saved him from that name?" Here the speaker turned to Jean Thompson, and changed his speech to English. "A lady sez to me today: 'Père Jerome, 'ow dat is a dreadfool dat 'e gone at de coas' of Cuba to be one corsair! Aint it?' 'Ah, Madame,' I sez, ' 'tis a terrible! I 'ope de good God will fo'give me an' you fo' dat!' "

Jean Thompson answered quickly:

"You should not have let her say that."

"*Mais,* fo' w'y?"

"Why, because, if you are partly responsible, you ought so much the more to do what you can to shield his reputation. You should have said,"— the attorney changed to French,—" 'He is no pirate; he has merely taken out letters of marque and reprisal under the flag of the republic of Carthagena!' "

"*Ah, bah!*" exclaimed Doctor Varrillat, and both he and his brother-in-law, the priest, laughed.

"Why not?" demanded Thompson.

"Oh!" said the physician, with a shrug, "say id thad way iv you wand."

Then, suddenly becoming serious, he was about to add something else, when Père Jerome spoke.

"I will tell you what I could have said. I could have said: 'Madame, yes; 'tis a terrible fo' him. He stum'le in de dark; but dat good God will mek it a *mo' terrible* fo' dat man, oohever he is, w'at put 'at light out!' "

"But how do you know he is a pirate?" demanded Thompson, aggressively.

"How do we know?" said the little priest, returning to French. "Ah! there is no other explanation of the ninety-and-nine stories that come to us, from every port where ships arrive from the north coast of Cuba, of a commander of pirates there who is a marvel of courtesy and gentility——"

"And whose name is Lafitte," said the obstinate attorney.

"And who, nevertheless, is not Lafitte," insisted Père Jerome.

"Daz troo, Jean," said Doctor Varrillat. "We hall know daz troo."

Père Jerome leaned forward over the board and spoke, with an air of secrecy, in French.

"You have heard of the ship which came into port here last Monday. You have heard that she was boarded by pirates, and that the captain of the ship himself drove them off."

"An incredible story," said Thompson.

"But not so incredible as the truth. I have it from a passenger. There was on the ship a young girl who was very beautiful. She came on deck, where the corsair stood, about to issue his orders, and, more beautiful than ever in the desperation of the moment, confronted him with a small missal spread open, and, her finger on the Apostles' Creed, commanded him to read. He read it, uncovering his head as he read, then stood gazing on her face, which did not quail; and then, with a low bow, said: 'Give me this book and I will do your bidding.' She gave him the book and bade him leave the ship, and he left it unmolested."

Père Jerome looked from the physician to the attorney and back again, once or twice, with his dimpled smile.

"But he speaks English, they say," said Jean Thompson.

"He has, no doubt, learned it since he left us," said the priest.

"But this ship-master, too, says his men called him Lafitte."

"Lafitte? No. Do you not see? It is your brother-in-law, Jean Thompson! It is your wife's brother! Not Lafitte, but" (softly) "Lemaitre! Lemaitre! Capitaine Ursin Lemaitre!"

The two guests looked at each other with a growing drollery on either face, and presently broke into a laugh.

"Ah!" said the doctor, as the three rose up, "you juz kip dad cog-an'-bull fo' yo' negs summon."

Père Jerome's eyes lighted up.

"I goin' to do it!"

"I'll tell you," said Evariste, turning upon him with sudden gravity, "iv dad is troo, I tell you w'ad is sure-sure! Ursin Lemaitre din kyare nut'n fo' doze creed; *he fall in love!*"

Then, with a smile, turning to Jean Thompson, and back again to Père Jerome:

"But anny'ow you tell it in dad summon dad 'e kyare fo' dad creed."

Père Jerome sat up late that night, writing a letter. The remarkable effects upon a certain mind, effects which we shall presently find him attributing solely to the influences of surrounding nature, may find for some a more sufficient explanation in the fact that this letter was but one of a series, and that in the rover of doubted identity and incredible eccentricity Père Jerome had a regular correspondent.

Chapter V

The Cap Fits

About two months after the conversation just given, and therefore somewhere about the Christmas holidays of the year 1821, Père Jerome delighted the congregation of his little chapel with the announcement that he had appointed to preach a sermon in French on the following Sabbath—not there, but in the cathedral.

He was much beloved. Notwithstanding that among the clergy there were two or three who shook their heads and raised their eyebrows, and said he would be at least as orthodox if he did not make quite so much of the Bible and quite so little of the dogmas, yet "the common people heard him gladly." When told, one day, of the unfavorable whispers, he smiled a little and answered his informant,—whom he knew to be one of the whisperers himself,—laying a hand kindly upon his shoulder:

"Father Murphy,"—or whatever the name was,—"your words comfort me."

"How is that?"

"Because—'*Væ quum benedixerint mihi homines!*' "*

The appointed morning, when it came, was one of those exquisite days in which there is such a universal harmony, that worship rises from the heart like a spring.

"Truly," said Père Jerome to the companion who was to assist him in the mass, "this is a Sabbath day which we do not have to make holy, but only to *keep* so."

May be it was one of the secrets of Père Jerome's success as a preacher, that he took more thought as to how he should feel, than as to what he should say.

The cathedral of those days was called a very plain old pile, boasting neither beauty nor riches; but to Père Jerome it was very lovely; and before its homely altar, not homely to him, in the performance of those solemn offices, symbols of heaven's mightiest truths, in the hearing of the organ's harmonies, and the yet more eloquent interunion of human voices in the choir, in overlooking the worshiping throng which knelt under the soft, chromatic lights, and in breathing the sacrificial odors of the chancel, he found a deep and solemn joy; and yet I guess the finest thought of his soul the while was one that came thrice and again:

"Be not deceived, Père Jerome, because saintliness of feeling is easy here; you are the same priest who overslept this morning, and overate yes-

---

*"Woe unto me, when all men speak well of me!"

terday, and will, in some way, easily go wrong to-morrow and the day after."

He took it with him when—the Veni Creator sung—he went into the pulpit. Of the sermon he preached, tradition has preserved for us only a few brief sayings, but they are strong and sweet.

"My friends," he said,—this was near the beginning,—"the angry words of God's book are very merciful—they are meant to drive us home; but the tender words, my friends, they are sometimes terrible! Notice these, the tenderest words of the tenderest prayer that ever came from the lips of a blessed martyr—the dying words of the holy Saint Stephen, 'Lord, lay not this sin to their charge.' Is there nothing dreadful in that? Read it thus: 'Lord, lay not this sin to *their* charge.' Not to the charge of them who stoned him? To whose charge then? Go ask the holy Saint Paul. Three years afterward, praying in the temple at Jerusalem, he answered that question: 'I stood by and consented.' He answered for himself only; but the Day must come when all that wicked council that sent Saint Stephen away to be stoned, and all that city of Jerusalem, must hold up the hand and say: 'We, also, Lord—we stood by.' Ah! friends, under the simpler meaning of that dying saint's prayer for the pardon of his murderers is hidden the terrible truth that we all have a share in one another's sins."

Thus Père Jerome touched his key-note. All that time has spared us beside may be given in a few sentences.

"Ah!" he cried once, "if it were merely my own sins that I had to answer for, I might hold up my head before the rest of mankind; but no, no, my friends—we cannot look each other in the face, for each has helped the other to sin. Oh, where is there any room, in this world of common disgrace, for pride? Even if we had no common hope, a common despair ought to bind us together and forever silence the voice of scorn!"

And again, this:

"Even in the promise to Noë, not again to destroy the race with a flood, there is a whisper of solemn warning. The moral account of the antediluvians was closed off and the balance brought down in the year of the deluge; but the account of those who come after runs on and on, and the blessed bow of promise itself warns us that God will not stop it till the Judgment Day! O God, I thank thee that the day must come at last when thou wilt destroy the world, and stop the interest on my account!"

It was about at this point that Père Jerome noticed, more particularly than he had done before, sitting among the worshipers near him, a small, sad-faced woman, of pleasing features, but dark and faded, who gave him profound attention. With her was another in better dress, seemingly a girl still in her teens, though her face and neck were scrupulously concealed by a heavy veil, and her hands, which were small, by gloves.

"Quadroones," thought he, with a stir of deep pity.

Once, as he uttered some stirring word, he saw the mother and daughter (if such they were), while they still bent their gaze upon him, clasp each other's hand fervently in the daughter's lap. It was at these words:

"My friends, there are thousands of people in this city of New Orleans to whom society gives the ten commandments of God with all the *nots* rubbed out! Ah! good gentlemen! if God sends the poor weakling to purgatory for leaving the right path, where ought some of you to go who strew it with thorns and briers!"

The movement of the pair was only seen because he watched for it. He glanced that way again as he said:

"O God, be very gentle with those children who would be nearer heaven this day had they never had a father and mother, but had got their religious training from such a sky and earth as we have in Louisiana this holy morning! Ah! my friends, nature is a big-print catechism!"

The mother and daughter leaned a little farther forward, and exchanged the same spasmodic hand-pressure as before. The mother's eyes were full of tears.

"I once knew a man," continued the little priest, glancing to a side aisle where he had noticed Evariste and Jean sitting against each other, "who was carefully taught, from infancy to manhood, this single only principle of life: defiance. Not justice, not righteousness, not even gain; but defiance: defiance to God, defiance to man, defiance to nature, defiance to reason; defiance and defiance and defiance."

"He is going to tell it!" murmured Evariste to Jean.

"This man," continued Père Jerome, "became a smuggler and at last a pirate in the Gulf of Mexico. Lord, lay not that sin to his charge alone! But a strange thing followed. Being in command of men of a sort that to control required to be kept at the austerest distance, he now found himself separated from the human world and thrown into the solemn companionship with the sea, with the air, with the storm, the calm, the heavens by day, the heavens by night. My friends, that was the first time in his life that he ever found himself in really good company.

"Now this man had a great aptness for accounts. He had kept them— had rendered them. There was beauty, to him, in a correct, balanced, and closed account. An account unsatisfied was a deformity. The result is plain. That man, looking out night after night upon the grand and holy spectacle of the starry deep above and the watery deep below, was sure to find himself, sooner or later, mastered by the conviction that the great Author of this majestic creation keeps account of it; and one night there came to him, like a spirit walking on the sea, the awful, silent question: 'My account with God—how does it stand?' Ah! friends, that is a question which the book of nature does not answer.

"Did I say the book of nature is a catechism? Yes. But, after it answers the first question with 'God,' nothing but questions follow; and so, one day, this man gave a ship full of merchandise for one little book which answered those questions. God help him to understand it; and God help you, monsieur, and you, madame, sitting here in your *smuggled clothes*, to beat upon the breast with me and cry, 'I, too, Lord—I, too, stood by and consented.'"

Père Jerome had not intended these for his closing words; but just there, straight away before his sight and almost at the farthest door, a man rose slowly from his seat and regarded him steadily with a kind, bronzed, sedate face, and the sermon, as if by a sign of command, was ended. While the Credo was being chanted he was still there, but when, a moment after its close, the eye of Père Jerome returned in that direction, his place was empty.

As the little priest, his labor done and his vestments changed, was turning into the Rue Royale and leaving the cathedral out of sight, he just had time to understand that two women were purposely allowing him to overtake them, when the one nearer him spoke in the Creole patois, saying, with some timid haste:

"Good-morning, Père—Père Jerome; Père Jerome, we thank the good God for that sermon."

"Then, so do I," said the little man. They were the same two that he had noticed when he was preaching. The younger one bowed silently; she was a beautiful figure, but the slight effort of Père Jerome's kind eyes to see through the veil was vain. He would presently have passed on, but the one who had spoken before said:

"I thought you lived in the Rue des Ursulines."

"Yes; I am going this way to see a sick person."

The woman looked up at him with an expression of mingled confidence and timidity.

"It must be a blessed thing to be so useful as to be needed by the good God," she said.

Père Jerome smiled:

"God does not need me to look after his sick; but he allows me to do it, just as you let your little boy in frocks carry in chips." He might have added that he loved to do it, quite as much.

It was plain the woman had somewhat to ask, and was trying to get courage to ask it.

"You have a little boy?" asked the priest.

"No, I have only my daughter;" she indicated the girl at her side.

Then she began to say something else, stopped, and with much nervousness asked:

"Père Jerome, what was the name of that man?"

"His name?" said the priest. "You wish to know his name?"

"Yes, Monsieur" (or *Miché*, as she spoke it); "it was such a beautiful story." The speaker's companion looked another way.

"His name," said Father Jerome,—"some say one name and some another. Some think it was Jean Lafitte, the famous; you have heard of him? And do you go to my church, Madame ——?"

"No, Miché; not in the past; but from this time, yes. My name"—she choked a little, and yet it evidently gave her pleasure to offer this mark of confidence—"is Madame Delphine—Delphine Carraze."

Chapter VI

A Cry of Distress

Père Jerome's smile and exclamation as some days later he entered his parlor in response to the announcement of a visitor were indicative of hearty greeting rather than surprise.

"Madame Delphine!"

Yet surprise could hardly have been altogether absent, for though another Sunday had not yet come around, the slim, smallish figure sitting in a corner, looking very much alone, and clad in dark attire, which seemed to have been washed a trifle too often, was Delphine Carraze on her second visit. And this, he was confident, was over and above an attendance in the confessional, where he was sure he had recognized her voice.

She rose bashfully and gave her hand, then looked to the floor, and began a faltering speech, with a swallowing motion in the throat, smiled weakly and commenced again, speaking, as before, in a gentle, low note, frequently lifting up and casting down her eyes, while shadows of anxiety and smiles of apology chased each other rapidly across her face. She was trying to ask his advice.

"Sit down," said he; and when they had taken seats she resumed, with downcast eyes:

"You know,—probably I should have said this in the confessional, but ——"

"No matter, Madame Delphine; I understand; you did not want an oracle, perhaps; you want a friend."

She lifted her eyes, shining with tears, and dropped them again.

"I"—she ceased. "I have done a"—she dropped her head and shook it despondingly—"a cruel thing." The tears rolled from her eyes as she turned away her face.

Père Jerome remained silent, and presently she turned again, with the evident intention of speaking at length.

"It began nineteen years ago—by"—her eyes, which she had lifted, fell lower than ever, her brow and neck were suffused with blushes, and she murmured—"I fell in love."

She said no more, and by and by Père Jerome replied:

"Well, Madame Delphine, to love is the right of every soul. I believe in love. If your love was pure and lawful I am sure your angel guardian smiled upon you; and if it was not, I cannot say you have nothing to answer for, and yet I think God may have said: 'She is a quadroone; all the rights of her womanhood trampled in the mire, sin made easy to her—almost compulsory,—charge it to account of whom it may concern.'"

"No, no!" said Madame Delphine, looking up quickly, "some of it might fall upon——" Her eyes fell, and she commenced biting her lips and nervously pinching little folds in her skirt. "He was good—as good as the law would let him be—better, indeed, for he left me property, which really the strict law does not allow. He loved our little daughter very much. He wrote to his mother and sisters, owning all his error and asking them to take the child and bring her up. I sent her to them when he died, which was soon after, and did not see my child for sixteen years. But we wrote to each other all the time, and she loved me. And then—at last——" Madame Delphine ceased speaking, but went on diligently with her agitated fingers, turning down foolish hems lengthwise of her lap.

"At last your mother-heart conquered," said Père Jerome.

She nodded.

"The sisters married, the mother died; I saw that even where she was she did not escape the reproach of her birth and blood, and when she asked me to let her come——." The speaker's brimming eyes rose an instant. "I know it was wicked, but—I said, come."

The tears dripped through her hands upon her dress.

"Was it she who was with you last Sunday?"

"Yes."

"And now you do not know what to do with her?"

"*Ah! c'est ça, oui!*—that is it."

"Does she look like you, Madame Delphine?"

"Oh, thank God, no! you would never believe she was my daughter; she is white and beautiful!"

"You thank God for that which is your main difficulty, Madame Delphine."

"Alas! yes."

Père Jerome laid his palms tightly across his knees with his arms bowed out, and fixed his eyes upon the ground, pondering.

"I suppose she is a sweet, good daughter?" said he, glancing at Madame Delphine without changing his attitude.

Her answer was to raise her eyes rapturously.

"Which gives us the dilemma in its fullest force," said the priest, speaking as if to the floor. "She has no more place than if she had dropped upon a strange planet." He suddenly looked up with a brightness which almost as quickly passed away, and then he looked down again. His happy thought was the cloister; but he instantly said to himself: "They cannot have overlooked that choice, except intentionally—which they have a right to do." He could do nothing but shake his head.

"And suppose you should suddenly die," he said; he wanted to get at once to the worst.

The woman made a quick gesture, and buried her head in her handkerchief, with the stifled cry:

"Oh, Olive, my daughter!"

"Well, Madame Delphine," said Père Jerome, more buoyantly, "one thing is sure: we *must* find a way out of this trouble."

"Ah!" she exclaimed, looking heavenward, "if it might be!"

"But it must be!" said the priest.

"But how shall it be?" asked the desponding woman.

"Ah!" said Père Jerome, with a shrug, "God knows."

"Yes," said the quadroone, with a quick sparkle in her gentle eye; "and I know, if God would tell anybody, He would tell you!"

The priest smiled and rose.

"Do you think so? Well, leave me to think of it. I will ask Him."

"And He will tell you!" she replied. "And He will bless you!" She rose and gave her hand. As she withdrew it she smiled. "I had such a strange dream," she said, backing toward the door.

"Yes?"

"Yes. I got my troubles all mixed up with your sermon. I dreamed I made that pirate the guardian of my daughter."

Père Jerome smiled also, and shrugged.

"To you, Madame Delphine, as you are placed, every white man in this country, on land or on water, is a pirate, and of all pirates, I think that one is, without doubt, the best."

"Without doubt," echoed Madame Delphine, wearily, still withdrawing backward. Père Jerome stepped forward and opened the door.

The shadow of some one approaching it from without fell upon the threshold, and a man entered, dressed in dark blue cottonade, lifting from his head a fine Panama hat, and from a broad, smooth brow, fair where the hat had covered it and dark below, gently stroking back his very soft, brown locks. Madame Delphine slightly started aside, while Père Jerome reached silently, but eagerly, forward, grasped a larger hand than his own, and motioned its owner to a seat. Madame Delphine's eyes ventured no higher than to discover that the shoes of the visitor were of white duck.

"Well, Père Jerome," she said, in a hurried under-tone, "I am just going to say Hail Marys all the time till you find that out for me!"

"Well, I hope that will be soon, Madame Carraze. Good-day, Madame Carraze."

And as she departed, the priest turned to the new-comer and extended both hands, saying, in the same familiar dialect in which he had been addressing the quadroone:

"Well-a-day, old playmate! After so many years!"

They sat down side by side, like husband and wife, the priest playing with the other's hand, and talked of times and seasons past, often mentioning Evariste and often Jean.

Madame Delphine stopped short half-way home and returned to Père Jerome's. His entry door was wide open and the parlor door ajar. She passed through the one and with downcast eyes was standing at the other, her hand lifted to knock, when the door was drawn open and the white duck shoes passed out. She saw, besides, this time the blue cottonade suit.

"Yes," the voice of Père Jerome was saying, as his face appeared in the door—"Ah! Madame——"

"I lef' my para*sol*," said Madame Delphine, in English.

There was this quiet evidence of a defiant spirit hidden somewhere down under her general timidity, that, against a fierce conventional prohibition, she wore a bonnet instead of the turban of her caste, and carried a parasol.

Père Jerome turned and brought it.

He made a motion in the direction in which the late visitor had disappeared.

"Madame Delphine, you saw dat man?"

"Not his face."

"You couldn' billieve me iv I tell you w'at dat man pur*pose* to do!"

"Is dad so, Père Jerome?"

"He's goin' to hopen a bank!"

"Ah!" said Madame Delphine, seeing she was expected to be astonished.

Père Jerome evidently longed to tell something that was best kept secret; he repressed the impulse, but his heart had to say something. He threw forward one hand and looking pleasantly at Madame Delphine, with his lips dropped apart, clenched his extended hand and thrusting it toward the ground, said in a solemn undertone:

"He is God's own banker, Madame Delphine."

Chapter VII

Miché Vignevielle

Madame Delphine sold one of the corner lots of her property. She had almost no revenue, and now and then a piece had to go. As a consequence of the sale, she had a few large bank-notes sewed up in her petticoat, and one day—may be a fortnight after her tearful interview with Père Jerome —she found it necessary to get one of these changed into small money. She was in the Rue Toulouse, looking from one side to the other for a bank which was not in that street at all, when she noticed a small sign hanging above a door, bearing the name "Vignevielle." She looked in. Père Jerome had told her (when she had gone to him to ask where she should apply for change) that if she could only wait a few days, there would be a new concern opened in Toulouse street,—it really seemed as if Vignevielle was the name, if she could judge; it looked to be, and it was, a private banker's,— "U. L. Vignevielle's," according to a larger inscription which met her eyes as she ventured in. Behind the counter, exchanging some last words with a busy-mannered man outside, who, in withdrawing, seemed bent on running over Madame Delphine, stood the man in blue cottonade, whom she had met in Père Jerome's door-way. Now, for the first time, she saw his face, its strong, grave, human kindness shining softly on each and every bronzed feature. The recognition was mutual. He took pains to speak first, saying, in a re-assuring tone, and in the language he had last heard her use:

" 'Ow I kin serve you, Madame?"

"Iv you pliz, to mague dad bill change, Miché."

She pulled from her pocket a wad of dark cotton handkerchief, from which she began to untie the imprisoned note. Madame Delphine had an uncommonly sweet voice, and it seemed so to strike Monsieur Vignevielle. He spoke to her once or twice more, as he waited on her, each time in English, as though he enjoyed the humble melody of its tone, and presently, as she turned to go, he said:

"Madame Carraze."

She started a little, but bethought herself instantly that he had heard her name in Père Jerome's parlor. The good father might even have said a few words about her after her first departure; he had such an overflowing heart.

"Madame Carraze," said Monsieur Vignevielle, "doze kine of note wad you *'an'* me juz now is bein' contreft. You muz tek kyah from doze kine of note. You see——" He drew from his cash-drawer a note resembling the one he had just changed for her, and proceeded to point out certain tests of genuineness. The counterfeit, he said, was so and so.

"Bud," she exclaimed, with much dismay, "dad was de manner of my bill! Id muz be—led me see dad bill wad I give you,—if you pliz, Miché."

Monsieur Vignevielle turned to engage in conversation with an employé and a new visitor, and gave no sign of hearing Madame Delphine's voice. She asked a second time, with like result, lingered timidly, and as he turned to give his attention to a third visitor, reiterated:

"Miché Vignevielle, I wizh you pliz led——"

"Madame Carraze," he said, turning so suddenly as to make the frightened little woman start, but extending his palm with a show of frankness, and assuming a look of benignant patience, " 'ow I kin fine doze note now, mongs' all de rez? Iv you pliz nod to mague me doze troub'."

The dimmest shadow of a smile seemed only to give his words a more kindly authoritative import, and as he turned away again with a manner suggestive of finality, Madame Delphine found no choice but to depart. But she went away loving the ground beneath the feet of Monsieur U. L. Vignevielle.

"Oh, Père Jerome!" she exclaimed in the corrupt French of her caste, meeting the little father on the street a few days later, "you told the truth that day in your parlor. *Mo conné li à ç't heure.* I know him now; he is just what you called him."

"Why do you not make him *your* banker, also, Madame Delphine?"

"I have done so this very day!" she replied, with more happiness in her eyes than Pére Jerome had ever before seen there.

"Madame Delphine," he said, his own eyes sparkling, "make *him* your daughter's guardian; for myself, being a priest, it would not be best; but ask him; I believe he will not refuse you."

Madame Delphine's face grew still brighter as he spoke.

"It was in my mind," she said.

Yet to the timorous Madame Delphine many trifles became, one after another, an impediment to the making of this proposal, and many weeks elapsed before further delay was positively without excuse. But at length, one day in May (1822), in a small private office behind Monsieur Vignevielle's banking-room,—he sitting beside a table, and she, more timid and demure than ever, having just taken a chair by the door,—she said, trying, with a little bashful laugh, to make the matter seem unimportant, and yet with some tremor of voice:

"Miché Vignevielle, I bin maguing my will." (Having commenced their acquaintance in English, they spoke nothing else.)

" 'Tis a good idy," responded the banker.

"I kin mague you de troub' to kib dad will fo' me, Miché Vignevielle?"

"Yez."

She looked up with grateful re-assurance; but her eyes dropped again as she said:

"Miché Vignevielle——" Here she choked, and began her peculiar motion of laying folds in the skirt of her dress, with trembling fingers. She lifted her eyes, and as they met the look of deep and placid kindness that was in his face, some courage returned, and she said:

"Miché."

"Wad you wand?" asked he, gently.

"If it arrive to me to die——"

"Yez?"

Her words were scarcely audible:

"I wand you teg kyah my lill' girl."

"You 'ave one lill' gal, Madame Carraze?"

She nodded with her face down.

"An' you godd some mo' chillen?"

"No."

"I nevva know dad, Madame Carraze. She's a lill' small gal?"

Mothers forget their daughters' stature. Madame Delphine said:

"Yez."

For a few moments neither spoke, and then Monsieur Vignevielle said:

"I will do dad."

"Lag she been you' h-own?" asked the mother, suffering from her own boldness.

"She's a good lill' chile, eh?"

"Miché, she's a lill' hangel!" exclaimed Madame Delphine, with a look of distress.

"Yez; I teg kyah 'v 'er, lag my h-own. I mague you dad promise."

"But——" There was something still in the way, Madame Delphine seemed to think.

The banker waited in silence.

"I suppose you will want to see my lill' girl?"

He smiled; for she looked at him as if she would implore him to decline.

"Oh, I tek you' word fo' hall dad, Madame Carraze. It mague no differend wad she loog lag; I don' wan' see 'er."

Madame Delphine's parting smile—she went very shortly—was gratitude beyond speech.

Monsieur Vignevielle returned to the seat he had left, and resumed a newspaper,—the "Louisiana Gazette" in all probability,—which he had laid down upon Madame Delphine's entrance. His eyes fell upon a paragraph which had previously escaped his notice. There they rested. Either he read it over and over unwearingly, or he was lost in thought. Jean Thompson entered.

"Now," said Mr. Thompson, in a suppressed tone, bending a little across the table, and laying one palm upon a package of papers which lay in the other, "it is completed. You could retire from your business any day inside of six hours without loss to anybody." (Both here and elsewhere, let it be understood that where good English is given the words were spoken in good French.)

Monsieur Vignevielle raised his eyes and extended the paper to the attorney, who received it and read the paragraph. Its substance was that a certain vessel of the navy had returned from a cruise in the Gulf of Mexico and Straits of Florida, where she had done valuable service against the pirates—having, for instance, destroyed in one fortnight in January last twelve pirate vessels afloat, two on the stocks, and three establishments ashore.

"United States brig *Porpoise*," repeated Jean Thompson. "Do you know her?"

"We are acquainted," said Monsieur Vignevielle.

Chapter VIII

She

A quiet footstep, a grave new presence on financial sidewalks, a neat garb slightly out of date, a gently strong and kindly pensive face, a silent bow, a new sign in the Rue Toulouse, a lone figure with a cane, walking in meditation in the evening light under the willows of Canal Marigny, a long-darkened window relighted in the Rue Conti—these were all; a fall of dew would scarce have been more quiet than was the return of Ursin Lemaitre-Vignevielle to the precincts of his birth and early life.

But we hardly give the event its right name. It was Capitaine Lemaitre who had disappeared; it was Monsieur Vignevielle who had come back. The pleasures, the haunts, the companions, that had once held out their charms to the impetuous youth, offered no enticements to Madame Delphine's banker. There is this to be said even for the pride his grandfather had taught him, that it had always held him above low indulgences; and though he had dallied with kings, queens, and knaves through all the mazes of Faro, Rondeau, and Craps, he had done it loftily; but now he maintained a peaceful estrangement from all. Evariste and Jean, themselves, found him only by seeking.

"It is the right way," he said to Père Jerome, the day we saw him there. "Ursin Lemaitre is dead. I have buried him. He left a will. I am his executor."

"He is crazy," said his lawyer brother-in-law, impatiently.

"On the contr-y," replied the little priest, " 'e 'as come ad hisse'f."

Evariste spoke.

"Look at his face, Jean. Men with that kind of face are the last to go crazy."

"You have not proved that," replied Jean, with an attorney's obstinacy. "You should have heard him talk the other day about that newspaper paragraph. 'I have taken Ursin Lemaitre's head; I have it with me; I claim the reward, but I desire to commute it to citizenship.' He is crazy."

Of course Jean Thompson did not believe what he said; but he said it, and, in his vexation, repeated it, on the *banquettes* and at the clubs; and presently it took the shape of a sly rumor, that the returned rover was a trifle snarled in his top-hamper.

This whisper was helped into circulation by many trivial eccentricities of manner and by the unaccountable oddness of some of his transactions in business.

"My dear sir!" cried his astounded lawyer, one day, "you are not running a charitable institution!"

"How do you know?" said Monsieur Vignevielle. There the conversation ceased.

"Why do you not found hospitals and asylums at once," asked the attorney, at another time, with a vexed laugh, "and get the credit of it?"

"And make the end worse than the beginning," said the banker, with a gentle smile, turning away to a desk of books.

"Bah!" muttered Jean Thompson.

Monsieur Vignevielle betrayed one very bad symptom. Wherever he went he seemed looking for somebody. It may have been perceptible only to those who were sufficiently interested in him to study his movements; but those who saw it once saw it always. He never passed an open door or gate but he glanced in; and often, where it stood but slightly ajar, you might see him give it a gentle push with his hand or cane. It was very singular.

He walked much alone after dark. The *guichinangoes* (garroters, we might say), at those times the city's particular terror by night, never crossed his path. He was one of those men for whom danger appears to stand aside.

One beautiful summer night, when all nature seemed hushed in ecstasy, the last blush gone that told of the sun's parting, Monsieur Vignevielle, in the course of one of those contemplative, uncompanioned walks which it was his habit to take, came slowly along the more open portion of the Rue Royale, with a step which was soft without intention, occasionally touching the end of his stout cane gently to the ground and looking upward among his old acquaintances, the stars.

It was one of those southern nights under whose spell all the sterner energies of the mind cloak themselves and lie down in bivouac, and the fancy and the imagination, that cannot sleep, slip their fetters and escape, beckoned away from behind every flowering bush and sweet-smelling tree, and every stretch of lonely, half-lighted walk, by the genius of poetry. The air stirred softly now and then, and was still again, as if the breezes lifted their expectant pinions and lowered them once more, awaiting the rising of the moon in a silence which fell upon the fields, the roads, the gardens, the walls, and the suburban and half-suburban streets, like a pause in worship. And anon she rose.

Monsieur Vignevielle's steps were bent toward the more central part of the town, and he was presently passing along a high, close, board-fence, on the right-hand side of the way, when, just within this inclosure, and almost overhead, in the dark boughs of a large orange-tree, a mocking-bird began the first low flute-notes of his all-night song. It may have been only the nearness of the songster that attracted the passer's attention, but he paused and looked up.

And then he remarked something more,—that the air where he had stopped was filled with the overpowering sweetness of the night-jasmine. He looked around; it could only be inside the fence. There was a gate just there. Would he push it, as his wont was? The grass was growing about it in a thick turf, as though the entrance had not been used for years. An iron staple clasped the cross-bar, and was driven deep into the gate-post. But now an eye that had been in the blacksmithing business—an eye which had later received high training as an eye for fastenings—fell upon that staple, and saw at a glance that the wood had shrunk from it, and it had sprung from its hold, though without falling out. The strange habit asserted itself; he laid his large hand upon the cross-bar; the turf at the base yielded, and the tall gate was drawn partly open.

At that moment, as at the moment whenever he drew or pushed a door or gate, or looked in at a window, he was thinking of one, the image of whose face and form had never left his inner vision since the day it had met him in his life's path and turned him face about from the way of destruction.

The bird ceased. The cause of the interruption, standing within the opening, saw before him, much obscured by its own numerous shadows, a broad, ill-kept, many-flowered garden, among whose untrimmed rose-trees and tangled vines, and often, also, in its old walks of pounded shell, the coco-grass, and crab-grass had spread riotously, and sturdy weeds stood up in bloom. He stepped in and drew the gate to after him. There, very near by, was the clump of jasmine, whose ravishing odor had tempted him. It stood just beyond a brightly moonlit path, which turned from him in a curve toward the residence, a little distance to the right, and escaped the view at a point where it seemed more than likely a door of the house might open upon it. While he still looked, there fell upon his ear, from around that curve, a light footstep on the broken shells,—one only, and then all was for a moment still again. Had he mistaken? No. The same soft click was repeated nearer by, a pale glimpse of robes came through the tangle, and then, plainly to view, appeared an outline—a presence—a form—a spirit—a girl!

From throat to instep she was as white as Cynthia. Something above the medium height, slender, lithe, her abundant hair rolling in dark, rich waves back from her brows and down from her crown, and falling in two heavy plaits beyond her round, broadly girt waist and full to her knees, a few escaping locks eddying lightly on her graceful neck and her temples,—her arms, half hid in a snowy mist of sleeve, let down to guide her spotless skirts free from the dewy touch of the grass,—straight down the path she came!

Will she stop? Will she turn aside? Will she espy the dark form in the deep shade of the orange, and, with one piercing scream, wheel and vanish? She draws near. She approaches the jasmine; she raises her arms, the sleeves falling like a vapor down to the shoulder; rises upon tiptoe, and plucks a spray. O Memory! Can it be? *Can it be?* Is this his quest, or is it lunacy? The ground seems to M. Vignevielle the unsteady sea and he to stand once more on a deck. And she? As she stands now, if she but turn toward the orange, the whole glory of the moon will shine upon her face. His heart stands still; he is waiting for her to do that. She reaches up again; this time a bunch for her mother. That neck and throat! Now she fastens a spray in her hair. The mocking-bird cannot withhold; he breaks into song— she turns—she turns her face—it is she, it is she! Madame Delphine's daughter is the girl he met on the ship.

Chapter IX

Olive

She was just passing seventeen—that beautiful year when the heart of the maiden still beats quickly with the surprise of her new dominion, while with gentle dignity her brow accepts the holy coronation of womanhood. The forehead and temples beneath her loosely bound hair were fair without paleness, and meek without languor. She had the soft, lack-luster beauty of the South; no ruddiness of coral, no waxen white, no pink of shell; no heavenly blue in the glance; but a face that seemed, in all its other beauties, only a tender accompaniment of the large, brown, melting eyes, where the openness of child-nature mingled dreamily with the sweet mysteries of maiden thought. We say no color of shell on face or throat; but this was no deficiency, that which took its place being the warm, transparent tint of sculptured ivory.

This side door-way which led from Madame Delphine's house into her garden was overarched partly by an old remnant of vine-covered lattice, and partly by a crape-myrtle, against whose small, polished trunk leaned a rustic seat. Here Madame Delphine and Olive loved to sit when the twilights were balmy or the moon was bright.

"*Chérie*," said Madame Delphine on one of these evenings, "why do you dream so much?"

She spoke in the *patois* most natural to her, and which her daughter had easily learned.

The girl turned her face to her mother, and smiled, then dropped her glance to the hands in her own lap, which were listlessly handling the end of a ribbon. The mother looked at her with fond solicitude. Her dress was white again; this was but one night since that in which Monsieur Vignevielle had seen her at the bush of night-jasmine. He had not been discovered, but had gone away, shutting the gate, and leaving it as he had found it.

Her head was uncovered. Its plaited masses, quite black in the moonlight, hung down and coiled upon the bench, by her side. Her chaste drapery was of that revived classic order which the world of fashion was again laying aside to re-assume the mediæval bondage of the stay-lace; for New Orleans was behind the fashionable world, and Madame Delphine and her daughter were behind New Orleans. A delicate scarf, pale blue, of lightly netted worsted, fell from either shoulder down beside her hands. The look that was bent upon her changed perforce to one of gentle admiration. She seemed the goddess of the garden.

Olive glanced up. Madame Delphine was not prepared for the movement, and on that account repeated her question:

"What are you thinking about?"

The dreamer took the hand that was laid upon hers between her own palms, bowed her head and gave them a soft kiss.

The mother submitted. Wherefore, in the silence which followed, a daughter's conscience felt the burden of having withheld an answer, and Olive presently said, as the pair sat looking up into the sky:

"I was thinking of Père Jerome's sermon."

Madame Delphine had feared so. Olive had lived on it ever since the day it was preached. The poor mother was almost ready to repent having ever afforded her the opportunity of hearing it. Meat and drink had become of secondary value to her daughter; she fed upon the sermon.

Olive felt her mother's thought and knew that her mother knew her own; but now that she had confessed, she would ask a question:

"Do you think, *maman,* that Père Jerome knows it was I who gave that missal?"

"No," said Madame Delphine, "I am sure he does not."

Another question came more timidly:

"Do—do you think he knows *him?*"

"Yes, I do. He said in his sermon he did."

Both remained for a long time very still, watching the moon gliding in and through among the small dark-and-white clouds. At last the daughter spoke again.

"I wish I was Père—I wish I was as good as Père Jerome."

"My child," said Madame Delphine, her tone betraying a painful summoning of strength to say what she had lacked the courage to utter,— "my child, I pray the good God you will not let your heart go after one whom you may never see in this world!"

The maiden turned her glance, and their eyes met. She cast her arms about her mother's neck, laid her cheek upon it for a moment, and then, feeling the maternal tear, lifted her lips, and, kissing her, said:

"I will not! I will not!"

But the voice was one, not of glad consent, but of desperate resolution.

"It would be useless, anyhow," said the mother, laying her arm around her daughter's waist.

Olive repeated the kiss, prolonging it passionately.

"I have nobody but you," murmured the girl; "I am a poor quadroone!"

She threw back her plaited hair for a third embrace, when a sound in the shrubbery startled them.

"*Qui ci ça?*" called Madame Delphine, in a frightened voice, as the two stood up, holding to each other.

No answer.

"It was only the dropping of a twig," she whispered, after a long holding of the breath. But they went into the house and barred it everywhere.

It was no longer pleasant to sit up. They retired, and in course of time, but not soon, they fell asleep, holding each other very tight, and fearing, even in their dreams, to hear another twig fall.

Chapter X

Birds

Monsieur Vignevielle looked in at no more doors or windows; but if the disappearance of this symptom was a favorable sign, others came to notice which were especially bad,—for instance, wakefulness. At well-nigh any hour of the night, the city guard, which itself dared not patrol singly, would meet him on his slow, unmolested, sky-gazing walk.

"Seems to enjoy it," said Jean Thompson; "the worst sort of evidence. If he showed distress of mind, it would not be so bad; but his calmness,— ugly feature."

The attorney had held his ground so long that he began really to believe it was tenable.

By day, it is true, Monsieur Vignevielle was at his post in his quiet "bank." Yet here, day by day, he was the source of more and more vivid astonishment to those who held preconceived notions of a banker's calling. As a banker, at least, he was certainly out of balance; while as a promenader, it seemed to those who watched him that his ruling idea had now veered about, and that of late he was ever on the quiet alert, not to find, but to evade, somebody.

"Olive, my child," whispered Madame Delphine one morning, as the pair were kneeling side by side on the tiled floor of the church, "yonder is Miché Vignevielle! If you will only look at once—he is just passing a little in—— Ah, much too slow again; he stepped out by the side door."

The mother thought it a strange providence that Monsieur Vignevielle should always be disappearing whenever Olive was with her.

One early dawn, Madame Delphine, with a small empty basket on her arm, stepped out upon the *banquette* in front of her house, shut and fastened the door very softly, and stole out in the direction whence you could faintly catch, in the stillness of the daybreak, the songs of the Gascon butchers and the pounding of their meat-axes on the stalls of the market-house. She was going to see if she could find some birds for Olive,—the child's appetite was so poor; and, as she was out, she would drop an early prayer at the cathedral. Faith and works.

"One must venture something, sometimes, in the cause of religion," thought she, as she started timorously on her way. But she had not gone a dozen steps before she repented her temerity. There was some one behind her.

There should not be anything terrible in a footstep merely because it is masculine; but Madame Delphine's mind was not prepared to consider that. A terrible secret was haunting her. Yesterday morning she had found a shoe-track in the garden. She had not disclosed the discovery to Olive, but she had hardly closed her eyes the whole night.

The step behind her now might be the fall of that very shoe. She quickened her pace, but did not leave the sound behind. She hurried forward almost at a run; yet it was still there—no farther, no nearer. Two frights were upon her at once—one for herself, another for Olive, left alone in the house; but she had but the one prayer—"God protect my child!" After a fearful time she reached a place of safety, the cathedral. There, panting, she knelt long enough to know the pursuit was, at least, suspended, and then arose, hoping and praying all the saints that she might find the way clear for her return in all haste to Olive.

She approached a different door from that by which she had entered, her eyes in all directions and her heart in her throat.

"Madame Carraze!"

She started wildly and almost screamed, though the voice was soft and mild. Monsieur Vignevielle came slowly forward from the shade of the wall. They met beside a bench, upon which she dropped her basket.

"Ah, Miché Vignevielle, I thang de good God to mid you!"

"Is dad so, Madame Carraze? Fo' w'y dad is?"

"A man was chase me all dad way since my 'ouse!"

"Yes, Madame, I sawed him."

"You sawed 'im? Oo it was?"

" 'Twas only one man wad is a foolizh. De people say he's crezzie. *Mais,* he don' goin' to meg you no 'arm."

"But I was scare' fo' my lill' girl."

"Noboddie don' goin' trouble you' lill' gal, Madame Carraze."

Madame Delphine looked up into the speaker's strangely kind and patient eyes, and drew sweet re-assurance from them.

"Madame," said Monsieur Vignevielle, "wad pud you hout so hearly dis morning?"

She told him her errand. She asked if he thought she would find anything.

"Yez," he said, "it was possible—a few lill' *bécassines-de-mer,* ou somezin' ligue. But fo' w'y you lill' gal lose doze hapetide?"

"Ah, Miché,"—Madame Delphine might have tried a thousand times again without ever succeeding half so well in lifting the curtain upon the whole, sweet, tender, old, old-fashioned truth,—"Ah, Miché, she wone tell me!"

"Bud, anny'ow, Madame, wad you thing?"

"Miché," she replied, looking up again with a tear standing in either eye, and then looking down once more as she began to speak, "I thing—I thing she's lonesome."

"You thing?"

She nodded.

"Ah! Madame Carraze," he said, partly extending his hand, "you see? 'Tis impossible to mague you' owze shud so tighd to priv-en dad. Madame, I med one mizteg."

"Ah, *non,* Miché!"

"Yez. Thar har nod one poss'bil'ty fo' me to be dad guardian of you' daughteh!"

Madame Delphine started with surprise and alarm.

"There is ondly one wad can be," he continued.

"But oo, Miché?"

"God."

"Ah, Miché Vignevielle——" She looked at him appealingly.

"I don' goin' to dizzerd you, Madame Carraze," he said.

She lifted her eyes. They filled. She shook her head, a tear fell, she bit her lip, smiled, and suddenly dropped her face into both hands, sat down upon the bench and wept until she shook.

"You dunno wad I mean, Madame Carraze?"

She did not know.

"I mean dad guardian of you' daughteh godd to fine 'er now one 'uzban'; an' noboddie are hable to do dad egceb de good God 'imsev. But, Madame, I tell you wad I do."

She rose up. He continued:

"Go h-open you' owze; I fin' you' daughteh dad 'uzban'."

Madame Delphine was a helpless, timid thing; but her eyes showed she was about to resent this offer. Monsieur Vignevielle put forth his hand —it touched her shoulder—and said, kindly still, and without eagerness:

"One w'ite man, Madame; 'tis prattycabble. I *know* 'tis prattycabble. One w'ite jantleman, Madame. You can truz me. I goin' fedge 'im. H-ondly you go h-open you' owze."

Madame Delphine looked down, twining her handkerchief among her fingers.

He repeated his proposition.

"You will come firz by you'se'f?" she asked.

"Iv you wand."

She lifted up once more her eye of faith. That was her answer.

"Come," he said, gently, "I wan' sen' some bird ad you' lill' gal."

And they went away, Madame Delphine's spirit grown so exaltedly bold that she said as they went, though a violent blush followed her words:

"Miché Vignevielle, I thing Père Jerome mighd be ab'e to tell you someboddie."

Chapter XI

Face to Face

Madame Delphine found her house neither burned nor rifled.

"*Ah! ma piti sans popa!* Ah! my little fatherless one!" Her faded bonnet fell back between her shoulders, hanging on by the strings, and her dropped basket, with its "few lill' *bécassines-de-mer*" dangling from the handle, rolled out its okra and soup-joint upon the floor. "*Ma piti!* kiss!——kiss!—kiss!"

"But is it good news you have, or bad?" cried the girl, a fourth or fifth time.

"*Dieu sait, ma c'ère; mo pas conné!* God knows, my darling; I cannot tell!"

The mother dropped into a chair, covered her face with her apron, and burst into tears, then looked up with an effort to smile, and wept afresh.

"What have you been doing?" asked the daughter, in a long-drawn, fondling tone. She leaned forward and unfastened her mother's bonnet-strings. "Why do you cry?"

"For nothing at all, my darling; for nothing—I am such a fool."

The girl's eyes filled. The mother looked up into her face and said:

"No, it is nothing, nothing, only that—" turning her head from side to side with a slow, emotional emphasis, "Miché Vignevielle is the best—*best* man on the good Lord's earth!"

Olive drew a chair close to her mother, sat down and took the little yellow hands into her own white lap, and looked tenderly into her eyes. Madame Delphine felt herself yielding; she must make a show of telling something:

"He sent you those birds!"

The girl drew her face back a little. The little woman turned away, trying in vain to hide her tearful smile, and they laughed together, Olive mingling a daughter's fond kiss with her laughter.

"There is something else," she said, "and you shall tell me."

"Yes," replied Madame Delphine, "only let me get composed."

But she did not get so. Later in the morning she came to Olive with the timid yet startling proposal that they would do what they could to brighten up the long-neglected front room. Olive was mystified and troubled, but consented, and thereupon the mother's spirits rose.

The work began, and presently ensued all the thumping, the trundling, the lifting and letting down, the raising and swallowing of dust, and the smells of turpentine, brass, pumice, and woolen rags that go to characterize a housekeeper's *émeute;* and still, as the work progressed, Madame Delphine's heart grew light, and her little black eyes sparkled.

"We like a clean parlor, my daughter, even though no one is ever coming to see us, eh?" she said, as entering the apartment she at last sat down, late in the afternoon. She had put on her best attire.

Olive was not there to reply. The mother called, but got no answer. She rose with an uneasy heart, and met her a few steps beyond the door that opened into the garden, in a path which came up from an old latticed bower. Olive was approaching slowly, her face pale and wild. There was an agony of hostile dismay in the look, and the trembling and appealing tone with which, taking the frightened mother's cheeks between her palms, she said:

"*Ah! ma mère, qui vini 'ci ce soir?* Who is coming here this evening?"

"Why, my dear child, I was just saying, we like a clean——"

But the daughter was desperate:

"Oh, tell me, my mother, *who* is coming?"

"My darling, it is our blessed friend, Miché Vignevielle!"

"To see me?" cried the girl.

"Yes."

"Oh, my mother, what have you done?"

"Why, Olive, my child," exclaimed the little mother, bursting into tears, "do you forget it is Miché Vignevielle who has promised to protect you when I die?"

The daughter had turned away, and entered the door; but she faced around again, and extending her arms toward her mother, cried:

"How can—he is a white man—I am a poor——"

"Ah! *chérie*," replied Madame Delphine, seizing the outstretched hands, "it is there—it is there that he shows himself the best man alive! He sees that difficulty; he proposes to meet it; he says he will find you a suitor!"

Olive freed her hands violently, motioned her mother back, and stood proudly drawn up, flashing an indignation too great for speech; but the next moment she had uttered a cry, and was sobbing on the floor.

The mother knelt beside her and threw an arm about her shoulders.

"Oh, my sweet daughter, you must not cry! I did not want to tell you at all! I did not want to tell you! It isn't fair for you to cry so hard. Miché Vignevielle says you shall have the one you wish, or none at all, Olive, or none at all."

"None at all! none at all! None, none, none!"

"No, no, Olive," said the mother, "none at all. He brings none with him to-night, and shall bring none with him hereafter."

Olive rose suddenly, silently declined her mother's aid, and went alone to their chamber in the half-story.

Madame Delphine wandered drearily from door to window, from window to door, and presently into the newly furbished front room, which now seemed dismal beyond degree. There was a great Argand lamp in one corner. How she had labored that day to prepare it for evening illumination! A little beyond it, on the wall, hung a crucifix. She knelt under it, with her eyes fixed upon it, and thus, silently, remained until its outline was undistinguishable in the deepening shadows of evening.

She arose. A few minutes later, as she was trying to light the lamp, an approaching step on the sidewalk seemed to pause. Her heart stood still. She softly laid the phosphorus-box out of her hands. A shoe grated softly on the stone step, and Madame Delphine, her heart beating in great thuds, without waiting for a knock, opened the door, bowed low, and exclaimed in a soft, perturbed voice:

"Miché Vignevielle!"

He entered, hat in hand, and with that almost noiseless tread which we have noticed. She gave him a chair and closed the door; then hastened, with words of apology, back to her task of lighting the lamp. But her hands paused in their work again,—Olive's step was on the stairs; then it came off the stairs; then it was in the next room, and then there was the whisper of soft robes, a breath of gentle perfume, and a snowy figure in the door. She was dressed for the evening.

"Maman?"

Madame Delphine was struggling desperately with the lamp, and at that moment it responded with a tiny bead of light.

"I am here, my daughter."

She hastened to the door, and Olive, all unaware of a third presence, lifted her white arms, laid them about her mother's neck, and, ignoring her effort to speak, wrested a fervent kiss from her lips. The crystal of the lamp sent out a faint gleam; it grew; it spread on every side; the ceiling, the walls lighted up; the crucifix, the furniture of the room came back into shape.

"Maman!" cried Olive, with a tremor of consternation.

"It is Miché Vignevielle, my daughter——"

The gloom melted swiftly away before the eyes of the startled maiden, a dark form stood out against the farther wall, and the light, expanding to the full, shone clearly upon the unmoving figure and quiet face of Capitaine Lemaitre.

Chapter XII

The Mother Bird

One afternoon, some three weeks after Captain Lemaitre had called on Madame Delphine, the priest started to make a pastoral call and had hardly left the gate of his cottage, when a person, overtaking him, plucked his gown:

"Père Jerome——"

He turned.

The face that met his was so changed with excitement and distress that for an instant he did not recognize it.

"Why, Madame Delphine——"

"Oh, Père Jerome! I wan' see you so bad, so bad! *Mo oulé dit quiç'ose,*—I godd some' to tell you."

The two languages might be more successful than one, she seemed to think.

"We had better go back to my parlor," said the priest, in their native tongue.

They returned.

Madame Delphine's very step was altered,—nervous and inelastic. She swung one arm as she walked, and brandished a turkey-tail fan.

"I was glad, yass, to kedge you," she said, as they mounted the front, outdoor stair; following her speech with a slight, unmusical laugh, and fanning herself with unconscious fury.

"*Fé chaud,*" she remarked again, taking the chair he offered and continuing to ply the fan.

Pére Jerome laid his hat upon a chest of drawers, sat down opposite her, and said, as he wiped his kindly face:

"Well, Madame Carraze?"

Gentle as the tone was, she started, ceased fanning, lowered the fan to her knee, and commenced smoothing its feathers.

"Père Jerome——" She gnawed her lip and shook her head.

"Well?"

She burst into tears.

The priest rose and loosed the curtain of one of the windows. He did it slowly—as slowly as he could, and, as he came back, she lifted her face with sudden energy, and exclaimed:

"Oh, Père Jerome, de law is brogue! de law is brogue! I brogue it! 'Twas me! 'Twas me!"

The tears gushed out again, but she shut her lips very tight, and dumbly turned away her face. Père Jerome waited a little before replying; then he said, very gently:

"I suppose dad muss 'ave been by accyden', Madame Delphine?"

The little father felt a wish—one which he often had when weeping women were before him—that he were an angel instead of a man, long enough to press the tearful cheek upon his breast, and assure the weeper God would not let the lawyers and judges hurt her. He allowed a few moments more to pass, and then asked:

"*N'est-ce-pas,* Madame Delphine? Daz ze way, aint it?"

"No, Père Jerome, no. My daughter—oh, Père Jerome, I bethroath my lill' girl—to a w'ite man!" And immediately Madame Delphine commenced savagely drawing a thread in the fabric of her skirt with one trembling hand, while she drove the fan with the other. "Dey goin' git marry."

On the priest's face came a look of pained surprise. He slowly said: "Is dad possib', Madame Delphine?"

"Yass," she replied, at first without lifting her eyes; and then again, "Yass," looking full upon him through her tears, "yass, 'tis tru'."

He rose and walked once across the room, returned, and said, in the Creole dialect:

"Is he a good man—without doubt?"

"De bez in God's world!" replied Madame Delphine, with a rapturous smile.

"My poor, dear friend," said the priest, "I am afraid you are being deceived by somebody."

There was the pride of an unswerving faith in the triumphant tone and smile with which she replied, raising and slowly shaking her head:

"Ah-h, no-o-o, Miché! Ah-h, no, no! Not by Ursin Lemaitre-Vignevielle!"

Pére Jerome was confounded. He turned again, and, with his hands at his back and his eyes cast down, slowly paced the floor.

"He *is* a good man," he said, by and by, as if he thought aloud. At length he halted before the woman.

"Madame Delphine——"

The distressed glance with which she had been following his steps was lifted to his eyes.

"Suppose dad should be true w'at doze peop' say 'bout Ursin."

"*Qui ci ça?* What is that?" asked the quadroone, stopping her fan.

"Some peop' say Ursin is crezzie."

"Ah, Père Jerome!" She leaped to her feet as if he had smitten her, and putting his words away with an outstretched arm and wide-open palm, suddenly lifted hands and eyes to heaven, and cried: "I wizh to God—*I wizh to God*—de whole worl' was crezzie dad same way!" She sank, trembling, into her chair. "Oh, no, no," she continued, shaking her head, " 'tis not Miché Vignevielle w'at's crezzie." Her eyes lighted with sudden fierceness. " 'Tis dad *law!* Dad *law* is crezzie! Dad law is a fool!"

A priest of less heart-wisdom might have replied that the law is—the law; but Père Jerome saw that Madame Delphine was expecting this very response. Wherefore he said, with gentleness:

"Madame Delphine, a priest is not a bailiff, but a physician. How can I help you?"

A grateful light shone a moment in her eyes, yet there remained a piteous hostility in the tone in which she demanded:

"*Mais, pou'quoi yé fé cette méchanique là?* What business had they to make that contraption?"

His answer was a shrug with his palms extended and a short, disclamatory "Ah." He started to resume his walk, but turned to her again and said:

"Why did they make that law? Well, they made it to keep the two races separate."

Madame Delphine startled the speaker with a loud, harsh, angry laugh. Fire came from her eyes and her lip curled with scorn.

"Then they made a lie, Père Jerome! Separate! No-o-o! They do not want to keep us separated; no, no! But they *do* want to keep us despised!" She laid her hand on her heart, and frowned upward with physical pain. "But, very well! from which race do they want to keep my daughter separate? She is seven parts white! The law did not stop her from being that; and now, when she wants to be a white man's good and honest wife, shall that law stop her? Oh, no!" She rose up. "No; I will tell you what that law is made for. It is made to—punish—my—child—for—not—choosing—her—father! Père Jerome—my God, what a law!" She dropped back into her seat. The tears came in a flood, which she made no attempt to restrain.

"No," she began again—and here she broke into English—"fo' me I don' kyare; but, Père Jerome,—'tis fo' dat I come to tell you,—dey *shall not* punizh my daughter!" She was on her feet again, smiting her heaving bosom with the fan. "She shall marrie oo she want!"

Père Jerome had heard her out, not interrupting by so much as a motion of the hand. Now his decision was made, and he touched her softly with the ends of his fingers.

"Madame Delphine, I want you to go at 'ome. Go at 'ome."

"Wad you goin' mague?" she asked.

"Nottin'. But go at 'ome. Kip quite; don' put you'se'f sig. I goin' see Ursin. We trah to figs dat law fo' you."

"You kin figs dad!" she cried, with a gleam of joy.

"We goin' to try, Madame Delphine. Adieu!"

He offered his hand. She seized and kissed it thrice, covering it with tears, at the same time lifting up her eyes to his and murmuring:

"De bez man God evva maque!"

At the door she turned to offer a more conventional good-bye; but he was following her out, bareheaded. At the gate they paused an instant, and then parted with a simple adieu, she going home and he returning for his hat, and starting again upon his interrupted business.

Before he came back to his own house, he stopped at the lodgings of Monsieur Vignevielle, but did not find him in.

"Indeed," the servant at the door said, "he said he might not return for some days or weeks."

So Père Jerome, much wondering, made a second detour toward the residence of one of Monsieur Vignevielle's employés.

"Yes," said the clerk, "his instructions are to hold the business, as far as practicable, in suspense, during his absence. Everything is in another name." And then he whispered:

"Officers of the Government looking for him. Information got from some of the prisoners taken months ago by the United States brig *Porpoise*. But"—a still softer whisper—"have no fear; they will never find him: Jean Thompson and Evariste Varrillat have hid him away too well for that."

Chapter XIII

Tribulation

The Saturday following was a very beautiful day. In the morning a light fall of rain had passed across the town, and all the afternoon you could see signs, here and there upon the horizon, of other showers. The ground was dry again, while the breeze was cool and sweet, smelling of wet foliage and bringing sunshine and shade in frequent and very pleasing alternation.

There was a walk in Père Jerome's little garden, of which we have not spoken, off on the right side of the cottage, with his chamber window at one end, a few old and twisted, but blossom-laden, crape-myrtles on either hand, now and then a rose of some unpretending variety and some bunches of rue, and at the other end a shrine, in whose blue niche stood a small figure of Mary, with folded hands and uplifted eyes. No other window looked down upon the spot, and its seclusion was often a great comfort to Père Jerome.

Up and down this walk, but a few steps in its entire length, the priest was walking, taking the air for a few moments after prolonged sitting in the confessional. Penitents had been numerous this afternoon. He was thinking of Ursin.

The officers of the Government had not found him, nor had Père Jerome seen him; yet he believed they had, in a certain indirect way, devised a simple project by which they could at any time "figs dad law," providing only that these Government officials would give over their search; for, though he had not seen the fugitive, Madame Delphine had seen him, and had been the vehicle of communication between them. There was an orange-tree, where a mocking-bird was wont to sing and a girl in white to walk, that the detectives wot not of. The law was to be "figs" by the departure of the three frequenters of the jasmine-scented garden in one ship to France, where the law offered no obstacles.

It seemed moderately certain to those in search of Monsieur Vignevielle (and it was true) that Jean and Evariste were his harborers; but for all that the hunt, even for clues, was vain. The little banking establishment had not been disturbed. Jean Thompson had told the searchers certain facts about it, and about its gentle proprietor as well, that persuaded them to make no move against the concern, if the same revelations did not even induce a relaxation of their efforts for his personal discovery.

Père Jerome was walking to and fro, with his hands behind him, pondering these matters. He had paused a moment at the end of the walk furthest from his window, and was looking around upon the sky, when, turning, he beheld a closely veiled female figure standing at the other end, and knew instantly that it was Olive.

She came forward quickly and with evident eagerness.

"I came to confession," she said, breathing hurriedly, the excitement in her eyes shining through her veil, "but I find I am too late."

"There is no too late or too early for that; I am always ready," said the priest. "But how is your mother?"

"Ah!——"

Her voice failed.

"More trouble?"

"Ah, sir, I have *made* trouble. Oh, Père Jerome, I am bringing so much trouble upon my poor mother!"

Père Jerome moved slowly toward the house, with his eyes cast down, the veiled girl at his side.

"It is not your fault," he presently said. And after another pause: "I thought it was all arranged."

He looked up and could see, even through the veil, her crimson blush.

"Oh, no," she replied, in a low, despairing voice, dropping her face.

"What is the difficulty?" asked the priest, stopping in the angle of the path, where it turned toward the front of the house.

She averted her face, and began picking the thin scales of bark from a crape-myrtle.

"Madame Thompson and her husband were at our house this morning. *He* had told Monsieur Thompson all about it. They were very kind to me at first, but they tried——" She was weeping.

"What did they try to do?" asked the priest.

"They tried to make me believe he is insane."

She succeeded in passing her handkerchief up under her veil.

"And I suppose then your poor mother grew angry, eh?"

"Yes; and they became much more so, and said if we did not write, or send a writing, to *him,* within twenty-four hours, breaking the——"

"Engagement," said Père Jerome.

"They would give him up to the Government. Oh, Père Jerome, what shall I do? It is killing my mother!"

She bowed her head and sobbed.

"Where is your mother now?"

"She has gone to see Monsieur Jean Thompson. She says she has a plan that will match them all. I do not know what it is. I begged her not to go; but oh, sir, she *is* crazy,—and—I am no better."

"My poor child," said Père Jerome, "what you seem to want is not absolution, but relief from persecution."

"Oh, father, I have committed mortal sin,—I am guilty of pride and anger."

"Nevertheless," said the priest, starting toward his front gate, "we will put off your confession. Let it go until to-morrow morning; you will find me in my box just before mass; I will hear you then. My child, I know that in your heart, now, you begrudge the time it would take; and that is right. There are moments when we are not in place even on penitential knees. It is so with you now. We must find your mother. Go you at once to your house; if she is there, comfort her as best you can, and *keep her in, if possible,* until I come. If she is not there, stay; leave me to find her; one of you, at least, must be where I can get word to you promptly. God comfort and uphold you. I hope you may find her at home; tell her, for me, not to fear,"—he lifted the gate-latch,—"that she and her daughter are of more value than many sparrows; that God's priest sends her that word from Him. Tell her to fix her trust in the great Husband of the Church, and she shall yet see her child receiving the grace-giving sacrament of matrimony. Go; I shall, in a few minutes, be on my way to Jean Thompson's, and shall find her, either there or wherever she is. Go; they shall not oppress you. Adieu!"

A moment or two later he was in the street himself.

Chapter XIV

By an Oath

Père Jerome, pausing on a street-corner in the last hour of sunlight, had wiped his brow and taken his cane down from under his arm to start again, when somebody, coming noiselessly from he knew not where, asked, so suddenly as to startle him:

"*Miché, commin yé 'pellé la rie ici?*—how do they call this street here?"

It was by the bonnet and dress, disordered though they were, rather than by the haggard face which looked distractedly around, that he recognized the woman to whom he replied in her own *patois:*

"It is the Rue Burgundy. Where are you going, Madame Delphine?"
She almost leaped from the ground.

"Oh, Père Jerome! *mo pas conné,*—I dunno. You know w'ere's dad 'ouse of Miché Jean Tomkin? *Mo courri 'ci, mo courri là,—mo pas capabe li trouvé.* I go (run) here—there—I cannot find it." She gesticulated.

"I am going there myself," said he; "but why do you want to see Jean Thompson, Madame Delphine?"

"I *'blige'* to see 'im!" she replied, jerking herself half around, one foot planted forward with an air of excited preoccupation; "I god some' to tell 'im wad I *'blige'* to tell 'im!"

"Madame Delphine——"

"Oh! Père Jerome, fo' de love of de good God, show me dad way to de 'ouse of Jean Tomkin!"

Her distressed smile implored pardon for the rudeness.

"What are you going to tell him?" asked the priest.

"Oh, Père Jerome,"—in the Creole *patois* again,—"I am going to put an end to all this trouble—only I pray you do not ask me about it now; every minute is precious!"

He could not withstand her look of entreaty.

"Come," he said, and they went.

Jean Thompson and Doctor Varrillat lived opposite each other on the Bayou road, a little way beyond the town limits as then prescribed. Each had his large, white-columned, four-sided house among the magnolias,—his huge live-oak overshadowing either corner of the darkly shaded garden, his broad, brick walk leading down to the tall, brick-pillared gate, his square of bright, red pavement on the turf-covered sidewalk, and his railed platform spanning the draining-ditch, with a pair of green benches, one on each edge, facing each other crosswise of the gutter. There, any sunset hour, you were sure to find the householder sitting beside his cool-robed matron, two or three slave-nurses in white turbans standing at hand, and an excited throng of fair children, nearly all of a size.

Sometimes, at a beckon or call, the parents on one side of the way would join those on the other, and the children and nurses of both families would be given the liberty of the opposite platform and an ice-cream fund! Generally the parents chose the Thompson platform, its outlook being more toward the sunset.

Such happened to be the arrangement this afternoon. The two husbands sat on one bench and their wives on the other, both pairs very quiet, waiting respectfully for the day to die, and exchanging only occasional comments on matters of light moment as they passed through the memory. During one term of silence Madame Varrillat, a pale, thin-faced, but cheerful-looking lady, touched Madame Thompson, a person of two and a half times her weight, on her extensive and snowy, bare elbow, directing her attention obliquely up and across the road.

About a hundred yards distant, in the direction of the river, was a long, pleasantly shaded green strip of turf, destined in time for a sidewalk. It had a deep ditch on the nearer side, and a fence of rough cypress palisades on the farther, and these were overhung, on the one hand, by a row of bitter-orange trees inside the inclosure, and, on the other, by a line of slanting china-trees along the outer edge of the ditch. Down this cool avenue two figures were approaching side by side. They had first attracted Madame Varrillat's notice by the bright play of sunbeams which, as they walked, fell upon them in soft, golden flashes through the chinks between the palisades.

Madame Thompson elevated a pair of glasses which were no detraction from her very good looks, and remarked, with the serenity of a reconnoitering general:

"*Père Jerome et cette milatraise.*"

All eyes were bent toward them.

"She walks like a man," said Madame Varrillat, in the language with which the conversation had opened.

"No," said the physician, "like a woman in a state of high nervous excitement."

Jean Thompson kept his eyes on the woman, and said:

"She must not forget to walk like a woman in the State of Louisiana," —as near as the pun can be translated. The company laughed. Jean Thompson looked at his wife, whose applause he prized, and she answered by an asseverative toss of the head, leaning back and contriving, with some effort, to get her arms folded. Her laugh was musical and low, but enough to make the folded arms shake gently up and down.

"Père Jerome is talking to her," said one. The priest was at that moment endeavoring, in the interest of peace, to say a good word for the four people who sat watching his approach. It was in the old strain:

"Blame them one part, Madame Delphine, and their fathers, mothers, brothers, and fellow-citizens the other ninety-nine."

But to everything she had the one amiable answer which Père Jerome ignored:

"I am going to arrange it to satisfy everybody, all together. *Tout à fait.*"

"They are coming here," said Madame Varrillat, half articulately.

"Well, of course," murmured another, and the four rose up, smiling courteously, the doctor and attorney advancing and shaking hands with the priest.

No—Père Jerome thanked them—he could not sit down.

"This, I believe you know, Jean, is Madame Delphine——"

The quadroone courtesied.

"A friend of mine," he added, smiling kindly upon her, and turning, with something imperative in his eye, to the group. "She says she has an important private matter to communicate."

"To me?" asked Jean Thompson.

"To all of you; so I will—— Good-evening." He responded nothing to the expressions of regret, but turned to Madame Delphine. She murmured something.

"Ah! yes, certainly." He addressed the company: "She wishes me to speak for her veracity; it is unimpeachable. Well, good-evening." He shook hands and departed.

The four resumed their seats, and turned their eyes upon the standing figure.

"Have you something to say to us?" asked Jean Thompson, frowning at her law-defying bonnet.

"*Oui,*" replied the woman, shrinking to one side, and laying hold of one of the benches, "*mo oulé di' tou' ç'ose*—I want to tell everything. *Miché Vignevielle la plis bon homme di moune*—the best man in the world; *mo pas capabe li fé tracas*—I cannot give him trouble. *Mo pas capabe non; m'olé di' tous ç'ose.*" She attempted to fan herself, her face turned away from the attorney, and her eyes rested on the ground.

"Take a seat," said Doctor Varrillat, with some suddenness, starting from his place and gently guiding her sinking form into the corner of the bench. The two ladies rose up; somebody had to stand; the two races could not both sit down at once—at least not in that public manner.

"Your salts," said the physician to his wife. She handed the vial. Madame Delphine stood up again.

"We will all go inside," said Madame Thompson, and they passed through the gate and up the walk, mounted the steps, and entered the deep, cool drawing-room.

Madame Thompson herself bade the quadroone be seated.

"Well?" said Jean Thompson, as the rest took chairs.

"*C'est drole*—it's funny," said Madame Delphine, with a piteous effort to smile, "that nobody thought of it. It is so plain. You have only to look and see. I mean about Olive." She loosed a button in the front of her dress and passed her hand into her bosom. "And yet, Olive herself never thought of it. She does not know a word."

The hand came out holding a miniature. Madame Varrillat passed it to Jean Thompson.

"*Ouala so popa,*" said Madame Delphine. "That is her father."

It went from one to another, exciting admiration and murmured praise.

"She is the image of him," said Madame Thompson, in an austere under-tone, returning it to her husband.

Doctor Varrillat was watching Madame Delphine. She was very pale. She had passed a trembling hand into a pocket of her skirt, and now drew out another picture, in a case the counterpart of the first. He reached out for it, and she handed it to him. He looked at it a moment, when his eyes suddenly lighted up and he passed it to the attorney.

"*Et là*"—Madame Delphine's utterance failed—"*et là, ouala sa moman.*" (That is her mother.)

The three others instantly gathered around Jean Thompson's chair. They were much impressed.

"It is true beyond a doubt!" muttered Madame Thompson.

Madame Varrillat looked at her with astonishment.

"The proof is right there in the faces," said Madame Thompson.

"Yes! yes!" said Madame Delphine, excitedly; "the proof is there! You do not want any better! I am willing to swear to it! But you want no better proof! That is all anybody could want! My God! you cannot help but see it!"

Her manner was wild.

Jean Thompson looked at her sternly.

"Nevertheless, you say you are willing to take your solemn oath to this."

"Certainly——"

"You will have to do it."

"Certainly, Miché Thompson, *of course* I shall; you will make out the paper and I will swear before God that it is true! Only"—turning to the ladies—"do not tell Olive; she will never believe it. It will break her heart! It——"

A servant came and spoke privately to Madame Thompson, who rose quickly and went to the hall. Madame Delphine continued, rising unconsciously:

"You see, I have had her with me from a baby. She knows no better. He brought her to me only two months old. Her mother had died in the ship, coming out here. He did not come straight from home here. His people never knew he was married!"

The speaker looked around suddenly with a startled glance. There was a noise of excited speaking in the hall.

"It is not true, Madame Thompson!" cried a girl's voice.

Madame Delphine's look became one of wildest distress and alarm, and she opened her lips in a vain attempt to utter some request, when Olive appeared a moment in the door, and then flew into her arms.

"My mother! my mother! my mother!"

Madame Thompson, with tears in her eyes, tenderly drew them apart and let Madame Delphine down into her chair, while Olive threw herself upon her knees, continuing to cry:

"Oh, my mother! Say you are my mother!"

Madame Delphine looked an instant into the upturned face, and then turned her own away with a long, low cry of pain, looked again, and laying both hands upon the suppliant's head, said:

"*Oh, chère piti à moin, to pa' ma fie!*" (Oh, my darling little one, you are not my daughter!) Her eyes closed, and her head sank back; the two gentlemen sprang to her assistance, and laid her upon a sofa unconscious.

When they brought her to herself, Olive was kneeling at her head, silently weeping.

"*Maman, chère maman!*" said the girl softly, kissing her lips.

"*Ma courri c'ez moin*" (I will go home), said the mother, drearily.

"You will go home with me," said Madame Varrillat, with great kindness of manner—"just across the street here; I will take care of you till you feel better. And Olive will stay here, with Madame Thompson. You will be only the width of the street apart."

But Madame Delphine would go nowhere but to her home. Olive she would not allow to go with her. Then they wanted to send a servant or two to sleep in the house with her for aid and protection; but all she would accept was the transient service of a messenger to invite two of her kins-people—man and wife—to come and make their dwelling with her.

In the course of time these two—a poor, timid, helpless pair—fell heir to the premises. Their children had it after them; but, whether in those hands or these, the house had its habits and continued in them; and to this day the neighbors, as has already been said, rightly explain its close-sealed, uninhabited look by the all-sufficient statement that the inmates "is quad-roons."

Chapter XV

Kyrie Eleison

The second Saturday afternoon following was hot and calm. The lamp burning before the tabernacle in Père Jerome's little church might have hung with as motionless a flame in the window behind. The lilies of St. Joseph's wand, shining in one of the half-opened panes, were not more completely at rest than the leaves on tree and vine without, suspended in the slumbering air. Almost as still, down under the organ-gallery, with a single band of light falling athwart his box from a small door which stood ajar, sat the little priest, behind the lattice of the confessional, silently wiping away the sweat that beaded on his brow and rolled down his face. At distant intervals the shadow of some one entering softly through the door would obscure, for a moment, the band of light, and an aged crone, or a little boy, or some gentle presence that the listening confessor had known only by the voice for many years, would kneel a few moments beside his waiting ear, in prayer for blessing and in review of those slips and errors which prove us all akin.

The day had been long and fatiguing. First, early mass; a hasty meal; then a business call upon the archbishop in the interest of some projected charity; then back to his cottage, and so to the banking-house of "Vigne-vielle," in the Rue Toulouse. There all was open, bright, and re-assured, its master virtually, though not actually, present. The search was over and the seekers gone, personally wiser than they would tell, and officially reporting that (to the best of their knowledge and belief, based on evidence, and especially on the assurances of an unexceptionable eye-witness, to wit, Monsieur Vignevielle, banker) Capitaine Lemaitre was dead and buried. At noon there had been a wedding in the little church. Its scenes lingered before Père Jerome's vision now—the kneeling pair: the bridegroom, rich in all the excellences of man, strength and kindness slumbering interlocked in every part and feature; the bride, a saintly weariness on her pale face, her awesome eyes lifted in adoration upon the image of the Saviour; the small knots of friends behind: Madame Thompson, large, fair, self-contained; Jean Thompson, with the affidavit of Madame Delphine showing through his tightly buttoned coat; the physician and his wife, sharing one expression of amiable consent; and last—yet first—one small, shrinking female figure, here at one side, in faded robes and dingy bonnet. She sat as motionless as stone, yet wore a look of apprehension, and in the small, restless black eyes which peered out from the pinched and wasted face, betrayed the peace-lessness of a harrowed mind; and neither the recollection of bride, nor of groom, nor of potential friends behind, nor the occupation of the present hour, could shut out from the tired priest the image of that woman, or the sound of his own low words of invitation to her, given as the company left the church—"Come to confession this afternoon."

By and by a long time passed without the approach of any step, or any glancing of light or shadow, save for the occasional progress from station to station of some one over on the right who was noiselessly going the way of the cross. Yet Père Jerome tarried.

"She will surely come," he said to himself; "she promised she would come."

A moment later, his sense, quickened by the prolonged silence, caught a subtle evidence or two of approach, and the next moment a penitent knelt noiselessly at the window of his box, and the whisper came tremblingly, in the voice he had waited to hear:

"*Bénissez-moin, mo' Père, pa'ce que mo péché.*" (Bless me, father, for I have sinned.)

He gave his blessing.

"*Ainsi soit-il*—Amen," murmured the penitent, and then, in the soft accents of the Creole *patois*, continued:

" 'I confess to Almighty God, to the blessed Mary, ever Virgin, to blessed Michael the Archangel, to blessed John the Baptist, to the holy Apostles Peter and Paul, and to all the saints, that I have sinned exceedingly in thought, word, and deed, *through my fault, through my fault, through my most grievous fault.*' I confessed on Saturday, three weeks ago, and received absolution, and I have performed the penance enjoined. Since then——" There she stopped.

There was a soft stir, as if she sank slowly down, and another as if she rose up again, and in a moment she said:

"Olive *is* my child. The picture I showed to Jean Thompson is the half-sister of my daughter's father, dead before my child was born. She is the image of her and of him; but, O God! Thou knowest! Oh Olive, my own daughter!"

She ceased, and was still. Père Jerome waited, but no sound came. He looked through the window. She was kneeling, with her forehead resting on her arms—motionless.

He repeated the words of absolution. Still she did not stir.

"My daughter," he said, "go to thy home in peace." But she did not move.

He rose hastily, stepped from the box, raised her in his arms, and called her by name:

"Madame Delphine!" Her head fell back in his elbow; for an instant there was life in the eyes—it glimmered—it vanished, and tears gushed from his own and fell upon the gentle face of the dead, as he looked up to heaven and cried:

"Lord, lay not this sin to her charge!"

Charles Waddell Chesnutt
(1858-1932)

Charles Waddell Chesnutt was born in Cleveland, Ohio, on June 20, 1858, the son of Andrew Jackson and Ann Maria Sampson Chesnutt, both free Negroes who had left North Carolina two years earlier to seek greater freedom and security in the Northwest. Shortly thereafter the Chesnutts moved to Oberlin, Ohio, but were back in Cleveland by the time the Civil War began. Andrew Chesnutt enlisted in the Union Army as a teamster and served throughout the war. Ann Maria and her sons (now three) remained in Cleveland, where Charles began attending the Cleveland Public Schools.

After the war, Andrew Chesnutt remained in North Carolina to be with his aged father and sent for Ann Maria and the children to join him. Though reluctant to leave the opportunities and freedom of the North, she brought her sons back South in 1866. In Fayetteville Charles attended the newly established Howard School, whose principal, Robert Harris, a remarkable man, exerted a great deal of influence over him. When Charles was thirteen, his mother died, leaving him to help care for two brothers and three sisters. For the next several years young Chesnutt taught in remote rural schools in North and South Carolina while continuing to pursue his own education largely by himself. In his free time he studied music, algebra, Latin, history, and read or re-read many of the classics.

In 1877 Chesnutt returned to Fayetteville, where he was appointed as first assistant to Robert Harris in the newly established Normal School there. He was teacher of reading, writing, spelling, composition, and related subjects in this school, whose purpose was to train teachers for the Negro schools. Charles married Susan Perry, a teacher at the Howard School and daughter of a prominent local businessman. He began studying stenography in hopes of obtaining a job in the North as a reporter. It was also about this time that he expressed in his journal his aspirations for writing.

In the fall of 1880, after the the death of Harris, Chesnutt became principal of the Normal School. He was only twenty-two at the time. He remained dissatisfied with the restrictions and hostility of life in the South, however, and continued to practice stenography in hopes of using this skill to secure employment in the North. At the end of the school year in 1883 he submitted his resignation to the school board and, despite the misgivings of those closest to him, headed north. After six months in New York, he moved to Cleveland, the city of his birth, where he found employment with a railroad company and began reading law. In 1887 he was admitted to the bar, standing at the head of his class. It was also about this time that he began writing short stories and submitting them to periodicals. His first published story, "Uncle Peter's House," appeared in the Cleveland *News and Herald* in 1885, but his first big break into the world of literature was the acceptance of his story "The Goophered Grapevine" by the *Atlantic Monthly*.

When Chesnutt's story "The Wife of His Youth" appeared in the *Atlantic Monthly* in July, 1898, it created a very favorable critical impression. Chesnutt's first published volume was a collection of stories entitled *The Conjure Woman* (1899). These tales, all of which are told in the North Carolina Negro dialect of "Uncle Julius," involve incidents of "conjuring." Later in the same year, a second volume of stories was published, *The Wife of His Youth and Other Stories of the Color Line*. The sub-title, which was suggested by Chesnutt's editor, Walter Hines Page, indicates the unifying theme of the volume. Although some of the tales in this collection had appeared earlier in periodicals, "A Matter of Principle" never received separate periodical printing and was first published in *The Wife of His Youth*.

Chesnutt's first novel, *The House Behind the Cedars,* appeared in 1900, followed closely by his second, *The Marrow of Tradition* (1901), both with strong racial themes. During this time Chesnutt was still writing short stories for periodicals, polemical articles on the race issue, and a biography of Frederick Douglass. His last published novel, *The Colonel's Dream* (1905), is really more the work of a pamphleteer than that of a novelist. After 1905 Chesnutt's literary endeavors ceased. It was in that year, however, that he received what he considered to be an accolade to his literary career: he was invited to attend Mark Twain's seventieth birthday party at Delmonico's in New York City, proclaimed one of the most festive events in the history of American literature and certainly a high point in Chesnutt's career.

The remainder of Chesnutt's life was spent quietly at his home in Cleveland, where he continued to be an active and respected member of the community. He died there in November, 1932.

Textual note

The text is that of the first edition of *The Wife of His Youth and Other Stories of the Color Line* (Boston and New York: Houghton, Mifflin and Company, 1899).

A Matter of Principle

"What our country needs most in its treatment of the race problem," observed Mr. Cicero Clayton at one of the monthly meetings of the Blue Vein Society, of which he was a prominent member, "is a clearer conception of the brotherhood of man."

The same sentiment in much the same words had often fallen from Mr. Clayton's lips,—so often, in fact, that the younger members of the society sometimes spoke of him—among themselves of course—as "Brotherhood Clayton." The sobriquet derived its point from the application he made of the principle involved in this oft-repeated proposition.

The fundamental article of Mr. Clayton's social creed was that he himself was not a negro.

"I know," he would say, "that the white people lump us all together as negroes, and condemn us all to the same social ostracism. But I don't accept this classification, for my part, and I imagine that, as the chief party in interest, I have a right to my opinion. People who belong by half or more of their blood to the most virile and progressive race of modern times have as much right to call themselves white as others have to call them negroes."

Mr. Clayton spoke warmly, for he was well informed, and had thought much upon the subject; too much, indeed, for he had not been able to escape entirely the tendency of too much concentration upon one subject to make even the clearest minds morbid.

"Of course we can't enforce our claims, or protect ourselves from being robbed of our birthright; but we can at least have principles, and try to live up to them the best we can. If we are not accepted as white, we can at any rate make it clear that we object to being called black. Our protest cannot fail in time to impress itself upon the better class of white people;

for the Anglo-Saxon race loves justice, and will eventually do it, where it does not conflict with their own interests."

Whether or not the fact that Mr. Clayton meant no sarcasm, and was conscious of no inconsistency in this eulogy, tended to establish the racial identity he claimed may safely be left to the discerning reader.

In living up to his creed Mr. Clayton declined to associate to any considerable extent with black people. This was sometimes a little inconvenient, and occasionally involved a sacrifice of some pleasure for himself and his family, because they would not attend entertainments where many black people were likely to be present. But they had a social refuge in a little society of people like themselves; they attended, too, a church, of which nearly all the members were white, and they were connected with a number of the religious and benevolent associations open to all good citizens, where they came into contact with the better class of white people, and were treated, in their capacity of members, with a courtesy and consideration scarcely different from that accorded to other citizens.

Mr. Clayton's racial theory was not only logical enough, but was in his own case backed up by substantial arguments. He had begun life with a small patrimony, and had invested his money in a restaurant, which by careful and judicious attention had grown from a cheap eating-house into the most popular and successful confectionery and catering establishment in Groveland. His business occupied a double store on Oakwood Avenue. He owned houses and lots, and stocks and bonds, had good credit at the banks, and lived in a style befitting his income and business standing. In person he was of olive complexion, with slightly curly hair. His features approached the Cuban or Latin-American type rather than the familiar broad characteristics of the mulatto, this suggestion of something foreign being heightened by a Vandyke beard and a carefully waxed and pointed mustache. When he walked to church on Sunday mornings with his daughter Alice, they were a couple of such striking appearance as surely to attract attention.

Miss Alice Clayton was queen of her social set. She was young, she was handsome. She was nearly white; she frankly confessed her sorrow that she was not entirely so. She was accomplished and amiable, dressed in good taste, and had for her father by all odds the richest colored man—the term is used with apologies to Mr. Clayton, explaining that it does not necessarily mean a negro—in Groveland. So pronounced was her superiority that really she had but one social rival worthy of the name,—Miss Lura Watkins, whose father kept a prosperous livery stable and lived in almost as good style as the Claytons. Miss Watkins, while good-looking enough, was not so young nor quite so white as Miss Clayton. She was popular, however, among their mutual acquaintances, and there was a good-natured race between the two as to which should make the first and best marriage.

Marriages among Miss Clayton's set were serious affairs. Of course marriage is always a serious matter, whether it be a success or a failure, and there are those who believe that any marriage is better than no marriage. But among Miss Clayton's friends and associates matrimony took on an added seriousness because of the very narrow limits within which it could take place. Miss Clayton and her friends, by reason of their assumed superiority to black people, or perhaps as much by reason of a somewhat morbid shrinking from the curiosity manifested toward married people of strongly contrasting colors, would not marry black men, and except in rare instances white men would not marry them. They were therefore restricted for a choice to the young men of their own complexion. But these, unfortunately for the girls, had a wider choice. In any State where the laws permit freedom of the marriage contract, a man, by virtue of his sex, can find a wife of whatever complexion he prefers; of course he must not always ask too much in other respects, for most women like to better their social position when they marry. To the number thus lost by "going on the other side," as the phrase went, add the worthless contingent whom no self-respecting woman would marry, and the choice was still further restricted; so that it had become fashionable, when the supply of eligible men ran short, for those of Miss Clayton's set who could afford it to go traveling, ostensibly for pleasure, but with the serious hope that they might meet their fate away from home.

Miss Clayton had perhaps a larger option than any of her associates. Among such men as there were she could have taken her choice. Her beauty, her position, her accomplishments, her father's wealth, all made her eminently desirable. But, on the other hand, the same things rendered her more difficult to reach, and harder to please. To get access to her heart, too, it was necessary to run the gauntlet of her parents, which, until she had reached the age of twenty-three, no one had succeeded in doing safely. Many had called, but none had been chosen.

There was, however, one spot left unguarded, and through it Cupid, a veteran sharpshooter, sent a dart. Mr. Clayton had taken into his service and into his household a poor relation, a sort of cousin several times removed. This boy—his name was Jack—had gone into Mr. Clayton's service at a very youthful age,—twelve or thirteen. He had helped about the housework, washed the dishes, swept the floors, taken care of the lawn and the stable for three or four years, while he attended school. His cousin had then taken him into the store, where he had swept the floor, washed the windows, and done a class of work that kept fully impressed upon him the fact that he was a poor dependent. Nevertheless he was a cheerful lad, who took what he could get and was properly grateful, but always meant to get more. By sheer force of industry and affability and shrewdness, he forced his employer to promote him in time to a position of recognized authority in the establishment. Any one outside of the family would have perceived in him a very suitable husband for Miss Clayton; he was of about the same age, or a year or two older, was as fair of complexion as she, when she was not powdered, and was passably good-looking, with a bearing of which the natural manliness had been no more warped than his training and racial status had rendered inevitable; for he had early learned the law of growth, that to bend is better than to break. He was sometimes sent to accompany Miss Clayton to places in the evening, when she had no other escort, and it is quite likely that she discovered his good points before her parents did. That they should in time perceive them was inevitable. But even then, so accustomed were they to looking down upon the object of their former bounty, that they only spoke of the matter jocularly.

"Well, Alice," her father would say in his bluff way, "you'll not be absolutely obliged to die an old maid. If we can't find anything better for you, there's always Jack. As long as he does n't take to some other girl, you can fall back on him as a last chance. He'd be glad to take you to get into the business."

Miss Alice had considered the joke a very poor one when first made, but by occasional repetition she became somewhat familiar with it. In time it got around to Jack himself, to whom it seemed no joke at all. He had long considered it a consummation devoutly to be wished, and when he became aware that the possibility of such a match had occurred to the other parties in interest, he made up his mind that the idea should in due course of time become an accomplished fact. He had even suggested as much to Alice, in a casual way, to feel his ground; and while she had treated the matter lightly, he was not without hope that she had been impressed by the suggestion. Before he had had time, however, to follow up this lead, Miss Clayton, in the spring of 187–, went away on a visit to Washington.

The occasion of her visit was a presidential inauguration. The new President owed his nomination mainly to the votes of the Southern delegates in the convention, and was believed to be correspondingly well disposed to the race from which the Southern delegates were for the most part recruited. Friends of rival and unsuccessful candidates for the nomination had more than hinted that the Southern delegates were very substantially rewarded for their support at the time when it was given; whether this was true or not the parties concerned know best. At any rate the colored politicians did not see it in that light, for they were gathered from near and far to press their claims for recognition and patronage. On the evening following the White House inaugural ball, the colored people of Washington gave an "inaugural" ball at a large public hall. It was under the management of their leading citizens, among them several high officials holding over from the last administration, and a number of professional and business men. This ball was the most noteworthy social event that colored circles up to that time had ever known. There were many visitors from various parts of the country. Miss Clayton attended the ball, the honors of which she carried away easily. She danced with several partners, and was introduced to innumerable people whom she had never seen before, and whom she hardly expected ever to meet again. She went away from the ball, at four o'clock in the morning, in a glow of triumph, and with a confused impression of senators and representatives and lawyers and doctors of all shades, who had sought an introduction, led her through the dance, and overwhelmed her with compliments. She returned home the next day but one, after the most delightful week of her life.

II

One afternoon, about three weeks after her return from Washington, Alice received a letter through the mail. The envelope bore the words "House of Representatives" printed in one corner, and in the opposite corner, in a bold running hand, a Congressman's frank, "Hamilton M. Brown, M. C." The letter read as follows:—

HOUSE OF REPRESENTATIVES,
WASHINGTON, D. C., MARCH 30, 187–.

MISS ALICE CLAYTON, GROVELAND.

DEAR FRIEND (if I may be permitted to call you so after so brief an acquaintance),—I remember with sincerest pleasure our recent meeting at the inaugural ball, and the sensation created by your beauty, your amiable manners, and your graceful dancing. Time has so strengthened the impression I then received, that I should have felt inconsolable had I thought it impossible ever to again behold the charms which had brightened the occasion of our meeting and eclipsed by their brilliancy the leading belles of the capital. I had hoped, however, to have the pleasure of meeting you again, and circumstances have fortunately placed it in my power to do so at an early date. You have doubtless learned that the contest over the election in the Sixth Congressional District of South Carolina has been decided in my favor, and that I now have the honor of representing my native State at the national capital. I have just been appointed a member of a special committee to visit and inspect the Sault River and the Straits of Mackinac, with reference to the needs of lake navigation. I have made arrangements to start a week ahead of the other members of the committee, whom I am to meet in Detroit on the 20th. I shall leave here on the 2d, and will arrive in Groveland on the 3d, by the 7.30 evening express. I shall remain in Groveland several days, in the course of which I shall be pleased to call, and renew the acquaintance so auspiciously begun in Washington, which it is my fondest hope may ripen into a warmer friendship.

If you do not regard my visit as presumptuous, and do not write me in the mean while forbidding it, I shall do myself the pleasure of waiting on you the morning after my arrival in Groveland.

With renewed expressions of my sincere admiration and profound esteem, I remain,

Sincerely yours,

HAMILTON M. BROWN, M. C.

To Alice, and especially to her mother, this bold and flowery letter had very nearly the force of a formal declaration. They read it over again and again, and spent most of the afternoon discussing it. There were few young men in Groveland eligible as husbands for so superior a person as Alice Clayton, and an addition to the number would be very acceptable. But the mere fact of his being a Congressman was not sufficient to qualify him; there were other considerations.

"I've never heard of this Honorable Hamilton M. Brown," said Mr. Clayton. The letter had been laid before him at the supper-table. "It's strange, Alice, that you have n't said anything about him before. You must have met lots of swell folks not to recollect a Congressman."

"But he was n't a Congressman then," answered Alice; "he was only a claimant. I remember Senator Bruce, and Mr. Douglass; but there were so many doctors and lawyers and politicians that I could n't keep track of them all. Still I have a faint impression of a Mr. Brown who danced with me."

She went into the parlor and brought out the dancing programme she had used at the Washington ball. She had decorated it with a bow of blue ribbon and preserved it as a souvenir of her visit.

"Yes," she said, after examining it, "I must have danced with him. Here are the initials—'H. M. B.' "

"What color is he?" asked Mr. Clayton, as he plied his knife and fork.

"I have a notion that he was rather dark—darker than any one I had ever danced with before."

"Why did you dance with him?" asked her father. "You were n't obliged to go back on your principles because you were away from home."

"Well, father, 'when you're in Rome'—you know the rest. Mrs. Clearweather introduced me to several dark men, to him among others. They were her friends, and common decency required me to be courteous."

"If this man is black, we don't want to encourage him. If he's the right sort, we'll invite him to the house."

"And make him feel at home," added Mrs. Clayton, on hospitable thoughts intent.

"We must ask Sadler about him to-morrow," said Mr. Clayton, when he had drunk his coffee and lighted his cigar. "If he's the right man he shall have cause to remember his visit to Groveland. We'll show him that Washington is not the only town on earth."

The uncertainty of the family with regard to Mr. Brown was soon removed. Mr. Solomon Sadler, who was supposed to know everything worth knowing concerning the colored race, and everybody of importance connected with it, dropped in after supper to make an evening call. Sadler was familiar with the history of every man of negro ancestry who had distinguished himself in any walk of life. He could give the pedigree of Alexander Pushkin, the titles of scores of Dumas's novels (even Sadler had not time to learn them all), and could recite the whole of Wendell Phillips's lecture on Toussaint l'Ouverture. He claimed a personal acquaintance with Mr. Frederick Douglass, and had been often in Washington, where he was well known and well received in good colored society.

"Let me see," he said reflectively, when asked for information about the Honorable Hamilton M. Brown. "Yes, I think I know him. He studied at Oberlin just after the war. He was about leaving there when I entered. There were two H. M. Browns there—a Hamilton M. Brown and a Henry M. Brown. One was stout and dark and the other was slim and quite light; you could scarcely tell him from a dark white man. They used to call them 'light Brown' and 'dark Brown.' I did n't know either of them except by sight, for they were there only a few weeks after I went in. As I remember them, Hamilton was the fair one—a very good-looking, gentlemanly fellow, and, as I heard, a good student and a fine speaker."

"Do you remember what kind of hair he had?" asked Mr. Clayton.

"Very good indeed; straight, as I remember it. He looked something like a Spaniard or a Portuguese."

"Now that you describe him," said Alice, "I remember quite well dancing with such a gentleman; and I'm wrong about my 'H. M. B.' The dark man must have been some one else; there are two others on my card that I can't remember distinctly, and he was probably one of those."

"I guess he's all right, Alice," said her father when Sadler had gone away. "He evidently means business, and we must treat him white. Of course he must stay with us; there are no hotels in Groveland while he is here. Let's see—he'll be here in three days. That is n't very long, but I guess we can get ready. I'll write a letter this afternoon—or you write it, and invite him to the house, and say I'll meet him at the depot. And you may have *carte blanche* for making the preparations."

"We must have some people to meet him."

"Certainly; a reception is the proper thing. Sit down immediately and write the letter and I'll mail it first thing in the morning, so he'll get it before he has time to make other arrangements. And you and your mother put your heads together and make out a list of guests, and I'll have the invitations printed to-morrow. We will show the darkeys of Groveland how to entertain a Congressman."

It will be noted that in moments of abstraction or excitement Mr. Clayton sometimes relapsed into forms of speech not entirely consistent with his principles. But some allowance must be made for his atmosphere; he could no more escape from it than the leopard can change his spots, or the— In deference to Mr. Clayton's feelings the quotation will be left incomplete.

Alice wrote the letter on the spot and it was duly mailed, and sped on its winged way to Washington.

The preparations for the reception were made as thoroughly and elaborately as possible on so short a notice. The invitations were issued; the house was cleaned from attic to cellar; an orchestra was engaged for the evening; elaborate floral decorations were planned and the flowers ordered. Even the refreshments, which ordinarily, in the household of a caterer, would be mere matter of familiar detail, became a subject of serious consultation and study.

The approaching event was a matter of very much interest to the fortunate ones who were honored with invitations, and this for several reasons. They were anxious to meet this sole representative of their race in the —th Congress, and as he was not one of the old-line colored leaders, but a new star risen on the political horizon, there was a special curiosity to see who he was and what he looked like. Moreover, the Claytons did not did not often entertain a large company, but when they did, it was on a scale commensurate with their means and position, and to be present on such an occasion was a thing to remember and to talk about. And, most important consideration of all, some remarks dropped by members of the Clayton family had given rise to the rumor that the Congressman was seeking a wife. This invested his visit with a romantic interest, and gave the reception a practical value; for there were other marriageable girls besides Miss Clayton, and if one was left another might be taken.

III

On the evening of April 3d, at fifteen minutes of six o'clock, Mr. Clayton, accompanied by Jack, entered the livery carriage waiting at his gate and ordered the coachman to drive to the Union Depot. He had taken Jack along, partly for company, and partly that Jack might relieve the Congressman of any trouble about his baggage, and make himself useful in case of emergency. Jack was willing enough to go, for he had foreseen in the visitor a rival for Alice's hand,—indeed he had heard more or less of the subject for several days,—and was glad to make a reconnaissance before the enemy arrived upon the field of battle. He had made—at least he had thought so—considerable progress with Alice during the three weeks since her return from Washington, and once or twice Alice had been perilously near the tender stage. This visit had disturbed the situation and threatened to ruin his chances; but he did not mean to give up without a struggle.

Arrived at the main entrance, Mr. Clayton directed the carriage to wait, and entered the station with Jack. The Union Depot at Groveland was an immense oblong structure, covering a dozen parallel tracks and furnishing terminal passenger facilities for half a dozen railroads. The tracks ran east and west, and the depot was entered from the south, at about the middle of the building. On either side of the entrance, the waiting-rooms, refreshment rooms, baggage and express departments, and other administrative offices, extended in a row for the entire length of the building; and beyond them and parallel with them stretched a long open space, separated from the tracks by an iron fence or *grille*. There were two entrance gates in the fence, at which tickets must be shown before access could be had to trains, and two other gates, by which arriving passengers came out.

Mr. Clayton looked at the blackboard on the wall underneath the station clock, and observed that the 7.30 train from Washington was five minutes late. Accompanied by Jack he walked up and down the platform until the train, with the usual accompaniment of panting steam and clanging bell and rumbling trucks, pulled into the station, and drew up on the third or fourth track from the iron railing. Mr. Clayton stationed himself at the gate nearest the rear end of the train, reasoning that the Congressman would ride in a parlor car, would naturally come out by the gate nearest the point at which he left the train.

"You'd better go and stand by the other gate, Jack," he said to his companion, "and stop him if he goes out that way."

The train was well filled and a stream of passengers poured through. Mr. Clayton scanned the crowd carefully as they approached the gate, and scrutinized each passenger as he came through, without seeing any one that met the description of Congressman Brown, as given by Sadler, or any one that could in his opinion be the gentleman for whom he was looking. When the last one had passed through he was left to the conclusion that his expected guest had gone out by the other gate. Mr. Clayton hastened thither.

"Did n't he come out this way, Jack?" he asked.

"No, sir," replied the young man, "I have n't seen him."

"That's strange," mused Mr. Clayton, somewhat anxiously. "He would hardly fail to come without giving us notice. Surely we must have missed him. We'd better look around a little. You go that way and I'll go this."

Mr. Clayton turned and walked several rods along the platform to the men's waiting-room, and standing near the door glanced around to see if he could find the object of his search. The only colored person in the room was a stout and very black man, wearing a broadcloth suit and a silk hat, and seated a short distance from the door. On the seat by his side stood a couple of valises. On one of them, the one nearest him, on which his arm rested, was written in white letters, plainly legible,—

H. M. Brown, M. C.
"Washington, D. C."

Mr. Clayton's feelings at this discovery can better be imagined than described. He hastily left the waiting-room, before the black gentleman, who was looking the other way, was even aware of his presence, and, walking rapidly up and down the platform, communed with himself upon what course of action the situation demanded. He had invited to his house, had come down to meet, had made elaborate preparations to entertain on the following evening, a light-colored man,—a white man by his theory, an acceptable guest, a possible husband for his daughter, an avowed suitor for her hand. If the Congressman had turned out to be brown, even dark brown, with fairly good hair, though he might not have desired him as a son-in-law, yet he could have welcomed him as a guest. But even this softening of the blow was denied him, for the man in the waiting-room was palpably, aggressively black, with pronounced African features and woolly hair, without apparently a single drop of redeeming white blood. Could he, in the face of his well-known principles, his lifelong rule of conduct, take this negro into his home and introduce him to his friends? Could he subject his wife and daughter to the rude shock of such a disappointment? It would be bad enough for them to learn of the ghastly mistake but to have him in the house would be twisting the arrow in the wound.

Mr. Clayton had the instincts of a gentleman, and realized the delicacy of the situation. But to get out of his difficulty without wounding the feelings of the Congressman required not only diplomacy but dispatch. Whatever he did must be done promptly; for if he waited many minutes the Congressman would probably take a carriage and be driven to Mr. Clayton's residence.

A ray of hope came for a moment to illumine the gloom of the situation. Perhaps the black man was merely sitting there, and not the owner of the valise! For there were two valises, one on each side of the supposed Congressman. For obvious reasons he did not care to make the inquiry himself, so he looked around for his companion, who came up a moment later.

"Jack," he exclaimed excitedly, "I'm afraid we're in the worst kind of a hole, unless there's some mistake! Run down to the men's waiting-room and you'll see a man and a valise, and you'll understand what I mean. Ask that darkey if he is the Honorable Mr. Brown, Congressman from South Carolina. If he says yes, come back right away and let me know, without giving him time to ask any questions, and put your wits to work to help me out of the scrape."

"I wonder what's the matter?" said Jack to himself, but did as he was told. In a moment he came running back.

"Yes, sir," he announced; "he says he's the man."

"Jack," said Mr. Clayton desperately, "if you want to show your appreciation of what I've done for you, you must suggest some way out of this. I'd never dare to take that negro to my house, and yet I'm obliged to treat him like a gentleman."

Jack's eyes had worn a somewhat reflective look since he had gone to make the inquiry. Suddenly his face brightened with intelligence, and then, as a newsboy ran into the station calling his wares, hardened into determination.

"Clarion, special extry 'dition! All about de epidemic er dipt'eria!" clamored the newsboy with shrill childish treble, as he made his way toward the waiting-room. Jack darted after him, and saw the man to whom he had spoken buy a paper. He ran back to his employer, and dragged him over toward the ticket-seller's window.

"I have it, sir!" he exclaimed, seizing a telegraph blank and writing rapidly, and reading aloud as he wrote. "How's this for a way out?"—

"DEAR SIR,—I write you this note here in the depot to inform you of an unfortunate event which has interfered with my plans and those of my family for your entertainment while in Groveland. Yesterday my daughter Alice complained of a sore throat, which by this afternoon had developed into a case of malignant diphtheria. In consequence our house has been quarantined; and while I have felt myself obliged to come down to the depot, I do not feel that I ought to expose you to the possibility of infection, and I therefore send you this by another hand. The bearer will conduct you to a carriage which I have ordered placed at your service, and unless you should prefer some other hotel, you will be driven to the Forest Hill House, where I beg you will consider yourself my guest during your stay in the city, and make the fullest use of every convenience it may offer. From present indications I fear no one of our family will be able to see you, which we shall regret beyond expression, as we have made elaborate arrangements for your entertainment. I still hope, however, that you may enjoy your visit, as there are many places of interest in the city, and many friends will doubtless be glad to make your acquaintance.

"With assurance of my profound regret, I am   Sincerely yours,
"Cicero Clayton."

"Splendid!" cried Mr. Clayton. "You've helped me out of a horrible scrape. Now, go and take him to the hotel and see him comfortably located, and tell them to charge the bill to me."

"I suspect, sir," suggested Jack, "that I'd better not go up to the house, and you'll have to stay in yourself for a day or two, to keep up appearances. I'll sleep on the lounge at the store, and we can talk business over the telephone."

"All right, Jack, we'll arrange the details later. But for Heaven's sake get him started, or he'll be calling a hack to drive up to the house. I'll go home on a street car."

"So far so good," sighed Mr. Clayton to himself as he escaped from the station. "Jack is a deuced clever fellow, and I'll have to do something more for him. But the tug-of-war is yet to come. I've got to bribe a doctor, shut up the house for a day or two, and have all the ill-humor of two disappointed women to endure until this negro leaves town. Well, I'm sure my wife and Alice will back me up at any cost. No sacrifice is too great to escape having to entertain him; of course I have no prejudice against his color,—he can't help that,—but it is the *principle* of the thing. If we received him it would be a concession fatal to all my views and theories. And I am really doing him a kindness, for I'm sure that all the world could not make Alice and her mother treat him with anything but cold politeness. It'll be a great mortification to Alice, but I don't see how else I could have got out of it."

He boarded the first car that left the depot, and soon reached home. The house was lighted up, and through the lace curtains of the parlor windows he could see his wife and daughter, elegantly dressed, waiting to receive their distinguished visitor. He rang the bell impatiently, and a servant opened the door.

"The gentleman did n't come?" asked the maid.

"No," he said as he hung up his hat. This brought the ladies to the door.

"He did n't come?" they exclaimed. "What's the matter?"

"I'll tell you," he said. "Mary," this to the servant, a white girl, who stood in open-eyed curiosity, "we shan't need you any more to-night."

Then he went into the parlor, and, closing the door, told his story. When he reached the point where he had discovered the color of the honorable Mr. Brown, Miss Clayton caught her breath, and was on the verge of collapse.

"That nigger," said Mrs. Clayton indignantly, "can never set foot in this house. But what did you do with him?"

Mr. Clayton quickly unfolded his plan, and described the disposition he had made of the Congressman.

"It's an awful shame," said Mrs. Clayton. "Just think of the trouble and expense we have gone to! And poor Alice'll never get over it, for everybody knows he came to see her and that he's smitten with her. But you've done just right; we never would have been able to hold up our heads again if we had introduced a black man, even a Congressman, to the people that are invited here to-morrow night, as a sweetheart of Alice. Why, she would n't marry him if he was President of the United States and plated with gold an inch thick. The very idea!"

"Well," said Mr. Clayton, "then we've got to act quick. Alice must wrap up her throat—by the way, Alice, how *is* your throat?"

"It's sore," sobbed Alice, who had been in tears almost from her father's return, "and I don't care if I do have diphtheria and die, no, I don't!" and she wept on.

"Wrap up your throat and go to bed, and I'll go over to Doctor Pillsbury's and get a diphtheria card to nail up on the house. In the morning, first thing, we'll have to write notes recalling the invitations for to-morrow evening, and have them delivered by messenger boys. We were fools for not finding out all about this man from some one who knew, before we invited him here. Sadler don't know more than half he thinks he does, anyway. And we'll have to do this thing thoroughly, or our motives will be misconstrued, and people will say we are prejudiced and all that, when it is only a matter of principle with us."

The programme outlined above was carried out to the letter. The invitations were recalled, to the great disappointment of the invited guests. The family physician called several times during the day. Alice remained in bed, and the maid left without notice, in such a hurry that she forgot to take her best clothes.

Mr. Clayton himself remained at home. He had a telephone in the house, and was therefore in easy communication with his office, so that the business did not suffer materially by reason of his absence from the store. About ten o'clock in the morning a note came up from the hotel, expressing Mr. Brown's regrets and sympathy. Toward noon Mr. Clayton picked up the morning paper, which he had not theretofore had time to read, and was glancing over it casually, when his eye fell upon a column headed "A Colored Congressman." He read the article with astonishment that rapidly turned to chagrin and dismay. It was an interview describing the Congressman as a tall and shapely man, about thirty-five years old, with an olive complexion not noticeably darker than many a white man's, straight hair, and eyes as black as sloes.

"The bearing of this son of South Carolina reveals the polished manners of the Southern gentleman, and neither from his appearance nor his conversation would one suspect that the white blood which flows in his viens in such preponderating measure had ever been crossed by that of a darker race," wrote the reporter, who had received instructions at the office that for urgent business considerations the lake shipping interest wanted Representative Brown treated with marked consideration.

There was more of the article, but the introductory portion left Mr. Clayton in such a state of bewilderment that the paper fell from his hand. What was the meaning of it? Had he been mistaken? Obviously so, or else the reporter was wrong, which was manifestly improbable. When he had recovered himself somewhat, he picked up the newspaper and began reading where he had left off.

"Representative Brown traveled to Groveland in company with Bishop Jones of the African Methodist Jerusalem Church, who is *en route* to attend the general conference of his denomination at Detroit next week. The bishop, who came in while the writer was interviewing Mr. Brown, is a splendid type of the pure negro. He is said to be a man of great power among his people, which may easily be believed after one has looked upon his expressive countenance and heard him discuss the questions which affect the welfare of his church and his race."

Mr. Clayton stared at the paper. " 'The bishop,' " he repeated, " 'is a splendid type of the pure negro.' I must have mistaken the bishop for the Congressman! But how in the world did Jack get the thing balled up? I'll call up the store and demand an explanation of him.

"Jack," he asked, "what kind of a looking man was the fellow you gave the note to at the depot?"

"He was a very wicked-looking fellow, sir," came back the answer. "He had a bad eye, looked like a gambler, sir. I am not surprised that you did n't want to entertain him, even if he was a Congressman."

"What color was he—that's what I want to know—and what kind of hair did he have?"

"Why, he was about my complexion, sir, and had straight black hair."

The rules of the telephone company did not permit swearing over the line. Mr. Clayton broke the rules.

"Was there any one else with him?" he asked when he had relieved his mind.

"Yes, sir, Bishop Jones of the African Methodist Jerusalem Church was sitting there with him; they had traveled from Washington together. I drove the bishop to his stopping-place after I had left Mr. Brown at the hotel. I did n't suppose you'd mind."

Mr. Clayton fell into a chair, and indulged in thoughts unutterable.

He folded up the paper and slipped it under the family Bible, where it was least likely to be soon discovered.

"I'll hide the paper, anyway," he groaned. "I'll never hear the last of this till my dying day, so I may as well have a few hours' respite. It's too late to go back, and we've got to play the farce out. Alice is really sick with disappointment, and to let her know this now would only make her worse. May be he'll leave town in a day or two, and then she'll be in condition to stand it. Such luck is enough to disgust a man with trying to do right and live up to his principles."

Time hung a little heavy on Mr. Clayton's hands during the day. His wife was busy with the housework. He answered several telephone calls about Alice's health, and called up the store occasionally to ask how the business was getting on. After lunch he lay down on a sofa and took a nap, from which he was aroused by the sound of the door-bell. He went to the door. The evening paper was lying on the porch, and the newsboy, who had not observed the diphtheria sign until after he had rung, was hurrying away as fast as his legs would carry him.

Mr. Clayton opened the paper and looked it through to see if there was any reference to the visiting Congressman. He found what he sought and more. An article on the local page contained a résumé of the information given in the morning paper, with the following additional paragraph:—

"A reporter, who called at the Forest Hill this morning to interview Representative Brown, was informed that the Congressman had been invited to spend the remainder of his time in Groveland as the guest of Mr. William Watkins, the proprietor of the popular livery establishment on Main Street. Mr. Brown will remain in the city several days, and a reception will be tendered him at Mr. Watkins's on Wednesday evening."

"That ends it," sighed Mr. Clayton. "The dove of peace will never again rest on my roof-tree."

But why dwell longer on the sufferings of Mr. Clayton, or attempt to describe the feelings or chronicle the remarks of his wife and daughter when they learned the facts in the case?

As to Representative Brown, he was made welcome in the hospitable home of Mr. William Watkins. There was a large and brilliant assemblage at the party on Wednesday evening, at which were displayed the costumes prepared for the Clayton reception. Mr. Brown took a fancy to Miss Lura Watkins, to whom, before the week was over, he became engaged to be married. Meantime poor Alice, the innocent victim of circumstances and principles, lay sick abed with a supposititious case of malignant diphtheria, and a real case of acute disappointment and chagrin.

"Oh, Jack!" exclaimed Alice, a few weeks later, on the way home from evening church in company with the young man, "what a dreadful thing it all was! And to think of that hateful Lura Watkins marrying the Congressman!"

The street was shaded by trees at the point where they were passing, and there was no one in sight. Jack put his arms around her waist, and, leaning over, kissed her.

"Never mind, dear," he said soothingly, "you still have your 'last chance' left, and I'll prove myself a better man than the Congressman."

Occasionally, at social meetings, when the vexed question of the future of the colored race comes up, as it often does, for discussion, Mr. Clayton may still be heard to remark sententiously:—

"What the white people of the United States need most, in dealing with this problem, is a higher conception of the brotherhood of man. For of one blood God made all the nations of the earth."

Katherine O'Flaherty Chopin
(1851-1904)

Katherine O'Flaherty was born in St. Louis, Missouri, on February 8, 1851. Her father, Thomas O'Flaherty, had emigrated to America in 1823 from Ireland; and, establishing a profitable business in St. Louis, had married fifteen-year-old Eliza Faris, from a prominent local Creole family. Kate's heritage was thus a union of the aristocratic French tradition and the energetic pioneer spirit of the immigrant. In 1855, when Kate was only four years old, her father was one of seventeen passengers killed in a train wreck. This was the first in a series of personal tragedies which acquainted her with the reality of sudden death.

One of the most influential persons in Kate's life was her maternal great-grandmother, Madame Victoria Verdon Charleville. This grand old lady lived in the O'Flaherty home until her death in 1863 and undertook the training of her great-granddaughter. It was from her that Kate heard tales of the early days of St. Louis, and she was also responsible for awakening in the child an enduring interest in character, especially in that of independent, determined women.

During the Civil War the O'Flahertys' sympathies were with the Confederacy, although Missouri was a Union state. George O'Flaherty, Kate's half-brother who enlisted as a private in the "Missouri Mounted Infantry," died of typhoid fever in Arkansas in 1863, when he was twenty-three years old—another severe blow to the young girl's sensibilities.

In 1870 Kate married Oscar Chopin, the son of a wealthy New Orleans Creole doctor. After ten years in New Orleans Chopin's cotton business failed and he moved his wife and six children to Cloutierville, Louisiana, where he opened and operated a general store. During her ten years of married life in New Orleans, Kate Chopin did not write or take notes on her observations and experiences. Yet it is evident from her later writing that she was storing up information and impressions which she was to make good use of in her novels and short stories. The experience in Cloutierville was also a fortunate one for her writing career; there she became acquainted with rural and plantation life in Louisiana and associated with many different types of people.

One more of the many tragedies of Kate's life occurred in 1882: her husband died suddenly from a violent attack of "swamp fever." After his death, Kate and her children returned to St. Louis to live with her mother. She, too, died suddenly in 1885, leaving her daughter grief-stricken and alone. At thirty-four Kate Chopin had lost all those most dear to her except for her six children, the oldest of whom was only fourteen years old. It was probably desperation and loneliness coupled with her penetrating awareness of human suffering that caused her to turn to writing as a means of expression.

In 1889 Mrs. Chopin began to publish short stories and to write her first novel, *At Fault,* published in September, 1890. *Bayou Folk,* a collection of her Creole stories, was published in 1894, followed by her second collection of stories, *A Night in Acadie,* in 1897. The stories in this collection exhibit her fine handling of dialect and clear perception of the distinguishing features of characters. Included in it is "Athénaïse: A Story of A Temperament," which had first been published in the *Atlantic Monthly* of the preceding year. "Athénaïse" well illustrates the delicate charm of her style, infused with an intellectual and spiritual element which contributes to the importance of her work.

Kate Chopin's last and best novel, *The Awakening,* was published in 1889 by Herbert S. Stone and Company of Chicago. Though many reviews praised its artistic achievement, it was also greeted by a storm of harsh criticism, some of which attacked its author's motives and character.

On Saturday, August 20, 1904, Mrs. Chopin made her last of many visits to the St. Louis World's Fair. That night she suffered what was probably a cerebral hemorrhage and lapsed into unconsciousness. She died on Monday, August 22, 1904.

Textual note

Copy-text of "Athénaïse: A Story of A Temperament" is the first periodical printing, in the *Atlantic Monthly,* LXXVIII (August, 1896), 232–41; (September, 1896), 404–13. "Athénaïse" was reprinted in *A Night in Acadie* (Chicago: Way & Williams, 1897).

Athénaïse: A Story of A Temperament

I

Athénaïse went away in the morning to make a visit to her parents, ten miles back on rigolet du Bon Dieu. She did not return in the evening, and Cazeau, her husband, fretted not a little. He did not worry much about Athénaïse, who, he suspected, was resting only too content in the bosom of her family; his chief solicitude was manifestly for the pony she had ridden. He felt sure those "lazy pigs," her brothers, were capable of neglecting it seriously. This misgiving Cazeau communicated to his servant, old Félicité, who waited upon him at supper.

His voice was low pitched, and even softer than Félicité's. He was tall, sinewy, swarthy, and altogether severe looking. His thick black hair waved, and it gleamed like the breast of a crow. The sweep of his mustache, which was not so black, outlined the broad contour of the mouth. Beneath the under lip grew a small tuft which he was much given to twisting, and which he permitted to grow, apparently, for no other purpose. Cazeau's eyes were dark blue, narrow and overshadowed. His hands were coarse and stiff from close acquaintance with farming tools and implements, and he handled his fork and knife clumsily. But he was distinguished looking, and succeeded in commanding a good deal of respect, and even fear sometimes.

He ate his supper alone, by the light of a single coal-oil lamp that but faintly illumined the big room, with its bare floor and huge rafters, and its heavy pieces of furniture that loomed dimly in the gloom of the apartment. Félicité, ministering to his wants, hovered about the table like a little, bent, restless shadow.

She served him a dish of sunfish fried crisp and brown. There was nothing else set before him beside the bread and butter and the bottle of red wine which she locked carefully in the buffet after he had poured his second glass. She was occupied with her mistress's absence, and kept reverting to it after he had expressed his solicitude about the pony.

"Dat beat me! on'y marry two mont', an' got de head turn' a'ready to go 'broad. Ce n'est pas Chrétien, ténez!"

Cazeau shrugged his shoulders for answer, after he had drained his glass and pushed aside his plate. Félicité's opinion of the unchristian-like behavior of his wife in leaving him thus alone after two months of marriage weighed little with him. He was used to solitude, and did not mind a day or a night or two of it. He had lived alone ten years, since his first wife died, and Félicité might have known better than to suppose that he cared. He told her she was a fool. It sounded like a compliment in his modulated, caressing voice. She grumbled to herself as she set about clearing the table, and Cazeau arose and walked outside on the gallery; his spur, which he had not removed upon entering the house, jangled at every step.

The night was beginning to deepen, and to gather black about the clusters of trees and shrubs that were grouped in the yard. In the beam of light from the open kitchen door a black boy stood feeding a brace of snarling, hungry dogs; further away, on the steps of a cabin, some one was playing the accordion; and in still another direction a little negro baby was crying lustily. Cazeau walked around to the front of the house, which was square, squat, and one-story.

A belated wagon was driving in at the gate, and the impatient driver was swearing hoarsely at his jaded oxen. Félicité stepped out on the gallery, glass and polishing-towel in hand, to investigate, and to wonder, too, who could be singing out on the river. It was a party of young people paddling around, waiting for the moon to rise, and they were singing Juanita, their voices coming tempered and melodious through the distance and the night.

Cazeau's horse was waiting, saddled, ready to be mounted, for Cazeau had many things to attend to before bedtime; so many things that there was not left to him a moment in which to think of Athénaïse. He felt her absence, though, like a dull, insistent pain.

However, before he slept that night he was visited by the thought of her, and by a vision of her fair young face with its drooping lips and sullen and averted eyes. The marriage had been a blunder; he had only to look into her eyes to feel that, to discover her growing aversion. But it was a thing not by any possibility to be undone. He was quite prepared to make the best of it, and expected no less than a like effort on her part. The less she revisited the rigolet, the better. He would find means to keep her at home hereafter.

These unpleasant reflections kept Cazeau awake far into the night, notwithstanding the craving of his whole body for rest and sleep. The moon was shining, and its pale effulgence reached dimly into the room, and with it a touch of the cool breath of the spring night. There was an unusual stillness abroad; no sound to be heard save the distant, tireless, plaintiff notes of the accordion.

II

Athénaïse did not return the following day, even though her husband sent her word to do so by her brother, Montéclin, who passed on his way to the village early in the morning.

On the third day Cazeau saddled his horse and went himself in search of her. She had sent no word, no message, explaining her absence, and he felt that he had good cause to be offended. It was rather awkward to have to leave his work, even though late in the afternoon,—Cazeau had always so much to do; but among the many urgent calls upon him, the task of bringing his wife back to a sense of her duty seemed to him for the moment paramount.

The Michés, Athénaïse's parents, lived on the old Gotrain place. It did not belong to them; they were "running" it for a merchant in Alexandria. The house was far too big for their use. One of the lower rooms served for the storing of wood and tools; the person "occupying" the place before Miché having pulled up the flooring in despair of being able to patch it. Upstairs, the rooms were so large, so bare, that they offered a constant temptation to lovers of the dance, whose importunities Madame Miché was accustomed to meet with amiable indulgence. A dance at Miché's and a plate of Madame Miché's gumbo filé at midnight were pleasures not to be neglected or despised, unless by such serious souls as Cazeau.

Long before Cazeau reached the house his approach had been observed, for there was nothing to obstruct the view of the outer road; vegetation was not yet abundantly advanced, and there was but a patchy, straggling stand of cotton and corn in Miché's field.

Madame Miché, who had been seated on the gallery in a rocking-chair, stood up to greet him as he drew near. She was short and fat, and wore a black skirt and loose muslin sack fastened at the throat with a hair brooch. Her own hair, brown and glossy, showed but a few threads of silver. Her round pink face was cheery, and her eyes were bright and good humored. But she was plainly perturbed and ill at ease as Cazeau advanced.

Montéclin, who was there too, was not ill at ease, and made no attempt to disguise the dislike with which his brother-in-law inspired him. He was a slim, wiry fellow of twenty-five, short of stature like his mother, and resembling her in feature. He was in shirt-sleeves, half leaning, half sitting, on the insecure railing of the gallery, and fanning himself with his broad-rimmed felt hat.

"Cochon!" he muttered under his breath as Cazeau mounted the stairs,—"sacré cochon!"

"Cochon" had sufficiently characterized the man who had once on a time declined to lend Montéclin money. But when this same man had had the presumption to propose marriage to his well-beloved sister, Athénaïse, and the honor to be accepted by her, Montéclin felt that a qualifying epithet was needed fully to express his estimate of Cazeau.

Miché and his oldest son were absent. They both esteemed Cazeau highly, and talked much of his qualities of head and heart, and thought much of his excellent standing with city merchants.

Athénaïse had shut herself up in her room. Cazeau had seen her rise and enter the house at perceiving him. He was a good deal mystified, but no one could have guessed it when he shook hands with Madame Miché. He had only nodded to Montéclin, with a muttered "Comment ça va?"

"Tiens! something tole me you were coming to-day!" exclaimed Madame Miché, with a little blustering appearance of being cordial and at ease, as she offered Cazeau a chair.

He ventured a short laugh as he seated himself.

"You know, nothing would do," she went on, with much gesture of her small, plump hands, "nothing would do but Athénaïse mus' stay las' night fo' a li'le dance. The boys wouldn' year to their sister leaving."

Cazeau shrugged his shoulders significantly, telling as plainly as words that he knew nothing about it.

"Comment! Montéclin didn' tell you we were going to keep Athénaïse?" Montéclin had evidently told nothing.

"An' how about the night befo'," questioned Cazeau, "an las' night? It is n't possible you dance every night out yere on the Bon Dieu!"

Madame Miché laughed, with amiable appreciation of the sarcasm; and turning to her son, "Montéclin, my boy, go tell yo' sister that Monsieur Cazeau is yere."

Montéclin did not stir except to shift his position and settle himself more securely on the railing.

"Did you year me, Montéclin?"

"Oh yes, I yeard you plain enough," responded her son, "but you know as well as me it's no use to tell 'Thénaïse anything. You been talkin' to her yo'se'f since Monday; an' pa's preached himse'f hoa'se on the subject; an' you even had uncle Achille down yere yesterday to reason with her. W'en 'Thénaïse said she wasn' goin' to set her foot back in Cazeau's house, she meant it."

This speech, which Montéclin delivered with thorough unconcern, threw his mother into a condition of painful but dumb embarrassment. It brought two fiery red spots to Cazeau's cheeks, and for the space of a moment he looked wicked.

What Montéclin had spoken was quite true, though his taste in the manner and choice of time and place in saying it were not of the best. Athénaïse, upon the first day of her arrival, had announced that she came to stay, having no intention of returning under Cazeau's roof. The announcement had scattered consternation, as she knew it would. She had been implored, scolded, entreated, stormed at, until she felt herself like a dragging sail that all the winds of heaven had beaten upon. Why in the name of God had she married Cazeau? Her father had lashed her with the question a dozen times. Why indeed? It was difficult now for her to understand why, unless because she supposed it was customary for girls to marry when the right opportunity came. Cazeau, she knew, would make life more comfortable for her; and again, she had liked him, and had even been rather flustered when he pressed her hands and kissed them, and kissed her lips and cheeks and eyes, when she accepted him.

Montéclin himself had taken her aside to talk the thing over. The turn of affairs was delighting him.

"Come, now, 'Thénaïse, you mus' explain to me all about it, so we can settle on a good cause, an' secu' a separation fo' you. Has he been mistreating an' abusing you, the sacré cochon?" They were alone together in her room, whither she had taken refuge from the angry domestic elements.

"You please to reserve yo' disgusting expressions, Montéclin. No, he has not abused me in any way that I can think."

"Does he drink? Come, 'Thénaïse, think well over it. Does he ever get drunk?"

"Drunk! Oh, mercy, no,—Cazeau never gets drunk."

"I see; it's jus' simply you feel like me: you hate him."

"No, I don't hate him," she returned reflectively; adding with a sudden impulse, "It's jus' being married that I detes' an' despise. I hate being Mrs. Cazeau, an' would want to be Athénaïse Miché again. I can't stan' to live with a man: to have him always there; his coats an' pantaloons hanging in my room; his ugly bare feet—washing them in my tub, befo' my very eyes, ugh!" She shuddered with recollections, and resumed, with a sigh that was almost a sob: "Mon Dieu, mon Dieu! Sister Marie Angélique knew w'at she was saying; she knew me better than myse'f w'en she said God had sent me a vocation an' I was turning deaf ears. W'en I think of a blessed life in the convent, at peace! Oh, w'at was I dreaming of!" and then the tears came.

Montéclin felt disconcerted and greatly disappointed at having obtained evidence that would carry no weight with a court of justice. The day had not come when a young woman might ask the court's permission to return to her mamma on the sweeping grounds of a constitutional disinclination for marriage. But if there was no way of untying this Gordian knot of marriage, there was surely a way of cutting it.

"Well, 'Thénaïse, I'm mighty durn sorry you got no better groun's 'an w'at you say. But you can count on me to stan' by you w'atever you do. God knows I don' blame you fo' not wantin' to live with Cazeau."

And now there was Cazeau himself, with the red spots flaming in his swarthy cheeks, looking and feeling as if he wanted to thrash Montéclin into some semblance of decency. He arose abruptly, and approaching the room which he had seen his wife enter, thrust open the door after a hasty preliminary knock. Athénaïse, who was standing erect at a far window, turned at his entrance.

She appeared neither angry nor frightened, but thoroughly unhappy, with an appeal in her soft dark eyes and a tremor on her lips that seemed to him expressions of unjust reproach, that wounded and maddened him at once. But whatever he might feel, Cazeau knew only one way to act toward a woman.

"Athénaïse, you are not ready?" he asked in his quiet tones. "It's getting late; we havn' any time to lose."

She knew that Montéclin had spoken out, and she had hoped for a wordy interview, a stormy scene, in which she might have held her own as she had held it for the past three days against her family, with Montéclin's aid. But she had no weapon with which to combat subtlety. Her husband's looks, his tones, his mere presence, brought to her a sudden sense of hopelessness, an instinctive realization of the futility of rebellion against a social and sacred institution.

Cazeau said nothing further, but stood waiting in the doorway. Madame Miché had walked to the far end of the gallery, and pretended to be occupied with having a chicken driven from her parterre. Montéclin stood by, exasperated, fuming, ready to burst out.

Athénaïse went and reached for her riding-skirt that hung against the wall. She was rather tall, with a figure which, though not robust, seemed perfect in its fine proportions. "La fille de son père," she was often called, which was a great compliment to Miché. Her brown hair was brushed all fluffily back from her temples and low forehead, and about her features and expression lurked a softness, a prettiness, a dewiness, that were perhaps too childlike, that savored of immaturity.

She slipped the riding-skirt, which was of black alpaca, over her head, and with impatient fingers hooked it at the waist over her pink linen-lawn. Then she fastened on her white sunbonnet and reached for her gloves on the mantelpiece.

"If you don' wan' to go, you know w'at you got to do, 'Thénaïse," fumed Montéclin. "You don' set yo' feet back on Cane River, by God, unless you want to,—not w'ile I'm alive."

Cazeau looked at him as if he were a monkey whose antics fell short of being amusing.

Athénaïse still made no relpy, said not a word. She walked rapidly past her husband, past her brother; bidding goodby to no one, not even to her mother. She descended the stairs, and without assistance from any one mounted the pony, which Cazeau had ordered to be saddled upon his arrival. In this way she obtained a fair start of her husband, whose departure was far more leisurely, and for the greater part of the way she managed to keep an appreciable gap between them. She rode almost madly at first, with the wind inflating her skirt balloon-like about her knees, and her sunbonnet falling back between her shoulders.

At no time did Cazeau make an effort to overtake her until traversing an old fallow meadow that was level and hard as a table. The sight of a great solitary oak-tree, with its seemingly immutable outlines, that had been a landmark for ages—or was it the odor of elderberry stealing up from the gully to the south? or what was it that brought vividly back to Cazeau, by some association of ideas, a scene of many years ago? He had passed that old live-oak hundreds of times, but it was only now that the memory of one day came back to him. He was a very small boy that day, seated before his father on horseback. They were proceeding slowly, and Black Gabe was moving on before them at a little dog-trot. Black Gabe had run away, and had been discovered back in the Gotrain Swamp. They had halted beneath this big oak to enable the negro to take breath; for Cazeau's father was a kind and considerate master, and every one had agreed at the time that Black Gabe was a fool, a great idiot indeed, for wanting to run away from him.

The whole impression was for some reason hideous, and to dispel it Cazeau spurred his horse to a swift gallop. Overtaking his wife, he rode the remainder of the way at her side in silence.

It was late when they reached home. Félicité was standing on the grassy edge of the road, in the moonlight, waiting for them.

Cazeau once more ate his supper alone; for Athénaïse went to her room, and there she was crying again.

III

Athénaïse was not one to accept the inevitable with patient resignation, a talent born in the souls of many women; neither was she the one to accept it with philosophical resignation, like her husband. Her sensibilities were alive and keen and responsive. She met the pleasurable things of life with frank, open appreciation, and against distasteful conditions she rebelled. Dissimulation was as foreign to her nature as guile to the breast of a babe, and her rebellious outbreaks, by no means rare, had hitherto been quite open and aboveboard. People often said that Athénaïse would know her own mind some day, which was equivalent to saying that she was at present unacquainted with it. If she ever came to such knowledge, it would be by no intellectual research, by no subtle analyses or tracing the motives of actions to their source. It would come to her as the song to the bird, the perfume and color to the flower.

Her parents had hoped—not without reason and justice—that marriage would bring the poise, the desirable pose, so glaringly lacking in Athénaïse's character. Marriage they knew to be a wonderful and powerful agent in the development and formation of a woman's character; they had seen its effect too often to doubt it.

"And if this marriage does nothing else," exclaimed Miché in an outburst of sudden exasperation, "it will rid us of Athénaïse; for I am at the end of my patience with her! You have never had the firmness to manage her,"—he was speaking to his wife,—"I have not had the time, the leisure, to devote to her training; and what good we might have accomplished, that maudit Montéclin—Well, Cazeau is the one! It takes just such a steady hand to guide a disposition like Athénaïse's, a master hand, a strong will that compels obedience."

And now, when they had hoped for so much, here was Athénaïse, with gathered and fierce vehemence, beside which her former outbursts appeared mild, declaring that she would not, and she would not, and she would *not* continue to enact the rôle of wife to Cazeau. If she had had a reason! as Madame Miché lamented; but it could not be discovered that she had any sane one. He had never scolded, or called names, or deprived her of comforts, or been guilty of any of the many reprehensible acts commonly attributed to objectionable husbands. He did not slight nor neglect her. Indeed, Cazeau's chief offense seemed to be that he loved her, and Athénaïse was not the woman to be loved against her will. She called marriage a trap set for the feet of unwary and unsuspecting girls, and in round, unmeasured terms reproached her mother with treachery and deceit.

"I told you Cazeau was the man," chuckled Miché, when his wife had related the scene that had accompanied and influenced Athénaïse's departure.

Athénaïse again hoped, in the morning, that Cazeau would scold or make some sort of a scene, but he apparently did not dream of it. It was exasperating that he should take her acquiescence so for granted. It is true he had been up and over the fields and across the river and back long before she was out of bed, and he may have been thinking of something else, which was no excuse, which was even in some sense an aggravation. But he did say to her at breakfast, "That brother of yo's, that Montéclin, is unbearable."

"Montéclin? Par exemple!"

Athénaïse, seated opposite to her husband, was attired in a white morning wrapper. She wore a somewhat abused, long face, it is true,—an expression of countenance familiar to some husbands,—but the expression was not sufficiently pronounced to mar the charm of her youthful freshness. She had little heart to eat, only playing with the food before her, and she felt a pang of resentment at her husband's healthy appetite.

"Yes, Montéclin," he reasserted. "He's developed into a firs'-class nuisance; an' you better tell him, Athénaïse,—unless you want me to tell him,—to confine his energies after this to matters that concern him. I have no use fo' him or fo' his interference in w'at regards you an' me alone."

This was said with unusual asperity. It was the little breach that Athénaïse had been watching for, and she charged rapidly: "It's strange, if you detes' Montéclin so heartily, that you would desire to marry his sister." She knew it was a silly thing to say, and was not surprised when he told her so. It gave her a little foothold for further attack, however. "I don't see, anyhow, w'at reason you had to marry me, w'en there were so many others," she complained, as if accusing him of persecution and injury. "There was Marianne running after you fo' the las' five years till it was disgraceful; an' any one of the Dortrand girls would have been glad to marry you. But no, nothing would do; you mus' come out on the rigolet fo' me." Her complaint was pathetic, and at the same time so amusing that Cazeau was forced to smile.

"I can't see w'at the Dortrand girls or Marianne have to do with it," he rejoined; adding, with no trace of amusement, "I married you because I loved you; because you were the woman I wanted to marry, an' the only one. I reckon I tole you that befo'. I thought—of co'se I was a fool fo' taking things fo' granted—but I did think that I might make you happy in making things easier an' mo' comfortable fo' you. I expected—I was even that big a fool—I believed that yo' coming yere to me would be like the sun shining out of the clouds, an' that our days would be like w'at the storybooks promise after the wedding. I was mistaken. But I can't imagine w'at induced you to marry me. W'atever it was, I reckon you foun' out you made a mistake, too. I don' see anything to do but make the best of a bad bargain, an' shake han's over it." He had arisen from the table, and, approaching, held out his hand to her. What he had said was commonplace enough, but it was significant, coming from Cazeau, who was not often so unreserved in expressing himself.

Athénaïse ignored the hand held out to her. She was resting her chin in her palm, and kept her eyes fixed moodily upon the table. He rested his hand, that she would not touch, upon her head for an instant, and walked away out of the room.

She heard him giving orders to workmen who had been waiting for him out on the gallery, and she heard him mount his horse and ride away. A hundred things would distract him and engage his attention during the day. She felt that he had perhaps put her and her grievance from his thoughts when he crossed the threshold; whilst she—

Old Félicité was standing there holding a shining tin pail, asking for flour and lard and eggs from the storeroom, and meal for the chicks.

Athénaïse seized the bunch of keys which hung from her belt and flung them at Félicité's feet.

"Tiens! tu vas les garder comme tu as jadis fait. Je ne veux plus de ce train là, moi!"

The old woman stooped and picked up the keys from the floor. It was really all one to her that her mistress returned them to her keeping, and refused to take further account of the ménage.

IV

It seemed now to Athénaïse that Montéclin was the only friend left to her in the world. Her father and mother had turned from her in what appeared to be her hour of need. Her friends laughed at her, and refused to take seriously the hints which she threw out,—feeling her way to discover if marriage were as distasteful to other women as to herself. Montéclin alone understood her. He alone had always been ready to act for her and with her, to comfort and solace her with his sympathy and support. Her only hope for rescue from her hateful surroundings lay in Montéclin. Of herself she felt powerless to plan, to act, even to conceive a way out of this pitfall into which the whole world seemed to have conspired to thrust her.

She had a great desire to see her brother, and wrote asking him to come to her. But it better suited Montéclin's spirit of adventure to appoint a meeting-place at the turn of the lane, where Athénaïse might appear to be walking leisurely for health and recreation, and where he might seem to be riding along, bent on some errand of business or pleasure.

There had been a shower, a sudden downpour, short as it was sudden, that had laid the dust in the road. It had freshened the pointed leaves of the live-oaks, and brightened up the big fields of cotton on either side of the lane till they seemed carpeted with green, glittering gems.

Athénaïse walked along the grassy edge of the road, lifting her crisp skirts with one hand, and with the other twirling a gay sunshade over her bare head. The scent of the fields after the rain was delicious. She inhaled long breaths of their freshness and perfume, that soothed and quieted her for the moment. There were birds splashing and spluttering in the pools, pluming themselves on the fence-rails, and sending out little sharp cries, twitters, and shrill rhapsodies of delight.

She saw Montéclin approaching from a great distance,—almost as far away as the turn of the woods. But she could not feel sure it was he; it appeared too tall for Montéclin, but that was because he was riding a large horse. She waved her parasol to him; she was so glad to see him. She had never been so glad to see Montéclin before; not even the day when he had taken her out of the convent, against her parents' wishes, because she had expressed a desire to remain there no longer. He seemed to her, as he drew near, the embodiment of kindness, of bravery, of chivalry, even of wisdom; for she had never known Montéclin at a loss to extricate himself from a disagreeable situation.

He dismounted, and, leading his horse by the bridle, started to walk beside her, after he had kissed her affectionately and asked her what she was crying about. She protested that she was not crying, for she was laughing, though drying her eyes at the same time on her handkerchief, rolled in a soft mop for the purpose.

She took Montéclin's arm, and they strolled slowly down the lane; they could not seat themselves for a comfortable chat, as they would have liked, with the grass all sparkling and bristling wet.

Yes, she was quite as wretched as ever, she told him. The week which had gone by since she saw him had in no wise lightened the burden of her discontent. There had even been some additional provocations laid upon her, and she told Montéclin all about them,—about the keys, for instance, which in a fit of temper she had returned to Félicité's keeping; and she told how Cazeau had brought them back to her as if they were something she had accidentally lost, and he had recovered; and how he had said, in that aggravating tone of his, that it was not the custom on Cane River for the negro servants to carry the keys, when there was a mistress at the head of the household.

But Athénaïse could not tell Montéclin anything to increase the disrespect which he already entertained for his brother-in-law; and it was then he unfolded to her a plan which he had conceived and worked out for her deliverance from this galling matrimonial yoke.

It was not a plan which met with instant favor, which she was at once ready to accept, for it involved secrecy and dissimulation, hateful alternatives both of them. But she was filled with admiration for Montéclin's resources and wonderful talent for contrivance. She accepted the plan; not with the immediate determination to act upon it, rather with the intention to sleep and to dream upon it.

Three days later she wrote to Montéclin that she had abandoned herself to his counsel. Displeasing as it might be to her sense of honesty, it would yet be less trying than to live on with a soul full of bitterness and revolt, as she had done for the past two months.

V

When Cazeau awoke, one morning, at his usual very early hour, it was to find the place at his side vacant. This did not surprise him until he discovered that Athénaïse was not in the adjoining room, where he had often found her sleeping in the morning on the lounge. She had perhaps gone out for an early stroll, he reflected, for her jacket and hat were not on the rack where she had hung them the night before. But there were other things absent,—a gown or two from the armoire; and there was a great gap in the piles of lingerie on the shelf; and her traveling-bag was missing, and so were her bits of jewelry from the toilet tray—and Athénaïse was gone!

But the absurdity of going during the night, as if she had been a prisoner, and he the keeper of a dungeon! So much secrecy and mystery, to go sojourning out on the Bon Dieu! Well, the Michés might keep their daughter after this. For the companionship of no woman on earth would he again undergo the humiliating sensation of baseness that had overtaken him in passing the old oak-tree in the fallow meadow.

But a terrible sense of loss overwhelmed Cazeau. It was not new or sudden; he had felt it for weeks growing upon him, and it seemed to culminate with Athénaïse's flight from home. He knew that he could again compel her return as he had done once before,—compel her return to the shelter of his roof, compel her cold and unwilling submission to his love and passionate transports; but the loss of self-respect seemed to him too dear a price to pay for a wife.

He could not comprehend why she had seemed to prefer him above others; why she had attracted him with eyes, with voice, with a hundred womanly ways, and finally distracted him with love which she seemed, in her timid, maidenly fashion, to return. The great sense of loss came from a realization of having missed a chance for happiness,—a chance that would come his way again only through a miracle. He could not think of himself loving any other woman, and could not think of Athénaïse ever—even at some remote date—caring for him.

He wrote her a letter, in which he disclaimed any further intention of forcing his commands upon her. He did not desire her presence ever again in his home unless she came of her free will, uninfluenced by family or friends; unless she could be the companion he had hoped for in marrying her, and in some measure return affection and respect for the love which he continued and would always continue to feel for her. This letter he sent out to the rigolet by a messenger early in the day. But she was not out on the rigolet, and had not been there.

The family turned instinctively to Montéclin, and almost literally fell upon him for an explanation; he had been absent from home all night. There was much mystification in his answers, and a plain desire to mislead in his assurances of ignorance and innocence.

But with Cazeau there was no doubt or speculation when he accosted the young fellow. "Montéclin, w'at have you done with Athénaïse?" he questioned bluntly. They had met in the open road on horseback, just as Cazeau ascended the river bank before his house.

"W'at have you done to Athénaïse?" returned Montéclin for answer.

"I don't reckon you've considered yo' conduct by any light of decency an' propriety in encouraging yo' sister to such an action, but let me tell you"—

"Voyons, you can let me alone with yo' decency an' morality an' fiddlesticks. I know you mus' 'a' done Athénaïse pretty mean that she can't live with you; an' fo' my part, I'm mighty durn glad she had the spirit to quit you."

"I ain't in the humor to take any notice of yo' impertinence, Montéclin; but let me remine you that Athénaïse is nothing but a chile in character; besides that, she's my wife, an' I hole you responsible fo' her safety an' welfare. If any harm of any description happens to her, I'll strangle you, by God, like a rat, and fling you in Cane River, if I have to hang fo' it!" He had not lifted his voice. The only sign of anger was a savage gleam in his eyes.

"I reckon you better keep yo' big talk fo' the women, Cazeau," replied Montéclin, riding away.

But he went doubly armed after that, and intimated that the precaution was not needless, in view of the threats and menaces that were abroad touching his personal safety.*

VI

Athénaïse reached her destination sound of skin and limb, but a good deal flustered, a little frightened, and altogether excited and interested by her unusual experiences.

Her destination was the house of Sylvie, on Dauphine Street, in New Orleans,—a three-story gray brick, standing directly on the banquette, with three broad stone steps leading to the deep front entrance. From the second-story balcony swung a small sign, conveying to passers-by the intelligence that within were "chambres garnies."

It was one morning in the last week of April that Athénaïse presented herself at the Dauphine Street house. Sylvie was expecting her, and introduced her at once to her apartment, which was in the second story of the back ell, and accessible by an open, outside gallery. There was a yard below, paved with broad stone flagging; many fragrant flowering shrubs and plants grew in a bed along the side of the opposite wall, and others were distributed about in tubs and green boxes.

---

*The first installment ended here.

It was a plain but large enough room into which Athénaïse was ushered, with matting on the floor, green shades and Nottingham-lace curtains at the windows that looked out on the gallery, and furnished with a cheap walnut suit. But everything looked exquisitely clean, and the whole place smelled of cleanliness.

Athénaïse at once fell into the rocking-chair, with the air of exhaustion and intense relief of one who has come to the end of her troubles. Sylvie, entering behind her, laid the big traveling-bag on the floor and deposited the jacket on the bed.

She was a portly quadroon of fifty or thereabout, clad in an ample volant of the old-fashioned purple calico so much affected by her class. She wore large golden hoop-earrings, and her hair was combed plainly, with every appearance of effort to smooth out the kinks. She had broad, coarse features, with a nose that turned up, exposing the wide nostrils, and that seemed to emphasize the loftiness and command of her bearing,—a dignity that in the presence of white people assumed a character of respectfulness, but never of obsequiousness. Sylvie believed firmly in maintaining the color-line, and would not suffer a white person, even a child, to call her "Madame Sylvie,"—a title which she exacted religiously, however, from those of her own race.

"I hope you be please' wid yo' room, madame," she observed amiably. "Dat's de same room w'at yo' brother, M'sieur Miché, all time like w'en he come to New Orlean'. He well, M'sieur Miché? I receive' his letter las' week, an' dat same day a gent'man want I give 'im dat room. I say, 'No, dat room already ingage'.' Ev'body like dat room on 'count it so quite [quiet]. M'sieur Gouvernail, dere in nax' room, you can't pay 'im! He been stay t'ree year' in dat room; but all fix' up fine wid his own furn'ture an' books, 'tel you can't see! I say to 'im plenty time', 'M'sieur Gouvernail, w'y you don' take dat t'ree-story front, now, long it's empty?' He tell me, 'Leave me 'lone, Sylvie; I know a good room w'en I fine it, me.' "

She had been moving slowly and majestically about the apartment, straightening and smoothing down bed and pillows, peering into ewer and basin, evidently casting an eye around to make sure that everything was as it should be.

"I sen' you some fresh water, madame," she offered upon retiring from the room. "An w'en you want an't'ing, you jus' go out on de gall'ry an' call Pousette: she year you plain,—she right down dere in de kitchen."

Athénaïse was really not so exhausted as she had every reason to be after that interminable and circuitous way by which Montéclin had seen fit to have her conveyed to the city.

Would she ever forget that dark and truly dangerous midnight ride along the "coast" to the mouth of Cane River! There Montéclin had parted with her, after seeing her aboard the St. Louis and Shreveport packet which he knew would pass there before dawn. She had received instructions to disembark at the mouth of Red River, and there transfer to the first southbound steamer for New Orleans: all of which instructions she had followed implicitly, even to making her way at once to Sylvie's upon her arrival in the city. Montéclin had enjoined secrecy and much caution; the clandestine nature of the affair gave it a savor of adventure which was highly pleasing to him. Eloping with his sister was only a little less engaging than eloping with some one else's sister.

But Montéclin did not do the grand seigneur by halves. He had paid Sylvie a whole month in advance for Athénaïse's board and lodging. Part of the sum he had been forced to borrow, it is true, but he was not niggardly.

Athénaïse was to take her meals in the house, which none of the other lodgers did; the one exception being that Mr. Gouvernail was served with breakfast on Sunday mornings.

Sylvie's clientéle came chiefly from the southern parishes; for the most part, people spending but a few days in the city. She prided herself upon the quality and highly respectable character of her patrons, who came and went unobtrusively.

The large parlor opening upon the front balcony was seldom used. Her guests were permitted to entertain in this sanctuary of elegance,—but they never did. She often rented it for the night to parties of respectable and discreet gentlemen desiring to enjoy a quiet game of cards outside the bosom of their families. The second-story hall also led by a long window out on the balcony. And Sylvie advised Athénaïse, when she grew weary of her back room, to go and sit on the front balcony, which was shady in the afternoon, and where she might find diversion in the sounds and sights of the street below.

Athénaïse refreshed herself with a bath, and was soon unpacking her few belongings, which she ranged neatly away in the bureau drawers and the armoire.

She had revolved certain plans in her mind during the past hour or so. Her present intention was to live on indefinitely in this big, cool, clean back room on Dauphine Street. She had thought seriously, for moments, of the convent, with all readiness to embrace the vows of poverty and chastity; but what about obedience? Later, she intended, in some roundabout way, to give her parents and her husband the assurance of her safety and welfare; reserving the right to remain unmolested and lost to them. To live on at the expense of Montéclin's generosity was wholly out of the question, and Athénaïse meant to look about for some suitable and agreeable employment.

The imperative thing to be done at present, however, was to go out in search of material for an inexpensive gown or two; for she found herself in the painful predicament of a young woman having almost literally nothing to wear. She decided upon pure white for one, and some sort of a sprigged muslin for the other.

VII

On Sunday morning, two days after Athénaïse's arrival in the city, she went in to breakfast somewhat later than usual, to find two covers laid at table instead of the one to which she was accustomed. She had been to mass, and did not remove her hat, but put her fan, parasol, and prayer-book aside. The dining-room was situated just beneath her own apartment, and, like all the rooms of the house, was large and airy; the floor was covered with a glistening oil-cloth.

The small, round table, immaculately set, was drawn near the open window. There were some tall plants in boxes on the gallery outside; and Pousette, a little, old, intensely black woman, was splashing and dashing buckets of water on the flagging, and talking loud in her creole patois to no one in particular.

A dish piled with delicate river-shrimps and crushed ice was on the table; a caraffe of crystal-clear water, a few hors d'œuvres, beside a small golden-brown crusty loaf of French bread at each plate. A half-bottle of wine and the morning paper were set at the place opposite Athénaïse.

She had almost completed her breakfast when Gouvernail came in and seated himself at table. He felt annoyed at finding his cherished privacy invaded. Sylvie was removing the remains of a mutton-chop from before Athénaïse, and serving her with a cup of café au lait.

"M'sieur Gouvernail," offered Sylvie in her most insinuating and impressive manner, "you please leave me make you acquaint' wid Madame Cazeau. Dat's M'sieur Miché's sister; you meet 'im two t'ree time', you rec'lec', an' you been one day to de race wid 'im. Madame Cazeau, you please leave me make you acquaint' wid M'sieur Gouvernail."

Gouvernail expressed himself greatly pleased to meet the sister of Monsieur Miché, of whom he had not the slightest recollection. He inquired after Monsieur Miché's health, and politely offered Athénaïse a part of his newspaper,—the part which contained the Woman's Page and the social gossip.

Athénaïse faintly remembered that Sylvie had spoken of a Monsieur Gouvernail occupying the room adjoining hers, living amid luxurious surroundings and a multitude of books. She had not thought of him further than to picture him a stout, middle-aged gentleman, with a bushy beard turning gray, wearing large gold-rimmed spectacles, and stooping somewhat from much bending over books and writing material. She had confused him in her mind with the likeness of some literary celebrity that she had run across in the advertising pages of a magazine.

Gouvernail's appearance was, in truth, in no sense striking. He looked older than thirty and younger than forty, was of medium height and weight, with a quiet, unobtrusive manner which seemed to ask that he be let alone. His hair was light brown, brushed carefully and parted in the middle. His mustache was brown, and so were his eyes, which had a mild, penetrating quality. He was neatly dressed in the fashion of the day; and his hands seemed to Athénaïse remarkably white and soft for a man's.

He had been buried in the contents of his newspaper, when he suddenly realized that some further little attention might be due to Miché's sister. He started to offer her a glass of wine, when he was surprised and relieved to find that she had quietly slipped away while he was absorbed in his own editorial on Corrupt Legislation.

Gouvernail finished his paper and smoked his cigar out on the gallery. He lounged about, gathered a rose for his buttonhole, and had his regular Sunday-morning confab with Pousette, to whom he paid a weekly stipend for brushing his shoes and clothes. He made a great pretense of haggling over the transaction, only to enjoy her uneasiness and garrulous excitement.

He worked or read in his room for a few hours, and when he quitted the house, at three in the afternoon, it was to return no more till late in the night. It was his almost invariable custom to spend Sunday evenings out in the American quarter, among a congenial set of men and women,—des esprits forts, all of them, whose lives were irreproachable, yet whose opinions would startle even the traditional "sapeur," for whom "nothing is sacred." But for all his "advanced" opinions, Gouvernail was a liberal-minded fellow; a man or woman lost nothing of his respect by being married.

When he left the house in the afternoon, Athénaïse had already ensconced herself on the front balcony. He could see her through the jalousies when he passed on his way to the front entrance. She had not yet grown lonesome or homesick; the newness of her surroundings made them sufficiently entertaining. She found it diverting to sit there on the front balcony watching people pass by, even though there was no one to talk to. And then the comforting, comfortable sense of not being married!

She watched Gouvernail walk down the street, and could find no fault with his bearing. He could hear the sound of her rockers for some little distance. He wondered what the "poor little thing" was doing in the city, and meant to ask Sylvie about her when he should happen to think of it.

VIII

The following morning, towards noon, when Gouvernail quitted his room, he was confronted by Athénaïse, exhibiting some confusion and trepidation at being forced to request a favor of him at so early a stage of their acquaintance. She stood in her doorway, and had evidently been sewing, as the thimble on her finger testified, as well as a long-threaded needle thrust in the bosom of her gown; and she held a stamped but unaddressed letter in her hand.

And would Mr. Gouvernail be so kind as to address the letter to her brother, Mr. Montéclin Miché? She would hate to detain him with explanations this morning,—another time, perhaps,—but now she begged that he would give himself the trouble.

He assured her that it made no difference, that it was no trouble whatever; and he drew a fountain pen from his pocket and addressed the letter at her dictation, resting it on the inverted rim of his straw hat. She wondered a little at a man of his supposed erudition stumbling over the spelling of "Montéclin" and "Miché."

She demurred at overwhelming him with the additional trouble of posting it, but he succeeded in convincing her that so simple a task as the posting of a letter would not add an iota to the burden of the day. Moreover, he promised to carry it in his hand, and thus avoid any possible risk of forgetting it in his pocket.

After that, and after a second repetition of the favor, when she had told him that she had had a letter from Montéclin, and looked as if she wanted to tell him more, he felt that he knew her better. He felt that he knew her well enough to join her out on the balcony, one night, when he found her sitting there alone. He was not one who deliberately sought the society of women, but he was not wholly a bear. A little commiseration for Athénaïse's aloneness, perhaps some curiosity to know further what manner of woman she was, and the natural influence of her feminine charm were equal unconfessed factors in turning his steps towards the balcony when he discovered the shimmer of her white gown through the open hall window.

It was already quite late, but the day had been intensely hot, and neighboring balconies and doorways were occupied by chattering groups of humanity, loath to abandon the grateful freshness of the outer air. The voices about her served to reveal to Athénaïse the feeling of loneliness that was gradually coming over her. Notwithstanding certain dormant impulses, she craved human sympathy and companionship.

She shook hands impulsively with Gouvernail, and told him how glad she was to see him. He was not prepared for such an admission, but it pleased him immensely, detecting as he did that the expression was as sin-

cere as it was outspoken. He drew a chair up within comfortable conversational distance of Athénaïse, though he had no intention of talking more
than was barely necessary to encourage Madame— He had actually forgotten her name!

He leaned an elbow on the balcony rail, and would have offered an
opening remark about the oppressive heat of the day, but Athénaïse did not
give him the opportunity. How glad she was to talk to some one, and how
she talked!

An hour later she had gone to her room, and Gouvernail stayed smoking on the balcony. He knew her quite well after that hour's talk. It was
not so much what she had said as what her half saying had revealed to his
quick intelligence. He knew that she adored Montéclin, and he suspected
that she adored Cazeau without being herself aware of it. He had gathered
that she was self-willed, impulsive, innocent, ignorant, unsatisfied, dissatisfied; for had she not complained that things seemed all wrongly arranged
in this world, and no one was permitted to be happy in his own way? And
he told her he was sorry she had discovered that primordial fact of existence
so early in life.

He commiserated her loneliness, and scanned his bookshelves next
morning for something to lend her to read, rejecting everything that offered
itself to his view. Philosophy was out of the question, and so was poetry;
that is, such poetry as he possessed. He had not sounded her literary tastes,
and strongly suspected she had none; that she would have rejected The
Duchess as readily as Mrs. Humphry Ward. He compromised on a magazine.

It had entertained her passably, she admitted, upon returning it. A
New England story had puzzled her, it was true, and a creole tale had offended her, but the pictures had pleased her greatly, especially one which
had reminded her so strongly of Montéclin after a hard day's ride that she
was loath to give it up. It was one of Remington's Cowboys, and Gouvernail insisted upon her keeping it,—keeping the magazine.

He spoke to her daily after that, and was always eager to render her
some service or to do something towards her entertainment.

One afternoon he took her out to the lake end. She had been there once,
some years before, but in winter, so the trip was comparatively new and
strange to her. The large expanse of water studded with pleasure-boats, the
sight of children playing merrily along the grassy palisades, the music, all
enchanted her. Gouvernail thought her the most beautiful woman he had
ever seen. Even her gown—the sprigged muslin—appeared to him the most
charming one imaginable. Nor could anything be more becoming than the
arrangement of her brown hair under the white sailor hat, all rolled back in
a soft pluff from her radiant face. And she carried her parasol and lifted her

skirts and used her fan in ways that seemed quite unique and peculiar to herself, and which he considered almost worthy of study and imitation.

They did not dine out there at the water's edge, as they might have done, but returned early to the city to avoid the crowd. Athénaïse wanted to go home, for she said Sylvie would have dinner prepared and would be expecting her. But it was not difficult to persuade her to dine instead in the quiet little restaurant that he knew and liked, with its sanded floor, its secluded atmosphere, its delicious menu, and its obsequious waiter wanting to know what he might have the honor of serving to "monsieur et madame." No wonder he made the mistake, with Gouvernail assuming such an air of proprietorship. But Athénaïse was very tired after it all; the sparkle went out of her face, and she hung draggingly on his arm in walking home.

He was reluctant to part from her when she bade him good-night at her door and thanked him for the agreeable evening. He had hoped she would sit outside until it was time for him to regain the newspaper office. He knew that she would undress and get into her peignoir and lie upon her bed; and what he wanted to do, what he would have given much to do, was to go and sit beside her, read to her something restful, soothe her, do her bidding, whatever it might be. Of course there was no use in thinking of that. But he was surprised at his growing desire to be serving her. She gave him an opportunity sooner than he looked for.

"Mr. Gouvernail," she called from her room, "will you be so kine as to call Pousette an' tell her she fo'got to bring my ice-water?"

He was indignant at Pousette's negligence, and called severely to her over the banisters. He was sitting before his own door, smoking. He knew that Athénaïse had gone to bed, for her room was dark, and she had opened the slats of the door and windows. Her bed was near a window.

Pousette came flopping up with the ice-water, and with a hundred excuses: "Mo pa oua vou à tab c'te lanuite, mo cri vou pé gagni déja là-bas; parole! Vou pas cri conté ça Madame Sylvie?" She had not seen Athénaïse at table, and thought she was gone. She swore to this, and hoped Madame Sylvie would not be informed of her remissness.

A little later Athénaïse lifted her voice again: "Mr. Gouvernail, did you remark that young man sitting on the opposite side from us, coming in, with a gray coat an' a blue ban' aroun' his hat?"

Of course Gouvernail had not noticed any such individual, but he assured Athénaïse that he had observed the young fellow particularly.

"Don't you think he looked something,—not *very* much, of co'se,—but don't you think he had a little faux-air of Montéclin?"

"I think he looked strikingly like Montéclin," asserted Gouvernail, with the one idea of prolonging the conversation. "I meant to call your attention to the resemblance, and something drove it out of my head."

"The same with me," returned Athénaïse. "Ah, my dear Montéclin! I wonder w'at he is doing now?"

"Did you receive any news, any letter from him to-day?" asked Gouvernail, determined that if the conversation ceased it should not be through lack of effort on his part to sustain it.

"Not to-day, but yesterday. He tells me that maman was so distracted with uneasiness that finally, to pacify her, he was fo'ced to confess that he knew w'ere I was, but that he was boun' by a vow of secrecy not to reveal it. But Cazeau has not noticed him or spoken to him since he threaten' to throw po' Montéclin in Cane River. You know Cazeau wrote me a letter the morning I lef', thinking I had gone to the rigolet. An' maman opened it, an' said it was full of the mos' noble sentiments, an' she wanted Montéclin to sen' it to me; but Montéclin refuse' poin'blank, so he wrote to me."

Gouvernail preferred to talk of Montéclin. He pictured Cazeau as unbearable, and did not like to think of him.

A little later Athénaïse called out, "Good-night, Mr. Gouvernail."

"Good-night," he returned reluctantly. And when he thought that she was sleeping, he got up and went away to the midnight pandemonium of his newspaper office.

IX

Athénaïse could not have held out through the month had it not been for Gouvernail. With the need of caution and secrecy always uppermost in her mind, she made no new acquaintances, and she did not seek out persons already known to her; however, she knew so few, it required little effort to keep out of their way. As for Sylvie, almost every moment of her time was occupied in looking after her house; and, moreover, her deferential attitude towards her lodgers forbade anything like the gossipy chats in which Athénaïse might have condescended sometimes to indulge with her landlady. The transient lodgers, who came and went, she never had occasion to meet. Hence she was entirely dependent upon Gouvernail for company.

He appreciated the situation fully; and every moment that he could spare from his work he devoted to her entertainment. She liked to be out of doors, and they strolled together in the summer twilight through the mazes of the old French quarter. They went again to the lake end, and stayed for hours on the water; returning so late that the streets through which they passed were silent and deserted. On Sunday morning he arose at an unconscionable hour to take her to the French market, knowing that the sights and sounds there would interest her. And he did not join the intellectual coterie in the afternoon, as he usually did, but placed himself all day at the disposition and service of Athénaïse.

Notwithstanding all, his manner toward her was tactful, and evinced intelligence and a deep knowledge of her character, surprising upon so brief an acquaintance. For the time he was everything to her that she would have him; he replaced home and friends. Sometimes she wondered if he had ever loved a woman. She could not fancy him loving any one passionately, rudely, offensively, as Cazeau loved her. Once she was so naïve as to ask him outright if he had ever been in love, and he assured her promptly that he had not. She thought it an admirable trait in his character, and esteemed him greatly therefor.

He found her crying one night, not openly or violently. She was leaning over the gallery rail, watching the toads that hopped about in the moonlight, down on the damp flagstones of the courtyard. There was an oppressively sweet odor rising from the cape jessamine. Pousette was down there, mumbling and quarreling with some one, and seeming to be having it all her own way,—as well she might, when her companion was only a black cat that had come in from a neighboring yard to keep her company.

Athénaïse did admit feeling heart-sick, body-sick, when he questioned her; she supposed it was nothing but homesick. A letter from Montéclin had stirred her all up. She longed for her mother, for Montéclin; she was sick for a sight of the cotton-fields, the scent of the ploughed earth, for the dim, mysterious charm of the woods, and the old tumble-down home on the Bon Dieu.

As Gouvernail listened to her, a wave of pity and tenderness swept through him. He took her hands and pressed them against him. He wondered what would happen if he were to put his arms around her.

He was hardly prepared for what happened, but he stood it courageously. She twined her arms around his neck and wept outright on his shoulder; the hot tears scalding his cheek and neck, and her whole body shaken in his arms. The impulse was powerful to strain her to him; the temptation was fierce to seek her lips; but he did neither.

He understood a thousand times better than she herself understood it that he was acting as substitute for Montéclin. Bitter as the conviction was, he accepted it. He was patient; he could wait. He hoped some day to hold her with a lover's arms. That she was married made no particle of difference to Gouvernail. He could not conceive or dream of its making a difference. When the time came that she wanted him,—as he hoped and believed it would come,—he felt he would have a right to her. So long as she did not want him, he had no right to her,—no more than her husband had. It was very hard to feel her warm breath and tears upon his cheek, and her struggling bosom pressed against him, and her soft arms clinging to him, and his whole body and soul aching for her, and yet to make no sign.

He tried to think what Montéclin would have said and done, and to act accordingly. He stroked her hair, and held her in a gentle embrace, until the tears dried and the sobs ended. Before releasing herself she kissed him against the neck; she had to love somebody in her own way! Even that he endured like a stoic. But it was well he left her, to plunge into the thick of rapid, breathless, exacting work till nearly dawn.

Athénaïse was greatly soothed, and slept well. The touch of friendly hands and caressing arms had been very grateful. Henceforward she would not be lonely and unhappy, with Gouvernail there to comfort her.

X

The fourth week of Athénaïse's stay in the city was drawing to a close. Keeping in view the intention which she had of finding some suitable and agreeable employment, she had made a few tentatives in that direction. But with the exception of two little girls who had promised to take piano lessons at a price that it would be embarrassing to mention, these attempts had been fruitless. Moreover, the homesickness kept coming back, and Gouvernail was not always there to drive it away.

She spent much of her time weeding and pottering among the flowers down in the courtyard. She tried to take an interest in the black cat, and a mocking-bird that hung in a cage outside the kitchen door, and a disreputable parrot that belonged to the cook next door, and swore hoarsely all day long in bad French.

Beside, she was not well; she was not herself, as she told Sylvie. The climate of New Orleans did not agree with her. Sylvie was distressed to learn this, as she felt in some measure responsible for the health and well-being of Monsieur Miché's sister; and she made it her duty to inquire closely into the nature and character of Athénaïse's malaise.

Sylvie was very wise, and Athénaïse was very ignorant. The extent of her ignorance and the depth of her subsequent enlightenment were bewildering. She stayed a long, long time quite still, quite stunned, except for the short, uneven breathing that ruffled her bosom. Her whole being was steeped in a wave of ecstacy. When she finally arose from the chair in which she had been seated, and looked at herself in the mirror, a face met hers which she seemed to see for the first time, so transfigured was it with wonder and rapture.

One mood quickly followed another, in this new turmoil of her senses, and the need of action became uppermost. Her mother must know at once, and her mother must tell Montéclin. And Cazeau must know. As she thought of him, the first purely sensuous tremor of her life swept over her.

She half whispered his name, and the sound of it brought red blotches into her cheeks. She spoke it over and over, as if it were some new, sweet sound born out of darkness and confusion, and reaching her for the first time. She was impatient to be with him. Her whole passionate nature was aroused as if by a miracle.

She seated herself to write to her husband. The letter he would get in the morning, and she would be with him at night. What would he say? How would he act? She knew that he would forgive her, for had he not written a letter?—and a pang of resentment toward Montéclin shot through her. What did he mean by withholding that letter? How dared he not have sent it?

Athénaïse attired herself for the street, and went out to post the letter which she had penned with a single thought, a spontaneous impulse. It would have seemed incoherent to most people, but Cazeau would understand.

She walked along the street as if she had fallen heir to some magnificent inheritance. On her face was a look of pride and satisfaction that passers-by noticed and admired. She wanted to talk to some one, to tell some person; and she stopped at the corner and told the oyster-woman, who was Irish, and who God-blessed her, and wished prosperity to the race of Cazeaus for generations to come. She held the oyster-woman's fat, dirty little baby in her arms and scanned it curiously and observingly, as if a baby were a phenomenon that she encountered for the first time in life. She even kissed it!

Then what a relief it was to Athénaïse to walk the streets without dread of being seen and recognized by some chance acquaintance from Red River! No one could have said now that she did not know her own mind.

She went directly from the oyster-woman's to the office of Harding & Offdean, her husband's merchants; and it was with such an air of partnership, almost proprietorship, that she demanded a sum of money on her husband's account, they gave it to her as unhesitatingly as they would have handed it over to Cazeau himself. When Mr. Harding, who knew her, asked politely after her health, she turned so rosy and looked so conscious, he thought it a great pity for so pretty a woman to be such a little goose.

Athénaïse entered a dry-goods store and bought all manner of things,—little presents for nearly everybody she knew. She bought whole bolts of sheerest, softest, downiest white stuff; and when the clerk, in trying to meet her wishes, asked if she intended it for infant's use, she could have sunk through the floor, and wondered how he might have suspected it.

As it was Montéclin who had taken her away from her husband, she wanted it to be Montéclin who should take her back to him. So she wrote him a very curt note,—in fact it was a postal card,—asking that he meet her at the train on the evening following. She felt convinced that after what had gone before, Cazeau would await her at their own home; and she preferred it so.

Then there was the agreeable excitement of getting ready to leave, of packing up her things. Pousette kept coming and going, coming and going; and each time that she quitted the room it was with something that Athénaïse had given her,—a handkerchief, a petticoat, a pair of stickings with two tiny holes at the toes, some broken prayer-beads, and finally a silver dollar.

Next it was Sylvie who came along bearing a gift of what she called "a set of pattern',"—things of complicated design which never could have been obtained in any new-fangled bazaar or pattern-store, that Sylvie had acquired of a foreign lady of distinction whom she had nursed years before at the St. Charles Hotel. Athénaïse accepted and handled them with reverence, fully sensible of the great compliment and favor, and laid them religiously away in the trunk which she had lately acquired.

She was greatly fatigued after the day of unusual exertion, and went early to bed and to sleep. All day long she had not once thought of Gouvernail, and only did think of him when aroused for a brief instant by the sound of his foot falls on the gallery, as he passed in going to his room. He had hoped to find her up, waiting for him.

But the next morning he knew. Some one must have told him. There was no subject known to her which Sylvie hesitated to discuss in detail with any man of suitable years and discretion.

Athénaïse found Gouvernail waiting with a carriage to convey her to the railway station. A momentary pang visited her for having forgotten him so completely, when he said to her, "Sylvie tells me you are going away this morning."

He was kind, attentive, and amiable, as usual, but respected to the utmost the new dignity and reserve that her manner had developed since yesterday. She kept looking from the carriage window, silent, and embarrassed as Eve after losing her ignorance. He talked of the muddy streets and the murky morning, and of Montéclin. He hoped she would find everything comfortable and pleasant in the country, and trusted she would inform him whenever she came to visit the city again. He talked as if afraid or mistrustful of silence and himself.

At the station she handed him her purse, and he bought her ticket, secured for her a comfortable section, checked her trunk, and got all the bundles and things safely aboard the train. She felt very grateful. He pressed her hand warmly, lifted his hat, and left her. He was a man of intelligence, and took defeat gracefully; that was all. But as he made his way back to the carriage, he was thinking, "By Heaven, it hurts, it hurts!"

XI

Athénaïse spent a day of supreme happiness and expectancy. The fair sight of the country unfolding itself before her was balm to her vision and to her soul. She was charmed with the rather unfamiliar, broad, clean sweep of the sugar plantations, with their monster sugar-houses, their rows of neat cabins like little villages of a single street, and their impressive homes standing apart amid clusters of trees.There were sudden glimpses of a bayou curling between sunny, grassy banks, or creeping sluggishly out from a tangled growth of wood, and brush, and fern, and poison-vines, and palmettos. And passing through the long stretches of monotonous woodlands, she would close her eyes and taste in anticipation the moment of her meeting with Cazeau. She could think of nothing but him.

It was night when she reached her station. There was Montéclin, as she had expected, waiting for her with a two-seated buggy, to which he had hitched his own swift-footed, spirited pony. It was good, he felt, to have her back on any terms; and he had no fault to find since she came of her own choice. He more than suspected the cause of her coming; her eyes and her voice and her foolish little manner went far in revealing the secret that was brimming over in her heart. But after he had deposited her at her own gate, and as he continued his way toward the rigolet, he could not help feeling that the affair had taken a very disappointing, an ordinary, a most commonplace turn, after all. He left her in Cazeau's keeping.

Her husband lifted her out of the buggy, and neither said a word until they stood together within the shelter of the gallery. Even then they did not speak at first. But Athénaïse turned to him with an appealing gesture. As he clasped her in his arms, he felt the yielding of her whole body against him. He felt her lips for the first time respond to the passion of his own.

The country night was dark and warm and still, save for the distant notes of an accordion which some one was playing in a cabin away off. A little negro baby was crying somewhere. As Athénaïse withdrew from her husband's embrace, the sound arrested her.

"Listen, Cazeau! How Juliette's baby is crying! Pauvre ti chou, I wonder w'at is the matter with it?"

EMENDATIONS IN THE COPY-TEXT

Listed below are all changes in the copy-text with the exception of the regularization of quotation marks. The tables are keyed to page and line numbers in *Nineteenth-Century Southern Fiction.*

"A Legend of Maryland"

25.21   guarantied   ]   guaranteed

A Kentucky Cardinal

89.36   suffering,]   suffering

"Love and Consumption"

104.26   dont]   don't
111.26   inexperience]   in experience
111.27   Fred. the]   Fred. that
121.4   succeded]   succeeded
122.27   her's]   hers
123.7   took]   too

"The Gold-Bug"

149.34   lead]   led
155.38   fall it]   fall

"The Horse Swap"

162.34   jirked]   jerked

"The Big Bear of Arkansas"

179.1   says,]   says

Madame Delphine

238.29   up]   up.